GLOBAL CITIZEN

Grass Roots Activism and High Diplomacy

Carl Wright

With best wishes

H
HANSIB

First published in Great Britain by Hansib Publications in 2022

Hansib Publications Limited
76 High Street, Hertford, SG14 3TA, United Kingdom

info@hansibpublications.com
www.hansibpublications.com

ISBN 978-1-912662-64-7
ISBN 978-1-912662-65-4 (Kindle)
ISBN 978-1-912662-66-1 (ePub)

A CIP catalogue record for this book
is available from the British Library

Production by Hansib Publications
Printed in Great Britain

www.hansibpublications.com

To my dear wife, Adele, who is always cheerful and has put up with my frequent overseas travels, excessive workloads and political obsessions for forty years; and to our energetic English setter, Rupert, who keeps me fit and trim.

ACKNOWLEDGEMENTS

These recollections have been a labour of love. While I take responsibility for their content, I have benefitted by the thoughts, comments and edits of many friends and close associates. I am grateful to Hansib Publications and their Managing Director, Kash Ali, for taking on publication and for their helpful advice; I feel gratified to have the same publishers as Sir Shridath 'Sonny' Ramphal, a great Global Citizen, Commonwealth Secretary-General and huge inspiration for my own international work.

My writing is of a subjective nature and reflects my interactions with wonderful friends and colleagues across the world. In my book, I have tried to convey personal as well as professional experiences; 'what it was like to be there', and how it was to be an activist and a diplomat at times of historic change. I have further tried to include many anecdotes, including moments of despair, exhilaration and mirth. I am also honoured by the generous words of Helen Clark in her Foreword to the book.

This book is a personal account, although I hope with important messages about the need for global understanding at a time when our fragile international structures are under acute threat, when the threat of war looms large. I want to acknowledge the many friends, family and political and professional colleagues who have influenced and advanced my life and career and those who have been mentors and role models. I may have sometimes appeared irreverent or brash. This was mostly borne out of impatience with getting things done and a lack of tolerance for what I perceived, perhaps wrongly, as individual or political prejudices.

My core aim remains promoting international cooperation, and to be a truly Global Citizen.

Dr Carl Wilms Wright
May 2022

GLOSSARY

ACP	African, Caribbean and Pacific (states)
ACPLGP	African, Caribbean and Pacific Local Government Platform
ACTU	Australian Council of Trade Unions
AFL-CIO	American Federation of Labor-Congress of Industrial Organisations
ALG	Association of London Government
ALP	Australian Labor Party
ANC	African National Congress
ASEAN	Association of Southeast Asian Nations
ASTMS	Association of Scientific, Technical & Managerial Staff (UK; now merged into Manufacturing, Science & Finance, MSF)
AU	African Union
CAP	Common Agricultural Policy (of EU)
CAPAM	Commonwealth Association for Public Administration & Management
CARICOM	Caribbean Community
CHOGM	Commonwealth Heads of Government Meeting
CLC	Canadian Labour Congress
CIDA	Canadian International Development Agency (merged into now Department for Foreign Affairs & International Trade; now Global Affairs Canada)
CLGF	Commonwealth Local Government Forum
CMAG	Commonwealth Ministerial Action Group (of Foreign Ministers)
COP	Conference of the Parties (UN Climate Change Conference)
COSATU	Congress of South African Trade Unions
CPA	Commonwealth Parliamentary Association
CSO	Civil Society Organisation
CTUC	Commonwealth Trade Union Council

DEVCO	Directorate General International Cooperation & Development (EU; now Directorate International Partnerships)
DFAT	Department of Foreign Affairs & Trade (Australia; formerly AusAID)
DFID	Department for International Development (UK; now merged into Foreign, Commonwealth & Development Office, FCDO)
ECDPM	European Centre for Development Policy Management
EEC	European Economic Community
EPG	Eminent Persons Group (Commonwealth)
ERDF	European Regional Development Fund
ETUC	European Trade Union Council
EU	European Union
FCM	Federation of Canadian Municipalities
FRELIMO	Liberation Front of Mozambique
GLA	Greater London Authority (formerly Greater London Council, GLC)
G-77	Group of 77 (developing countries at UN)
ICFTU	International Confederation of Free Trade Unions; now International Trade Union Confederation, ITUC
ICLEI	International Council for Local Environmental Initiatives
ILO	International Labour Organisation
LGIG	Local Government International Bureau (UK)
IGO	Intergovernmental Organisation
IMF	International Monetary Fund
IULA	International Union of Local Authorities
LGA	Local Government Association (also LGA of England & Wales)
MDC	Movement for Democratic Change (Zimbabwe)
MDGs	Millennium Development Goals
MFAT	Ministry of Foreign Affairs & Trade (New Zealand)
MPLA	People's Movement for the Liberation of Angola
NACTU	National Council of Trade Unions (South Africa)
NALGO	National & Local Government Officers Association (UK; now merged into UNISON)
NGO	Non Governmental Organisation
NLD	National League for Democracy (Myanmar)
NUPE	National Union of Public Employees (UK; now merged into UNISON)
OECD	Organisation for Economic Co-operation & Development
PAC	Pan Africanist Congress of Azania (South Africa)

PLP	Parliamentary Labour Party (UK)
RCS	Royal Commonwealth Society
RENAMO	Mozambique National Resistance
SACTU	South African Congress of Trade Unions
SALGA	South African Local Government Association
SDGs	Sustainable Development Goals
SPD	Social Democratic Party of Germany
SUE	Students for a United Europe
SWAPO	South-West Africa People's Organisation
TGWU	Transport & General Workers Union (UK; now UNITE)
TUC	Trade Union Council (also of UK) or trade union centre
UCL	University College London
UCLG	United Cities and Local Governments
UDI	Universal Declaration of Independence (Rhodesia)
UK	United Kingdom
UN	United Nations
UNA	United Nations Association
UNITA	National Union for the Total Independence of Angola
UNCDF	United Nations Capital Development Fund
UNDP	United Nations Development Programme
UNPROFOR	United Nations Protection Force
US / USA	United States of America
WHO	World Health Organisation
ZANU-PF	Zimbabwe African Union-Patriotic Front

CONTENTS

PREFACE 13

FOREWORD 17
Rt Hon Helen Clark

PROLOGUE 19
Memories and Reflections

PART I
EUROPEAN UNION AND GLOBAL LABOUR (the 1970s)
Youthful Activism and International Engagement

1. Yes to Europe 24
2. First Brits in Brussels 32
3. Apparatchiks versus Politicos 40
4. Workers United 46
5. Fair Labour Rights 55
6. New International Economic Order 60
7. The 1970s – A Reflection 67

PART II
NEO-LIBERAL ASCENDENCY (the 1980s)
From Trade Union Action to Commonwealth Diplomacy

8. Fresh Beginnings 72
9. Recasting Global Paradigms 78
10. The Impact of Thatcherism 83

11. CHOGMs and Expert Groups 88
12. Rhodesia to Zimbabwe 92
13. Confronting Apartheid 95
14. Global Solidarity 101
15. On Her Majesty's Diplomatic List 108
16. Trade Union Relapse 114
17. The 1980s Assessed 119

PART III
THE END OF HISTORY (the 1990s)
Dealing with Global Change and Challenge

18. Step-change in International Relations 126
19. Aftermath of the Collapse of Communism 132
20. Fragile States and Inclusive Institutions 138
21. Post-apartheid Transition 142
22. Fair and Free Elections 151
23. Party Political Lotteries 156
24. The 1990s Remembered 164

PART IV
LOCAL GOVERNMENT CAMPAIGNS (towards 2000 and beyond)
Promoting People Empowerment

25. Challenge for the New Millennium 168
26. Networks and Partnerships 176
27. Advocacy for Local Democracy 184
28. Knowledge-sharing and Good Practices 194
29. Building Local Capacity 202
30. The 2000s Evaluated 212

PART V
NEW REALITIES (to the present time)
Unravelling of the Post-1945 Consensus

31. 9/11, 7/7 and Violent Extremism 222
32. Economic Crash, Austerity and the New Populists 229
33. A Little Local Difficulty 236

34. Millennium Development Goals to Sustainable
   Development Goals 242
35. Final Acts and New Roles 250
36. Post-2000 Appraisal 253

PART VI
ECHOES AND IMAGES (Old Memories and New Plans)

37. Royal Encounters 262
38. Shaping My Life 266
39. Greek Colonels and other Foreign Adventures 280
40. Facing Superpower Rivalries 284
41. Private Interludes and In-between Pastimes 291
42. A Luta Continua 300

EPILOGUE 308
Imagine

BIBLIOGRAPHY 319

INDEX 327

PREFACE

I RETIRED FROM FULL-TIME WORK IN 2016. AT A FINAL FUNCTION held at Commonwealth headquarters, Marlborough House my chief guest, HRH the Prince of Wales, Prince Charles, most generously said of my work that, "This... is a remarkable record of service by any measure, and I can only thank him for all that he has done for the people of the Commonwealth over that time."

I was therefore personally offended when not long afterwards British Prime Minister Theresa May described 'a citizen of the world as a citizen of nowhere'. Being a Global Citizen does not stop you being a patriot of your country. It does not curtail you serving as a committed member of your local community or region. It does not – as in my case – prevent you identifying as a proud European, or indeed a proud African, American, Asian or Pacific citizen.

As a Global Citizen you are still very much attached to 'somewhere': There is no contradiction. As a Global Citizen you can be pro-UN, pro-Commonwealth or pro-EU. What matters is that you reject narrow nationalism and uphold democratic values and human rights and that you are an internationalist, striving for global understanding. That is what makes you a Global Citizen.

My recollections accordingly focus on my international career over a period of almost fifty years. They give attention to the complex interplay between official intergovernmental organisations and international non-governmental or quasi-governmental bodies like associations of trade unions and mayors. I have been fortunate to work in all of these bodies at a senior level. I have been an activist and a diplomat; a poacher and a gamekeeper. I hope I can cast light on such official and informal structures interacting internationally, issues not much studied or understood.

My life has not been without excitement. I have come close to expending most of my mythical nine lives. I have travelled into active war zones in Angola, Mozambique, Sri Lanka and South Sudan; I narrowly missed IRA, al-Qaeda and Boko Haram bombings; and I had a death-defying experience in the diplomatic zone in Islamabad.

Sneaking around Sri Lanka tea estates at the depth of night as a young trade unionist, taking illicit photographs of the terrible workers' conditions, also had its risks. As did being Commonwealth election observer in Pakistan and Nigeria where I was accompanied throughout by armed bodyguards, automatic weapons at the ready. That is nothing to say of frequent lucky escapes on dangerous outback roads, dodgy ferries and rickety planes travelling across Africa, Asia, the Americas, the Pacific, and Europe.

I have certainly wandered around too many dimly light streets in dubious urban settings late at night for my own good. I must have had a guardian angel watching over me all this time, keeping me safe.

If had to pick one single political issue from among the many I engaged with, it is the fight against apartheid in Southern Africa. I first got involved in the 1970s as a young trade unionist and was active in the anti-apartheid movement throughout the 1980s. I visited Zimbabwe at its independence in 1980 and South Africa in 1987 to address the Congress of South African Trade Unions, COSATU, at the height of apartheid repression. At the Commonwealth Secretariat, I oversaw educational and other solidarity programmes to sustain the Liberation Movements in Namibia and South Africa.

By the early 1990s, I was coordinating Commonwealth policy to support the incoming Mandela Government and then assist in consolidating the new democratic local government structures. I have returned to the country, where I have many good friends, on innumerable occasions and hold fond memories of being an official guest at Nelson Mandela's historic inauguration as President, one of the highlights of my career.

I encountered numerous global leaders: Indira Gandhi, Julius Nyerere, Kenneth Kaunda, Nelson Mandela, Desmond Tutu, Fidel Castro, Shridath Ramphal, Willy Brandt and Ban Ki-moon, to name but a few. Some, like Cyril Ramaphosa of South Africa, Bob Hawke of Australia, Wim Kok of the Netherlands, Helen Clark of New Zealand, and Portia Simpson-Miller of Jamaica, I got to know well. I say this not to 'name drop', but to give an insight into the remarkable personalities I have had the privilege to meet.

There have been numerous occasions when I have met HM Queen Elizabeth and other members of the British Royal Family. I encountered the late Pope Paul VI in the Vatican and the Archbishop of Canterbury, Rowan Williams. However, as important as all these global leaders are, I have gained as much or more from engaging with dedicated local politicians, principled trade union activists, hard-working government officials and many tireless grass-root campaigners. These are the lifeblood of our democracy and civil society.

The book is divided broadly according to decades. After an introductory Prologue, Part I (Chapters 1-7) deals with the 1970s, Part II (Chapters 8-17) with the 1980s and Part III (Chapters 18-24) with the 1990s. Part IV (Chapters 25-30) is mainly devoted the Commonwealth Local Government Forum, CLGF, which spans the period 1995-2016 and Part V (Chapters 31-36) deals with wider developments since the year 2000. Part VI (Chapters 37-42) looks at how my early life has impacted on my later work. It concludes with thoughts for the future, making the point that *a luta continua* – the fight goes on. An Epilogue reflects on lessons from the past fifty years, especially for our young generation.

Given the growth of multi-party democracy and decentralisation of public services, my local government work receives in-depth attention. I hope that my writings will be of special interest to the many dedicated local government mayors, politicians and officials across the world; as well as to central and provincial government policy-makers; and to academics interested in comparative local government structures in the Commonwealth and globally.

There is just one Human Race.

In a Global World we are all Global Citizens.

FOREWORD

Rt Hon Helen Clark, Prime Minister of New Zealand (1999-2008) and Administrator UNDP (2009-2017)

Our world order, established post-1945, based on the rule of law and liberal democracy, is under serious attack. The failure to ensure the necessary vaccination supplies to developing countries to tackle Covid-19 is a symptom of this breakdown, as is the hitherto inadequate global response to the spiralling climate crisis. The spread of political populism, exemplified by the UK's Brexit from the European Union and the Trump Presidency represent further examples of the abandonment of global cooperation.

I have known Carl Wright for many years and value his sound knowledge of the workings of governments and legislatures in many countries and his numerous international professional and personal contacts. His record in actively promoting internationalism over fifty years is set out well in these pages and makes for inspiring reading. It is heartening to read his principled opposition to narrow nationalism and xenophobia which promote so much intolerance and conflict across the world.

Global Citizen is unique in that it examines not only the workings of intergovernmental organisations but also how key interest groups like trade unions and associations of mayors interact within the global system. These, like the Commonwealth Trade Union Council and the Commonwealth Local Government Forum, and their many other counterparts, have come to play an increasingly important role. As such *Global Citizen* will be of interest to a wide audience, not only those specialising in international relations, but also to governmental and non-governmental decision-makers in areas like the promotion of labour rights, democratic principles and good governance, and sustainable development.

This is a personal record, underscored by many individual encounters with grass roots activists as well as political leaders. Above all, however, it is a much-needed defence of international cooperation and adhering to being truly 'Global Citizens'.

Rt Hon Helen Clark

PROLOGUE

Memories and Reflections

AS I AM CONCLUDING MY REFLECTIONS IN EARLY 2022, THE world has turned into a yet more dangerous place with the Russian invasion of Ukraine in flagrant disregard of international law. In Asia and the Far East, the growth of Chinese geopolitical assertion over Taiwan is causing further tension. Liberal democracies of the West have seen division with much damage done by the Trump Presidency and the UK's Brexit from the European Union. Everywhere, international organisations such as the UN and the Commonwealth are being challenged and the very nature of our carefully constructed post-1945 system of global relations is under threat. Developing countries are not receiving the support they had been promised under the 2030 *Agenda for Sustainable Development* and climate change is becoming an existential crisis for humankind and especially the world's most vulnerable states and people. Now more than ever it is necessary to promote international cooperation and resolve conflict, to act as Global Citizens.

Covid-19 burst onto the global scene in January 2020. In little over a month, it started to spread from China to Europe and the US. By March 2020, I and my wife Adele were in self-isolation in our home while the grim death toll from the virus got ever higher. Many mistakes were made in the responses to the pandemic by the UK and other governments. A year later we received our Covid vaccines which provided some assurance, but as the events of 2021 showed, the virus will be with us for much longer.

My life has been an odd, but complementary, mix of grass roots activism and of high diplomacy at international level. Insofar as there is a *Leitmotif* running through my writing, it is the impact of international relations on politics and global development. These are issues to which I have been engaged with all my professional life. My recollections start in the 1970s when I was a youthful activist, immersed in student politics and increasingly the Labour Movement. They recount taking on my initial job in 1972 before becoming one of the very first Brits to work in Brussels for what was then the European Economic Community or EEC in 1973-74.

It all started on a cold winters' morning on 3 January 1973 when I departed London for Brussels – the start of the UK's membership of the European Union. An idealistic young man, I had set out with great excitement at a new political dawn, driving my little second-hand Austin mini, strewn with a few suitcases, onto the ferry boat from Dover to Ostend. This was of course well before the Channel Tunnel.

I arrived in Brussels on a dark evening with little sense of direction. My subsequent career was then almost terminated as I drove into what I thought was a road underpass but turned out to be a tram tunnel. In a panic I saw bright tram lights approaching me rapidly with no apparent way to avoid a fatal collision. At the very last moment I discovered a side exit which I managed to divert into just in time – a fortunate escape.

After my period at the European Commission, I engaged globally as a trade union activist, 1974-88, first in Brussels at the International Confederation of Free Trade Unions, ICFTU, and later as Director of the new Commonwealth Trade Union Council, CTUC, in London. This entailed fighting for fair labour rights and opposing the growing global neo-liberal political ascendancy. Throughout this period, I was also active in the British Labour Party and narrowly missed Labour Party selection in highly winnable parliamentary seats as Member of Parliament and Member of the European Parliament. There is accordingly a fair amount of discussion about the minutiae of UK politics, especially as it relates to European and international affairs.

The 1990s were the moment when communism collapsed, and I discuss if this dramatic global event really signalled 'the end of history'. By then I had become a Commonwealth diplomat (1988-94), and saw how intergovernmental structures operated from the inside, rather than the outside. This gave me a broader perspective of international cooperation. I experienced the politics of international diplomacy at the highest level, interacting with many ministers and heads of state and government. However, being a life-long grass roots activist, I was an unlikely diplomat.

The years after 1995 saw my efforts to promote local democracy around the world. As Secretary-General of the Commonwealth Local Government Forum (CLGF), 1995-2016, which I set up, my work was devoted to encouraging people empowerment – what I have termed 'local campaigns'. This allowed me to deploy both my skills as activist and as diplomat, to promote community-level action and yet also advocate for global cooperation.

I was born in 1950 and had a frugal but loving family upbringing. My generation benefitted from free education, and I was able to excel academically. My early experiences during the 1950s and 1960s, growing up in different European countries in the aftermath of World War Two and during the tensions of the Cold War, did much to determine who I am. It shaped my world views and professional career choices and I record these personal memories.

By the time of my birth, India, Pakistan, Ceylon, Burma and Indonesia had achieved independence, signalling the dismantling of European overseas possessions. Struggles for independence were growing across the world. At times, as in Indochina and Algeria, and also Vietnam, these involved much bloodshed. By 1960, British Prime Minister Harold Macmillan spoke of the *'Winds of Change'* blowing across Africa, although they took a long time to reach the southern part of the continent, which was not fully free until 1994.

Well into the 1960s, my school atlas still presented the world under European colonial control. It showed great swathes of red across the globe, signifying the extent of a British Empire on which the sun never set. My early knowledge of countries around the world came through small cards showing the flags of different nations which I avidly collected and stuck into albums. Each card was contained in a packet of Brooke Bond leaf tea, as teabags were not yet in common use.

On one occasion, my primary school teacher asked my class to contact foreign embassies for information about their countries. Other children wrote to France, Spain or Switzerland, and duly got nice glossy tourist brochures. Bizarrely, I wrote off to remote Papua New Guinea. The country was not even independent but under Australian administration. I heard nothing for two months, then a thick envelope arrived in the post. It contained photographs of scantily clad head-hunters – or so my imagination would have it – and of exotic plants and animals. I was the envy of my schoolmates and this no doubt installed in me a desire to visit mysterious places in remote parts of the world.

By 1972, when I left university, the process of decolonisation was largely complete. What had been the British Commonwealth had turned into a Commonwealth of independent states, mostly republics, with no link to the British Crown. It was an organisation with which I was to be intimately engaged with professionally for forty years and got to know inside out.

Over the years I notched up official missions to some 100 countries worldwide, including just about every one of the 54 member states of the Commonwealth. These embraced visits to big and small states, highly developed and under-developed nations, fragile states and countries undergoing democratic transition, many still struggling to implement good governance. Most of the visits were short and intensive with no time for sightseeing.

My travels embraced two of the least visited countries in the world, Kiribati in the mid-Pacific and Moldova in Eastern Europe. I have clocked up all too many air miles. Not a proud environmental record. However, spread over many years, undertaken in the service of the public good and mostly in uncomfortable economy class, it was hardly glamorous jet-setting.

Towards the end of my career, senior Board members suggested I should put my name forward for election as Commonwealth Secretary-General. I could have marshalled the support of some Heads of Government from Africa, the Caribbean and elsewhere. But I was highly unlikely to get support from my own UK Government, having never worked for them and, as an international civil servant, always consciously maintained a distance.

On occasions, like the Greek mythical hero Icarus, I flew too close to the sun and had my feathers singed. Yet I have avoided crashing down to the ground. My work across the world has been rich in personal experiences and in job satisfaction. I feel that I have been able to make a difference and I hope I have made a worthwhile contribution to society. This has been an immense privilege.

Over the last fifty years I have engaged with colleagues of all creeds, convictions and ethnicities from around the world. Yet prior to 1966, I had not even met a Black person. I soon discovered that everyone has their own culture, traditions and beliefs, political or religious, but it has been my experience that all human beings are fundamentally similar. All of us share the same emotions, of joy and sadness.

In the words of Shakespeare's Shylock, in the *Merchant of Venice*:

'Hath not a Jew hands, organs, dimensions, senses, affections, passions? If you prick us, do we not bleed? If you tickle us, do we not laugh?'

PART I

EUROPEAN UNION AND GLOBAL LABOUR (the 1970s)

Youthful Activism and International Engagement

"The world's third great industrial power (after the US and USSR) will be American industry in Europe."

JEAN-JACQUES SERVAN-SCHREIBER,
FRENCH WRITER IN 'LE DEFI AMERICAIN'

The 1970s saw advances for democracy, human rights and moves towards a progressive global order. Aged only 22, I got a chance to put my idealism into practice as one of the first 'Brits' to work at the European Commission and then as grass roots trade union activist.

1.

Yes to Europe

THE ISSUE OF THE UK'S MEMBERSHIP OF WHAT IS NOW THE European Union, has dominated British politics for over fifty years. As one of the first ten UK nationals to work at the European Commission in Brussels in 1973 and having been involved in the political lead-up to UK membership, I can offer an insider record of those historical days.

By the mid-1960s the economic success of the European Economic Community, the EEC, often simply called the Common Market, and the desirability of British accession was evident. Post-Suez 1956, there was a growing lobby for British membership, led by the cross-party European Movement, supported by much of British business. The late 1960s saw Labour's Prime Minister Harold Wilson's attempt to bring Britain into membership, but foundered on the opposition of the French President, General De Gaulle. The subsequent demise of De Gaulle, succeeded by the more pragmatic President Pompidou, kept the issue alive.

The election of Conservative pro-European Ted Heath in 1970 was to move things on, with Heath being a driving force for British accession. Membership was, after lengthy negotiations, finally agreed in 1972. It however required ratification by the House of Commons. Here formidable opposition built-up through the Labour Party, influenced by party political considerations. There was also a significant minority of Tories fundamentally opposed to Europe and who saw EEC membership as a sell-out of British values, clinging to traditional Empire ties to the white Commonwealth Dominions of Australia, Canada and New Zealand.

The prospect of UK membership of the EEC was hotly debated. Within the Labour Party opinion was split, with much of the British Left seeing the EEC as a capitalist club whose mainly Right-wing-led governments would undermine progressive politics and impose free market economics. But there was a minority of MPs, largely from Labour's centre-Right, who enthused about UK membership. They included many of its brightest

24

young intake such as David Marquand, Dick Taverne, John Roper and Michael Barnes. Other leading pro-Europeans included Cabinet Ministers George Thomson and Shirley Williams, and two other young MPs, John Smith from Scotland and David Owen from the West Country. They were led by Roy Jenkins, the previous Home Secretary and Chancellor of the Exchequer, who was looking to become Labour leader. A good deal of the political manoeuvrings around Europe up to 1973 was thus motivated by the desire to position Jenkins as the successor to Harold Wilson, who had been Prime Minister 1964-70.

Having a European background, I had naturally been drawn to a strong British role in Europe. As a new undergraduate at University College London (UCL) in the autumn of 1968, I joined the small European Movement students' club at Freshers' Week and quickly got involved in its activities. The club was chaired by an older student called Richard Arndell who lived in a run-down flat just off the fashionable Kings Road in Chelsea. This was where, three years later, I held my 21st birthday party, ending up with an awful hangover the morning after, having consumed too much cheap wine. Richard, like several contemporaries, later became an official at the European Commission in Brussels, an institution which we saw as the champion of the European cause.

The University European club held monthly meetings with interesting speakers, and its committee members, which I soon joined, had the privilege of taking these out for dinner beforehand, often to the local Spaghetti House. Another dinner venue was the much-missed Schmidt's Restaurant in nearby Charlotte Street, where they served a good and reasonably priced schnitzel, and where the waiters insulted you in true Basil Fawlty style from the BBC sitcom *Fawlty Towers*, while the elderly lady at the till – I assume Frau Schmidt – spouted a remarkable moustache on her lip. One of the speakers I was impressed by was the well-known British writer Anthony Sampson, who had just published a book on Europe and who was also intimately involved with South Africa's liberation movements. Many years later I would work closely with him on a Commonwealth expert group examining South Africa's post-apartheid development.

Looking back, our means of communication was truly primitive. Word processors and PCs had not yet been invented and I cannot even recall having access to a photocopier. Producing our club newsletters involved laboriously typing-up the text manually onto a flimsy and easily torn paper stencil wedged into an old-fashioned typewriter. This was then put on a rotating stencil machine which would reproduce the required number of copies with much mess, effort and many ink blobs: in fact, our technology was not far removed from Guttenberg's original printing press of 1450.

In 1968, our European club was dominated by the student Left, with close links to the radical student movements on the continent such as the German Young Socialists, the 'Jusos'. The latter included activists like Jo Leinen who went on to be elected to the European Parliament. It was also linked to the Young European Federalists, who had a vision of a united, federal states of Europe and in turn lent strongly to the Left. The European federalist idea never really caught on in the UK and gave rise of suspicions of seeking to create a European superpower. Ironically, the UK would itself later move to a quasi-federal system of government among its four constituent nations of England, Wales, Scotland and Northern Ireland.

This international dimension attracted me more than the narrow domestic student politics of the National Union of Students. The latter was headed by a young Jack Straw, later Home Secretary under Tony Blair. The late 1960s were a time when relatively few students, perhaps except for those at Oxbridge, many of whom came from Eton and the public schools, bothered about formal party politics. There was much cynicism about the Wilson Labour Government. On foreign policy especially, there was disdain over perceived support for the United States in the Vietnam War; inability to quell the Rhodesian Unilateral Declaration of Independence under the racist regime of Ian Smith which denied Black people their vote; and British failure to help resolve the horrendous Biafra War raging in Nigeria.

It was appropriate that my first participation in a mass public demonstration was not in London, but in The Hague, where the EEC Heads of States were meeting in late 1969. Here the European Movement and its youth wing were demonstrating on the streets for greater European integration and in support of Britain's EEC membership.

After surviving a rough and stormy overnight ferry crossing from Harwich, I and my fellow students from the UK disembarked at Hook in Holland. I recall joining our continental comrades with great excitement, noting that they bore a revolutionary flag with a blood-red red letter 'E' for Europe, not the traditional green-coloured 'E' of the European Movement. As I learnt about their thinking, I was drawn to their concept of a United Socialist States of Europe. This was the 'Red Europe', which would be a progressive counterweight in the world to the rampant capitalism of the USA and the repressive authoritarianism of the Soviet Union, but not a new superpower for its own sake.

Another memorable overseas visit, again by overnight ferry across a rough Irish sea, was to a European youth conference in Dublin. I have vivid recollections of arriving bleary-eyed and being met at the dockside by a friendly Irish politician. This turned out to be none other than future Fine Gael Taoiseach (Prime Minister) Garret FitzGerald, who had risen at the crack of dawn to meet a scruffy bunch of British students and take them to their lodgings. Truly remarkable Irish hospitality.

These developments put our London University European club, whose chairman I had meanwhile become, in the political limelight. There were similar student European clubs elsewhere in the UK, linked in a national confederation under the overall umbrella of the British section of the European Movement. With the imminence of a Conservative Government taking Britain into Europe in 1971, together with a gradual demise of the student Left, the influence of the Right-wing Federation of Conservative Students grew. They took interest in Europe and began to put their members into existing clubs, while founding new ones elsewhere. As a result, the clubs, which now went under the somewhat sexist-sounding acronym of SUE, Students for a United Europe, were no longer Left-dominated.

Nonetheless, a manifesto issued by SUE in October 1971 on the eve of the critical House of Commons vote on EEC membership, which I helped to write, had a distinctly progressive nature. It supported EEC enlargement based on ten key demands, the implementation of many of which I was to be directly involved with subsequently, and most being realised in later years:

• Development and direct election of the European Parliament
• Increased aid to Third World through multilateral arrangements
• European regional and social policy
• East-West détente
• Pollution control
• Control of multi-national business
• Common foreign policy
• Technological co-operation
• Economic union
• Co-operation in education policies

In addition, the manifesto envisaged 'progressing towards world harmony and an eventual World Community', highlighting the link between European integration and broader internationalism. I have always felt that this link was essential: if you were an internationalist, you should be pro-EU, pro-UN or for that matter pro-Commonwealth, to name just a few bodies which I was to be professionally engaged with. I suppose it was the beginning of my conscious engagement as a Global Citizen.

Things came to a head in 1970/71 at the SUE elections for its UK chair position, for which I was standing. I had previously annoyed my Tory colleagues on the SUE committee by sending a letter of protest to the Conservative Home Secretary at the expulsion of Left-wing German student leader, Rudi Dutschke, from Britain. Dutschke, together with 'Red' Daniel Cohn-Bendit, had been one of the leading lights of the student movement in the 1960s. He had come to Britain after a brutal assassination attempt in 1968 in Berlin, from which he was still recovering. I found it cowardly and mean that an ill and convalescing man was being expelled by the Tory Government on narrow ideological grounds.

As a result of my action, the Right sought to prevent my election as SUE Chair and encouraged the then President of the Oxford Union, Julian Priestley, a Labour Party member, but a centrist politically, to stand against me. As it happened, we tied the vote. The organisation had no constitutional provision to resolve this, and we agreed to share the term of office between us, much to the annoyance of our Tory adversaries. Julian and I subsequently became good friends and we worked together well. He was later to obtain high office in Europe as the most senior official of the European Parliament, its Secretary-General. Sadly, he died at much too young an age.

One young Tory contemporary was Andrew Neil, who after a stint as adviser to the Conservative Minister Peter Walker, became editor of the *Sunday Times*, helping to mastermind the defeat of the print unions at Wapping under the direction of Rupert Murdoch. He then became a prominent Right-wing British TV presenter. Having become a Euro-sceptic, he was distinctly uncomfortable when I met him many years later and reminded him of his leading role in the Young European Federalist movement and of his editorship of our student newspaper which had strongly campaigned for a federal Europe,

After successfully completing my bachelor's degree in Geography at UCL in 1971, I had the opportunity to further deepen my knowledge of

European affairs by taking a Master's degree in Contemporary European Studies at the University of Reading. Here I researched and wrote on the politics of European integration and on its economic implications. At the same time, I continued my active engagement with the European student movement.

My active involvement in European student politics and links with the European Movement had brought me into contact with its Labour Party wing, the Labour Committee for Europe. This led me to join the British Labour Party in 1972; at the same time, I became a member of the powerful Transport and General Workers Union, TGWU, as well as of the Fabian Society, which represents the intellectual wing of the Labour Movement, going back to the days of such luminaries as George Bernard Shaw and H G Wells. I was to retain Labour Party membership for some forty years and was a grass roots party activist for much of this time and in the 1980s, and into the 1990s I narrowly missed becoming an elected Labour parliamentarian.

I recall attending my first Labour Party Conference in Blackpool. Here I made my debut with a bit of a splash by challenging senior Labour politician Tony Benn on his anti-European policy on a live BBC TV *Question Time* debate. This was chaired by the late Robin Day and it seems my rather lurid bright red shirt drew the attention of the famous broadcaster.

My role in these historic events leading up to British membership of the EEC was close to the action. It involved coordinating student and youth support for the European cause and seeking media attention with our slogan 'Say Yes to Europe'. Our key initial aim was a big parliamentary majority in the vote to confirm EEC membership in late 1971. Focus then shifted on ensuring parliamentary approvals at the subsequent committee stages of the EEC accession legislation throughout 1972. This was an exciting task.

In the House of Commons formidable opposition had built-up in the Labour Party. Labour in Opposition had shifted against EEC entry on what many opportunistically viewed as 'Tory terms'. Former Prime Minister Harold Wilson saw an opportunity of defeating Heath on a critical issue of confidence for the Conservative Government, and thereby bringing down the government and forcing an election which he hoped to win.

Owing to opposition within his own ranks, Heath looked to the pro-European Labour Party 'Jenkinsites' for support in the vital vote. Nothing seemed certain until the last minute and the parliamentary vote was in the balance. In the event, Labour's pro-Europeans refused to play party politics with Britain's future in Europe. Despite mounting pressure by grass-root activists, who accused them of supporting the Tory Government, they stood firm. When the decisive vote came in the House of Commons I and other student activists assembled outside Big Ben and Parliament waiting with bated breath for the result. Which way would Parliament divide?

We cheered loudly on hearing that more than sixty Labour pro-Europeans had defied the party whip to vote in favour of the negotiated terms with another twenty abstaining, thereby guaranteeing Edward Heath a clear majority. Britain's membership of the EEC on 1 January 1973 was now assured. My delight on hearing the outcome of the vote was a little spoilt when the Young Conservatives in our demonstration marched off to nearby Lord North Street to jeer Harold Wilson outside his Westminster house: my interest lay in a 'Red Europe', and not a 'blue' Conservative one.

Labour's pro-Europeans needed still more political courage when it came to support the Government in subsequent votes on the Parliamentary Committee stages of the draft legislation in 1972, and to ensure that all due legislative approval was secured.

For some, like Dick Taverne in Lincoln, personal vilification was vehement and he was hounded from his parliamentary seat by strident young Left-winger Margaret Beckett, who later went on to hold senior Labour ministerial positions.

Once parliamentary approvals had been agreed, the old EEC of six nations, France, Germany, Italy and the Benelux countries, was all set to expand to nine in January 1973, to include the UK, the Irish Republic and Denmark. Norway, which had also originally looked to membership, had decided to go its own way.

After attaining my Masters at Reading in 1972 as top of my year, I could have continued my studies towards an academic career. I was however keen to get hands-on involvement and was hooked on Europe. When the opportunity arose in to become full-time youth officer of the British European Movement, I grabbed it with both hands. Working with the UK branch of the European Movement from its London offices in 1, Whitehall Place gave me my first proper job and salary, a paltry £1,500 per year. But I was now being paid for something I had previously done voluntarily.

My thoughts now turned to what more I could do after January 1973. This led me to put out feelers about employment at the European Commission in Brussels. I had strong academic and linguistic qualifications, quite apart from my European political involvement. British staff recruitment was however being coordinated by the Foreign Office and the response I received from Whitehall was negative; it appeared they were only interested in putting seasoned civil servants into Brussels, not bright young graduates.

To my delight the Labour European Commissioner-designate, George Thomson, a former Commonwealth minister and close ally of Roy Jenkins, took an interest in me, prompted by his daughter Caroline, an active member of our European youth movement. After an interview at the Cabinet Office, he offered me a position as policy adviser in his private office or 'cabinet'. This was to be based at European Commission Headquarters, the Berlaymont building in Brussels, starting as soon as 1 January 1973. For me this was nothing less than a youthful idealistic dream come true.

In anticipation of my new position, and significantly increased salary, I acquired an American Express credit card, at a time when other credits cards like Visa were unusual and old-fashioned cheques were still the main form of non-cash payment.

I was therefore well equipped for my exciting new European voyage.

2.

First Brits in Brussels

MY WORK AT THE EUROPEAN COMMISSION IN 1973-74 PUT me right at the heart of senior policy making. It also meant going to lively European Parliament sessions in Luxembourg and Strasbourg.

As a cabinet member I had to attend high-level Commission policy meetings on behalf of my Commissioner George (later Lord) Thomson and brief him on their outcome with a view to formulating our position. Although all Commissioners were supposedly neutral and appointed on merit, the reality was that they looked in varying degrees after the interests of their home country and the Government which had nominated them. Policy meetings often involved highly specialised subjects outside my own expertise. They were frequently held in complex French without interpretation, which presented problems to my rudimentary schoolboy French. On occasions however my more fluent German was an asset especially when dealing with German Commission staff. It is ironic that today, even after Brexit, English has become the main working language of the EU, but that was certainly not the case back in 1973.

In the 1970s, there was no word processor, no email and no internet to fall back on to make office work easier; instead, you relied on your personal secretary – inevitably a young woman – to type up your letters and documents. Interestingly, I do recall participating in EEC Commission policy discussions on implications of computer technology back in 1973. It was however only in 1978 that I had a real taste of what was to come when I was invited to take part in an 'International Dialogue on the Future of Economic Liberalism'. This was organised by the European Management Institute, which fed into the annual Davos Symposium discussions. This dialogue involved me and three US based experts and another three experts in Europe, all linked in real-time by computer texting.

At the time this technology was still revolutionary and required the installation of a bulky Texas Instruments computer terminal in my

Brussels office. I was therefore one of the first individuals to engage in an embryonic type of webcast. But it was only in 1986, that I installed my own office computer, an Apricot ZEN, the capacity of which was a fraction of today's handheld smart phones. Proper internet usage and emails did not really start until the late 1990s, around the same time as somewhat less chunky and more reliable cell phones came on the market.

Commission meetings could be gruelling, like the EEC Energy Council which finished at 5am on the morning of 23 May 1973. Sometimes there were farcical moments. Once, an emergency Commission meeting was called late at night to discuss a crisis in Common Agricultural Policy (CAP) pricing policy. The unscheduled meeting went on so late that the interpreters left at midnight and the debate staggered on with aides whispering impromptu interpretations into their respective Commissioners ears. Some of these interpretations were not up to scratch and the Danish Commissioner agreed to a change in the price of bacon which almost brought down the Danish Government the next day.

The main responsibility of my boss, George Thomson was European regional policy, a relatively new area of EEC interest. He was assisted by a Director-General, or permanent secretary, Italian Renato Ruggiero, who would later go on to become the first head of the World Trade Organisation (WTO). Their efforts in 1973 were designed to establish a new European Regional Development Fund, ERDF, which was achieved after much initial negotiation among EEC member states and haggling about its budget. The ERDF had been one of the aims of the British Government and represented an attempt to diversify the EEC Budget away from predominately agricultural expenditure which was largely benefitting France and European rural regions.

Regional economic policy was an area on which I have considerable academic knowledge. Just a year earlier in 1972, I had co-authored a research study on the consequences of European monetary integration on regional economic policy, together with Geoffrey Denton, one of my tutors at the University of Reading. The study had warned, long before the Euro came into existence, that in a monetary union, peripheral EEC regions and countries would suffer economically, losing vital jobs and investment to the central economic hub of Germany and Benelux. We counselled that to offset this, EEC countervailing monetary, fiscal and regional policies were required. I was tempted to dust off this study and send it to Brussels when the post-2008 Eurozone crisis blew up in southern and peripheral Eurozone countries like Greece, Ireland and Portugal, in the absence of just such countervailing policies.

There were great political sensitivities around creating the Regional Fund among EEC member states and the extent to which the UK and its regions would benefit. Much of the negotiations took place behind closed doors. I am pleased to have been present at the birth of the new Fund and to have contributed to its establishment as a member of the Thomson Cabinet. At the time I did not realise how important the Fund was to become, helping many deprived regions across Europe, including in places like Wales, where I had grown up, and in East Kent, where I came to reside. I also did not foresee how its financial support would be earnestly sought by UK and those local authorities I would be involved with later in my career when I came to head the Commonwealth Local Government Forum in the 1990s.

Among the more interesting assignments was regular attendance at monthly European Parliament sessions in Strasbourg and Luxembourg. Here parliamentarians from EU member states, at the time still nominated by their own parliaments, not directly elected by the people, and with limited powers, sought to scrutinise the work of the European Commission.

Representing Labour-nominated Commissioner George Thomson, I often attended meetings of the Parliament's Socialist Group. The Group was at that time still being boycotted by the Labour Party, with Dick Taverne as the only UK social democrat present. In private discussions with Taverne in 1973, I learnt that he was contemplating launching a nationwide 'Democratic Labour' network. This idea became a reality a decade later when the 'Social Democrats' under Roy Jenkins broke away from the Labour Party in the early 1980s. In many ways this represented a continuation of past ideological splits in the Labour Party between the Right and Left, not only on the issue of Europe. It also contributed to a long period of Conservative political ascendency in the UK under Margaret Thatcher.

I got on well with the Group's secretary, German socialist Manfred Michel, and other parliamentarians, and almost ended up working for the Group after I left the Commission in 1974. A good friend was Anne Hennon (later Harris), an intelligent young Irish woman, who like me had also just been recruited and went on to a senior career at the European Parliament. Many years later she courageously published a book about her traumatic experiences as a young unmarried mother at a notorious

Catholic institution where her baby son was taken away from her, although happily she was able to reunite with him in later life.

There was a memorable occasion when returning by train to Brussels from a European Parliament session in Luxembourg. I was tired and asked the train's waiter for a beer. To my surprise, he refused to accept payment in Luxembourg francs, indicating that he would only take Belgian francs – this of course being many years before the introduction of the euro. This was despite the interchangeability of the two currencies and the fact we were still on the territory of the Grand Duchy, which admittedly, given its small geographic size, would not be for long.

As I argued with the waiter, a distinguished elderly gentleman, who had been quietly sitting opposite me reading *Le Monde* suddenly thrust down his paper. In no uncertain terms he told the waiter 'Monsieur, I am the Prime Minister and Finance Minister of Luxembourg, and you can jolly well take our currency'. It was indeed Prime Minister Pierre Werner of Luxembourg. It was ironic that he had recently been the author of the so-called Werner Plan, proposing European Monetary Union thirty years before it was actually to happen. Needless to say, I got my beer.

Looking back, I was proud to be one the very first 'Brits' to arrive to work at the European Commission, together with other members of the 'Thomson cabinet' and the cabinet of the Conservative Commissioner, Sir Christopher Soames. The Head of the Private Office, or 'Chef-de-Cabinet' was Welshman and former deputy General Secretary of the Labour Party, Gwyn Morgan. The number two was Foreign Office high-flyer Michael Jenkins. Our cabinet was a strange mix of career Whitehall officials, junior secretarial staff and ex-Labour Party employees, including two admin staff, John Randall and Sue Lewis. All were newcomers to the Commission apart from one 'old hand', Bob Cox, who had been previously working in the media section.

At only 22, soon to be 23, I was the baby of the cabinet and the Commission. My young years were a constant source of surprise to fellow Commission employees. Many of these had to do military service after school and then not finished lengthy university studies before their mid or late twenties, followed by a stint as intern or 'stagiaire', and had only then taken up Commission employment at the age of thirty or even older.

Inevitably, the Labour Party members of the cabinet clubbed together, soon to be joined by new recruits to Brussels such as ex MP Maurice Foley who had resigned his West Midlands parliamentary seat, trade unionist Jack Peel, former Transport House employee Ian Flintoff, media specialist Brian Murphy and Welshmen Hywel Ceri Jones and Nye Hughes. Together, especially those with Welsh connections like myself, we became known as the Welsh Mafia or 'Tafia'. Another early – but certainly non-Labour Party recruit – who I recall having lunch with was Stanley Johnson, the father of the later Mayor of London and Prime Minister, Boris Johnson, who had just taken a job in the Commission dealing with environmental issues.

Gwyn Morgan was a key player who had had an active career as Labour's International Secretary. He had recently narrowly missed out on becoming its General Secretary on account of the casting vote by Tony Benn, who was making his mark as the Leader of the British Left. While exuding bonhomie, Gwyn was a calculating politician who sought to use his professional skills in the new arena of Brussels. I quickly fell for his Welsh charm and silver tongue. I only realised much later that I had often been an innocent pawn in office politics. He was however a man of genuine compassion and at times showed me considerable personal consideration when I experienced personal problems.

I developed empathy for another member of our cabinet, Sue Lewis. Despite her young years, Sue was already a veteran of 10 Downing Street in the 1960s, where she had worked as secretary with Marcia Williams, PA to Prime Minister Harold Wilson. Her sister Liz had also worked closely with Wilson and her mother Betty was a long-standing employee at Labour Party HQ in Transport House, where she could be relied upon to pick up all the latest political gossip.

Although she could be sharp-tongued, I was to grow fond of Betty and her good-natured husband Bert, who was Head Waiter at London's posh West End Cafe Royale and hailed from London's East End. The Lewis's had a large council flat in Chelsea's salubrious Tite Street, not far from swinging Kings' Road. They were known for social generosity and lively parties and their flat saw many political get-togethers with senior Transport House staff, journalists, MPs and aspiring MPs, such as the then general manager of Jaguar cars, and later Coventry MP, Geoffrey Robinson.

Sue and I became quickly attached to each other, helped by being initially put up in the same Brussels hotel and we were to marry two years later. Our relationship was cemented during a dramatic incident when Sue was rushed into the nearest hospital with life-threatening peritonitis. Happily, she recovered quickly and much appreciated my concern, but her health was always a little suspect, not helped by her heavy smoking.

Soon we were living together in a small one-bedroom flat which I rented in Brussels' fashionable Uccle – or Ukkel in Flemish. This was just to the south of the city centre and had many attractive turn-of-the-century Art Noveau buildings. Sue had had several traumatic personal relationships before we had met. She saw in me someone different from the cynical political figures she had known and who had sought to use her to enhance their political careers. I, in turn, was fascinated by her and her family's deep commitment to, and engagement with, the Labour Movement, which spoke to my youthful idealism.

My old second-hand mini got me around Brussels and I subsequently replaced it with an equally small, but top-of the range bright red Mini GT 1275. Despite that, I frequently missed the Ostend car ferry to Dover and had to wait for the next one. On one occasion the police back home on the M2 Kent motorway stopped me for speeding. Seeing my Belgian number plates, they gave me a lecture, speaking very slowly to what seemed an ignorant foreigner. I complied by politely saying simply 'qui, Monsieur'. Luckily, they had not seen my British passport on the dashboard, so I was let off without points on my driving license.

Matters in Brussels were not helped by working together late hours in a small, incestuous office located on the top floor of the Berlaymont Commission building. The intensity of work was enormous, with much pressure and frequent late-night Commission meetings, sometimes lasting beyond midnight. There was also quite a lot of official travel back to the UK by plane as there was no Eurostar link as well as visits around the EEC.

There was a damaging drinking culture among Labour Party recruits to the Commission. Gwyn Morgan had an extremely well-stacked drinks cabinet in his office. We would start with whiskey or gins early evening and continue when work concluded, normally at 7 or 8 pm, This would climax in a much too late and boozy communal dinner, mostly at a local Italian restaurant, Alfredo's, around the corner from the Berlaymont. For good measure, the dinner party would then adjourn to the nearby British pub, The Drum, until the small hours. I still shudder at the amount of alcohol consumed, but as a young man I was able to absorb it without too much consequence the next day.

One reason for my recruitment to the cabinet had been my close involvement with the European Movement as its Youth Officer in 1972.

There was a need for George Thomson to maintain political contact with UK politicians, especially Labour's pro-Europeans. This was the time when much of the Labour Party's position towards the EEC remained highly negative. Party policy envisaged a British withdrawal from membership on assuming office unless significantly better conditions than the so-called 'Tory terms' could be negotiated. Labour Leader Harold Wilson was moreover still displeased at the defeat he had suffered in Parliament as a result of the vote for EEC membership by Thomson and his fellow Labour pro-Europeans.

A considerable amount of my time in 1973-74 was accordingly spent on looking after British MPs, trade unionists and Labour Party activists brought over to Brussels under the auspices of the Labour Committee for Europe. These included sceptics as well committed supporters, and aspiring politicians and future MPs, such as future Labour minister Ann Taylor. One visitor was Robert Kilroy-Silk, who already at that time showed the sex appeal which was to be a feature of his career as TV chat show host after the conclusion of his parliamentary career.

I believe our role in cementing links with key Labour Party opinion formers and demonstrating to them the practical value of Brussels to the UK, played a part in ensuring a more positive role towards the EEC, especially after Harold Wilson became Prime Minister again. It also contributed to the successful 'Yes' vote at the 1975 UK referendum on EEC membership.

On reflection, it is remarkable just how many Labour and trade union officials were hosted, and wined and dined, in a successful effort to convince them of the virtues of the EEC. In this work we collaborated closely with our Labour colleagues in the UK. These included another former European student activist, Geoff Harris, who went on to take a senior position as official in the Socialist Group of the European Parliament. We first met at my Brussels flat, together with young activists like the late Freddy Thielemans who became mayor of Brussels. Geoff was to author a thought-provoking book on the extreme Right in Europe in the 1980s, an issue even more relevant today. We became good friends and have kept up links over the years.

The need for advocacy work on Europe was shown at the TUC Congress held in September 1973. Here anti-EEC union leaders won a narrow vote deciding on a boycott of EEC institutions, despite opposition by the TUC's governing General Council. At the subsequent Labour Party Conference there was overwhelming support for the boycott policy.

A formal motion to withdraw from the EEC was only just defeated. It seemed the fight to say 'Yes to Europe' was not over but hotting up.

I have many amusing and not so amusing memories. Once I got stuck in a lift at midnight for an hour with the amiable Hampstead MP Ben Whitaker. Another time, a well-tanked former Labour Foreign Secretary, George Brown, threatened to have our young and inexperienced Commission driver dismissed. The poor guy was new and had got lost driving us around Brussels. I was appalled by Brown's attitude and also by his overtly Right-wing politics. I ended up arguing with him over dinner about his dire prediction of future splits in the Labour Party, which did prove to be prophetic given what happened in the early 1980s.

Another time, at a meeting, Gwyn Morgan kept falling asleep after a boozy Brussels lunch. We were with a senior British Coal Board delegation, headed by its Chairman, Sir Derek Ezra and National Union of Mineworkers leader, Joe Gormley. Every time Gwyn nodded off his not inconsiderable weight would transfer itself to his end of the large conference table around which we were seated. The table would then tip upwards, much to the merriment of all present.

On a further occasion, I was a last-minute substitute for Gwyn as an after-dinner speaker at the Welsh CBI in Llandudno. I gave what must have been a very boring and not well-delivered speech. This was not helped by wearing a light-coloured summer business suit when everyone else wore black tie. The only laugh of the evening came when, sitting down after speaking, my chair collapsed, and I ended up on my backside.

Happily, I got better at after-dinner speeches in later life.

3.

Apparatchiks versus Politicos

THERE IS AN INTRINSIC CONFLICT BETWEEN THE TRADITIONAL British concept of a minister's Private Office, and the continental concept of a 'cabinet'. The former has professional civil servants providing policy briefings, whereas the latter brings in appointed party-political advisers.

In truth, the Thomson cabinet combined Whitehall mandarins, mainly from the Foreign and Commonwealth Office and Labour Party activists. The civil servants had little time for what they saw as unprofessional and unruly Party politicos. We in turn disdained what we viewed as the unduly conservative attitudes of Whitehall apparatchiks. These tensions are of course not so different to those existing between ministerial political advisers and Whitehall civil servants today and have been brilliantly portrayed in the BBC sitcom *Yes Minister*.

There were several examples of the clash of policy and ideology within the Thomson cabinet. One of these concerned the regulation of multinational companies, or transnational corporations. In the later 1960s there had been increasing concern about the dominance of US companies in Europe as highlighted in Servan-Schreiber's best-selling book, *Le Defi American*, and high-profile political scandals involving big corporations such as ITT, the International Telephone and Telegraph Corporation. More generally, the growing power of multinational companies globally had attracted increased political concern among the Left and had, by the early 1970s, produced a wide range of literature and policy tracts.

In September 1973, following a suggestion by the Danish Government, Italian Commissioner Alterio Spinelli, an ex-communist and political prisoner under Mussolini and one of the European founding fathers, produced a policy paper on 'multinational firms'. This proposed European-level action to, among other things, safeguard workers' rights and protect developing countries from the actions of multinational companies. Significantly, the Spinelli proposal also noted the need for transnational trade unionism. Although I did not realise it at the time, this particular emphasis anticipated my future work in the trade union movement.

In my internal briefing note to George Thomson, I strongly argued that we support the proposal and 'resist attempts to water it down' as it 'puts pay to the argument that the Community is only concerned with enhancing capitalism and offsets demands aimed at confining countervailing action at the national level'. Here I was responding to the then prevailing attitude of the British Left that the EEC was a just a capitalist club.

The Spinelli policy paper set off alarm bells among pro-business conservatives in Whitehall. A new briefing paper put to George Thomson by the Whitehall members of his office argued that contrary to my advice, the Spinelli paper was 'badly drafted', and 'not well-worked out'. It noted that the paper was seen as 'anti-American' and 'anti-big business for purely political reasons' by the British Director-General of Industrial and Technological Affairs at the Commission, Ronald Grierson. Grierson, a former banker – and ex British Army officer with the Special Air Service (SAS) – who had been nominated for his position by the Heath Government. It proceeded to suggest that the proposal should be subsumed in a broader EEC paper on industrial policy by Grierson, which would no doubt have emasculated any radical ideas from Spinelli.

A watered-down version of the Spinelli paper was subsequently agreed by the Commission, and I hope my arguments in its support had helped it to survive. Despite this lesser version, the paper sent an important signal to the outside world of the EEC's seriousness in seeking international action on multinational – or transnational – companies.

Another key area I was involved with was new proposals on key EEC institutional reforms. These were based on an initial Commission paper of May 1973 and envisaged major changes in the period up to 1980, leading towards a 'European Union'. They included giving the European Parliament more powers, especially budgetary, and having direct elections to the Parliament at a time when its members were national MPs nominated by their governments. It further called for regular summit meetings of Heads of Government, which were not common, and it proposed Economic and Monetary Union.

These were reforms which were subsequently realised and had been advocated by the European Movement and by our student wing, SUE, in its 1971 manifesto. At the time they were looked on with great suspicion by the Heath Government and Whitehall. With my academic expertise in this area, I put up a strong case for supporting the proposed institutional reforms. Again, the British civil service members of the cabinet advised instead on a negative or minimalist response, questioning the very value of focusing on institutional reform at all. They also argued that we should not allow the European Parliament any jurisdiction over our new Regional Fund, which I found quite outrageous from a democratic point of view.

This inherent policy conflict soon festered into something nasty, with Gwyn Morgan and FCO Michael Jenkins competing for the ear of George Thomson. The raucous lifestyles of the 'Tafia' members did not help. Thomson himself was a kind man but had a reserved and frugal Scottish personality in sharp contrast to the Welsh bonhomie of Morgan. His idea of fun was singing Scottish folk songs around the piano with his wife Grace. In May 1973, there was to be a blazing row between Thomson and Morgan about an apparently unauthorised press briefing which Morgan had held in London, announcing the new EEC Regional Fund, pre-empting his boss. This soured relations.

British press gossip by journalist Terry Lancaster in *The People* newspaper about 'Morgan's Tafia' and the Labour Party 'exiles' did not help. Matters soon got worse, with accusations of professional incompetence flying around and personal animosities growing. Within a few months, the services of Labour activist John Randall were terminated. Sue Lewis lasted until the end of 1973. She had been appointed on account of her Labour Party experience but she, like Randall, had been given the incredibly tedious job of archivist, for which she had little interest and was given no training. This lack of archive knowledge was used as an excuse to terminate her employment.

Sue, with whom I was living at that stage, had played a big role in looking after visiting Labour Movement delegations throughout the year. This was something she continued to do even after having left the employment of the Commission. Together with other British colleagues we founded the Brussels Labour Group which sought regular interaction with the British Labour Party. With my German links, I moreover took part in meetings of the local German Social Democratic Party SDP group and even joined them for a weekend trip to canvass in a German State election campaign, which was great fun.

Sue subsequently worked for a Brussels-based Left-wing journal, *Agenor*, at a nominal salary. *Agenor* was a trailblazer, pioneering the new environmental and Green movement with policy papers such as

'The Greening of Marx'. It addressed women's rights and other equality issues. One of the dedicated environmentalists I met through *Agenor* was the forceful, if physically frail, co-founder of the German Green Party and environmental campaigner, Petra Kelly. Tragically in 1992, she and her lover and fellow Green politician, former Army General Gerd Bastian, were found shot dead in her house in Bonn. It seemed a double suicide pact, although the dramatic circumstances of their death have lent themselves to many conspiracy theories.

Given my personal relationship with Sue I was now in an awkward position. I was under increasing professional pressure. Often, I was asked to write policy briefs on complex subjects, such as the Common Agricultural Policy, energy, education, and consumer policy. These were subjects about which I had little prior knowledge. Most documents were often issued at short notice with a brief that was required immediately, while papers were frequently made available only in French, of which I had a poor understanding. In retrospect, I wonder if I was given this work to make my position untenable and to push me out of the cabinet. What perhaps made me more of a marked man was my principled refusal to leak – unlike others – confidential Commission working documents to UK Government representatives in Brussels and my overtly European federalist stance.

October 1973 saw the Middle East Yom Kippur or Ramadan War. The subsequent global economic crisis, triggered by the war, saw a quadrupling of oil prices from US$3 to US$12 a barrel. This had a serious impact on western economies, with inflation rates soaring in many countries. It also caused late night emergency meetings at the European Commission, where I held the energy brief in the Thomson cabinet and was able to follow developments intimately. Coming not long after the historic 1972 Stockholm Conference on the Human Environment, which established the UN Environmental Programme, the 1973 oil crisis raised serious policy issues about sustainability and reliance on carbon-based fossil fuels, especially oil. I well recall when, living in Brussels, an immediate response to the crisis was to introduce car-free Sundays for a while. Yet it took another thirty plus years and the 2008 global economic crisis before sustainability and climate change were seriously addressed.

Aside from my regular duties, I had something of a role as private secretary to the Commissioner. This initially included the writing of some of Thomson's more political speeches. However, the subtle nuances of this task, as opposed to putting down academic facts and figures, was not within my 23-year-old expertise. This work did though have its exciting and adventurous moments, when George and I toured the German regional development zone, flying along the Iron Curtain marking the East German border in a small, rather vulnerable, helicopter. On another occasion we flew, together with Commissioner Christopher Soames, through a torrid winter snowstorm from Strasbourg to Brussels. Our small eight-seater private plane was buffeted while the pilot kept flashing his wing lights to see if the plane's propeller blades were icing up. Happily, we landed safely in Brussels.

At the end of 1973, the Whitehall civil servants in the cabinet were firmly in the ascendancy. I felt increasingly isolated in the political positions I was taking, whether on multinational companies or EU institutional reforms. While there was little question of my being directly sacked from the Commission, I was 'offered' the opportunity to take a technically more secure full-time position at the same grade outside of the Thomson cabinet. This was to work with Maurice Foley in the Commission department dealing with international development policy, an area which became the centre of my subsequent professional career.

Under any normal circumstances, taking such an important post in an ideologically attractive area of work would have been extremely satisfying and I would have jumped at it. Indeed, it is usual for cabinet members, who are only temporary appointees, to look for more permanent jobs within the main Commission. Many younger ex-cabinet members of my time, such as my colleague Karel van Miert, a Belgian socialist, took other positions in the Commission; Karel would later rise to being European Commissioner.

I however, felt deeply upset at the time, seeing this offer as part of a wider conspiracy by the Whitehall apparatchiks to rid the cabinet of the remaining Labour Party members. In my youthful idealism and strong-headedness I obstinately refused the offer. Soon thereafter, the gossip column of the UK's *Guardian* newspaper reported on my imminent departure from the Thomson Cabinet and put it within the context of the general exodus of Labour Party activists. This was politically damaging to George Thomson at a time when a British General Election was looming, and Harold Wilson was threatening EEC withdrawal.

My love affair with Europe had gone sour. However, I always maintained my belief in European unity and kept close professional engagement with the EU throughout my career, supporting the 'Yes' cause in the 1975 UK referendum on the EEC and opposing Brexit in the 2016 vote. My deep commitment to the European ideal and to the concept of a United States of Europe has not wavered. What altered after my departure from the Commission in 1974 was my hitherto exclusive focus on EU institutions and my personal engagement with Labour's pro-European wing, who I had increasingly found too Right-wing for my liking. This led me to rediscover my earlier radical socialist instincts. As a result, I took of a leftward turn politically, like so many other *soixante-huitards* (sixty-eighters) and Labour activists in the 1970s.

In July 1974, not long after I had left the Thomson cabinet, *The Guardian* published a letter in which I criticised the conservatism of the British civil service. My letter called for support for the demands of civil service unions for basic political freedoms for their members and pointedly advocated the appointment of party-political advisers to Labour ministers. I concluded by asking for less hypocrisy from the Conservatives who I pointed out were 'quite content to continue rubbing shoulders with the higher placed Whitehall mandarins in the clubs of Pall Mall'. I guess it was a commentary on my experiences at the Commission.

In retrospect, my time in the Thomson cabinet was influenced by youthful naiveté, professional inexperence and my failure to develop better personal interaction with my boss, the late Lord George Thomson, for whose integrity and consistency I maintain a high respect. Certainly, I now hold him in greater esteem than Gwyn Morgan, now also deceased, who came unstuck when he himself was ousted as Thomson's Chef de Cabinet and ended up with peripheral EU jobs. I probably also took too much of a narrow and negative view of professional civil servants, whose expertise and integrity I came to value and understand in my interaction with them in future years.

My short period at the Commission gave me valuable inside knowledge of the practical workings of European institutions. This in turn benefitted my future professional career and ongoing engagement with the EU.

Perhaps fate pushed me in the right direction.

4.

Workers United

FEBRUARY 1974 SAW PRIME MINISTER HEATH CALLING THE so-called Miners' election on 'Who governs Britain'. This followed industrial action by the National Union of Mineworkers against his Government and his imposition of a three-day working week to ensure essential coal supplies.

I dropped everything and hurried over to London. Here I got a temporary unpaid staff assignment in the lead-up to the election. This involved working with Labour's Head of Research, Terry Pitt, at Party HQ in Transport House. In the event, Heath failed to secure a majority and Harold Wilson, as head of the largest party, formed a new Labour Government. Our private polls at Transport House had indicated a change in voter opinion during the last weekend of the campaign and I felt it had been a privilege to have been part of the HQ team which helped to turn things around. In contrast, George Thomson and Gwyn Morgan must have felt uneasy as only a month previously Wilson had criticised them in highly personal terms during a private dinner with French President Giscard d'Estaing. Potentially it was they who could now face the sack.

Following Labour's election, I and Sue Lewis had high hopes of returning to London and taking on a political job. Sue understandably was disappointed with Brussels and was anxious to return home and be with her family and friends. In my case Terry Pitt had moved to a senior policy adviser position at the Cabinet Office and had indicated that an opportunity might arise for me there to work with him. But our return to the UK in 1974 did not materialise because Terry did not stay at the Cabinet Office. Although a brilliant thinker, who had masterminded much of Labour's recent policy work, Terry had a bad drinking problem which was to do him much damage. He soon left for work overseas in Papua New Guinea for several years. My chances of working at the heart of the Wilson Labour government had disappeared and so I stayed in Brussels.

Terry returned to Britain and British politics some years later, physically and mentally restored, now a strict teetotaller. He proceeded to get himself elected as member of the European Parliament for his native Wolverhampton and seemed set on a great new career. It was good to see him in such revived spirits. Then returning late one night from Strasbourg, he fell asleep in the taxi which was taking him home from Birmingham airport. Tragically he choked to death on chewing gum lodged in his throat before the taxi could reach a hospital. It was with a sense of great sadness in my heart and personal loss of a good friend and comrade that I attended his subsequent funeral in Wolverhampton.

Having perhaps foolishly refused the offer of a good position in the European Commission, by mid-1974 I was in acute need of new employment. Hopes of a possible position with the Socialist Group of the European Parliament in Luxembourg, which had looked promising, did not materialise. I was staring unemployment in the eye just a bit over a year after I had landed my dream job. My options in Brussels seemed limited and I had nothing concrete to return to back home in the UK.

For a few months I took a poorly paid but interesting job as youth officer of the European Federalist Movement, based at their HQ in Brussels. This allowed me to revert to a little student politics. In cahoots with Julian Priestly and other young European Labour activists, I managed to undermine the Conservatives voting strength at a forthcoming Young European Federalist congress. This involved a prior trip to Norway. Here I was able to gather documentary evidence that much of their claimed youth membership – and voting strength – was fictitious. As a result, and much to their fury, we prevented their planned takeover of key posts at the European youth congress.

I then had a stroke of luck. One of my close political contacts was Dr Ernst Piehl, from the German Trade Union Council or TUC, the Deutsche Gewerksschaftsbund. Ernst had a friend, Renate Peltzer, who in turn worked for the International Confederation of Free Trade Unions, ICFTU, with its headquarters in Brussels. The ICFTU's prime concern was promoting worker's solidarity across frontiers. It also sought to represent trade union interest at international and global level, notably within the UN and its specialised agencies such as the International Labour Organisation, the ILO.

The 1970s were a time when progressive political movements and trade unions were on the ascendancy. They were also forging cross-frontier links to counteract the power of multinational companies. In the UK and many other western countries, unions were a powerful political force, with the British TUC approaching a membership of 12 million. It is today often forgotten what crucial role unions played in securing decent wages and living standards, how they fought for social benefits for ordinary workers and their families, and how strong they were in key industrial sectors such as manufacturing and mining.

Unions were frequently at the forefront of defending human and labour standards globally. Trade union leaders had led the earlier fight against colonialism and were now striving for national liberation against apartheid. After independence, many of these same union leaders in Africa, the Caribbean and elsewhere, took senior government posts, at times becoming Prime Minister or President of their country. Working with unions, especially internationally, therefore had great political appeal for me.

Through Renate I learnt of a vacancy as assistant in the Economic and Social Department of the ICFTU, which I successfully applied for. While considerably less well paid than at the European Commission, and lacking its tax free and other perks, this was a job strongly suited to my ideological interests. It also chimed with my professional qualifications in the area of research and policy formulation. Appropriately I started my new job on 1 May – international workers' day. I therefore left Europe to join the wider world, working for the global Labour Movement and becoming an active Global Citizen.

My new employer, the ICFTU, was an odd choice of career for a youthful ideologically-committed Left-wing Labour activist. The organisation had been set up at the height of the Cold War to fight communist-led unions – hence the word 'Free' in its title. There had been allegations of past CIA funding via its powerful American affiliate, the AFL-CIO, headed by Right-wing union boss, George Meany. The ICFTU was a bitter opponent to the rival communist World Federation of Trade Unions, based in Prague, and eschewed any contacts or cooperation just at a time when East-West détente was getting underway.

In the mid-1970s, when I joined, the ICFTU was being affected by the global winds of change. Meany, in an act of pique, had withdrawn the AFL-CIO from the organisation, claiming that it was going soft on communism. What had certainly changed was that the ICFTU was getting more responsive to demands for industrial democracy, for greater control of big business and multinational companies and for re-examination of global economic relationships, especially as they affected the developing world. It was now actively supporting key progressive causes like opposing apartheid in South Africa. This change was symbolised by my boss, the ICFTU's General Secretary, Otto Kersten, who had joined from the German TUC and represented a younger, more politically progressive post-war generation.

Much later, after the end of the Cold War, the ICFTU became the ITUC or International Trade Union Confederation, dropping the word 'free', associated as it was with Western Cold War ideology. It continues to do vital work in support of workers' rights throughout the world, which is as important ever. I was pleased to see that it recently elected Owen Tudor, a highly committed and effective TUC official, as its Deputy General Secretary.

The ICFTU was located in *Rue Montagne aux Herbes Potageres*, translating colourfully as the 'street of the mountain of vegetable herbs (or soup herbs)'. We were based close to Brussels' historic Grand Place and conveniently next to one of the lovely old Brussels pubs with the even more wonderful name of La Mort Subite, 'the Sudden Death'. Here I learnt about the ICFTU's colourful folklore. One of the amusing stories concerned two past staff members who were having an affair. They were caught in a highly comprising position after office hours on the personal desk of the then Secretary-General. The latter, on hearing about this, called for the two to be dismissed. Being a trade union after all, he relented and agreed on a severe reprimand on the condition that 'you get rid of that desk.'

The 1970s saw attempts to relax brutal Cold War divisions in Europe, which had been highlighted by the building of the Berlin Wall back in 1961. The leader of the German Social Democratic Party, the SPD, Willy Brandt, was a political inspiration to my generation. Brandt had been in exile during the Second World War and was not tainted by the shame of National Socialism. On becoming German Chancellor in 1969, he took a lead in forging a thaw in East-West relations. His humility was demonstrated when he dropped on his knees at a Jewish memorial in Poland seeking forgiveness for German war crimes: an admission of a terrible guilt, for which a younger generation of Germans have had to atone for their elders. He had deservedly received the Nobel Peace Prize in 1971.

Willy Brandt was one of my political heroes. I encountered Brandt personally when he visited Brussels to give an address and was much impressed by his humanity and personal charisma. He was someone who came across as a very warm human being. My other encounter with him was attending an SPD Congress in the mid-1970s. This was marked by an amusing incident at the opening ceremony. The letters 'SPD' had been suspended from the ceiling high above the assembled party executive on the podium. Halfway through the ceremony, one of the letters, happily only made from cardboard, came crashing down. Apparently, the hot TV lights had served to unfasten the adhesive tape that had secured it. While the party executive kept a solemn expression, I and foreign guests were highly amused.

I came across Willy Brandt's successor as German Chancellor, Helmut Schmidt, a bit later. He was a highly articulate, chain-smoking politician who did not suffer fools gladly. Schmidt had been invited to speak at the annual Labour Party Conference, which he did in his usual impeccable English. Here too, an amusing incident occurred. Unbeknown to the Chancellor, a heated debate on Britain and the European Economic Community, the EEC, was underway. This was, after all, the days of 'Old' Labour.

As he was arriving, one agitated Labour delegate rushed to the front of the hall, near where Schmidt was sitting, demanding to speak. The German Chancellor's bodyguards, not versed in the democratic ways of the Labour Party Conference, thought an attack on their boss was imminent and visibly reached for their concealed weapons. Happily, the Conference Chair resumed control before any Party delegates were forced to withdraw to their seats at gunpoint.

I soon found my feet in the global Labour Movement. Within two years of joining, I was put in charge of the ICFTU's economic policy formulation as secretary to its Economic and Social Committee. This involved directing key working parties on multinational companies and on international trade and development policy. An innovation I oversaw was publication of an annual *'Review of the World Economic Situation'* looked at from the standpoint of the employee. In this research work I could draw on the know-how of experienced union experts from member organisations such as the Swedish TUC, as well as the British TUC.

My work brought me close contact with top union and political leaders from across the world. One of these was the young Wim Kok, who headed the Dutch unions and was subsequently to become Labour Prime Minister in The Netherlands. I well remember us having fun together, indulging at games of 'bar football' at local pubs with a beer or two. Others included

Bob Hawke, soon to become Australian Prime Minister, and Dr Devan Nair, who ended up as President of Singapore. On the British side there was the head of the powerful Transport and General Workers' Union, Jack Jones, who became something of a personal mentor to me, and the TUC's thoughtful General Secretary, Len Murray.

On occasions I represented the ICFTU on fraternal bodies, including an economic policy committee of the Socialist International. The latter organisation brought together the world's Socialist, Social Democratic and Labour parties and was headed by French socialist and future Prime Minister Michel Rocard, who I encountered at several meetings.

In all this work, Kersten and his Belgian deputy, Johnny Vanderveken, my immediate boss, gave me much personal encouragement and remarkable professional freedom of action for an earnest and rather brash young man who was only in his mid-20s. This allowed me to grow professionally for which I am grateful, and I retain fond memories of my time at the ICFTU, cooperating with colleagues from all over the world and becoming good friends with colleagues like Christa Deistler who worked in the accounts department.

What was different from my previous European work was that I was now engaged in a truly global international environment: I had colleagues from Africa, Asia and the Americas, all under the overall direction of a Canadian President, Donald MacDonald, who was succeeded in 1975 by a Malaysian, Dr P.P. Narayanan. Here English, not French, was the lingua franca. Combined with living in a Flemish-speaking part of Brussels, Ukkel, my French never really got fluent. This is something I regretted years later when I represented the Commonwealth at French-speaking meetings in Paris, Dakar and elsewhere. I usually got by and understood the gist of what was being said, but my French grammar was awful.

My work at the ICFTU coincided with the establishment of the autonomous new European Trade Union Council (ETUC). Unlike the ICFTU, the ETUC sought to bring together different ideological groupings in Western Europe, drawn also from the Leftist-Christian World Confederation of Labour and later, much to the disgust of George Meany, the Italian Euro-communist union TUC CGIL. This initially caused unease at the ICFTU.

Within a few months of taking over my new job, I was sent on my first visit to Asia and the Far East, to Thailand, Indonesia, and Singapore where I encountered its astute post-independence leader Lee Kuan Yew and union boss Devan Nair. My return included a stop to meet unions in

Sri Lanka of which more later. I was very spoilt on the trip as it was sponsored by a well-heeled international organisation which provided a first-class air ticket. This was one of the very few occasions in my entire career I have been able to indulge in this luxury. My regular ICFTU and most subsequent professional flights were strictly economy class as is the norm with not-for-profit bodies.

Not long after I was paying my first-ever visit to the African continent. I still remember the excitement of touching down in Nairobi, not realising that the coming decades I would be making the journey to Africa many times over. In Kenya, British colonial troops had fought against the indigenous Mau Mau insurgency. In doing so, the British used brutal and unethical methods which were later to result in legal cases being brought against the UK Government. Looking back on this dark chapter in European colonisation, which tends not to be taught in British schools, I am reminded of the image attributed to Kenya's first President, Jomo Kenyatta, who said "When the white man came and we had our land, they brought us the bible and taught us to pray. When we opened our eyes after praying, we had the bible and they had the land".

In its work, the ICFTU was closely allied with the so-called International Trade Secretariats. These included the International Metalworkers Federation, the International Transport Workers Federation and the International Union of Food and Allied Workers. Such organisations brought together individual unions from particular sectors like engineering, transport and the food industries, whereas the ICFTU and the ETUC were umbrella bodies for national federations of trade unions, the 'TUCs'.

In 1975, I got to travel to Mexico City for the ICFTU's World Congress. In preparation, I had written a policy paper on global experiences of Industrial Democracy, which was formally adopted by ICFTU members at the Congress. This paper may have played a part in influencing the British TUC towards adopting a more open-minded attitude towards co-determination and worker participation on company boards, as opposed to the UK's traditional 'them-and-us' confrontation with employers, which relied only on collective bargaining.

It is interesting in retrospect to speculate whether Margaret Thatcher would have been able to enact her subsequent anti-union legislation to quite such an extent if British unions had had the kind of entrenched legal system of industrial democracy which their counterparts in Germany or Sweden enjoyed. Such a legal system was proposed in the late 1970s by the Bullock Report under the Callaghan Labour Government but got mothballed by the advent of the Thatcher Government in 1979.

The year 1975 was also the year Sue Lewis and I tied the knot, having lived together for two years and become engaged in 1974. Our wedding was a grand affair and was reported in British newspapers like *The Guardian*. We married in the historic St James's Church, Piccadilly, built by Sir Christopher Wren. I was wearing a smart grey morning suit and Sue wore a glamorous long white wedding dress. I well remember how our wedding party outside the church was subject to snapshots by passing Japanese tourists. The wedding ceremony was followed by a posh reception at the nearby Café Royale where Sue's dad was in charge of the catering services. A more relaxed and noisier 'knees-up' was to take place in the evening at the Lewis' large council flat in Chelsea.

Amusingly, the wedding had been postponed at short notice for two weeks from the original date 'because of national events beyond our control': a special Labour Party meeting. This would have prevented many guests attending, including potentially my future mother-in-law, Betty. At least one guest, my former university professor from Reading, Hugh Thomas (later Lord Thomas), ended up arriving two weeks early on the original wedding date to find an empty church.

The wedding turned out to be a Labour Party society event. Present were many Labour Party officials, several MPs and Peers. Among the telegrams read out was a message of congratulations from the Prime Minister, Harold Wilson, for whom Sue had worked in the 1960s and who was represented by his personal aide, Sue's earlier boss, Marcia Williams (later Lady Falkender).

There were telegrams wishing us a close 'European Union' and a good 'Social Contract' – the latter referring to the recent agreement between the then Labour government and the unions. The wedding coincided with trade union solidarity action I was coordinating through the ICFTU to support tea workers in Sri Lanka. To my delight, *The Guardian* gave front-page treatment to the campaign on the very day of my wedding. A reference to our Sri Lanka campaign accordingly provided a key part of my somewhat unconventional wedding speech. More conventional family guests must have been confused at all the political language and rousing rendering of the 'Red Flag', not a song heard too often at the Café Royale.

My family members attending the wedding included my parents, grandmother and a small contingent of my German relatives on my mothers' side. These included my grandmother's younger brother and my favourite great uncle, Curt Ackermann, looking extremely smart in evening attire. Uncle Curt was a class act of his own. He lived in the comfortable West Berlin suburb of Lichterfelde with his wife Eleanor, a former dancer of Hungarian and Austrian descent.

Curt had been an actor in pre-war Berlin. He had never hidden his disgust of the Nazis, and it was said on one famous occasion had refused to shake the hand of Nazi propaganda minister Joseph Goebbels at quite some personal risk. One of his riveting stories was how, despite being able-bodied, he had avoided being drafted into the German Army. Faced with his call-up orders at the time of Hitler's *Goettersdaemmerung* (Twilight of the Gods) in 1945, a dubious Hungarian doctor prescribed him tablets which turned his skin yellow. This allowed him to claim jaundice and avoid almost certain death in facing Soviet troops advancing on Berlin.

Sadly, two factors subsequently worked against our marriage: continuing to live in Brussels where Sue was very unhappy; and my frequent absences overseas on account of my work, which often left her alone bored in a foreign city, looking for company. I was aware of Sue's homesickness, and we did pay frequent visits back to London, driving my little red Mini at crazy speeds to catch the last ferry from Ostend or Calais to Dover.

Increasingly, we drifted apart. I sought to keep the marriage going, taking Sue with me on visits to Africa and the USA in 1977, but it was too late. We separated and Sue returned to London with divorce following in 1978. I was happy when she later married *Guardian* journalist David Gow, whom she had met in Brussels and went to live in Wales. However, I failed to keep up contact after I, myself, re-married in 1980. Then in 2000, I heard the awful news that poor Susan, still young, had contracted a brain tumour. She died within the year, and it was with a tear in my eye that I attended her funeral on a miserable wet day in Wales and laid a red rose on her grave.

My years had their ups and downs, but despite personal setbacks I have always believed in the glass being half full rather than half empty.

5.

Fair Labour Rights

I WAS NOW CAMPAIGNING FOR FAIR LABOUR RIGHTS, DECENT conditions of employment, proper wages and recognition of trade unions. This was at the very heart of what I believed in as a grass roots activist.

The International Labour Organisation in Geneva is the guardian of global labour rights. These rights are enshrined in ILO conventions and number in excess of 100. Once ratified by governments, the ILO seeks to ensure their application, mainly by public exposure of abuses and by applying moral persuasion; it has no army to enforce its standards on sovereign governments. Among the more important ILO conventions are fair labour standards, such as those dealing with the prevention of child labour and recognition of trade union rights, notably ILO Conventions 87 and 98.

The ILO took a lead role in exposing repressive regimes like Pinochet's Chile and apartheid South Africa, providing a public global platform for their opponents. Non-democratic countries, military regimes and One Party-states were frequently in the dock. Nor did the ILO shrink from publicly criticising Western states as in the case with Margaret Thatcher's ban on union membership in the intelligence gathering Government Communications Headquarters, GCHQ, which contravened fair labour standards.

The ILO was housed in a large dull grey, but imposing, building, flanked by the lofty Jura Mountains and overlooking tranquil Lake Geneva. It is the only UN institution that predates the Second World War. Unlike other purely intergovernmental agencies, the ILO has a unique tripartite governance structure composed of government, employers' and trade union representatives. Once a year in June, the International Labour Conference meets in the elegant splendour of the Palais de Nations, attended by hundreds of delegates from around the world. In the 1970s the conference and associated Governing Body meetings amazingly lasted a whole month or longer. This provided delegates with ample opportunity for weekend tours around the beautiful lake and excursions into the stunning Swiss and French mountains, as well as a host of other extra-curricular activities.

Inevitably the ILO, like other UN bodies, got sucked into the vortex of Cold War politics. For a while the US Government, under the influence of George Meany, withdrew from ILO membership on the basis that, like the ICFTU, it too was going soft on communism and also taking a too pro-Arab and anti-Israel stance. My own work as a union activist was, frankly, made possible by the absence of the AFL-CIO from the ICFTU and ILO. I doubt the latter would have agreed 'Leftist' policies whether on industrial democracy or on global development policy which I managed to steer through the ICFTU.

Ironically, I spent a fair bit of time cultivating American unions during frequent trips to the USA and was a regular visitor to AFL-CIO headquarters and the US Department of Labor in Washington. My visits made me aware of the progressive wing of the US movement represented by the United Autoworkers Union which I hoped would replace the moribund AFL-CIO leadership of George Meany and his dour and equally conservative-minded successor Lane Kirkland.

The ICFTU, had its own office in Geneva and played a central role in the politics of the ILO, acting as the unofficial secretariat of the ILO's Workers' Group and lobbying for key trade union interests. Starting in 1975, I became a regular participant at the annual ILO conferences, usually being assigned as the ICFTU secretary to the important Resolutions Committee which was at the heart of the political battles being fought each year. It was an event I looked forward to, and usually drove my little red mini all the way from Brussels to Geneva through picturesque French countryside, arriving tired in the evening having navigated the Jura mountains down steep zig-zagging roads.

The politics of the ILO were complex. There were times when the Workers' Group colluded with the Employers' Group against the Governments. At other times alliances were forged with friendly governments against the Employers. It was a little like a three-dimensional game of chess. More often than not, we were successful in getting the trade union position approved and securing important advances in fair labour standards, especially for workers in the developing world. They could then use and refer to those ILO standards when fighting for their rights back home.

My most notable grass roots activism in pursuit of ILO standards concerned the battle to protect the rights of Sri Lankan tea workers. Their plight was highlighted in a British Granada ITV documentary which looked at employment on the estates of British multi-nationals such as Brooke Bond Liebig and Lonrho. During a visit to the tea estates in Sri Lanka in late 1974, I witnessed the appalling working and living conditions of the Tamil tea workers and their families, especially on the Lonrho estates. I saw how companies failed to provide the most elementary housing and sanitation for their workforce and how they paid starvation wages. This made me determined to try and achieve change for the better.

My visit was organised by the Ceylon Workers Congress and its then leader and future Government Minister, Savumiamoorthy Thondaman, and had its cloak-and-dagger aspects. As union access to many estates was restricted by the employers, I had to resort to visiting the estates illegally at the depth of night. I would then, as quietly as possible, document my findings with the use of an old-fashioned camera and flashbulbs. The harrowing black and white photographs I took revealed the callous exploitation that existed and were later used for a high-profile international campaign in the British media.

The one occasion I sought to pay a daytime visit to a remote Lonrho-owned tea estate, I got into deep trouble. On arriving, I and my Sri Lankan union colleague were immediately surrounded by angry management thugs. They had large sticks and were beginning to threaten us. At this stage I feared the worst: a severe beating could have been on the cards, and, as no-one knew our whereabouts, we could easily have 'disappeared' without trace. I was at a loss as to what to do. It was too late to run away, and I started to sweat.

Luckily, my accompanying union official had much presence of mind. He persuaded the thugs to frogmarch us unceremoniously to the local Sri Lankan managers' bungalow. On seeing us the manager started shouting and screaming, demanding to know what we were up to. I feared the worst. My colleague then showed his brilliance. He demanded the manager phone his head office in Colombo to confirm we had permission to visit the estate. This of course we had not, and I was uncertain how this tactic would help. But sure enough, not being able to get through to Colombo by landline, this being before the advent of mobile phones, the manager fell for our bluff. He smiled and waved away the 'heavies', offering us a nice cup of tea instead.

On leaving the estate, I asked my union colleague how he could have known the manager would be unable to get through to Colombo by phone. He smirked and his cheerful reply was that 'the phones never work when it is raining' – which indeed it was. He also disclosed that his wife worked on the local telephone exchange and had been under strict instruction not to put any calls from the estate's manager through to Colombo. I was able to wipe the sweat from my brow. It was good to be with a colleague who was canny and streetwise.

While my bosses at the ICFTU gave me full encouragement in my efforts in support of the tea workers, I encountered indifference on the part of the organisation which should have been giving the lead, the British TUC. This was not because of the TUC leadership under its able and highly professional General Secretary Len (later Lord) Murray. I always greatly respected Len and many of the leading British trade unionists were strongly internationalist and supportive of my work. The reason instead lay in the cynicism and bureaucratic approach of the then Head of the TUC 'FCO' or International Department, Alan Hargreaves. I was to have other battles with him. He reminded me of the very Foreign Office bureaucrats I had fallen out with at the European Commission.

Refusing to take no for an answer, I incurred Hargreaves' wrath by side-stepping him and approaching a senior trade union friend, Alec Kitson, for help. Alec was a blunt-speaking Scot with a heart of gold, and Assistant General Secretary of my own union, the powerful Transport and General Workers Union. He was also Chair of the Labour Party's International Committee run by another political friend, Jenny Little. Alec's response was uncompromisingly supportive. As a result, and by linking-up with the committed investigative journalists on ITV's *World in Action*, our campaign in support of the Sri Lanka tea workers took off.

Our actions on Sri Lanka had considerable impact. Soon the issue of the tea workers was raised at the AGMs of the companies concerned. An official House of Commons fact-finding mission was sent to Sri Lanka. This called on the British employers to make urgent changes. Newspapers like *The Guardian* provided extensive coverage. The Sri Lanka Government now took notice of the international outrage and decided to nationalise the tea estates with a view to improving conditions.

Faced with bad publicity and marginal profits in the growing of tea, the companies decided to let the Sri Lanka government go ahead with nationalisation. As a result, they were able to divest themselves of the embarrassing responsibility over the conditions and pay of the workforce while cleverly maintaining control over the more profitable marketing and selling of tea. They thus escaped their direct responsibilities for the work force and forced us to focus on getting the Sri Lanka Government to take positive action instead. This was complicated by the ethnic divide between the minority Tamils on the tea estates and the majority Singhalese. Nonetheless, much to my personal satisfaction, conditions did improve significantly after some time.

My early battles with the TUC bureaucracy made me understand why another TUC employee, who I met also working in the economic field at this time, decided to quit the organisation in frustration. This was fellow member of the Young European Left, later Labour cabinet minister and European Trade Commissioner, (now Lord) Peter Mandelson. However, as time went on, I became skilled in dealing with TUC procedures and allying myself to key union leaders, most of which were genuinely supportive of global engagement to enforce fair labour rights.

I soon got to understand the trade union slogan *Solidarity Forever*.

6.

New International Economic Order

BY THE END OF THE DECADE THERE WAS MUCH TALK ABOUT establishing better and more equitable global economic relations. This gave rise to the UN's call for a New International Economic Order.

The new global order was to address poverty and employment, with fair labour standards governing world trade and international guidelines to guide flows of capital across borders by multinational companies. The demand was spearheaded by the Group of 77 developing countries at the UN; it was also closely aligned to what the ICFTU and progressive political parties of the Left were seeking. In consequence, I was able to align international union policy with efforts to reform the world economic structures. We also deployed our close links with the Socialist International and with Labour and Social Democratic governments. This was after all a time when trade unions in the developed countries, especially in Europe, were highly influential politically and when Social Democratic governments held power.

The ICFTU was to be actively involved with the *Brandt Commission on North-South Relations* which made radical proposal for global reforms. The Commission was headed by the by the ex-German Chancellor, which *inter alia* included the President of the Canadian Labour Congress, a key ICFTU affiliate, as well as my future boss, Shridath Ramphal, the Commonwealth Secretary-General. The many other notables on the Commission included former prime ministers; Britain's Edward Heath and Sweden's Olaf Palme. It published its influential findings in 1980 and a year later I was, myself, a contributor to a report setting out international responses to its recommendations, alongside a wide range of high-level authors including Helmut Schmidt and Margaret Thatcher.

Trade union support for the New International Economic Order was not unqualified. What we demanded was more equality not only between but also within nations. We argued, with considerable justification, that a new global system was of limited value if the benefits only went to local elites and did not help the mass of the people. Our policy had been set out in an ICFTU 'Development Charter', which I was able to guide through our Economic and Social Committee and had been approved by the ICFTU members at our Congress in Mexico City in 1975.

The union advocacy for a New International Economic Order centred on negotiations for fairer trade relations. Here the ILO had an influential role. In 1976, I served in the secretariat and drafting committee of the extraordinary ILO World Employment Conference which had been convened as the ILO's input to the debate on the New International Economic Order. The global conference was to adopt an important Action Programme. This dealt with the right to work and what were termed 'basic needs' such as housing, health and education, a concept which was to have a lasting legacy. Among those involved with the ILO and developing the concept of basic needs were distinguished economists such as Sir Richard Jolly, who I came to know well and who later became UNICEF Deputy Executive Director, where he played a key role in global development strategies.

The World Employment Conference, like EEC meetings in Brussels, had involved all-night drafting sessions and 'stopping the clock' to approve a last-minute deal. One of our more difficult tasks during a hot Geneva summer's night was finding ways of keeping our elderly chairman, the Minister from Indonesia, from dropping off asleep in the early hours. We achieved this by periodically opening the windows for a blast of fresh air, there being no air conditioning, but this was accompanied by swarms of buzzing insects from Lake Geneva. Swatting these was also a good way to keep ourselves awake.

Apart from politics, there was much social activity in Geneva, which revolved around nightly receptions hosted by different national delegations. These were often held in the residences of various ambassadors with breathtakingly beautiful views of the lake and the mountains. There was rarely a lack of free alcohol. On one occasion the reception was hosted by a teetotal Indian Minister, and I suddenly noticed that my gin and tonic had only tonic in it. Perhaps predictively, that reception was over in record time.

Geneva in June was when many top trade union leaders from around the world attended. Among those I got particularly friendly with were the union leader from Australia, Bob Hawke and from New Zealand,

Jim Knox. Jim was a large burly man who got easily excited but had a heart of gold; one of his party pieces being to do a Mâori war dance, the Hakka, on top of a dinner table which happily survived his substantial weight.

Bob Hawke, who in 1983 became Leader of the Australian Labor Party and not long thereafter Prime Minister, was in a class of his own. Bob was lean and handsome, had enormous charisma with many attractive female admirers in tow. He was also a great drinker, and I believe he is still listed in the *Guinness Book of Records* for consuming a yard of ale in just eleven seconds.

Hawke was a shrewd and highly intelligent tactician, an able chairman of the ILO Resolutions Committee, with whom I worked closely throughout my time in Geneva. I frankly fell under his spell and became part of his personal entourage. As one of Bob's 'mates' on at least one occasion I was called to assist him in dealing with the fallout from a more dubious amorous adventure the previous night. I am not being indiscreet here, as much of this was set out in his authorised biography which helped endear him to the Aussie electorate. Bob in return was always incredibly supportive and never failed to see me or refuse his support when he became Prime Minister, including at key Commonwealth conferences such as in Nassau in 1985.

One of my most memorable recollections concerns a late-night ILO Resolutions Committee meeting in Geneva. This finished around midnight. Returning to the narrow, cobbled streets of the old medieval town, which were largely deserted, a small group of 'mates', led by Hawke, resolved to have a drink to celebrate our successes at the Committee. Unfortunately, local pubs had already closed, or, seeing us coming, quickly shut their doors.

In desperation, walking down the quiet Geneva side street, Hawke led us in a raucous chorus of *'Waltzing Matilda'*. As if by magic, the door of a parked VW kombi-bus opened, and two Aussie youngsters peered out, amazed at seeing the head of their trade unions in full voice.

Almost immediately a street party materialised, with bottles of wine and cans of Fosters beer passed from the kombi-bus. The party finished when a local lady in an upstairs flat, enraged at all the noise, tipped something nasty down on us from her window. She also threatened to call the police, so we decided to move on. The booze had at any rate been exhausted by then. The moral of the story, as I reminded Prime Minister Bob Hawke when I once met him at Parliament House, Canberra, was that if you are ever desperate for a drink, sing *'Waltzing Matilda'* and a can of Fosters will materialise from nowhere.

Of all the political policy instruments to which I was able to help formulate during my time as head of the ICFTU's Economic and Social Committee, one of the most enduring and important was the so-called 'social clause' for international trade. This policy was overwhelmingly agreed by trade unionists from developed as well as developing countries, with the only dissenters being a few state-controlled unions from the Far East. The social clause is a simple concept: in order to ensure fair labour standards throughout the world and avoid the exploitation of child labour or non-union labour, governments benefitting from international trade concessions must subscribe to core ILO fair labour standards. If they do not, it was proposed that trade concessions be withdrawn and, if necessary, trade sanctions imposed on the country concerned.

The proposal has aroused controversy for many years and continues to be revived periodically at the World Trade Organisation and elsewhere. Opposition to the social clause comes from an unholy alliance of elites in developing countries hostile to organised labour, and greedy employers wanting to exploit cheap labour in order to maximise profits. There are some development economists who rate unhindered free trade over anything, regardless of the human cost, and wrongly claim that the social clause is a protectionist measure for Western workers. In fact, it is the exploited work force in both developed and developing countries and those marginalised by globalisation, that stand to benefit most from it. It is also nonsense to say that a social clause will only benefit that minority of the workforce which is currently in a trade union: the historical evidence points to unions helping to secure social and economic rights for all the working population.

One of my key responsibilities was to coordinate an ICFTU Working Party on Multinational Companies, which sought to initiate union policy towards transnational capital. Here I was building on my previous engagement on this issue while still at the European Commission, having worked on the earlier Spinelli initiative. This, too, was part of seeking to forge the New International Economic Order.

By the mid-1970s, the growing power of international capital had become evermore apparent. It was seriously undermining trade unions at national level, particularly in developing countries, where the level of union organisation was often weak and bad employers felt they could flex their muscles. Indeed, in many undemocratic places around the world, less scrupulous employers lent on, or openly bribed, local regimes to enact repressive anti-union legislation. They would also set up free enterprise zones with lower working rights and even bans on unions.

Already in 1971, the value added by each of the top ten multinationals was in excess of US$ 3 billion, greater than the GNP of eighty countries at the time. A number of scandals had focused public attention on the negative role of international capital. As a result, the Council of Europe and many national legislatures, including the US Congress, the UK House of Commons and the German Bundestag held special hearings or investigations. These were devoted to assessing the impact of multinationals and I gave evidence to several of these.

I wrote about these issues in a pamphlet published by the Fabian Society, *Transnational Corporations: A Strategy for Control* in 1977. Like other Fabian pamphlets, this was not an arid academic tract, but contained serious policy proposals designed to influence the thinking of Government. My suggestions included enhanced trade union cooperation and securing greater controls at national and international level. I also proposed that such a strategy for control should feature in the manifestos of socialist parties campaigning for direct elections to the European Parliament in 1978.

The strategy of the unions was accordingly two-fold: strengthening our own sister union organisations, especially in developing countries, alongside targeted 'solidarity' campaigns against bad employers; and calling for greater national and international regulation of the activities of multinationals by governments. The latter involved drawing up international codes of conduct, ideally legally binding; however, counter-lobbying by employers ensured they turned out to be mostly voluntary in nature.

An important idea was to seek mandatory consultation by companies of their workforce representatives prior to major investment decisions or indeed company closures. This strategy was linked to growing demands, which had originated in Germany in the late 1960s, for 'co-determination' or industrial democracy at the workplace. In some cases, there was even a call for full-blooded 'workers' control', involving bottom-up socialisation, rather than top-down nationalisation, of the means of production.

The 1970s saw practical efforts to address the vastly increased post-war power of international capital and the multinational or transnational companies. This included the establishment of a new UN Commission of Transnational Corporations, based in New York, to draw up an international code of conduct to govern their behaviour. Partly to pre-empt the UN, a somewhat milder code was agreed by Western OECD countries, although some of its provisions were tightened a bit on the urging of its Paris-based Trade Union Advisory Committee, the meetings of which I attended. Specialised codes were also drawn up by various other agencies such as the ILO.

In recognition of the importance of the proposed UN code, I was assigned to be the adviser at the UN Commission, taking advantage of the ICFTU's consultative status at the UN. This assignment meant frequent visits to New York, where I rented a small apartment off East 54th Street in heart of Manhattan. I soon got to know and love the Big Apple. It also meant I became familiar with the inside workings of the UN HQ and was able to navigate my way around the complex geography of its chambers, corridors and delegate lounge. The lounge incidentally served excellent expresso coffee, good for keeping you awake in sometimes highly laborious UN sessions.

In New York, I worked closely with David (now Lord) Lea, then head of the TUC economic department who was one of several appointed trade union experts to the UN Commission. David had a brilliant mind and a good sense of tactics but could be abrasive. This probably stopped him becoming the successor to Len Murray as TUC General Secretary. Rather than David, the TUC chose the jovial, but less effective, Norman Willis of the TGWU as new TUC General Secretary. Sadly, Norman presided over the acute decline and marginalisation of the organisation under the onslaught of the Thatcher government and the chaos of the Miners' Strike in the 1980s, spearheaded by its firebrand General Secretary of the National Union of Miners, Arthur Scargill.

We had some strange bedfellows in New York, progressive Western Governments, but also the Group of 77 developing countries (G-77) and the communist bloc. Occasionally we managed to put political and moral pressure on Western governments, and in one instance got the UK delegation to do a *volte face* by going over their heads direct to 10 Downing Street. On the other side were business representatives who, unlike us, had whole teams of lawyers and advisers to help them; business could also count on the support of many Western Government representatives.

We had a good line to the Finnish Director of the UN Commission, Klaus Sahlgren and his personal adviser, Kari Tapiola, a former Finnish trade unionist, who was to become a good friend and later held senior positions at the ILO. During this time, I became close to one of the senior UK Government representatives, Pamela Denham. Another great friend was Aracelly Santana, from Ecuador, an able and highly politically committed UN official.

Much effort was put into the work on the UN code and after many lengthy negotiations a relatively definitive draft was close to completion. David Lea and I were particularly pleased that we had been able to include provisions for what we hoped would be mandatory advance consultation of trade unions by multinationals on key investment and other decisions. This was also a battle which was to be fought for in the provisions of the future European Social Charter.

It seemed that the world was at the onset of a new progressive era.

7.

The 1970s – A Reflection

MY CAREER STARTED AT THE TENDER AGE OF 22. BEFORE long I was travelling the world and stalking the international corridors of power.

As a student in the early 1970s I had been involved at the political campaign to secure British membership of the EEC and this engagement provided me with early skills in the art of political advocacy; it also turned me into a grass roots Labour Party activist, becoming intimately acquainted and involved with the machinations of the wider Labour Movement.

This meant I had strong political convictions from an early age, which did not always sit well when I was employed in formal intergovernmental organisations, be it the European Commission in 1973-74 or indeed later in the Commonwealth Secretariat 1988-94. However, the experience of working inside these official structures gave me a thorough understanding of how these bodies function and how to influence them from the outside, which was invaluable in my later advocacy work. It also provided me with a great network of professional contacts and friends who could be drawn on for support.

The expansion of the EEC in 1973, and the UK's clear 'Yes to Europe' vote in the 1975 EU referendum, set the scene for greater European integration. As one of the first Brits to work in Brussels in 1973, I was present at the birth of the European Regional Development Fund, the early efforts at EU policy on multinational companies and the beginnings of the drive towards greater democratisation and integration, including through the European Parliament.

These were things which I had written my university Masters theses on just a year previously. I was now able to engage with all of this at a senior policy level and see how things played out in practice. This work experience allowed me to test my earlier theoretical knowledge against the innermost workings of European relations and the complex intergovernmental mechanisms and institutional processes involved.

By the mid-1970s, my focus had switched to the global scene as a trade union official employed by the ICFTU. My union work required extensive travels around the world in support of labour rights and much grass roots activism, not without danger, as during my exploits on the Sri Lanka tea estates. It further involved direct exposure to the functioning of the global structures of the UN, especially the ILO. As a result, I came to understand the workings of high diplomacy and got engaged in important international decision-making processes, for example on the drafting committee of the 1976 Word Employment Conference and through my advisory role at the UN Commission on Transnational Corporations.

Looking back on it, my contribution to ensure the adoption of the 1976 ILO basic-needs strategy gives me particular professional satisfaction. The basic needs approach was to foreshadow later developmental thinking and it anticipated the 2000 Millennium Development Goals, MDGs, a quarter of a century later, with their focus on the setting of goals to meet basic needs such as water, sanitation, health, education and housing provision. These in turn led to the Sustainable Development Goals, SDGs, in 2015 which cover the same, but also many other basic needs. Sadly, it was only then that governments accepted a new UN Sustainable Development Goal, SDG 10, on reducing inequality within and among countries, reflecting the earlier language of the 1970s.

My ICFTU work gave me comprehension of the complex interrelationship between government and non-governmental organisations, NGOs, especially at international level. Strictly speaking the ICFTU, a Labour Movement body, was not a NGO, as it has a distinct political dimension on account of its trade union membership across the world. While some of the same parameters and rules applied, for example with regard to formal status and representation at UN meetings, trade unions clearly had much greater political clout than most NGOs. This was on account of their close relationship with socialist and social democratic parties, many of which were in government in the 1970s and sympathetic to trade union aims.

This work taught me an important lesson, which is that to be an effective advocate at international level, it is vital to have political influence at national level, given that the UN and other bodies are composed of nation states. The ILO with its tripartite nature was a bit different, and some aspects of EU policy making by the European

Commission has always had an element of independence from national government, but ultimately it is the latter who call the tune and pay the bills. This is why, if I wanted, say, the UK Delegation at the UN support a key proposal, it paid to get the British TUC to first lobby the Labour Government of the time and make sure that the responsible UK ministry, usually but not always, the Foreign Office, gave the necessary instructions to its UN delegation.

I realised that at international level, as much as at national level, it was valuable to develop good personal working relations with the senior officials, especially those responsible for drafting relevant policy documents. I also learnt that many officials, particularly but not only those working in international organisations, were progressive and open to ideas. Such personal relations are actually more important than having beautifully argued policy papers, although you do have to have a well-argued case to present if you were to be taken seriously.

Too many NGOs naively think the force of their arguments and passion will win the day, but this is not how the world works. In intergovernmental organisations, advocacy is highly time consuming and laborious but pays dividends. Taking the time to have a coffee or drink with the responsible official and getting them on side can make a huge difference.

While it is essential to have a specific government's support especially to formally table your proposals at the relevant negotiations, at international level it is necessary to secure support from as many other governments as possible, so as to create a momentum. Ideally this should encompass individual governments from different regions or, even better, entire groups such as the EU or Group of 77 developing countries. Having support from a whole bloc of countries will obviously have more impact and avoid being seen as representing only a particular narrow national interest. In my later work on the UN code for transnational corporations, I therefore successfully sought wide-ranging support from progressive Western countries, the G-77 developing countries and even the Eastern Bloc.

An issue I became increasingly drawn to through my trade union work and involvement at the ILO and UN was the fight against the apartheid regime in Pretoria and the accompanying liberation struggles in Southern Africa, including Rhodesia, where white minority rule remained entrenched. In fact, one of my favourite personal newspaper clippings from that time shows a photo of a young Carl with the bold headline above it proclaiming, *'War against apartheid'*.

In my work at the ILO and the UN, I had shared the high hopes for establishment of a New International Economic Order to address global poverty and other injustices. International cooperation and multilateralism appeared in the ascendancy, raising hopes of a departure from the sterile bipolar politics of the Cold War, with the G-77 at the UN playing a growing role. One consequence was the EU placing greater emphasis on development cooperation policy under the Yaounde, and later the Lomé and Cotonou Conventions, a partnership with former African, Caribbean and Pacific colonies, an area of work I was increasingly engaged with. However, the dawn of neo-liberalism marked by the election of Margaret Thatcher in the UK in 1979 and Ronald Reagan in the USA in 1980 was to bring much of these worthy aspirations to an abrupt stop by the end of the decade.

Despite the imminent change of political fortunes at the end of the 1970s, I hope my work throughout the decade allowed me to make small, but significant, contributions to progressive thinking on European unity, North-South relations, global basic needs strategy, industrial democracy and policy towards multinational companies. I must have got a bit of a Left-wing reputation because in a live radio interview in Nairobi and I was introduced not as 'Mr Carl Wright' but as 'Mr Karl Marx'. I wonder if the interviewer's slip of the tongue created panic at the CIA headquarters in Langley, hearing 'Karl Marx' was alive and well.

I was now a fully paid-up Global Citizen.

PART II

NEO-LIBERAL ASCENDENCY
(the 1980s)

From Trade Union Action to Commonwealth Diplomacy

"There is no such thing [as society]"
"I do not support sanctions [on South Africa]"
MARGARET THATCHER, BRITISH PRIME MINISTER

The 1980s saw neo-liberal economic policies sweeping the world, led by Margaret Thatcher and Ronald Reagan. Returning to the UK in 1980, I continued my trade union and international work within the Commonwealth, with a focus on fighting apartheid.

8.

Fresh Beginnings

COMING HOME TO LONDON IN 1980, I WAS IN CHARGE OF MY own organisation for the first time and became immersed in the Commonwealth. I was also looking for a new personal relationship.

Against the growing global neo-liberal ascendency, trade union grass roots activism offered a way to counteract the onward march of the Right. I had enjoyed the work at the ICFTU and could have continued there quite easily. It is not too fanciful to imagine that I could eventually have become its General Secretary. Indeed quite a few years later, when the position had become vacant, that very course of action was suggested to me by its then President, Sir LeRoy Trotman of Barbados. I could also have used the ICFTU and my growing range of senior political contacts in securing an important position at the ILO or another international agency or body such as the Socialist International. In fact, Guy Ryder, a junior TUC colleague at my time, followed this career path, rising to ICFTU General Secretary and then Director-General of the ILO.

My heart however was with the British Labour Movement. I increasingly felt motivated to return to Britain and continue my international work from there. I also wanted to keep open the option of a domestic political career in Parliament and join the fight against neo-liberalism at home. This was impossible from Brussels. An opportunity finally presented itself for returning to the UK in 1980, while continuing my international work with the Labour Movement. This was by becoming Director of a new body, the Commonwealth Trade Union Council, CTUC.

For many years trade unionists from around the Commonwealth had met once a year during the ILO for a one-day conference. This was followed by a raucous dinner at the Hotel des Bergues, a top Geneva establishment, whose staff must have dreaded the boisterous annual event. The dinner was an occasion when the delegates from around the

Commonwealth would sing, dance and make merry, giving a rousing rendering of their various national anthems and songs. I remember on one occasion, to the horror of the waiters, a Fijian delegate grabbed a large leg of lamb from a beautiful silver platter and waived it around his head in order to parody his culture's supposed cannibalistic traditions.

In 1979, John Harker, a young, intelligent British immigrant to Canada who had become head of the international department of the Canadian Labour Congress (CLC) in Ottawa, secured agreement for the establishment of a small secretariat in London, of what was to become the Commonwealth TUC – the CTUC. John and his wife Eunice were close friends, whose home in Ottawa I visited on many occasions. He was aware of my interest in returning to London.

In this respect the Commonwealth, unlike most other international organisations, has a long-standing practice of having established numerous professional, non-governmental and quasi-governmental organisations alongside the formal intergovernmental Commonwealth bodies. While most of these tend to be limited in resources, they provide a vital element of wide-ranging Commonwealth cooperation which significantly complements the work of the official structures and gives the Commonwealth as a whole important legitimacy and outreach. The CTUC was therefore to be an important addition to this wider family of Commonwealth organisations.

After consultation with Commonwealth unions, I was offered the position of Director of the new body operating from a tiny office in TUC headquarters, Congress House in London's Bloomsbury, close to my old university haunts. I started work there aided by a single secretary, Wendy Mallard, in March 1980. A number of other staff soon followed, including David Clement and Stephen Faulkner, who led on trade union training programmes, and Annie Watson. Much of my early work was designed to establish and resource the organisation and to ensure that it was able to influence the work of Commonwealth Governments and the Commonwealth Secretariat in particular.

Around this time, I decided to discard my former double-barrelled surname 'Wilms-Wright' and just become plain 'Carl Wright', although I did keep the 'Wilms' as a middle name. On reflection this was really a way of my wanting to integrate fully in the British way of life on my return to London, and consciously seeking to avoid what was often regarded as an upper-class affectation, not suited to a trade union activist. Perhaps I was too sensitive about this in the same way as I always was when someone tried to tease out 'what accent' I had and where I came from.

Settling in West Hampstead on return to Britain in 1980, I soon met Adele Maxwell-Miles, a talented dance teacher – who did have a double-barrelled surname but actually came from a modest family background. Adele lived in the next street along and ran her own children's dance and ballet school in London's Cricklewood and Willesden. When we did meet again, it was with her then young part-time pianist and student, Joanna McGregor. Joanna was soon to make the big time as a highly acclaimed concert pianist, then became a member of the Arts Council and Head of Piano at the Royal Academy of Music.

Adele was very different from the tough political women I had previously met and dated, having had no contact with politics; but she was vibrant and full of good fun. She is a very genuine person, concerned with supporting people in the local community, mainly leaving worrying about the wider world to me. However, she has also organised a number of successful charity events to raise funds for good causes in developing countries and cares deeply about poverty and injustice.

Adele owned a dog, William, who to my dismay followed her everywhere, even the bedroom, something I was not used to, having had no pets as a child. With my strong Labour Movement convictions and internationalist views, I must have been like a being from Mars to her and her Conservative-voting family. Despite this, we immediately hit it off and were soon involved in an intense relationship, which has, despite ups and downs, survived well for forty years.

It was not long before we – and William – started to live together in a small semi-detached house at 97 Cotswold Gardens in the Golders Green Estate, on which I had taken out my first mortgage. Within a year of our meeting, when I was 31, we felt sufficiently strong about each other to want to marry.

My second wedding in 1981 turned out to be very distinct from my first rather grand event at St James Piccadilly and the Café Royal. I wanted something different and more personal and made the romantic proposal that we should wed on the other side of the world in Sydney, Australia. This would be followed by an exotic honeymoon in Bali, with its rich Hindu cultural heritage and colourful Bangkok, with its gleaming golden Buddhist temples. Adele readily agreed.

The opportunity to marry in Australia had come by my attending my first Commonwealth Heads of Government Meeting (CHOGM) in

Melbourne. Following this event, Adele, who had previously travelled little overseas, courageously flew alone all the way out to Sydney, a journey of over 24 hours. We were duly married at Sydney's Sutherland registry office in the presence of my dear godmother Helga Pettitt, a close friend of my mother, and her husband Gordon. Apart from telegrams sent by family and friends, we received a lovely bouquet of flowers from Bob Hawke, soon to become Prime Minister of Australia in 1983. We then chilled out on the nearby golden sandy beach of Manley. All a far cry from dour and wet north-west London.

It was due to my godmother Helga that we were able to marry legally. This required an appearance before an Australian magistrate, who was a good friend of Gordon and proved flexible in interpreting legal restrictions for marriage. Occasionally, I tease Adele about the legality of the event, as well as our anniversary date. Given the ten-hour time difference between Sydney and London, it was only just the same date in the UK, which otherwise would have been a perfect excuse for forgetting the anniversary date.

The following year we had the good fortune to be able to buy the big semi-detached house next door to my new parents-in-law. This was just before London property prices went sky high. Appropriately, the house was at 13 Menelik Road, West Hampstead, with the road named after the African Emperor Menelik II of Abyssinia, who gave the Italians a bloody nose when they tried to invade the country at the end of the nineteenth century. It was fascinating to visit the emperor's tomb in Addis Ababa some years later and to pay homage to this great African leader.

We were to spend thirty years in Menelik Road and had many good times there. It was a comfortable neighbourhood only twenty minutes' walk from Hampstead Heath. During this time, we held lots of parties and social events, both with our own family and neighbours as well as with a wider group of friends. We also entertained many political associates there including Commonwealth Secretary-General Chief Emeka Anyaoku, Tanzanian Foreign Minister Joseph Rwegasira, future Labor leader Simon Crean from Australia, Bernt Carlsson, then UN High Commissioner for Namibia, and UK politicians like local government minister Nick Raynsford.

My close friend from school in Wales, Gary Smith and his wife Andrea, lived just around the corner. Like me Gary, working in the world of big oil, travelled much internationally. There was a scary episode when he disappeared while in Saudi Arabia. While seeking to console

Andrea, who was beside herself with worry, I contacted the FCO and the British Ambassador who frankly were of little help. Then Gary re-appeared – he had been locked up in a Saudi political jail for being in the wrong place at the wrong time near Mecca. He was glad to get away, telling us chilling stories about the anguished screams of prisoners being tortured. I find it a disgrace that to this day the UK is avidly supplying arms to what is still one of the most reactionary and repressive regimes in the world.

Ever-present in London were our various faithful dogs, which after the demise of Adele's William, were always handsome, if scatty, English setters – Wellington, Berkley, Bertie, Mr Darcy and later our loveable Rupert. Some of these turned out to be champions at the prestigious Crufts dog show. For a while we had a beautiful snow-white cat, Worsley. We also had an African dog, Mini Minor, of which more later. After my mother in law's death, we inherited a small tortoise, Horace. He is nearly 100 and going strong and will no doubt outlive us. His distinctive features are that he knows his name and follows us around the garden; he is also sex-crazed, getting amorous with shoes as a substitute for the real thing.

Menelik Road was to remain our sole home until 1991 when we bought a small 150-year-old cottage in the hamlet of Maypole, Hoath, in East Kent, near the ancient cathedral city of Canterbury. This cottage overlooked idyllic golden cornfields with the nearby North Sea glimmering silver in the distance. On moving in, we discovered to our amazement that the cottage had been built and owned by a distant relative of Adele's, as her father's side of her family, came from that part of Kent. It was obviously meant to be.

There was an odd Kent connection with our home area in West Hampstead too. Percy Cotton-Powell had been the property developer who had built the houses in Menelik Road and neighbouring streets of West Hampstead and Kilburn in the early nineteenth century. He had lived near Broadstairs, Kent and decided the London streets should be named after local Kent villages like Minister and Fordwich. Other street names such as Menelik originated not in East Kent, but in East Africa. They had come from his African safaris and exotic names included Asmara Road, where my friend Gary lived, and Gondor Gardens, home to author Doris Lessing.

To this day, the Cotton-Powell country mansion near Broadstairs contains a stuffed elephant brought back from his travels; more than I ever managed to fit into my suitcase. I did however over the years pick up quite a collection of wonderful African, Asian and many other overseas artefacts. One of the nicest is a beautiful Makonde wood carving presented to me by the Tanzanian trade unions, I also have some superb Ashanti-style bronzes acquired from Ghana and Nigeria. There is an intricately engraved bronze metal horse from Pakistan and many ceremonial masks and wooden carvings from such far-flung places as the Congo and Papua New Guinea.

It was satisfying to settle into a new life back home and remain immersed in Labour Movement work.

9.

Recasting Global Paradigms

NEO-LIBERALISM WAS TO REIGN SUPREME. THE WORLD BECAME a very different place and hopes of a New International Economic Order were soon buried.

The 1980s saw an ideological sea-change in global politics following the election of Margaret Thatcher and Ronald Reagan. The New Right focused on free markets and unfettered operation of the capitalist system, with loosening of financial and capital controls and promotion of globalisation. This became known as the *Washington Consensus* and proved to be a sworn enemy of Keynesian interventionist economic policies; it strongly opposed a strong State sector, seeking instead the privatisation of public assets. This neo-liberal policy was ruthlessly enforced by bodies like the International Monetary Fund, IMF, often resulting in the withdrawal of vital social benefits and subsidies for poorer people especially in developing countries.

There were valiant attempts to take forward the ideas of the New International Economic Order through initiatives such as 1980 *Brandt Commission Report,* the 1982 *Commission on Common Security* under Sweden's Olaf Palme and the 1985 *Global Challenge Report* under Jamaica's Michael Manley. But their implementation was blocked by the New Right ideologues.

However, the environment hit the headlines in the 1980s. When the Chernobyl nuclear disaster occurred in 1986, I recall all too well the radioactive fallout which reached us in the UK and caused justified panic as far as the Welsh hills. With a depleting ozone layer, the environment, sustainability, and green politics became global issues. This was highlighted in the 1987 Brundtland report *Our Common Future*. In addition, the AIDS epidemic started taking its toll worldwide, but especially in Africa, while in the Horn of Africa acute famine raged, leading to the Live Aid initiative which saw an unprecedented 1.6 billion TV viewers donating a remarkable $75 million to charity.

The 1980s had their ugly side with both the Soviet Union and the US shooting down passenger planes with great loss of life; the subsequent Pan Am Lockerbie terrorist outrage of 1988, plane hijackings and high-profile political assassinations. In 1984, the iconic Indian leader, Indira Gandhi was murdered. I had met her officially in New Delhi in 1982 and again in 1983. The first visit was a courtesy call, alongside my Indian trade union colleagues, but during the second meeting we discussed the role of the Commonwealth in more detail, as well as the impact of the US invasion of Grenada which had just taken place, concluding there was little realistically that could be done in response.

I consider it a privilege to have encountered Indira Gandhi and was impressed by her sharp intelligence and easy-going manner. Some years later, I was to meet her son Rajiv Gandhi, a charming young leader, who had succeeded her as Prime Minister, but who was also tragically assassinated not long after.

Navigating my way through the changing global and domestic political environment my prime focus was on setting up the new CTUC, building on my past trade union experience at the ICFTU. The CTUC was different from the ICFTU in that its membership was based on the Commonwealth and all its members spoke English and shared common traditions. Most had similar legislative and professional practices and there was no need for interpreters or translations.

The CTUC was distinct in that membership was open to all national trade union centres or associations, regardless of ideology; controversially, members included the respective pro-Moscow and pro-Beijing communist organisations in India. While I did meet with these in run-down offices in New Delhi, they did not take an active part in our work, viewing it with quite some suspicion. In addition, we had many non-aligned union centres in Africa as members, which belonged to neither to the Western ICFTU nor the Communist World Federation of Trade Unions, but only to the continental Organisation of African Trade Union Unity, headed by a canny Kenyan, Denis Akumu, who I got to know and collaborate with.

Although I continued to take part in ICFTU meetings as observer, including its important sub-committee on South Africa, this open, non-aligned, position of the CTUC aroused suspicion from my old employers, as well as from the more conventional bureaucrats of the TUC who were still engaged in Cold War politics. It was to present me with tough political choices on occasions as I was keen to demonstrate the impartiality of the new organisation. To have done otherwise would have meant it would have been politically stillborn and lack influence with Commonwealth Governments, especially from Africa.

I received initial funding support from the Canadian Labour Congress and the Canadian Government, which involved visits to Ottawa, usually combined with trips to New York and Washington. My CTUC Chairperson was the President of the Canadian Labour Congress, Dennis McDermott. Denis was a no-nonsense autoworker who, like John Harker, had originally come from Britain and had been in the Marines with tattoos on his arm to prove it. Regretfully, the British TUC, although providing office space at Congress House, was at best lukewarm. Fortunately, the TUC General Secretary, Len Murray, was himself positive and saw the value of Commonwealth links.

A new TUC International Secretary, Michael Walsh, had now taken over, and although younger and more open-minded, he still viewed the CTUC as a rival. Of course, not all TUC staff were bureaucrats and I worked well with many of them. These included David Lea and Bill Callaghan in the TUC's economic department; and two future TUC General Secretaries, John Monks and Brendan Barber whose wife Mary worked in the International Department. Later, too, more progressively minded officials like Owen Tudor took over the direction of the TUC's international work, resulting in a more enlightened approach.

In confronting the dead hand of TUC bureaucracy, I was able to call on the support of the internationally minded members of the TUC General Council. This included both Left-wingers like Clive Jenkins of the white-collar union ASTMS (later MSF) and Right-wingers like Geoffrey Drain of NALGO (later UNISON). Another close associate was to be Rodney Bickerstaffe of NUPE. Later Ron Todd, who took over from Jack Jones as TGWU General Secretary, was very supportive.

I was soon given observer status at the TUC's monthly meeting of its International Committee where I presented regular reports. After repeated battles about recognition at the annual TUC Congress, I eventually won a prestigious platform seat on the annual Congress, alongside the TUC General Council members and international visitors. I was also invited to the annual General Council dinner, a jovial and relaxed affair at which Labour leaders like Neil Kinnock literally sang for their dinner.

My colleagues in Congress House must have viewed me as an exotic creature with my constant global travel and preoccupation with internationalism. My quixotic image was reinforced by the somewhat ostentatious Japanese Mitsubishi car I parked in the TUC underground garage each day: hardly the best advert for the domestic British car industry. I had however got the Mitsubishi, which was right-hand drive, second-hand from my friend Gary when my own brand-new car had unexpectedly given up. It was subsequently graced by a prestigious parking space on The Mall when I went to work for the Commonwealth Secretariat. I then sold it on to an African colleague and the last I heard it was being exported to Sierra Leone, where it is now doubt still in active service.

Selling the Mitsubishi gave me a chance to revert again to a British brand, a Rover, on three subsequent occasions and my last one, a top of the range 623 model, is still serving me well after thirty years. Looking back now, it seems incredible to have driven to work daily for all of the 1980s and much of the 1990s and to have had a free personal parking space in central London. These were the days prior to growing gridlock on the capital's roads and the imposition of the much-needed London congestion and emission charges. It was at a time when we were blissfully unaware of the harmful impact of car emissions on health and their carbon emissions. Today, I stick solidly to the excellent, if expensive, public transport system in London, assisted by the generous Freedom Pass which gives all Londoners over the age of sixty free travel.

One of the towering figures of the Labour Movement in the 1970s was Jack Jones, General Secretary of the almost two million strong TGWU. It was the union I had joined in 1971 and have remained as a member for fifty years, including under its new branding of Unite. I have always had the greatest respect for Jack for his dedication, seriousness and internationalism which went back to the time he had fought in the International Brigades against Franco's fascists during the Spanish Civil War.

Clive Jenkins was a particularly close ally. Clive, a Welshman, was a bit of a gadfly and had a sharp mind but also a weakness for the good things in life. More than once, he entertained me at swish restaurants with vintage wines, for example when Simon Crean, the leader of the Australian trade unions came to London. I always remember the great anguish on Clive's face when, at an international solidarity conference in Arusha, Tanzania, he was forced to sample the local – and rather vinegary – Rosé wine.

The visit by Simon Crean, who had taken over from Bob Hawke as ACTU – Australian TUC – President was of significance. It was to study what had gone wrong in the British Labour Party's 'Social Contract' with the unions in 1978-79, resulting in the election of Margret Thatcher. I helped organise Simon's programme, including meetings with key architects of the British Social Contract between the TUC and the previous Labour Government such as Jack Jones. I like to think that the lessons learnt by Simon and applied in Australia were a contributory factor in the subsequent electoral successes of Bob Hawke and his Australian Labor Party after 1983. I was over the years to maintain good contacts with Simon who went on to hold important ministerial positions in future Labor Governments in Australia and served as Labor Leader in opposition 2001-03. Here was a good example on how political parties in the Commonwealth interacted and learnt from each other's experience – and mistakes.

What I did not realise was how much UK trade unions would be under political attack.

10.

The Impact of Thatcherism

MY TIMING IN RETURNING TO THE UK IN 1980 COULD NOT have been worse from a political point of view. Margaret Thatcher had just been elected Prime Minister and with the help of Right-wing ideologues like Norman Tebbit began her neo-liberal crusade.

A key element of Thatcher's plan was to emasculate the trade unions which she regarded as 'the enemy within'. She subsequently showed her disdain of the very concept of society and collective action, which she was to spell out in a notorious interview in 1987, where she claimed: "There is no such thing [as society]".

Trade unions, previously at the centre of government, were now ostracised and cast to the outer periphery of decision-making. This was possible because of the political mistakes made by the trade union movement during the 1978-79 'winter of discontent', when strikes against the Labour Government's pay policy had resulted in heaps of rubbish in the street. For a time, even some dead were left unburied. This was exaggerated out of all proportion by the Right-wing media, but it alienated the electorate which had been upset by repeated global economic crises. It had been further compounded by the failure of Labour Prime Minister, Jim Callaghan, to call an election, as expected, in late 1978, when Labour might still have been able to pull off a victory.

Margret Thatcher was an ideologically driven politician who was highly successful politically and did much to change the UK and beyond. When an objective history of the time is finally written, it will be seen that far from the heroic champion of freedom and rebuilding Britain which she is made out to be by the political Right, she will be seen as a Prime Minister who did great damage to the UK's political, economic and social fabric.

She did this through undermining key democratic and civil structures such as local government and trade unions; her wanton destruction of manufacturing and mining; and her run-down of public sector services through privatisation. Social housing, too, has never recovered from her decision to sell off council houses. The consequence was the devastation of whole communities and regions, especially in former industrial heartlands. Internationally, too, Thatcher's Cold War rhetoric and her support for the racist apartheid regime in South Africa caused much harm to Britain's image. At one stage she came close to breaking up the Commonwealth by her refusal to join other Commonwealth countries in imposing sanctions on Pretoria.

Clive Jenkins used to tell the story of one of the last TUC delegations to visit 10 Downing Street in the early 1980s. After an unproductive meeting with Margaret Thatcher, the then Chancellor, Geoffrey Howe, was politely showing the delegation to the front door of Number 10. Suddenly they heard a shrill female voice calling, "Come along now Geoffrey, no more time to waste", an indication of the disdain with which the Prime Minister regarded not only trade unions, but even her own senior ministers.

By the early 1980s the British Labour Movement started to self-destruct. This was a reaction to the success of Tony Benn and the Bennite Left and led to the breakaway 'Gang of Four' – Right-wingers Roy Jenkins, Shirley Williams, David Owen and Bill Rodgers who set up the new Social Democratic Party, SDP. The latter were all leaders I had met and knew personally through my earlier engagement in the European Movement. I however disagreed with their decision to split-off from the Labour Party and felt vindicated in having loosened my political ties with them after having left the European Commission.

I was witness to the penultimate chapter leading to the split, when at the 1980 Special Labour Party Conference in Wembley delegates directed most of their anger against their own Party leadership, rather than the Tory Government. The resulting schism in the Labour Party and the defection of a large number of Labour MPs to the SDP, coupled with the Leftward lurch of the Party and the election of the ineffective and other-worldly Michael Foot as Leader, meant that Labour was set for almost two decades in the political wilderness. Something similar was to happen after Labour's election defeats in 2010 and 2015, cumulating eventually in the emphatic general election victory of Boris Johnson in 2019.

Dealing with international work, I was relatively isolated from the brutality of UK domestic politics. Happily, my close relation with Bob Hawke and other Commonwealth leaders compensated from what was happening in my home country. Nonetheless, working for the Labour Movement and being a Labour Party activist meant that I was not unaffected. What that time demonstrated to me was the importance of political parties staying united if they want to achieve power, and not indulging in ideological schisms, something the Left is all too prone to.

Having just returned from overseas in Brussels and preoccupied with establishing the new CTUC and global work, I did not at the time see the scale of the political disaster in the making. I was in fact attracted by many of the policy reforms proposed by the so-called 'Bennites' which were in line with my own progressive politics, although I did not like their anti-EU postures. I turned a blind eye when my personal assistant, Wendy Mallard, spent much time in ensuring that Left-winger Tony Banks unseated the sitting 'Old' Labour MP in Newham. Perhaps I was unduly influenced by the professional links I had developed with Tony when he had been political adviser of Judith Hart, who had been overseas development minister under the previous Labour Government.

Apart from the unions, the other big political target of the Thatcher Government was the Labour-controlled local government councils in London and other big cities. This was the time of the so-called 'loony Left', especially in London's local government, including my own council in Camden. The Left excelled on unpopular policies aimed at enforcing political correctness, which were seized upon by the Tory press.

A key Tory target was the Greater London Council, GLC, housed in County Hall just across the river Thames from Parliament, headed by Ken Livingstone. The GLC was active in opposing the Thatcher Government and its measures. But this was its democratic right. Incredibly, in response Thatcher was able to dissolve and formally abolish the elected GLC by forcing through an Act of Parliament. This was a show of undemocratic vandalism worthy of any Third World dictator, depriving London of a collective voice enjoyed by other cities throughout the world. This vital democratic structure and the position of elected Mayor of London was only restored by the Blair Government in 2000, resulting in the return of Livingstone as mayor.

It is a little-known fact that the dominant amount of legislation during the Thatcher years was local government legislation, all designed to weaken the powers of Labour councils. As a result, whereas in 1979 UK councils had been responsible for raising some 80 per cent of their own revenue through local rates and other taxes, by 1990 this had been reduced to around 20 per cent. Now councils were reliant on central government grants which could be cut at any time. This has made the UK one of the most centralised countries in the world and has fatally undermined local democracy in the country. Local government in the UK today has not truly recovered. Under Labour (1997-2010) own revenues did go up to some 40 per cent; still low by international standards. Recently, in part due to cuts in central grants, this percentage nudged upwards.

Attending local Labour Party meetings in the 1980s was an unpleasant and fractious experience. When I went to my first Labour Party branch meeting in West Hampstead after returning from Brussels, instead of being welcomed as a valued trade union activist, I was labelled a 'bloody Congress House bureaucrat': somewhat ironic in view of my own battles with those same bureaucrats. This acrimony accelerated the haemorrhage of party members and supporters of what was viewed as an increasingly out-of-touch party.

Long-standing friendships suffered from the growing political divisions. I had already lost touch with student colleagues like Dick (now Lord) Newby who joined the Social Democratic Party (SDP) and who was to rise to become the Secretary-General of the later Liberal Democrats. It was not until the late 1990s that I met again briefly with old associates like Dick and Caroline Thomson, but by then our previous links had broken.

Even close personal friendships with those who remained within the Labour Party, as with Dianne Hayter, then General Secretary of the Fabian Society, who I had dated after my divorce, were affected by political disputes; this prevented deeper attachments. In later years, our political and social interests diverged further, and I now have had little connection with previous associates, many of which sit in the House of Lords as a reward for their party loyalties.

One of my first political acquaintances just before returning to the UK in 1980 was Left-winger Jeremy Corbyn, later Leader of the Labour Party. Labour HQ had assigned me to campaign with him in the Labour marginal seat of Hornsey in north London in the 1979 General Election. At the time Jeremy was the agent for unsuccessful candidate 'Red' Ted Knight, the ultra-Left Leader of Lambeth Council. He then became MP for Islington in 1983 and for many decades was renowned as a Left-wing Labour rebel and a fighter for human rights and against neo-liberalism.

I kept on first name terms with Jeremy over the years, given his strong support for human rights and international causes, but I was never a fan of his confrontational Leftist politics. Once he became Labour Leader, he faced the onslaught of the Right-wing media for his often-principled positions as well as opposition by much of his own MPs. To my mind, his credibility was fatally undermined by the weak position he took in the 2016 Brexit referendum in support of EU membership. Although he did well in the 2017 election, almost winning against Prime Minister Theresa May, thereafter his poor leadership and failure to champion the cause of remaining in Europe, as well as his ineffective action on dealing with anti-Semitism in the Labour Party, was highly damaging electorally in 2019.

The 1980s were not a good time for the Labour Movement.

11.

CHOGMs and Expert Groups

AS DIRECTOR OF THE COMMONWEALTH TUC, I HAD CLOSE contact with the Commonwealth Secretariat. This was based within the elegant splendour of Marlborough House in London's Pall Mall.

Marlborough House is a royal palace and a former home of the Prince of Wales. It maintains its royal grandeur, especially the beautiful Blenheim Saloon, which was later used for receptions and hosted my retirement party in 2016. Some of the rooms still resemble royal bedrooms. I remember one Secretariat colleague having an office where a past heir to the throne used to entertain his mistresses. Much of the room consisted of bookcases and one had a false door which swung open on pulling out a book from the bookcase entitled 'The Way Out' – not something the royal mistresses would have known.

The Commonwealth Secretariat was set up under Harold Wilson in 1965 and functions like a mini United Nations. It has a Secretary-General, elected by Commonwealth Heads of Government and a small multi-national staff, drawn from countries around the world. The first Secretary-General was the Canadian Arnold Smith, who was succeeded by the flamboyant and highly effective Sir Shridath or 'Sonny' Ramphal from Guyana. He was in turn succeeded by Nigerian Chief Emeka Anyaoku, Don Mckinnon from New Zealand, Kamalesh Sharma from India and Patricia Scotland who was born in Dominica in the Caribbean but has lived and worked in the UK all her life.

Many Londoners confuse the Secretariat with the former Commonwealth Institute in Kensington, which used to cater largely for UK schools and cultural activities. The Secretariat is anything but a 'British' body, indeed the number of Brits employed there are a distinct minority. When I went to work there, I was only one of handful of Brits appointed at senior diplomatic level like the able Peter Williams who headed the education section. The only concession to tradition was earmarking one of the then three Deputy Secretary-General positions to a UK Foreign Office grandee, a practice now abandoned.

Every two years Commonwealth leaders Heads of Government hold a summit meeting, the CHOGM or Commonwealth Heads of Government Meeting . This is a remarkable event when some fifty Presidents and Prime Ministers from around the global come together, including an intimate 'retreat' when they exclude their ministers and advisers so they can talk freely among themselves. It is opened by HM the Queen as Head of the Commonwealth and is the one time where she delivers a political speech of her own. More recently her son, HRH Prince Charles, has taken on some of her Commonwealth duties.

On these occasions leaders maintained a 'family' spirit not found in other, more formal international gatherings, and as a result often reach agreement on issues which eluded other global other events. Originally these gatherings would last up to a week, and even take in the odd Cricket test match. Like much else in modern life, CHOGMs have now been whittled down to a streamlined 2-3 days at most; even the famous 'retreat' is just a few hours, greatly reducing its intimacy and value.

Originally an opportunity for just Commonwealth leaders to meet, the CHOGMs soon attracted a large media following and many fringe events, organised by diverse accredited Commonwealth organisations, which found them a great opportunity to showcase their activities and meet with senior Commonwealth representatives from around the word. In more recent years, each CHOGM has been accompanied by a Peoples' Forum, gathering varied civil society and professional bodies, a Business Forum for the private sector, as well as Youth Forum and a Women's Forum.

This large number of associated events has brought its own logistical and security issues, resulting in sometimes too rigid barriers for interaction. This has most recently been overcome, in part, by having a structured dialogue between foreign ministers and Commonwealth organisations at CHOGM, as well as allowing a limited number of accredited organisations to observe the preparatory meetings of foreign ministers which take place prior to the executive meetings of heads of government.

My first experience of a Commonwealth Summit was in Melbourne in 1981. This was followed by going to New Delhi in 1983, Nassau in 1985 and Vancouver in 1987. At these events I organised senior trade union delegations to meet with the hosting Prime Ministers and other leaders and present them with our views. As a result, I was successful in ensuring reference to the CTUC and trade unions concerns in the CHOGM outcome statements, the CHOGM Communique.

There used to be regional CHOGMs in the Asia/Pacific region. In 1982, I attended the regional CHOGM in Delhi where I had my unique experience of having my first personal meeting with Mrs Indira Gandhi. I also vividly recall a regional event in Fiji. This was memorable, not least because of local workmen splashing thick green emulsion on the parched grass outside the hotel where Heads of Government would be staying the next day. As a result, it looked like a lush lawn, but I can only hope that none of the leaders walked on it and ended up with green feet.

The CHOGMs had other amusing moments. In Nassau in 1985, our CTUC delegation met with the CHOGM Chairperson, The Bahamas Prime Minister Lynden Pindling. Unfortunately, the Prime Minister had one glass eye, which was very noticeable. To our great embarrassment, the leader of our delegation, Shirley Carr of Canada, made the Freudian open statement: "Mr Prime Minister, would you please like to cast an eye over our submission ..." As we all cringed, the Prime Minister's single good eye looked at us distinctly unamused.

Pindling had a tough time on account of demonstrations against him by his domestic political opposition. Noisy demonstrators were lined up on the route that Heads of Government were to take from their posh beach hotel to dine with the Queen on the Royal Yacht Britannia. As a result, some bright spark decided they could avoid unpleasantness by shipping the leaders to the Royal Yacht by boat, thereby avoiding the roadside demonstrators. What had however been overlooked, was that a boat ride takes much longer than a car ride. As a result, Her Majesty was kept waiting for a long time and several elderly leaders almost fell into the water while trying to transfer from their small boat onto the Britannia.

I developed a good personal relationship with the dynamic Shridath 'Sonny' Ramphal, who I greatly admired and who was supportive and attended one of our first CTUC meetings in Geneva. Seeing Sonny in action was a delight – the kind of leader who oozed charisma and charm as well as high intellect and real gravitas. It was always refreshing to see him at the centre of key global issues and how he was unafraid to take on big member states like the UK if they went against the Commonwealth consensus – something I also had to do in my own Commonwealth roles.

One of the senior Secretariat staff I got to know well was the Director of the Economic Affairs Division, the late Dr Vishnu Persaud, who, like his boss Sonny Ramphal, came from the Caribbean. Bishnu as he was known, had an impressive record of bringing together senior experts from across the Commonwealth and was someone who could spot and act on key global trends. These experts would meet and agree a policy report on vital issues of the day, which would then be published and submitted to Heads of Government for implementation.

It was through Bishnu's support that I represented the CTUC on two key Commonwealth Expert Groups, on Technological Change in 1984-85 and Jobs for Young People in 1986-87. Both ground-breaking reports were duly presented to Heads of Government for endorsement, and I was able to ensure they contained a strong element of trade union views, for example dealing with job loss through the introduction of new technology.

I was able to kick-start an important institutional innovation with support from Bishnu Persaud and to the bemusement of his boss, the amiable and experienced British diplomat and Deputy Secretary-General, Sir Peter Marshall. This involved holding regular meetings of Commonwealth ministers of employment and labour. These took place on the fringes of the annual ILO conference and took off thanks to the presence of most of the ministers and our own CTUC union counterparts in Geneva, so it was not too difficult to find a slot for meetings.

Essentially the ministers would hold their own gathering, convened by the Commonwealth Secretariat, although I was able to influence the agenda; then there would be an interaction and dialogue with a senior CTUC delegation which I organised. This served to give labour and trade union issues a real profile within the Commonwealth which had not existed previously. It also allowed for ministers to report to CHOGM, which further served to enhance high-level focus on issues of concern to us.

By the mid-1980s, I was fully immersed in Commonwealth affairs.

12.

Rhodesia to Zimbabwe

IN 1979, THE CHOGM HAD MET IN LUSAKA. IT ACHIEVED A remarkable breakthrough in securing democratic elections in Rhodesia, soon to become Zimbabwe.

My first task as CTUC Director in April 1980 was to fly to Zimbabwe to witness the country's independence celebrations and to hold discussions on support for the local trade union movement. One of my immediate aims was to encourage the coming together of previous racially segregated trade union bodies into a unified Zimbabwe Congress of Trade Unions, the ZCTU. This was to be followed by extensive CTUC trade union training programmes funded by Commonwealth governments.

The Zimbabwe independence celebrations were an exciting event. They were held at a large football stadium in what was then still called Salisbury, later renamed Harare. Bob Marley got the loudest applause of the night with a haunting rendition of his song 'Zimbabwe'. At one stage we feared political sabotage when an all-white schoolgirls' choir marched in and started to sing the old UDI anthem in English, only to lapse into a perfect Shona language version of the new Zimbabwe anthem, to symbolise the political transition. This got a great cheer from the mainly Black crowd.

The predominately white police were less successful in adapting when during the ceremony they over-reacted to a minor crowd disturbance by discharging tear gas. The noxious fumes drifted across the stadium and even had the Prince of Wales clutching a handkerchief over his mouth, forcing a temporary abandonment of proceedings. Clearly much still had to change.

I soon discovered just how long it would take the old regime to adapt. During my April visit I made arrangements for the first-ever Commonwealth meeting in Zimbabwe held shortly afterwards, organised by the CTUC. For this historic event we invited senior Black African trade union leaders who had previously been barred entry to the country. Unknown to me as I was waiting for them on the other side of airport immigration, most were refused entry by the white immigration officials and forced to turn back.

This situation threatened to turn into a major diplomatic incident. On learning what had happened, the head of the local unions, Albert Mugabe, a half-brother of the newly elected Prime Minister, arranged for us to immediately see Robert Mugabe at his residence late that night. The barred trade unionists had been put on a flight back to Nairobi which was due to arrive there shortly. Urgent action was necessary.

In our presence, the Prime Minister, casually dressed in sweater and slacks, telephoned the Foreign Minister of Kenya, asking him to convey his personal apologies to our colleagues and requesting them to return on the next flight to Harare. This they duly did the following day so our meeting could proceed. I was pleased to note on my next visit to what was now Harare, the previous racist immigration personnel had disappeared.

Over the next thirty plus years I visited Harare once or twice a year. We soon had a small CTUC office in Harare which was co-ordinating our training activities in Zimbabwe and undertaking work in neighbouring countries. Much of the training was done at Ranche House College, Harare, a private training institution which had defied the UDI Government of Ian Smith in his heyday and which I would deploy later to support the training of Namibian and South African trade unionists.

An unexplained incident happened during this time. Dramatically, union leader Albert Mugabe was found dead at the bottom of his swimming pool one night. It was never clear whether the cause was accidental or otherwise. This was at the time of the notorious Government atrocities in the Ndebele areas, known for their political opposition to Mugabe's Zanu-PF party, to which the international community, to their shame, turned a blind eye. I sometime wonder if his death was more sinister than appeared at the time.

My visits were often eventful. On one occasion, I was waiting to see the Minister of Labour and Social Welfare outside his office and ended up caught up in a violent demonstration by war veterans. The ministry had been stormed by a crowd of angry veterans demanding welfare payments and were now surging up to the Minister's office on the 10th floor. Finding myself in front of an angry mob, I beat a hasty retreat only to find that most officials had locked themselves in their offices for safety, leaving me to fend for myself. Luckily, the permanent secretary found me just in time and rescued me by taking me quickly out by the back stairs before things got too nasty.

Over the years I developed many Zimbabwean friendships. These included senior ministers like John Nkomo who served as both labour minister and minister of local government and went on to be Deputy President. John hosted our events held on Harare and joined us in meetings in Ghana and elsewhere. When things took a turn for the worse in later years under Mugabe, he was one of the few reasonable voices remaining.

On many visits, the atmosphere in the city was relaxed. I recall with fondness visiting Harare's local clubs with their vibrant African jazz and talented female singers. Harare in the 1980s seemed ready for good times with a strong economy and apparently stable leadership. It appeared set to become an ideal model for democracy in Africa and the Commonwealth, but this was not to be. Few could then have predicted the sad state to which the country would sink to by the late 1990s, with political intolerance, abuse of human rights and economic deprivation, and entrenchment of a political elite in the ruling ZANU-PF that was prone to personal enrichment.

If there is a lesson, not confined to Zimbabwe or Africa, it is that power corrupts and absolute power corrupts absolutely. This is especially the case when, as with Robert Mugabe, power is exercised unchecked over a long period of time and if a narrow clique is allowed to dominate politics. There is lot to be said for limiting the time in office of any leader to ten years at most and allow new and younger leaders to take over.

It is sad to reflect on how promising the new political dawn had been in Zimbabwe in 1980.

13.

Confronting Apartheid

ZIMBABWE HAD ATTAINED INDEPENDENCE IN 1980 ALONGSIDE the collapse of the Portuguese colonial empire in Angola and Mozambique. The big unfinished business was the liberation of Namibia and South Africa, controlled by the brutal apartheid regime.

The decade saw an increasingly bitter and bloody anti-apartheid struggle in South Africa and neighbouring frontline states. This was an arena where the Commonwealth, under the dynamic leadership of Sonny Ramphal was to play a central role, both in leading the fight to impose sanctions on Pretoria and in pushing for meaningful domestic political dialogue. Global public opinion, especially among the young, was mobilised in support of the release of Nelson Mandela and political prisoners.

For my generation, which became politically active in the late 1960s, agitating for democratic majority rule in Southern Africa became a central act of faith. The release of ANC leader Nelson Mandela was repeatedly demanded at huge anti-apartheid demonstrations in Trafalgar Square, held outside the South African Embassy, and popular rock concerts at Wembley were held in his honour. This raised global awareness of the Liberation Struggle in Southern Africa.

I had been involved in the anti-apartheid trade union actions at the ICFTU from the mid-1970s. Then I had tried to encourage the imposition of international codes of conduct on foreign multinationals operating in South Africa, and to incorporate these codes into broader ILO and UN initiatives. Although these codes were often derided as being too little and too late, they nonetheless included a key provision: the recognition of Black trade unions which employers increasingly observed. Once established, the Black unions were to play a central role in the overthrow of apartheid and I am proud to have played a small role in this process.

One of the obstacles facing the Liberation Movements, the ANC and PAC in South Africa and SWAPO in Namibia, was the political polarisation of the Cold War. Although the ANC and SWAPO received help from the West, especially from Sweden and the Scandinavian countries, their prime support, including for their military wings, came from the Soviet Bloc. They were therefore, wrongly, seen as beholden to Moscow, a view firmly held by Right-wing leaders like Ronald Reagan and Margaret Thatcher who naively viewed them as communist terrorists.

Thatcher, despite recent attempts to whitewash her image, had no time for sanctions against South Africa. She vigorously opposed any attempt to move in this direction by the Commonwealth. I well recall having sent a letter to the British Prime Minister on behalf the CTUC in 1986, asking her to impose sanctions. As expected, an official Downing Street letter duly came back signed by Margaret Thatcher. In this she reiterated that, "I do not support sanctions". Her strong headedness on this issue was highlighted by the way she had underlined the word 'not' in thick black ink: the message could not have been clearer.

South Africa was to dominate the 1985 CHOGM in Nassau. Sanctions were being sought by nearly all Commonwealth countries and the resistance to these by Margaret Thatcher and the UK Government threatened to break-up of the Commonwealth, with key African countries contemplating walking out. It looked as if the end of the Commonwealth was imminent.

To encourage compromise, our CTUC trade union delegation in Nassau, which was also arguing for sanctions, came up a clever compromise. We proposed that the Commonwealth start a political dialogue with Pretoria aiming at the release of Mandela and instigation of democratic reforms and domestic negotiations to end apartheid. However, if that failed, as seemed likely, the full force of economic and other sanctions should kick in. Our idea was bought by our close friend Prime Minister Hawke of Australia who in turn agreed it with Salim Salim of Tanzania and Shridath Ramphal. Other leaders and, reluctantly, the UK under Margaret Thatcher, then went along with the concept.

Following subsequent high-level consultations, our proposal was to result in the formal decision to establish the Commonwealth Eminent Persons Group, EPG. The EPG initiative was driven by the dynamism of Sonny Ramphal, ably assisted by his deputy and successor, Emeka Anyaoku. Ramphal deserves full credit for implementation of the proposal. He was generous enough to acknowledge in his autobiography that the original idea for this had come from Bob Hawke, who had taken up the idea put to him by CTUC delegation which I had led in Nassau.

The EPG, chaired by Malcolm Fraser of Australia and General Obasanjo of Nigeria, did indeed go to South Africa, met Nelson Mandela in his prison cell and tried to negotiate with Pretoria. They were able to start an initial political dialogue aimed at a negotiation framework to end apartheid and all of a sudden, things looked really positive. An early settlement was however sabotaged by Pretoria's hardliners, who without warning sent their air force to bomb the ANC headquarters in Lusaka.

This brutal action duly scuttled the mission of the Eminent Persons. As a result, and in line with the deal made in Nassau, the way to economic sanctions on Pretoria was open, although the UK continued to drag its feet. Nonetheless our Commonwealth initiative of 1985 was to inspire the conduct of actual transitional arrangements agreed later between President F.W. de Klerk and Nelson Mandela following the latter's release in 1990.

In addition to lobbying for sanctions we looked to take direct action in support of the Black South African trade union movement. This involved helping the newly established Congress of South African Trade Unions, COSATU, which was close to the ANC, and the National Council of Trade Unions, NACTU, linked the Pan-African Congress, PAC. African members of the CTUC Steering Committee led the call for this, notably my good friend Joseph Rwegasira, a highly skilled, likeable and soft-spoken diplomat who would later go on to become Tanzania's Foreign Minister.

By 1986, the demand for international sanctions against South Africa was becoming irresistible. In August of that year senior Commonwealth leaders including Bob Hawke, convened in London where I arranged to meet with them. There they agreed, but without the UK, a tough line on sanctions.

In a letter of 27 August, sent to ACTU President Simon Crean, Hawke acknowledged that meeting the CTUC delegation in London had given him the authority to counteract the argument that sanctions would hurt the Black population most; it had further allowed him to say that the Black opposition was not intent on destroying the country but was rather seeking a new, democratic and non-racial South Africa. He went on to recognise 'the valuable work of the CTUC in providing training for Black trade unionists in southern Africa'; and pledged continued support from his government for our work. A powerful endorsement for the policies we were implementing, and an indication of how a well organised advocacy group can have impact at the highest political level.

Another diplomatic coup was organising the first ever-meeting between the then head of the ANC, Oliver Tambo and senior CTUC and other trade unionists during the ILO conference in Geneva in 1986. This included top TUC and CLC representatives at a time when they had never had a formal meeting with the ANC. Hitherto their official line had been not to talk to a non-trade union Liberation Movement, and I was pleased this misguided position changed after our Geneva meeting and was hurriedly erased from institutional memory.

In our endeavours we came up against the jealousy of my old employers, the ICFTU. The latter wanted to monopolise contacts with Black South African unions and avoid interference by the fledgling CTUC with, as they saw it, dangerous non-aligned and Leftist leanings. They were particularly upset that we set up close working links with the COSATU leadership and secured COSATU as a formal CTUC member.

The ICFTU line was supported by the TUC and, to an increasing extent, by the CLC, once its President Denis McDermott had retired and been replaced as CLC President and CTUC Chairperson by the more Right-wing Shirley Carr. The new TUC General Secretary, Norman Willis, was also less supportive than Len Murray had been. Initially, I had been able to maintain support of either the TUC or the CLC for a more activist CTUC involvement, but with both now aligned against me this became increasingly difficult. As a consequence, my own position as CTUC Director came under threat.

Matters came to a crisis at a meeting in Canada in 1986, attended by Norman Willis. The atmosphere was sour, and I was threatened with removal as CTUC Director unless I backed off our engagement with South Africa. I decided to stay firm, having the full support of my staff, who were incensed by the strong-armed tactics being deployed. However, my big card was the active support of our African Steering Committee members and, significantly, COSATU General Secretary Jay Naidoo. A critical negotiating point came when the Nigerian trade union delegation in Ottawa produced a substantial financial grant earmarked for CTUC action in support of COSATU. This was handed over to me at the meeting in US dollars and strengthened my hand.

My firm position was to pay off. Agreement was reached that CTUC could engage in direct support of COSATU and other Black unions and play an important role in the subsequent political evolution. A cordial lunch followed with Norman Willis on my return to London. This was memorable in involving the consumption of two nice bottles of wine, admittedly most drunk by Norman.

The same year CTUC and the TUC co-hosted the first official visit of the COSATU leadership to London, who were put up in a modest hotel near the TUC off Russell Square in Bloomsbury. Returning to the hotel after dinner on their first night we were shocked to find that the room of Jay Naidoo had been broken into and his luggage ransacked. This was a stark reminder that the South African regime did not shrink from intimidation of its political opponents, even in London.

I was soon to obtain direct experience of just what appalling victimisation our South African friends were subjected to. On the invitation of COSATU, I paid my first visit to South African in July 1987 to address the Second Congress of COSATU, held at Wits University, Johannesburg. The COSATU HQ building had been bombed by the regime, its elderly President had his arm in plaster after being beaten up by the police, and trade unionists and activists were routinely detained without trial and tortured. Disgracefully, I learnt that even junior COSATU admin staff were being targeted and had found car bombs under their vehicles, narrowly escaping death.

My visit, together with Norman Willis and Michael Walsh of the TUC, almost did not materialise. It had been made clear to us by Pretoria that we would only get as far as the arrivals lounge of Jan Smuts airport and denied entry.

A frantic consultation ensued with the British Government, which was desperate to encourage 'constructive dialogue' with Pretoria, and therefore felt it had to support our visit. Following pressure by Her Majesty's Government, notably Foreign Office Minister Lynda Chalker, Pretoria grudgingly agreed to give us a fixed three-day visa. This was issued only a few short hours before the last possible flight connection to Johannesburg, to make our travel as difficult as possible. Having anticipated this delay, we had our bags ready packed and made it to Heathrow and our flight in the nick of time.

On arrival in South Africa, we had a hectic three days of non-stop activity. COSATU gave us a crash course in confronting apartheid. We attended and addressed their Congress, meeting the senior political leadership, including the charismatic leader of the National Union of Mineworkers and later President of South Africa, Cyril Ramaphosa, who acted as my personal interpreter during the Congress proceedings. I hold vivid memories, and quite a few photos, of that inspiring occasion, punctuated with fiery political speeches and vibrant toi-toi dancing.

We were shown Soweto and the sprawling Black townships, confined to the periphery of white Johannesburg, and saw the notorious single men's dormitories where workers were kept in prison-like conditions. A lighter moment came when Jay Naidoo introduced us to the excellent South African wine over dinner. Drinking South African wine was boycotted at home and on returning to the UK I had to wait many more years until I was able to drink it again 'legally'.

It was a visit I will not easily forget, and a highlight of my work with CTUC.

14.

Global Solidarity

THE CTUC HAD A BROAD-RANGING REMIT TO PROMOTE TRADE union and labour rights throughout the Commonwealth. This was to take me to many different countries.

In Nassau in 1985, our delegation had another important concern apart from apartheid: the release of Zambian trade union leader Freddy Chiluba, who had been jailed by his own government. In meeting with President Kenneth Kaunda, also known as KK, we were forceful in making the argument that we could not accept double standards when calling for trade union freedoms in South Africa and seeing them restricted in Zambia. KK struck me as a thoughtful leader who was open to reason, and who certainly played an important role within the Commonwealth.

Our intervention in Nassau helped to bring about the early release of Chiluba and other trade unionists. Chiluba was to become President of Zambia himself where I was to meet him later in the splendid surroundings of State House in Lusaka. He subsequently got his own back on KK when he also put him under detention for a while and vindictively sought to restrict his basic citizen rights. Regretfully, his Presidency was not a success and he left office under a cloud with allegations of corruption and other misdeeds.

My other encounter with KK, the father of Zambia, was at an international conference in Livingstone near Victoria Falls around the same period. He arrived several hours late for a lunch he had been due to host, having been delayed in important talks with Robert Mugabe on apartheid. Of course, we could not start the meal without him, and we were starving. Any annoyance was soon dispelled when, as well as giving the usual welcome greeting of 'One Zambia, One Nation' he quickly added 'and One Lunch', causing much laughter and mirth.

The same conference held other vivid memories. One was being stranded and stuck in deep mud, when we were taken by minibus to a safari park full of lions and dangerous wild animals. With a smile I recall the Soviet delegation trying to pull the bus out in one direction while at the same time the Americans were pushing in the opposite direction: something of a commentary on the Cold War. Luckily, we were soon rescued by a fleet of Land Rovers and driven to the safety of our hotel.

I recall being impressed by a highly committed young Zambian woman trade unionist, Alice Siame. We were to become good friends, and she was to play a prominent role especially in directing attention to the needs of women workers and supporting women trade unionists. This issue became a growing part of the CTUC's remit and her long-standing contribution to the international trade union movement has been significant.

Much of the CTUC's solidarity work was of a modest, but strategic nature. Our aim was to help trade unionists in developing countries to help themselves, in particular through trade union education and training. Training had traditionally been based on old fashioned classroom style teaching methods.

The CTUC was fortunate that in addition to my own staff, David Clement and Stephen Faulkner, we were able to draw on a young and committed group of British TUC education officers such as Graham Petersen, Ron Oswald and Arthur Johnson. TUC education had recently undergone a revolution in teaching methods and emphasised 'active learning' through modern participation and role plays, providing motivation for students, rather than boring lectures. This part of the CTUC's work, aimed at grass roots education and capacity-building, was a vital complement to its more political work. It was an activity which was to benefit future trade union leaders across the Commonwealth.

By drawing on modern learning methods we had a major impact with the small resources I was able to secure from AusAid in Australia, the UK Government's Overseas Development Ministry (ODA), the EU and other agencies. In this I was helped by the good political and personal links I had with Prime Minister Hawke and past British Labour ministers like Judith Hart and John Grant.

In this way my staff complement could grow, with representation based in different parts of the Commonwealth. In this CTUC was probably ahead of most Commonwealth organisations, which tended to operate out of their London offices and did not have the vision or resources to see the importance of having regional representation. The only exception was the Commonwealth Youth Programme, which did have offices in different regions, but which sadly no longer exists.

The CTUC's participatory approach to our members meant that no-one could accuse us of neo-colonialism, still less of promoting Cold War objectives. We sought wherever possible to employ local staff and resource persons and link-up with local institutions. The young UK TUC tutors we did deploy were all, as typical of their generation, highly motivated and politically committed.

This was to lead those jealous of our success to falsely accuse the CTUC of being ideologically Left-wing, even 'Trotskyite' at a time when that term was highly damaging in the British Labour Movement. In reply I can only point to how our pioneering educational approach has become mainstream. Indeed, the closest I ever personally came to Trotskyism was when, some years later, I visited the house in Mexico City where one of Stalin's henchmen put a pickaxe through the unfortunate Leon Trotsky's skull.

There were many occasions when I took lead in defending trade union and human rights, sometimes at personal risk.

I once flew to Accra following the ransacking of local union offices by militant groups after the takeover of power by Flight-Lt Jerry Rawlings. My visit to Ghana was beset by political and logistical difficulties, of which the least of my worries was being attacked by swarms of mosquitos in a hot and squalid hotel room. My presence in the country and our subsequent training programme in Ghana made a difference and helped to rebuild the local union movement. Likewise, I ensured support for our Nigerian trade union colleagues when the military took power in their country, making strong representations on their behalf to the Commonwealth Secretariat which in turn applied political pressure to seek the release of imprisoned trade unionists.

In East Africa, too, I was present at difficult moments. I vividly recall visiting Uganda in the early 1980s after the demise of Idi Amin. This was to render solidarity when the country was on its knees and in desperate need of help. It was a time when young kids were swaggering around the streets of a run-down Kampala toting AK-47 machine guns. Most donors were reluctant to engage their staff given the poor security and I admit I felt in quite some danger myself.

My visit did have a lighter moment when I was invited to the wedding of a Ugandan friend in Kampala and introduced to the delights of very potent home-made banana beer, the only alcoholic drink available. While it tasted great, it contrived to give me one of the worst hangovers of my life. I soon visited the country again and was able to initiate an ongoing programme of support to help re-build the local trade unions.

In Sierra Leone, I recall having lunch with the head of the trade unions and the minister of labour in Freetown. When I asked why the cheaper local beer was not available, only expensive imported lager, it turned out that the local brewery had recently closed. I then, unexpectedly, refereed a negotiation between the union leader and the minister about the Government re-opening the brewery. It seems my comment helped to save the local brewing industry and ensured that workers got their cheap beer again.

Our solidarity programmes extended to the Caribbean and the Pacific. In the Caribbean, I visited countries with strong unions like Barbados, Trinidad and Jamaica and also countries where unions were just being established such as Belize, formerly British Honduras. This involved starting trade union training programmes, mainly with EU funding, organised on a regional basis. I also arranged the first-ever visit by a Black South African delegation from COSATU to the region and ensured they met with the then political leadership in Jamaica under Hugh Shearer, who I also recall meeting at the time.

Following two visits to Belize, just before and after independence in 1981, I was able to secure Canadian support for a local trade union training initiative. CTUC engagement here played a role in pre-empting the sort of one-sided 'support' and control coming from Reagan's US which neighbouring Central American countries had seen. On one of these visits, I was bemused to see an official notice at the Belize City harbour informing employees that 'smoking marijuana is not permitted in the harbour area', but presumably allowed elsewhere. Certainly, some smaller countries have their own way of doing things.

I was always impressed by the sophistication of much of the Commonwealth Caribbean countries, which is reflected in their vibrant multi-party democracies and political pluralism. It was therefore not surprising that over the years the region has seen global political leaders like Michael Manley, Sonny Ramphal and many others, as well as renowned trade union leaders like Sir Frank Walcott of Barbados. I have been privileged to visit most of these countries and count many West Indian colleagues like Senator Bobby Montague of Jamaica among my close friends.

Apart from Fiji, trade unions in most of the small Pacific islands were in their infancy in the 1980s. One morning I was intrigued to receive a message asking for support for striking public sector workers in Kiribati. I learnt that this was the former Gilbert Islands, located a thousand miles north of Australia on the equator. In response I decided to send a 'nuclear deterrent' to Kiribati in the shape of trade union leader Jack Jones, who had recently retired. In fact, Jack did a great job in giving advice to the local unions, which he recalls with fondness in his autobiography. He later told me that seeing the nascent unions in Kiribati reminded him of his early days in the Liverpool docks.

Kiribati, pronounced Kiri-bass, consists of 33 tiny islands, spread over a vast ocean area of several million square kilometres. However, the largest island, Tarawa, is just ten kilometres long by 500 metres across. Already prone to storms, it is likely to disappear below the waves from global warming. When I visited Tarawa in 1982, I was hosted at the residence of the British High Commissioner for dinner, who told me that when it got stormy, he "went to sleep with a lifebelt on, just in case". I am not sure if he was joking either. With global warming this situation will of course get ever worse.

During my visit to Tarawa, I was feted as a friend of Kiribati and given a beach-side reception by the Minister of Labour under swaying palm trees and with the gentle blue waters of the Pacific Ocean all around. This involved eating delicious freshly caught seafood while sitting cross-legged on the beach, which though okay for the first hour, soon gave me backache. A surrealistic episode, worthy of a Monty Python comedy sketch, followed.

The elderly Minister dressed casually in a tee-shirt, sarong and wearing simple sandals, suddenly announced that dancing would now take place. Instead of the gracious South Sea Island music I had expected, an old battery record player was produced. Soon the sounds of a raucous Chubby Checker record from 1960 blared out inviting us all to 'twist again'. This the somewhat frail Minister in his flimsy sarong, duly proceeded to do, along with the rest of us. It did admittedly ease my backache.

The final touch was being presented with a genuine shark's teeth knife made of bamboo. I carefully wrapped this up in my shirts and put it in my suitcase. When I unpacked in London, I found that my garments had been torn to shreds by the sharpness of the shark's teeth. I am sure these days the knife would have been confiscated immediately upon check-in as a dangerous weapon. This it certainly is, and I keep it in a safe place at home, alongside the fearsome pointed wooden war club I once acquired in Vanuatu.

Getting to Kiribati was itself an adventure, involving an overnight stopover in Nauru, a tiny island state in the middle of nowhere.

Nauru is the UN's smallest country by population, only numbering 10,000 souls. It owes its existence and wealth to millions of years of bird droppings. This in turn resulted in highly profitable phosphate which has been extensively mined. In consequence, Nauru's people used to be very prosperous and tended to be on the large side physically on account of excessive food consumption. I was told of the local who had bought a sleek Lamborghini sport car only to find that he could not fit behind the seat and that there was not a sufficiently long road on the island to get the car beyond first gear. Sadly, prosperity was bought at great environmental cost with much of the island now being an open cast phosphate mine with little vegetation, and now that most of the phosphate has been mined, the money too has run out.

At the time I stopped-over, Nauru's tiny airport landing strip merged into its one and only real road which circumnavigated the island. The boundary between the two was marked by a sign announcing 'give way to aircraft'. Happily, aircraft only landed once a week and the road did not have too many cars.

I had a funny return journey after my visit to Kiribati, thanks to a long flight on Air Nauru from Nauru to Hong Kong. Going to stretch my legs halfway through the flight, I wandered to the end of the only cabin in the ageing Boeing jet. I then noticed a door which, being naturally curious, I decided to open. Slowly my eyes grew accustomed to the darkness. I then saw to my amazement what looked like the cargo hold. This was occupied by South Sea islanders sitting cross-legged on the floor among various boxes and cases. I realised then that this was the economy class, as they, unlike myself, had no seats, but only floor-space to sit on. In contrast, I, having an actual seat upfront, was travelling in the luxury of business class.

The Fiji Islands have a more developed economy than other countries in the Pacific. This was reflected in their more advanced political and trade union structures. In the mid-1980s, Fiji was led by a charismatic union leader, Mahendra Chaudhury, who set up a local Labour Party which went on to win the national elections in 1987 and became Prime Minister.

Although the Fiji Labour Party was non-racial, its large Indian component and the growing population of ethnic Indians, provoked a violent reaction by the indigenous Fijians, who feared being eclipsed.

Their military leader, Colonel Rabuka, seized power, deposing Chaudhury and dissolved parliament, proceeding to disenfranchise the Indian population, many of which then left the country for Australia and beyond.

This new mini-apartheid state in the Pacific became a hot issue for the Commonwealth. At the 1987 CHOGM in Vancouver, I recall arguing with my old friend, Prime Minister Bob Hawke, who was advocating too soft a response to the Fiji coup for my liking. Fiji was duly suspended from the Commonwealth and did not re-join until 1997 when democracy had been restored. I can claim a minor role in facilitating its return to the Commonwealth by having invited senior local government representatives, including the Lord Mayor of Suva, to a Commonwealth conference which I organised in Port Moresby early in 1997.

Fiji's absence from the Commonwealth meant that I did not visit the country for some ten years. When I did return in 1999, I was delighted to find that my trade union colleague Mahendra Chaudhury, who I was able meet and congratulate in person, had again been elected Prime Minister. Sadly, history was to repeat itself when Chaudhury was yet once more toppled in a racially inspired coup and the country was again suspended from the Commonwealth for many years. Once more, I tried to build bridges, but this proved difficult when the regime disbanded all elected local government in the country which I had sought to support. Although it has now returned to democracy and Commonwealth membership, it has to date failed to honour a promise to restore local democracy.

My absence from Fiji for many years did have the bonus of my not having to consume the traditional drink, Kava. The latter is a narcotic, made by mixing the powdered root of a tree with water and with saliva contributed by the village women who produce it and spit into it. It is a deadly brew: a tiny sip of this ill-tasting grey liquid will make your tongue go numb. If you drink more, the rest of your body will go numb.

Kava is consumed seemingly everywhere. A local taxi driver will offer it to you from a dirty plastic bucket. The former Lord Mayor gave it to you in a silver goblet. To my mind it easily competes with home-made Uganda banana beer in its potency. I was alarmed when, on a visit to my home in London, a Pacific staff member produced a sample of Kava for us all to try: It is banned as a narcotic in most places outside of Fiji, including in the UK.

Overseas travel certainly has its interesting moments.

15.

On Her Majesty's Diplomatic List

FROM 1988 UNTIL 1994, I WAS EMPLOYED AS A DIPLOMAT AT
the Commonwealth Secretariat. Here I held the senior position of
Assistant Director dealing with the Commonwealth *Victims of Apartheid*
programmes.

By 1987, I had worked for the international trade union movement
for fourteen years. I felt I had taken the CTUC as far as it would go in
the short term and was looking for new challenges. My heart was in
international work, and I was less focused on UK domestic politics,
although I remained active within my local Labour Party in Hampstead
where I was the Vice Chair.

Since my appointment as CTUC Director in 1980, I had been much
involved in the activities of the Commonwealth and was well-regarded
in Commonwealth Secretariat circles. In late 1997, a vacancy arose as
Assistant Director, in the Fellowships and Training Programme, FTP, of
the Secretariat. After talking to Bishnu Persaud and other Secretariat
friends, I decided to apply for the job. I would have preferred to apply
for a Director's position, with responsibility for a particular department
or for a senior role within a more political section such as the Political
Affairs Division of the Secretariat. However, I was still a young 37 and
hoped that, as the Secretariat had been an expanding organisation, a
Directorship would soon materialise.

The Secretariat job was a diplomatic position, and only Directors
and Assistant Directors are deemed to have this status. They are featured
on the official UK Diplomatic List, although in the case of UK nationals,
none of the generous tax concessions for which non-UK nationals qualify
apply. Indeed, the main perk is an annual invitation to the Buckingham
Palace Garden Party.

Following a successful interview, I was offered the position. I surprised
my trade union colleagues with deciding, with some reluctance, and a

little tear, to leave the CTUC which I had set up seven years earlier. Before going, I wrote a frank valedictory article which set out my thoughts about the organisation and voiced concern at some political difficulties it had recently faced internally, especially on South Africa. Sir Frank Walcott, my Steering Committee member from Barbados and a highly respected senior trade unionist, was kind enough to reproduce the article in his local newspaper, together with very complimentary comments about my work. I felt I was leaving the CTUC in a good position, organisationally and financially.

I had a nice going-away party at Congress House. A highlight was the presentation of a book on the early dockers union from my old mentor, Jack Jones. In giving it to me, he touchingly wrote that it was "a little of the real history of our movement which I know you will always respect in your new area of activity" and "Salud". I took this to heart in my subsequent professional and political endeavours and have kept up my union dues to this day.

In retrospect, my trade union colleagues thought that I was leaving for a prestigious and well-paid position, changing from being 'poacher' to 'gamekeeper'. In fact, the new job had less freedom of action and in strictly money terms, was only marginally better paid and had less perks. Certainly, I never earned a substantial salary throughout my life and Adele made very little if anything from her meagre children's dance school fees. Money has never been my main concern in life as long as I got by and was comfortable. On principle, I have never owed a commercial share or speculated, nor have I received a penny from unearned income other than from my pension scheme investments or small savings; nor have I ever received any significant family inheritance.

Insofar as in later life and on retirement Adele and I acquired a lovely home, this was largely because, like many others, we benefitted from massive London property price rises, having bought our first joint home on a 25-year mortgage in 1982. We also decided that having got remarried quite late in life, and both committed to our respective careers, we would not have children. With highly fulfilling jobs and many interactions with nephews, nieces, cousins and Adele's numerous dance school pupils, it is a decision we have had no reason to regret.

I started my new job with the Commonwealth Secretariat in January 1988 with high expectations. My immediate boss and Director of the FTP, Dr Mohan Kaul from India, seemed open-minded and progressive in his approach to things. The department where I was Assistant

Director – the Fellowships and Training Programme – FTP-had responsibility for training and capacity-building throughout the Commonwealth to improve public administration and senior management skills in developing country administrations. It also supported the work of Commonwealth professional bodies and civil society organisations.

What really interested me most was the *Victims of Apartheid* programme. This was administered by our department and offered scholarships and other support to the Namibian and South African Liberation Movements and was highly political. To these was soon added the Special Commonwealth Fund for Mozambique, the establishment and operation of which I was much involved with.

I soon got fully engaged with the programme, working with the coordinating project officer, Terry Dormer. This programme, based on the 1985 Nassau Fellowships Scheme had been expanded at the 1987 Vancouver CHOGM and in 1988-89 supported 302 students and another 1350 in distance learning. At the 1989 Kuala Lumpur CHOGM, it had been "agreed that the Commonwealth should continue to provide support to the victims and opponents of apartheid within South Africa. Of particular importance were educational programmes, including in particular the Nassau Fellowships, legal and humanitarian assistance to detainees and their families, support for the trade union movement, and economic and social development programmes including low-cost housing programmes".

In line with this mandate, it fell to me to extend the scope of the programme to more sensitive areas. These included instigating significant support for what was termed 'agents of change', notably the Black trade unions, as well as channelling resources to the new Skills for South Africa network, based at Oxford, which provided job attachments and other practical training to key South Africans in anticipation of their likely return home post-apartheid.

After initially serving under Sonny Ramphal from Guyana, the new Commonwealth Secretary-General was a Nigerian, Chief Anyaoko, my Departmental Director Mohan was Indian, and my colleagues came from all corners of the globe. Few colleagues were from the UK. I have throughout my professional life worked in a multi-national and multi-cultural environment whether in the EU, at the UN and now the Commonwealth, found it stimulating and have thrived on it. I have never worked in a solely British organisation or institution and would have felt uncomfortable in the absence of international colleagues.

As I had found out in my early career in Brussels in the 1970s, by the 1980s, the British FCO and much of UK civil service was still full of male ex-public school boys and I encountered them frequently in my new role. Quite a few of these British officials held antediluvian political, sexist and even racist attitudes towards the outside world, with deeply entrenched conservative values, with both a small 'c' and a big party-political 'C'. Coming from a comprehensive school in Wales and – horror of horrors – the trade unions, did not endear me to them.

However, by the 1990s, UK public sector reforms had begun to change this picture with a broader, more inclusive, intake including women and ethnic minorities. Happily, today's FCO and senior Whitehall officials are very different from what they used to be. They are much more diverse in background and outlook and today's public-school elite seem to be more represented in 10 Downing Street and the ruling political class rather than in the public service.

Working in a multi-cultural environment can have distinct problems. Even in Europe, a culture clash is apparent. I notice my German relatives, at least the older ones, introduce themselves to strangers quite abruptly by their surname and, unlike the practice in Anglo-Saxon countries, often bristle if work colleagues call them by their first name. Different nationalities have their own working cultures and procedures: some are at work at the crack of dawn, whilst others prefer to work late. Some grab a quick lunchtime sandwich while others insist on long lunch breaks in line with their own cultural practices. Not everyone can adapt easily to this mix.

My bosses at the Commonwealth Secretariat, although in many ways enlightened in their politics, often exhibited an engrained sense of hierarchy and deployed an old-fashioned top-down managerial style. When I started my work as Assistant Director, my immediate boss, Mohan Kaul, was the Director and we were the two senior-most staff. He had his office just two doors along from mine. Yet at first, if I wanted to talk to him, he asked me to make an appointment to see him through his secretary who had the office between us. This was something which I bluntly refused to do.

It all started badly when, on my very first assignment, perhaps a little cynically given my trade union background, I was sent to a meeting at a UK military-related training college, which was a bit of a culture shock. Mohan and I subsequently had many differences and he kept me away from representing the department at senior Secretariat management meetings. More seriously, the renewal of my initial two-year contract of employment came under threat in 1990. The cerebral but very particular, Deputy Secretary-General Moni Malhoutra, also an Indian national, backed Mohan against me on a number of occasions. However, I could count on the support of the new Secretary-General, Chief Anyaoku. Then, with renewal of my second contract, I was finally given more responsibility and was allowed to show what I could do. Subsequently Mohan and I worked closely together and became friendly; indeed, I was later one of the signatories for his UK naturalisation papers.

In retrospect I must have seemed brash and insufficiently deferential to my boss and many of my Commonwealth colleagues. In fact, as in Brussels in 1973, I have always deeply disliked bureaucratic, hierarchical structures or fancy job titles. I was never interested in giving attention to detailed and tedious paperwork which old-style civil servants – the 'Sir Humphreys' of that highly perceptive and funny British TV series *Yes Minister* – love so much. While I accept the need for clear staff responsibilities, I tire easily of petty office politics and gossip and prefer to concentrate on the strategic issues which really matter. I much prefer to delegate detailed implementation of work to my staff where possible and focus on the bigger picture.

My British Labour Movement links and associations certainly did not help. This was especially true when I had to deal with certain British colleagues who did not see me as 'one of them' politically. Once Mrs Thatcher had consolidated her political ascendancy, being an ex-trade union activist or sympathiser became to be almost treasonable in the UK public service, especially after her defeat of the British miners in the mid-1980s. When I joined the Secretariat in 1988, just a year after Mrs Thatcher's third triumphant election victory, the Labour Party seemed as far from power as ever. As a result, I felt I was being kept away from sensitive political issues and events I had been intimately involved with at the CTUC, including attendance at CHOGMs, and found this was very frustrating.

Thatcher's privatisation philosophy, if anything strengthened under her successor John Major after 1990, was copied by many Commonwealth governments in line with the neo-liberal philosophy of the time. My belief in a strong public sector, government intervention and employee rights, was looking out of place. Indeed, shortly after the unexpected fourth election defeat of Labour by the Conservatives in 1992, one of my British antagonists in the Secretariat was heard to utter the profound words that, "Now is the time to get Carl Wright". I suppose I should have been flattered and made sure that he did not succeed in his aim.

My time as Assistant Director corresponded with the transformation of my department from what was broadly a demand-driven scholarship programme, to a more management and results-orientated Management and Training Programme. Many of the public sector reforms we supported were necessary in countries which had bloated and inefficient bureaucracies, depleting stretched State finances. However, all too often for my liking, the Secretariat was an enthusiastic advocate of what became known as the 'new public sector initiative'. This was essentially a radical overhaul and reform of government services, often entailing down-sizing and whole-scale privatisation, the implementation of the very neo-liberalism I had fought against in the trade unions. As in the UK, it resulted in sell-offs at knockdown prices, with little benefit to the consumer, but big pay-outs for company directors and shareholders, with poorer service provision for consumers.

Some years on, Mohan made the transition as Director-General of the newly established Commonwealth Business Council and came to see the values of private-public sector partnerships and we collaborated on several initiatives. Much later, he sought to be elected Commonwealth Secretary-General, but was unsuccessful in getting support from the Indian Government which instead successfully nominated a serving Indian diplomat, Kamalesh Sharma. On reflection I feel Mohan would have been a successful Secretary-General.

Given my union background I agreed to serve on the Secretariat's internal staff association and became one of its officers. However, it did not have the clout or negotiating power of a true trade union and was only able to achieve small gains for the staff.

I began to miss my old labour movement activist work.

16.

Trade Unionism Relapse

LOOKING BACK ON SEVEN YEARS' SERVICE AT THE
Commonwealth Secretariat 1988-94, I take pride in my achievements.
My trade union work was however not yet done.

My record at the Secretariat was acknowledged in a warm thank-you
letter I received from Secretary-General Emeka Anyaoku when I left in
1994. My key activities had related to the anti-apartheid struggle and
had two broad phases: the period 1988-90 when we were actively
supporting the Liberation struggle and 1990-94, after the release of
Nelson Mandela from prison, which involved preparing the country for
the post-apartheid transition and its subsequent reconstruction on a
non-racial basis.

1988 was the year before the fall of the Berlin Wall. The prospects
for a free South Africa still seemed distant. However, momentum was
gathering on independence for Namibia. A good comrade and friend
from Sweden, the former General Secretary of the London-based Socialist
International, Bernt Carlsson, had been appointed UN Commissioner
for Namibia. I had met him a few months previously in New York and
discussed collaboration. He had joined me and Adele for a relaxed dinner
at our house in West Hampstead in London in late 1988. Just a few
weeks after hosting him I learnt with deep shock that Bernt had been a
passenger on the ill-fated Pan Am flight blown up by a terrorist bomb
over Lockerbie in Scotland.

Lockerbie was the worst terrorist outrage in living memory with
terrible loss of life. One of the many theories for the callous attack
stipulated a South African connection, possible aimed at the Namibian
peace process. Poor Bernt would have been a clear target. There was a
rumour that a senior South African delegation had been booked on the
flight but cancelled at the last moment. It is unlikely if the truth will ever
be known, and a Libyan or Iranian link seems more likely, but I recall

with great sadness that on that fateful day I lost a good and kind friend. The world also lost an internationalist and a statesman. I later drew some consolation when Glenys Kinnock agreed to my proposal that our new One World Action charity should also be called the 'Bernt Carlsson Trust' in Bernt's honour.

Given my close involvement in support of South Africa and its trade unions, I was keen to continue this in my new position as Assistant Director in collaboration with the CTUC, and I tried to encourage Secretariat funding for CTUC activities. This was in line with the 1987 CHOGM mandate on support for Black unions which I had been instrumental in getting endorsed. My problem was that my successor as CTUC Director was a TUC official, Patrick Quinn, with limited international experience, who had little interest in cooperating with me.

It was not long before Dave Clement, Steve Faulkner and other able CTUC staff left and in subsequent years I was saddened when Secretariat colleagues frequently asked me what had happened to the CTUC and if it still existed. Following some ups and downs the organisation was headed by Arthur Johnstone in 1994 and finally by the dedicated Annie Watson, who I had appointed. But it was already in decline with loss of key members such as Australian ACTU and in 2005 it was formally dissolved as an independent organisation and absorbed as the 'Commonwealth Group' of the ITUC, operating from Brussels. Recently, I was pleased to see it has shown signs of a renaissance in this guise and has been quite active at CHOGMs.

Back in 1988/89, I was faced with a dilemma when the opportunity arose to plough Secretariat funds into trade union work in support of our comrades in South Africa and Namibia. At the CTUC our policy had been to work with the internal Black unions like COSATU, but not their exiled counterparts like the South African Congress of Trade Unions (SACTU) with strong communist influence; the same applied to the National Union of Namibian Workers (NUNW), the exiled Namibian union linked to SWAPO. In contrast the Secretariat was more sensitive to the views of the ANC and SWAPO and had no such problem in putting money into SACTU or NUNW as well as into COSATU in recognition of their role as major agents of political change.

Given the evolving situation in Southern Africa, there were now growing contacts especially between the internal UDM and COSATU and the exiled ANC and SACTU. This meant that there was a desire for the internal and external trade union bodies to meet and agree common political strategies. This was usually done in neutral venues like Zimbabwe. As CTUC under its new leadership was not inclined to work with SACTU and NUNW, our South African and Namibian comrades looked to me and the Commonwealth Secretariat for assistance.

Having seen the strength and dynamism of COSATU and its leadership, I never bought the argument that they could somehow be taken over by SACTU or subject to communist control. I knew that if anything the reverse would happen, given the extent to which COSATU was the legitimate representative of Black workers and allied closely with the democratic structures of the UDF. I accordingly decided to directly help to organise and fund a substantial number of workshops and training events for the internal and external trade union movements of Namibia and South Africa.

These events were mostly held at the well-respected training college in Harare, Ranche House College. They played an important part in bringing about common action and eventual unity among the internal and external Liberation Movement structures by facilitating their coming together. As such they helped strengthen the capacity and strategic cohesiveness of the opposition to apartheid at a time when Nelson Mandela and his associates were still languishing in prison.

In my work I was helped by a young trade union tutor from Liverpool, Trevor Davies, who had previously done work for me in Southern Africa at the CTUC. Trevor was from the Leftist NUPE union, now part of the public service union UNISON. His work rate, political commitment and engagement in support of the anti-apartheid cause could not be questioned. NUPE, with the active support of its General Secretary Rodney Bickerstaffe, provided support by handling accounts for activities undertaken, thereby ensuring financial accountability and oversight.

The programme was to take on a substantial dimension and brought me open hostility from my former colleagues at the CTUC and the ICFTU who continued to worry that it was giving credibility to communist-dominated groups like SACTU. One consequence was that I was effectively ostracised by my old colleagues and became something of a non-person, not being invited to CTUC social functions for many years. This I found hurtful, having founded the organisation. My compensation came in the quiet satisfaction at what I had accomplished in support of the anti-apartheid struggle and the esteem I was held in by my trade union brothers and sisters in South Africa and throughout the Commonwealth.

Apart from managing the broader Secretariat solidarity programmes for Namibia and South Africa, I assumed responsibility for training activities under the newly created Commonwealth Special Fund for Mozambique. I travelled for the first time to Maputo in late 1988 to arrange the initial operations of the Fund at a time when Mozambique was embroiled in a vicious civil war, fermented by the Pretoria regime. During my visit Maputo was surrounded by the insurgent RENAMO (Mozambican National Resistance) troops. Travelling to the edge of what was then a war-racked and dilapidated city, I could see the outlying RENAMO military positions. I realised that I was in the middle of a war zone and in some danger. I beat a hasty retreat to the grand but run-down Polana Hotel in the city centre which was the only establishment still functioning to any extent.

Not very reassuringly, my office's travel service had informed me before my departure that during my stay in Maputo, my travel life insurance would be doubled because of the security risks involved. Happily, on subsequent visits, the RENAMO troops had been forced away from the capital and back into the bush, so I felt a lot safer. My missions to Maputo were to result in significant numbers of senior Mozambican officials receiving public administration training as well as English language tuition. Much of this involved my arranging work placements for officials in neighbouring countries like Zimbabwe.

I visited Botswana, Zambia, Tanzania and other African frontline states in connection with training and support for the Liberation Movements. These were countries which Pretoria had sought to destabilise, and several had been attacked militarily, an issue highlighted in a Commonwealth report on *'Apartheid Terrorism'*. In Tanzania I travelled overland to the main exile centre for South Africans in the south of the country and was impressed by its discipline and efficient organisation. In pursuit of this work, I became a trustee of the South African Extension Unit, a Tanzanian institution, based in Dar es Salaam, which was doing excellent work in providing adult education to large numbers of exiles through innovative distance learning methods and regularly attended its Board meetings.

During earlier visits to Tanzania, I stayed at the Hotel Kilimanjaro, the only large hotel in Dar at the time which had charms of sorts. When I had first lodged at the establishment, Tanzania's economy was in a rough state and this was reflected in the hotel services: breakfast comprised bread without butter, and coffee was served black without milk. The rooms were in an awful state and the large swimming pool had no water. I drew some consolation when I lamented about the pool to my friend Gary, who had just returned from Lagos. He shrugged his shoulders and said he had also not been able to use his hotel pool either, not because of lack of water, but because it contained a dead human body.

By the late 1980s, the 'Kili' as it was affectionately known, achieved a breakthrough by introducing air conditioning in the rooms. On arrival in my hotel room, I was met by an icy-cold blast coming through a metal grate positioned over my room door. This could not be turned down, so I called the front desk to fix it. An engineer emerged who duly removed the grate, placed some newspaper to cover the ensuing gaping hole and then, very tidily, put the grate back again. As a result, the icy blast was moderated, due to the wonders of appropriate technology: an old newspaper.

My new role had allowed me to help in the battle against apartheid.

17.

The 1980s Assessed

THE 1980s WERE A FORMATIVE PERIOD IN MY LIFE AND CAREER.
I regarded it as a compliment that, years later, Commonwealth colleagues
still referred to me as a 'union man'.

The decade saw the election of Ronald Reagan and Margaret Thatcher
and was marked by a distinct Right-wing turn in global politics after the
heady days of the 1970s with its hopes for a New International Economic
Order. Soon neo-liberalism with a return to harsh free market economics,
privatisation and restrictions on trade union and other rights was the
order of the day. This new Washington Consensus sought to impose itself
at the global level at the UN and at the Commonwealth. Accordingly,
much of my CTUC work in the 1980s was devoted to opposing neo-
liberalism through strengthening trade union structures and fighting for
progressive international policies.

The new political realities meant that there was little point in directing
my advocacy work at the British Government, as I had done successfully
during the previous Labour Governments of the 1970s. Now I had to
focus my energies on working closely with other sympathetic
governments, like the Australian Labor Government, headed by my 'mate'
Bob Hawke. This was a relationship I benefitted from, both in securing
resources for the work of CTUC and, more importantly, high level
political support, notably at the 1985 CHOGM when Prime Minister
Hawke took forward our CTUC proposals on South Africa.

In 1980, I had started a new phase of my career as Director of the
Commonwealth TUC based at Congress House, the TUC headquarters
in London. Running my own organisation for the first time, building it
up, and overseeing staff and budgets was a learning process and I relished
the challenge. I was soon expert in securing funds from official
organisations like the British ODA or the EU through submitting detailed
funding applications, bidding for tenders and ensuring close working

links with the responsible officials. Here, my old links with the EU gave me an advantage over other Commonwealth organisations; few if any having thought of securing funding from Brussels. I also learnt to recruit and manage my own staff, not an easy process.

My work allowed me to continue my grass roots activism in support of struggling labour and trade union movements across the world in far-flung places as Kiribati in the Pacific, Belize in the Caribbean and in post-conflict states like Uganda. It increasingly brought me into contact with high diplomacy within the Commonwealth when I attended meetings of Heads of Government, the CHOGMs, and met with leaders like Indira Gandhi, Kenneth Kaunda and Robert Mugabe.

Much of my focus during the decade was on the anti-apartheid struggle in Southern Africa. Appropriately my first official CTUC mission overseas was attending the 1980 Zimbabwe Independence celebrations, marked by a joyous rendition from Bob Marley. It was followed by many visits to support the newly established unions, including organising the first-ever Commonwealth event in the country through the CTUC. Thereafter, I was helping the global union movement to advocate for sanctions on Pretoria, notably at the 1985 Commonwealth Summit in Nassau where CTUC was also the instigator of the Eminent Persons' initiative on South Africa. This cumulated in my visit to address the COSATU Congress in Johannesburg in 1987, an unforgettable experience at the height of the apartheid brutalities. Subsequently, at the 1987 Vancouver Summit, I was able to ensure reference to support for Black unions in the official CHOGM statements.

As head of the CTUC, I got to know the complex workings not just of the intergovernmental Commonwealth Secretariat, but also the wide range of associated Commonwealth organisations, professional and civil society bodies with long-standing links across the world. I soon came to appreciate the unique nature of the Commonwealth which groups together so many diverse countries and cultures, bound by language and many historical ties.

For me the Commonwealth offered practical and political opportunities for strengthening understanding among peoples, defending human and trade union rights, fighting for greater global economic and social equalities and improving democracy and good governance. My admiration of the Commonwealth has stayed with me, but I always saw it as a vehicle for progressive change, rather than an organisation to be supported for its own sake, or out of historical sentimentality. Sadly, the perception of the Commonwealth, certainly in the UK, is all too often still confused with outdated nostalgia about Empire and wrong-headed perceptions of the role of the Royal Family.

In contrast I found that the sympathy that exists for the Commonwealth in so many of its other member states allowed me significant access to top policy makers without worrying too much about protocol. Here I built, as I had done at the ICFTU, on the political influence of our trade union member organisations in relation to progressive national governments. Thus, whenever I visited a country, they would arrange high level meetings with ministers or heads of state, as happened with my meetings with Indira Gandhi. This, too, gave the CTUC a comparative advantage over other Commonwealth organisations which were less political – but it could backfire when more conservative governments took power.

Another key to success, especially at CHOGMs and international gatherings, was assembling senior trade union leaders in our CTUC delegation who could call on their own respective heads of government and arrange for our delegation to meet with them. This then secured political support which worked to having our concerns reflected in the CHOGM communique by an appropriate paragraph drafted in advance in consultation with Secretariat officials. It also allowed bilateral discussions of issues of concern in a particular country, not least seeking to secure the release of detained union leaders from jail, as we successfully did in the case of Zambia after meeting Kenneth Kaunda.

Having top union leaders represented on my CTUC executive and present at CHOGM facilitated the task of dealing with Commonwealth heads of government. But you had to maintain close communications and cordial personal relationships with them at all times. This required face-to-face meetings and prior consultations, necessitating frequent overseas travel.

Likewise, having a nice paragraph in the CHOGM communique was only the start. The post-CHOGM skill was to use the political mandate contained in the communique to lobby national ministers and their governments to abide to what their President or Prime Minister had agreed, and at times seek to get them to change course. This was not easy. However, most ministers would be duly impressed when you showed them the relevant CHOGM paragraph and pointed out that their own political boss had signed up for it.

Although the Commonwealth Secretariat has its origin in Empire, by 1980 it was a progressive independent international organisation led by its dynamic Secretary-General Sonny Ramphal, who was taking a lead on many global North-South issues and in the fight against apartheid. It was an appropriate partner for the CTUC, and I was able to achieve a close relationship with it and to influence key policy decisions, including achieving representation on key expert groups reporting to CHOGM. An important innovation in this regard was to encourage holding regular meetings of Commonwealth employment and labour ministers during the ILO conference and interacting with them.

By 1988, I was on her Majesty's Diplomatic List as senior official in the Commonwealth Secretariat; this required some adjustment, and I was never really a true diplomat, on occasions using very undiplomatic language, which upset more sensitive souls. In my new role as Assistant Director, I had responsibility for a significant amount of funds and had to ensure that these were put to good use; this was the heyday of the Commonwealth Fund for Technical Cooperation, CFTC, and my department administered a great deal of this.

Working in a larger, intergovernmental body with what seemed to me, on occasions, excessive red tape and office intrigues, had its frustrations. As in any governmental or international bureaucracy, decision-making and taking action is not as easy as in small NGO or trade union organisation. I was moreover vulnerable on account of my strong association with the British Labour Movement, given that the Conservative Party was the unchallenged UK governing party throughout my period at the Secretariat.

My activities at the Commonwealth Secretariat continued the CTUC's focus on the struggle against apartheid, including ensuring support for the Liberation Movements and the Black trade unions in South Africa. I got to know their leaders, like Cyril Ramaphosa, Jay Naidoo and Sydney Mufamadi well. I was also able to help operationalise the new Commonwealth Special Fund for Mozambique which involved regular visits to post-war Maputo and African frontline states including Angola.

My work activities were diverse and involved innovative public sector training initiatives. My past expertise manifested itself in my work at the Secretariat. For example, I was able to use my previous know-how in dealing with multinational companies in helping to formulate a Secretariat programme designed to train government officials to negotiate with foreign investors. My political track record with the Southern Africa Liberation Movements ensured I had credibility with ANC, SWAPO and others. Ironically, given my earlier cynical view of the UK Foreign Office,

I helped design and establish a successful training programme for Commonwealth diplomats which is still in use today.

As Assistant Director I worked closely with colleagues both inside and outside the Secretariat, and many became good friends. These included the able Stuart Mole, who headed the Secretary General's private office and had stood for parliament as Liberal Democrat; he later went on to run the Royal Commonwealth Society. Together we organised joint Liberal Democrat-Labour Party discussion events on Commonwealth and international affairs, aiming to align the two parties' policies. Such coming together of progressive parties is I feel a real necessity in order to challenge the electoral success of the political Right in the UK and elsewhere.

I had many other Commonwealth friendships. There was Richard Bourne, former *Guardian* journalist and at the time with the Institute of Commonwealth Studies, who was a driving force behind many Commonwealth initiatives such as the Commonwealth Human Rights Initiative, with which I was also involved in establishing, and the Ramphal Institute. Another close associate was Mark Robinson, a former Tory MP who had worked with Sonny Ramphal, and was on the progressive wing of the Conservative Party. Of course, these were more than just friendships – they formed an intimate network of contacts who could be consulted and called upon when needed, an essential ingredient in advocacy work, whether at national or international level.

The dark side of the 1980s was underlined by the murder of political leaders such as Indira Gandhi and her son Rajiv Gandhi as well as the killing of Swedish Prime Minister Olaf Palme on the streets of Stockholm in 1986, a sinister assassination that has never been solved. There were many other atrocities, like the Lockerbie terrorist bombing which killed my dear friend Bernt Carlsson.

I was in New York on the day when former Beatle, John Lennon was shot dead in December 1980 and have vivid memories of this tragic event. After attending a UN meeting, I was walking near Times Square and heard a newsflash that Lennon had been shot. The next day, I and the whole world was deeply shocked at his untimely death. Throughout New York people showed their grief at the loss of this great musician, songwriter and peace campaigner.

John's anthem, *'Imagine'* with its haunting lyrics about achieving a better world without strife and possessions is one of the greatest songs ever. On subsequent trips to New York, I often passed *'Strawberry Fields'* in Central Park, dedicated to John's memory, near to the Dakota building where he was shot, to contemplate his remarkable legacy.

Reflecting on the decade, I felt I had fought a good fight in opposing neo-liberalism.

TOP: Fifty years after demonstrating to join the EU as a student, I was again on the streets to protest against Brexit, Canterbury, 2019

MIDDLE: Making the intellectual case for Europe. Published in 1972, Professor Hugh Thomas stated in his acknowledgements: "This book owes a great deal to my research assistant, Carl Wilms-Wright ... Many of the good ideas in this book are his. He guided me brilliantly over much tricky ground."

BOTTOM: Exposing exploitation of tea workers and their families on British-owned estates in Sri Lanka, 1975

TOP: ICFTU Board meeting in Rome with my colleague Andrew Kailembo, 1977

MIDDLE: Brussels life with my first wife Susan, 1976

BOTTOM: My Fabian pamphlet on transnational corporations, 1977

The ICFTU's 'war' against South Africa

MR. WILMS-WRIGHT . . . employment policies must be given absolute priority.

Q. Mr. Wilms-Wright, the ICFTU is known to have been a champion against apartheid in South Africa. What is the position now?

A. Our Executive Board is now proposing stronger measures than it has adopted in the past in opposing the apartheid regime of Vorster . . . . And it has expressed its solidarity with Black South African workers.

Q. In your campaign against the Vorster regime, you recently called for a global week of solidarity with Black South African workers. Was the campaign a flop or a success?

A. This was, I think a very successful event which the ICFTU organised about ten days ago. It consisted of big rallies especially in the industrialised countries. We tried to instigate major boycotts and interruptions of trade and investment activities.

Campaign

You have probably heard there was a big response in a number of countries such as Britain, West Germany and other key industrialised countries where the trade union centres affiliated to

A. Well, we were profoundly shocked by the recent developments as regards Rhodesia and the abrupt breaking off of the Geneva negotiations with the Smith regime. And here, too, we have in the past eve since the UDI condemned the actions of the Smith regime. We very much fear now that this latest action by the White minority regime will create large-scale bloodshed.

Q. Mr. Wilms-Wright, You were so much involved in the ICFTU-sponsored workshop on employment held in Nairobi. What do you think about the multinational companies? And what problems were discussed in dealing with them?

A. This was the key aspect which was discussed at the workshop by the delegates. It is also the subject to which the ICFTU has devoted a lot of time to. Here too, we have a permanent working party. At the last meeting of this working party, Mr. Juma Boy of Cotu was one of the participants in our discussion.

But regarding your specific point about the problems of multinationals, here I think, all the delegates felt very strongly

of the United Nations.

Q. How do you see the unemployment situation in Africa?

A. Well, this of course is very serious. And again one of the key aspects of our workshop in Nairobi was dealing with employment policies and means of reducing both unemployment and unemployment. We are aware that there is great unemployment in many developing countries including Africa. And we think that employment policies must be given absolute priority by the governments concerned.

Q. As far as your organisation is concerned, what do you understand as the basic needs for people in developing countries?

A. Well, the World Employment Conference organised by the International Labour Organisation last year to which much of the workshop discussions here in Nairobi were devoted to, set up the basic needs.

The conference defined them as things like food, shelter, housing, adequate sanitation and supply of drinking water as well as a range of basic community services such as medical care, transportation and education.

At the workshop we elaborated of

national conclusions.

What we want is really concrete follow-up action. What the delegates will do to disseminate information they have got to their members with a view to influencing governments and with a view to organising their

as the major disadvantages of these organisations as far as the labour movement is concerned?

A. One of the major disadvantages was once a employment. It is often said that multinational companies provide employment. But if you look at

Looking on in the presence of Pope Paul VI at the Vatican in 1977

CTUC wants better sugar deal for ACP

The Commonwealth Trade Union Council (CTUC) has promised to make representation to some European countries for a better deal for sugar growers in the African, Caribbean and Pacific (ACP) States of which Barbados is a member.

CTUC's Director Mr. Carl Wright gave the assurance yesterday in the wake of what he said was the CFTU's concern about arrangements for ACP sugar exports to the European Economic Community (EEC) under the Lomé Convention.

The operation of the sugar protocol which provides among other things for annual negotiations for a price for the ACP sugar exports has come in for severe criticism from these states. A big conference at which the future of sugar will be the main talking point.

sugar protocol and of the arrangements for cane sugar", Mr. Wright said.

He stated further: "On completion of that conference next month the CTUC will be in a position to lobby in Europe and elsewhere in support of the sugar cane growers".

He said he did not wish to pre-empt the conference at which the Barbados Workers Union (BWU) will be represented, "but I am sure the CTUC will be making approaches in line with the recommendations of the outcome of that conference."

This would be to ensure that the livelihood and the well being of workers in Barbados are safeguarded.

The CTUC was established in March 1980 and is a council grouping national trade union organisations in some 40

TOP: Discussions with Prime Minister Indira Gandhi in New Delhi, 1983

MIDDLE: Sonny Ramphal addressing CTUC, in Geneva, 1983. Also present is Glyn Lloyd of the TUC

BOTTOM: CTUC supports ACP sugar producers at the EEC. Front page article in the *Advocate-News*, 31 March 1983, Barbados

TOP: Meeting
Jamaica's Deputy Prime
Minister Hugh Shearer
in Kingston, Jamaica,
1985

MIDDLE: My trade
union mentor Jack
Jones of the TGWU and
Adele in 1987

BOTTOM: Addressing
the COSATU Congress
in Johannesburg in
1987 at the height of the
apartheid repression

TOP: With Cyril
Ramaphosa, COSATU
1987. Also present is
TUC General Secretary
Norman Willis and
Michael Walsh TUC

MIDDLE:
Commonwealth expert
group on post-apartheid
including Chair John
Harker and renowned
UK writer Anthony
Sampson, 1991

BOTTOM:
Commonwealth
Election Observer in
Pakistan, 1993

TOP: Commonwealth Diplomat, 1988-94, off to a reception at Buckingham Palace with Adele

MIDDLE: Sharing a joke with my 'mate' Prime Minister Bob Hawke of Australia in Pretoria, 1994

BOTTOM: A truly historic event. Seated next to Bishop Trevor Huddleston and President Julius Nyerere of Tanzania at Nelson Mandela's inauguration in Pretoria in 1994

TOP: The wonderful 'Arch', Desmond Tutu at the CLGF Conference in Aberdeen, 2005

MIDDLE: A big hug from Jamaica's Prime Minister and CLGF Patron, Portia Simpson-Miller in Kingston, Jamaica, 2006

BOTTOM: Former CLGF Chairpersons and good friends, Senator Bobby Montague of Jamaica and Basil Morrison of New Zealand in Freeport, The Bahamas, 2009

TOP: Agreeing a Memorandum of Understanding at the United Nations in New York with UNDP Administrator and former Prime Minister of New Zealand, Helen Clark. Also present is Lawrence Yule, CLGF Chairperson from New Zealand

MIDDLE: Conferring with Aung San Suu Kyi in London in 2012 about support for Myanmar

BOTTOM: Meeting with Rwanda's President Paul Kagame in Kampala in 2013. Also present is my dear friend the Hon. Adolf Mwesige from Uganda

With HM The Queen at the opening of the Commonwealth Hub in London, 2016

Welcoming HRH Prince Charles at my retirement party at Marlborough House in 2016. Also present is Commonwealth Secretary-General Patricia Scotland

TOP: At the Campaign Against Genocide Museum in Rwanda's capital, Kigali in 2018. A deeply shocking reminder of the scale of the 1994 Rwanda genocide against the Tutsi

MIDDLE: Attending the annual Commonwealth Day Service in Westminster Abbey with Adele, 2017

BOTTOM LEFT: Delivering my doctoral address at the University of KwZulu Natal in Duban, 2012

BOTTOM RIGHT: Delivering the keynote address at the UN Peace Service in Canterbury Cathedral, 2019

TOP: COP26 Glasgow. Highlighting the *Canterbury Commitment to Climate Action* with Lisa Carlson, Canterbury Business Improvement District, 2021

MIDDLE: Participating in the Ukraine peace demonstration in London's Trafalgar Square, 2022

BOTTOM RIGHT: Skiing with Adele in Austria, 2019

BOTTOM LEFT: Rupert keeping me company while I work at home in Kent, 2022

TOP: Fifty years after demonstrating to join the EU as a student, I was again on the streets to protest against Brexit, Canterbury, 2019

MIDDLE: Making the intellectual case for Europe. Published in 1972, Professor Hugh Thomas stated in his acknowledgements: "This book owes a great deal to my research assistant, Carl Wilms-Wright ... Many of the good ideas in this book are his. He guided me brilliantly over much tricky ground."

BOTTOM: Exposing exploitation of tea workers and their families on British-owned estates in Sri Lanka, 1975

transnational
corporations :
a strategy for control
Carl Wilms-Wright
fabian research series 334 75p

TOP: ICFTU Board
meeting in Rome with my
colleague Andrew
Kailembo, 1977

MIDDLE: Brussels life with
my first wife Susan, 1976

BOTTOM: My Fabian
pamphlet on transnational
corporations, 1977

PART III

THE END OF HISTORY
(the 1990s)

Dealing with Global Change
and Challenge

*"None are more hopelessly enslaved than those
who falsely believe they are free"*

JOHANN WOLFGANG VON GOETHE

The collapse of communism seemed to herald the 'End of History'. But key events continued throughout the 1990s and as a Commonwealth diplomat I had a ringside seat to witness global events.

18.

Step-change in International Relations

IN THE EARLY 1990S, US WRITER FRANCIS FUKUYAMA DULY proclaimed, 'the End of History'. In his view, this was marked by a decisive triumph of liberal democracy and free market capitalism over Marxist ideology and centrally planned economies.

The late 1980s had seen a thawing of East-West relations, accelerated by assumption of office by Mikhail Gorbachev in the Soviet Union. However, the threat of sudden nuclear Armageddon was never far from the surface with the eerie global 'doomsday clock' set at just a few minutes before midnight. But then communism collapsed dramatically and unexpectedly.

I was never starry-eyed about Moscow-style communism or Chinese Maoism, and the cruel restrictions of basic individual freedoms practices by the Soviet Union, Red China and their satellite states. My hopes of a reformed communist system in Eastern Europe had been high at the time of the 1968 Prague Spring, only to be dashed by the brutal suppression imposed by Soviet tanks. Back in the 1970s, I had visited and toured the old Soviet Union and had seen satellite states like East Germany, Hungary and Bulgaria, as well as well Yugoslavia, which was taking an independent line to Moscow. Later I met communist trade unionists, tough men like Mick McGahey of the UK National Union of Miners, hard-line Marxist politicians and even Maoist activists in India. I also dealt with sophisticated Soviet and Eastern bloc diplomats at the UN and the ILO.

Like much of my '68 generation, the *soixante-huitards*, I was opposed to Western confrontation with the East and did not want to see Third World War. Dialogue, as exemplified by Willy Brandt's *'Ostpolitik'* with its focus on reconciliation and cooperation had seemed the best way forward to overcome post-1945 divisions. To me and my youthful contemporaries, US and CIA subversive activities in Latin America, in

Asia and Africa differed little from Soviet and KGB manipulations. At times, as in Vietnam or Chile, the US appeared to cause even more suffering and loss of human life. I was never convinced about the rhetoric of the so-called 'Free World' with the USA as its unblemished champion and was accordingly sceptical about the advent of a new world order based on unrestricted capitalism.

The collapse of communism, when it came, was as much a surprise to me as to everyone else. There had been earlier signals through the reforms by Mikhail Gorbachev's radical *perestroika* policy and the USSR's withdrawal from Afghanistan. The post-Cold War era and the 1990s had begun in 1989 with free elections in former communist-controlled Poland, following the high-profile visit of Pope John Paul II and the sweeping into power the Solidarity movement of Lech Walesa in Warsaw. Walesa was a remarkable union leader who I had briefly met in my early trade union days when he had visited Brussels. I well recall his charisma and bonhomie and the excitement at listening to his vision of a new, liberated Europe, little dreaming he would later become President of a democratic Poland.

About the same time the communist system in Hungary was forced to dismantle itself, and to open its borders to the West, adding to the political meltdown in neighbouring Soviet-dominated Warsaw Pact states. Then free elections in Czechoslovakia propelled the renowned writer Vaclav Havel and his Civic Forum to the Presidency in Prague.

Most symbolic of all, that brutal and cruel totem of East-West conflict, the Berlin Wall, was finally burst open in late 1989. There was truly a wonderful demonstration of People Power in the German Democratic Republic, the GDR, starting in Leipzig and rapidly spreading elsewhere. At the time this dramatic change was not a forgone conclusion – in the GDR especially, the world came close to witnessing a bloody repression, but the regime decided against this at the last minute, influenced by Gorbachev's moderate line

I vividly remember sitting in a small house in north Wales in November 1989, where I was campaigning for a Labour Party parliamentary nomination, breathlessly watching live TV coverage from Berlin. I saw with growing disbelief, the jubilant scenes of joy when for the first time since 1961, East Germans from the communist GDR were able to freely cross the border to West Berlin. There they met their relatives and friends from the West, or just went to go to gaze at the bright city lights of West Berlin with its opulent shops and consumer wares. Before long the Wall itself was being pulled down by the people. It was appropriate that the beautiful *'Ode to Joy'* by Beethoven, set to the words of the German poet Schiller, and the official EU anthem, was performed at the Brandenburg Gate to mark the dismantling of the Wall and to celebrate the coming together of East and West Europe after decades of separation.

It made me think, with a cold shudder, of my visits to Berlin as a boy. Scary journeys in sealed railway carriages from West Germany across a sinister East Germany on to West Berlin. Where grim border guards armed with machine guns and handling ferocious dogs searched the trains. I had set sight of the Wall and its death strip where would-be refugees were shot down in cold blood.

On one occasion I had dared to venture through Checkpoint Charlie into East Berlin. I witnessed a bleak-looking communist city which, apart from the gleaming TV tower on the Alexanderplatz, had only faded and derelict grey buildings, still pockmarked by World War II bullets and shells. I recall having been struck by an impressive gastronomic menu at the Ratskeller, the Town Hall restaurant, only to find there were just two items on offer, soup and boiled pork. Not a good ad, I had thought, for the communist system and the choice it offered to consumers.

Excitement and chimes of freedom were in the air throughout Eastern Europe at the turn of the decade. The collapse of communism was rife everywhere. In Romania the brutal regime of Nicolae Ceausescu met a bloody end with the sudden execution of the dictator and his wife on Christmas Day 1989. Communist Bulgaria, too, followed down the democratic path. By 1990/91 the disintegration of the old Union of Soviet Socialist Republics, the USSR, itself was well underway.

The Baltic states, Estonia, Lithuania and Latvia, which had enjoyed statehood between the world wars, 1918-1939, before being swallowed up by Stalin in 1940, proclaimed their independence from Moscow. Events were moving rapidly and without warning. Soon, despite misgivings by some Western leaders, notably Margaret Thatcher, Germany achieved formal re-unification in November 1990: the first coming together of its people as one country since its collapse back in 1945.

Nor did USSR European republics like Georgia, Belarus, Moldova and even the Ukraine, the historic home place of the Russ, wait long to declare their independence from Moscow. They, too, renounced communism, although in places like Belarus authoritarian rulers merely switched political labels and continued with the previous repression.

The disintegration of the Soviet Union was to leave a legacy of unfinished geopolitical business to fester, such as the Russian population in the Crimea and Eastern Ukraine, which was to flare up later.

Soon I heard about the independence declarations of former USSR central Asian republics of Tajikistan, Turkmenistan, Kazakhstan and Uzbekistan, with far-flung capitals like Tashkent. I well recall my visit to Tashkent back in the 1970s and seeing the great Islamic centre of Samarkand with its beautiful mosques of blue and white marble. I had never imagined then these places could become independent of Moscow. Only in Mongolia did communist rule hold on a little bit longer, until 1995. Perhaps the 'End of History' had indeed arrived?

In Russia an epic of Shakespearian proportions was playing itself out. Authority was rapidly ebbing away from communist rule and from President Mikhail Gorbachev. 'Gorby', as he was affectionately known, had initiated and presided over the loosening of the Kremlin's reins. He had sought far-reaching economic and political reforms, while still seeking to maintain the communist system and the unity of the USSR. Now he was unable to keep control and prevent break-up.

I was in Kent in the summer of 1991. We had just purchased our small holiday cottage there and had not yet installed a TV. In a nearby town shop window TV, I noticed the dramatic scenes in Russia. A last-ditch coup attempt was made by Communist hardliners to oust Gorbachev, resulting in his detention in the Crimea. However, the plotters soon gave up their attempts to reinstall communism when faced by mass resistance, including 200,000 people on the streets of Leningrad alone.

I rushed back to watch a rapidly evolving crisis in the Soviet Union on a TV I had quickly purchased. Matters there were spinning out of control, with huge consequences for the entire world. As I witnessed history taking place, I heard that, Leningrad, symbolically, would revert to its old Imperial name of St Petersburg – a more apt description for that beautiful Baltic city of gentle waterways and graceful Tsarist places which I had toured nearly twenty years previously.

People Power now stormed the very citadel of communism in the Kremlin itself, in the heart of Red Square. This still contained the embalmed corpse of Lenin, the founder and iconic symbol of the communist revolution of 1917. The writing was truly on the wall. Events moved with breathtaking speed. Next the red hammer and sickle flag of the revolution was hauled down. It was replaced by the traditional white, blue and red tricolour of old Russia. The communist anthem, the

Internationale, was forsaken for a traditional piece of Russian music. Statues of Stalin were pulled down. Symbolically, McDonald's opened its first hamburger restaurant in Moscow in 1990.

Real political power was being irreversibly transferred to the new Executive President, Boris Yeltsin, and by the end of 1991 Gorbachev had resigned. The Soviet Union, which I had grown up with, had formally ceased to exist, a remarkable whirlwind of geopolitical transformation after seventy years of communist rule.

The USSR was thus consigned to the dustbin of history into which communists had thought capitalism would be dumped. It is still remembered in iconic songs like The Beatles' tongue-in-cheek rock rendition of *'Back in the USSR'*. I had once been offered top black-market prices for Beatles' records on the streets of Leningrad when these were still banned. Now it was not long before Paul McCartney performed in Moscow's Red Square to huge public acclaim. I subsequently enjoyed listening to Paul performing that great Beatles rock anthem live at concerts in London, accompanied by footage of the now defunct Soviet Union.

Yeltsin quickly went on to dismantle what was left of the communist economic system. He also strongly encouraged the adoption of western capitalist structures and foreign investment. Unfortunately, he did this in an uncontrolled and un-phased way, opening the flood gates to privatisation and unscrupulous capitalist entrepreneurs. At the same time, he abandoned much of the social protection and benefits which the old Soviet system, with all its inefficiencies, had afforded to its people. This led to a catastrophic collapse in average life expectancy in Russia, which slumped by a staggering eight years in the early 1990s.

Soon talk was of super-rich Russian oligarchs and a vicious mafia underworld 'vacuum cleaning' the Russian economy and reaping super profits. All this was irresponsibly encouraged by the West which allocated many millions of dollars to support privatisation. This was a process which the writer Alexander Solzhenitsyn, no friend of communism, aptly referred to as 'privateering'.

The new Russian oligarchs and billionaires went on to purchase luxury properties and Premier League football clubs in the UK. My new next-door neighbour in West Hampstead was a Russian who had apparently bought the not-inexpensive house with cash; he was collected each morning by a smart limousine driven by a sinister looking chauffeur with dark glasses.

Turmoil was to continue in Russia through much of the decade. Conflict was particularly pronounced in Muslim Chechnya. Unsuccessful attempts to break away from Moscow produced a death toll of close on 100,000 and huge destruction in its capital Grozny, only to unleash a wave of terrorist reprisal acts in Russia. More devastation was to follow in Georgia and the Ukraine later.

Ex-communist states were exposed to the full blast of free market competition, often with minimal transition. I witnessed the effects of neo-liberal policies in former East Germany, now merged with the capitalist West, where many Easterners or 'Ossies,' who had been employed in public services, such as teaching or the civil service, lost jobs and livelihood. This blighted German reunification and led to dissatisfaction and political tension. It offered life-support to what remained of communist movements, and the Linke (Left Party) was able to transform itself into a mainstream party. Later, eastern states like Brandenburg, Saxony and Mecklenburg, which I visited, turned to the far-Right AfD party, a reflection of feeling left behind.

There remained uncomfortable echoes of the past.

19

Aftermath of the Collapse of Communism

WAS THIS THEN THE 'END OF HISTORY' WHICH FRANCIS Fukuyama had predicted? Was this the victory of neo-liberal ascendancy and the triumph of free market economics?

The early 1990s saw attempts to reform global international relations. The 1992 Earth Summit, a result of growing global environmental and climate concern, in turn led to the UN Framework Convention of Climate Change UNFCC and the *Kyoto Protocol* in 1997, the first halting attempt to address the impact of climate change. There was also the work of the *Commission on Global Governance*, co-chaired by Sonny Ramphal and the former Swedish Prime Minister Ingvar Carlsson. However, these laudable initiatives lacked impact due to the predominant neo-liberal and free market political ascendancy.

Even when progressive forces re-asserted themselves in the 1990s under Bill Clinton in the USA in 1992 and Tony Blair in the UK in 1997, this involved a highly centrist policy or 'middle way' political agenda, which embraced markets, and was devoid of traditional Leftist policies. This approach was symbolised by Blair's political soulmate and strategist of New Labour, Peter Mandelson, who as a senior Labour Minister under Blair, voiced publicly that Labour was "intensely relaxed about people getting filthy rich", although he did insist they pay their taxes.

A more lasting geopolitical change resulted from the 1992 Maastricht Treaty which set out the foundations of the 'ever-closer' integration of what was now the European Union, the EU, accompanied by a new focus on social issues championed by Commission President Jacques Delors. Britain's physical link with the continent was cemented with the historic opening of the Channel Tunnel in 1994 and the start of the London-Paris and Brussels Eurostar high speed train. This provided city-to-city centre connections in some two hours, a connection I was to take so many times in the coming years. However, Maastricht was in many ways also the trigger for the growth of anti-EU political agitation in the UK which was to lead to Brexit in 2020.

I had grown up as child of the Cold War – first in West Germany, then in Britain – and under the constant threat of nuclear Armageddon, notably in 1962 and 1983. As a student and young activist, I had opposed East-West divisions. I had regularly experienced the unscrupulous power play of the USA and the USSR in international relations. I now felt great personal relief at the end of the Cold War.

For a time, Fukuyama's predictions appeared to hold. The collapse of communism in the USSR and Eastern Europe was followed by a sharp decline of autocratic regimes everywhere. A common consequence throughout the world, not only Eastern Europe, was the move towards multi-party democracy, underlain by the holding of fair and free elections, public sector decentralisation and privatisation of key services and an opening up towards civil society. As a result, Western-style liberal democracy and capitalist systems were established in many previously authoritarian and command economy states across the world.

I encountered this transition in Africa, in Asia and also in countries like Guyana. Centralised economic planning and single party rule were rapidly abandoned for new models of democratic market principles and party politics. It was somehow symbolic that the hotel I stayed in Georgetown had until recently been the Soviet Embassy – as witnessed by the high and foreboding former Embassy walls surrounding its premises.

A direct consequence of the end of communism was the removal of the existential threat to the Western capitalist system. This led to less consensual approach by employers and governments in economic and social policy, and to ever more-inequitable sharing of income and wealth. In consequence, trade unions and progressive movements in many places were weakened through restrictive legislation and lost membership.

Often market disciplines and profit motive were applied in a ruthless and uninhibited way, sweeping aside previous social protection almost overnight and resulting in unemployment, social deprivation and huge disparity in income and wealth. This accrued to oligarchs and the new super-rich elites, not the population as a whole: the one per cent as opposed to ninety-nine per cent. Indeed, disparities in income and wealth were, as shown by the economist Thomas Piketty and others, to grow ever larger in the coming years.

It seemed to me that the worship of free markets by governments led to excessive freeing up of previous controls and safeguards, especially over banks and the financial sector. These safeguards had dated back to the 1930s and aimed to protect against economic collapse and a recurrence of the Great Depression of 1929. The failure to remember the lessons of history ultimately led to the global economic crash of 2008, followed by unemployment and economic austerity, involving brutal cuts in public series. This was to accelerate yet further growth in income and wealth inequality in Western countries which had commenced in the 1980s under neo-liberalism.

I noticed that the demise of communism and their party regimes unleashed previously suppressed nationalist, religious and ethnic forces. In the Caucasus, in North Africa and in the Near East and Afghanistan, Islamic fundamentalism received a boost from the removal of secular one-party regimes backed by Moscow, which had kept control. This led to fragile, collapsing and failed states, where government authority and services disintegrated, a tragic example being Somalia, which has never really recovered. Often this entailed bloody civil wars with dreadful death tolls which were rarely given the global media exposure they warranted: over 100,000 perished in Algeria and possibly up to 800,000 in the Congo.

Nor was this nationalist and separatist fervour restricted to ex-communist states. Even prosperous Canada came within a hair's breadth of break-up in 1995 when the separatist aspirations of Quebec were rejected in a referendum by a tiny margin of just 50.58 per cent to 49.42 per cent. Catalonia is seeking to break away from Spain and South Sudan managed to secede from Sudan. In the UK too, separatist tendencies began to build, especially in Scotland which gained its own parliament and opted for an independence referendum in 2014 where the majority agreed to stay in the UK but with a sizeable vote against. Against this, a breakthrough occurred in the long-standing Northern Ireland problem with the signing of the 1997 *Good Friday Agreement* which made me hope that I would no longer have to experience IRA bombs in London.

More geopolitical instability followed the first Gulf War of 1990-91, triggered by the invasion of Kuwait by Iraq's Saddam Hussein and his defeat by an international coalition led by the US. I recall passing through the empty terminals of Heathrow Airport during the height of the war, when international travel came to a virtual standstill. However, in the Middle East, even in Iraq, one party and autocratic regimes maintained their undemocratic grip on power in defiance of the Fukuyama thesis. Nor did the much-vaunted 1994 *Oslo Accords* between Israel and the

Palestinians, brokered by President Clinton, lead to a truly autonomous Palestinian state and lasting peace.

In my professional work in the Commonwealth in the 1990s I dealt with the fallout of these historical changes and was actively involved to help countries in Africa and elsewhere establish and to consolidate their fragile new democracies. But it was this very fragility and the consequent political, economic and social convulsions, which soon put paid to the unrealistic notion that history had somehow stopped.

Over the years, the aftermath of communism led to a political counter-reaction, typified by the autocratic regime of Vladimir Putin and the rise of nationalist and populist movements in Eastern European countries, such as in Hungary and Poland. Russians today feel hard done-by, given that their geographic borders have shrunk to where they were hundreds of years before the Tsarist conquests in Europe and Asia. Their former East European allies are now embedded in NATO on their very borders, and there are uncomfortable parallels with an embittered Germany after its defeat in the First World War and its humiliation under the 1919 Treaty of Versailles.

This cannot excuse Russian aggression, its military annexation of the Crimea and it invasion of Ukraine in 2022 contrary to international law, still less the callous repression and assassination of political opponents by Vladimir Putin, but it does put Russian actions into historical perspective.

I have much sympathy for the individual Russian people who have had a rough deal since 1990 including under Putin and who share our common European history, culture and intellectual values through great composers and writers like Tchaikovsky, Shostakovich, Tolstoy, and Solzhenitsyn. For me, Russia is an integral part of the European mainstream and is not an alien offshoot as portrayed by Western neo-cons. I hope that when its democratic and human rights record is improved, it will gain associate membership of the EU in the same way as it is a member of the Council of Europe. In the short term there is little sign of this being possible.

There has been one major exception to the collapse of communism in the 1990s: China, which merits special consideration in the light of the Fukuyama thesis. China and a few communist countries like Cuba and Vietnam have stubbornly retained their One-Party systems. To ensure this Beijing oversaw a bloody massacre of protesters in Tiananmen Square in 1989 where army tanks brutally crushed any thought of replacing communism. Here history did end, at least temporarily, but it was a consolidation of hard-line communism, not Western liberal democracy.

While China has not seen significant change away from One-party communist rule, it has undergone a massive economic liberalisation and modernisation since the 1990s. In that sense the Fukuyama thesis may have some validity. This economic development has lifted hundreds of millions of Chinese citizens out of abject poverty and has created an amazingly successful export-orientated economy. At the same time, it has brought into being a new class of super-rich Chinese billionaire, a far cry from the Marxist dictatorship of the proletariat.

But there has been no real political relaxation, if anything, things have got significantly more totalitarian under President Xi Jinping in recent years. Human rights in the country are under growing threat, especially for the Muslim Uyghur people. In Hong Kong, too, the special political status and associated rights agreed in 1997 have increasingly been eroded contrary to international agreements; I can only admire those political activists and concerned citizens who have at much personal cost have left Hong Kong and sought to draw global attention to what is happening. There has been harsh and often cruel suppression of even the mildest internal criticism of the Chinese government. The harassment and pursuit of internal critics exiled opponents sadly reminds me of the practices of past autocratic regimes like Chile and South Africa. Such suppression of democratic rights and undermining of the Rule of Law has, as in Russia, no place in our modern world.

Apart from Hong Kong, I visited China for an international local government event, hosted by the Chinese government in Beijing. The visit including an enjoyable if exhausting excursion together with my African colleague, Jean-Pierre Mbassi, climbing up the Great Wall. This is a truly amazing structure which snakes along distant hill tops seemingly endlessly as far as the eye can see.

When I walked across the vast, largely empty Tiananmen Square, flanked by huge portraits of Chairman Mao, with the famous Forbidden City in the background, I perceived the ghosts of those killed by the regime in 1989. I could sense a cold blast coming from a cruel past. I felt uneasy at being feted by the communist leadership in the enormous Hall of the People, which is close by. In contrast, my contacts with ordinary Chinese people were warm and intimate; many had previously had little contact with Westerners and were eager to talk to find out about the outside world.

The strange fusion of communism and Western-style consumerism was brought home to me when I visited the Chinese National History Museum. The Museum is adjacent to Tiananmen Square and has a waxwork section, a bit like Madame Tussauds in London. There are life-size figures of the Communist greats including Marx, Engels, Lenin and of course Mao himself. Right in the middle of these Marxist luminaries stood British footballer David Beckham in his full soccer gear. I recall almost bursting out laughing when I saw this – perhaps there is something I did not know about David Beckham's ideological disposition.

I am critical of Chinese foreign policy having supported tyrants like Robert Mugabe in Zimbabwe and elsewhere. There is further much geopolitical calculation in the way China is pursuing its global 'Belt and Road' initiative, its 'New Silk Road'. All this is reflected in growing tensions with neighbouring countries like Australia, India and Japan and the confrontation with, in particular, the USA.

Historically China has suffered greatly through Western exploitation during the Opium wars of the nineteenth century. It then underwent a horrible occupation and brutal massacres under the Japanese following their invasion in the 1930s. There is a school of thought, which says that China is the new kid on the block, the new superpower which will upset the global power balance and flex its powerful muscles, and that it will precipitate World War and must be confronted. There are clearly worrying issues, such as aggressive Chinese policy in the East China Sea.

Even if there is not an actual military confrontation between the Superpowers, unforeseen historical accidents can do happen and ignite global conflict. This is why the Ukraine crisis is so dangerous; why China's belligerence towards Taiwan is a great worry. The consequences were seen all too tragically in 1914 in the lead-up to the First World War. This was a conflict which most historians now agree owed much to the Great Powers 'sleepwalking' into world war and I worry this could happen again.

History clearly continues to evolve.

20.

Fragile States and Inclusive Institutions

THE COLLAPSE OF COMMUNISM HAD A MAJOR GEOPOLITICAL
knock-on effect both in Europe and beyond. It was to lead to political
fragmentation in many countries.

By 1993/94, there was endemic and violent conflict in the Balkans,
ethnic cleansing of Catholic Croats, Orthodox Serbs and Muslim
Bosnians, massacres of innocent civilians at Srebrenica, indiscriminate
shelling and burning of towns and villages. I learnt what had happened
on the ground from my old friend from the UN, Aracelly Santana, who
took part in the UN Protection Force, UNPROFOR, and in subsequent
UN peace building.

Outside Europe, the ramifications of geopolitical splintering and
inter-ethnic conflict were as extreme. Upheavals and violent conflict in
diverse countries such as Afghanistan, Colombia, Fiji, Rwanda, Sierra
Leone, Sri Lanka and Sudan, to name just a few, showed that this was
hardly the 'End of History'. International attention, including by global
aid agencies, has accordingly become focused on fragile, failed and failing
states and how they could be assisted though developing inclusive
institutions, aimed at tackling ethnic and other conflicts. For the
Commonwealth, where I was working, this became a priority area
throughout the 1990s.

The sheer scale and brutality of bloody genocide against the Tutsi
which took place in Rwanda in the mid-1990s and claimed a million
lives must be one of the supreme evils of modern times. I realised just
how appalling this genocide had been, when accompanied by the city's
deputy mayor, I laid a memorial wreath at the main genocide site just
outside the capital Kigali. On this blood-soaked spot, a 100,000 innocent
men, women and children had been slain mercilessly. The deputy mayor
was in tears. She had lost many close relatives in the brutal killings.
Here, in a simple memorial site and museum on the fringe of the city,

surrounded by lush green hills around Kigali, the tragic history of the Rwanda genocide was portrayed all too starkly.

I was deeply moved when seeing the final room of the small genocide museum. This contained hundreds of black and white passport-style photographs pasted on its barren white walls. They were pictures of young children, even babies, who had been murdered in brutal ways. Underneath each photo was their name, their age, their favourite pastime and, most shockingly of all, how they had been killed – burnt alive in a church, hacked to death by machete, or killed in other unspeakable ways. This was a grim and disturbing reminder of the inhumanity human beings can show to each other. An inhumanity I thought had been left behind in the Holocaust. Even today the memory of those photos leaves a big lump in my throat.

The Rwanda genocide was an indictment of the former colonial power, Belgium, which had used and accentuated Hutu-Tutsi ethnic divisions under its rule. Equally, the French played a highly dubious role just prior to and even during the genocide, backing the murdering Hutu Government and then providing a safe haven for those responsible. It reminded me that the exploitation by Empire and evil deeds of colonialism, whether by the French in Algeria, the British in India or the Germans in Namibia, are all too easily forgotten and airbrushed from history books.

It is remarkable how Rwanda has now recovered from its past trauma and achieved national reconciliation. It has moved far away from being a failed state and has adopted progressive economic and social policies and has seen its people prosper. There is a well-functioning, decentralised system of local democracy. There are environmentally conscious policies such as banning plastic bags and instigating car-free Sundays where people jog and exercise on the streets of Kigali. Citizens also participate in joint community work (*umuganda*) every month.

Much of this change in Rwanda is due to the vision of President Kagame, whom I have met with on several occasions. These were meetings without much protocol, conducted in a relaxed and open manner. Kagame, like President Museveni in neighbouring Uganda, has maintained a tight political system and increasingly curbed opposing voices. I cannot condone democratic restrictions and human rights infringements, including growing repression of political opponents. But the bigger picture needs to be looked at. Kagame, like Museveni, has taken his country on a remarkable upward curve towards prosperity. Both have healed the deep wounds of genocide and internal conflict in their countries. It is the tragedy of many political leaders, not only in Africa, that they do not quit at the height of their achievements, but cling onto to power for too long.

Why nations fail is examined in the seminal academic work by Acemoglu and Robinson. The evidence shows that in order to prosper, citizens need 'inclusive institutions' which create virtuous circles of innovation, economic expansion and widely held wealth. Having democratic, accountable structures and good governance at local and central government is integral to this. This is why pluralistic countries like Botswana, have, as I saw many times at first hand, done so well. It is why they have been successful, and why other states like Zimbabwe, with their reliance on One-party dominance and an accompanying proneness to corruption by their elites, have abjectly failed.

Working at the Commonwealth Secretariat and then for the Commonwealth Local Government Forum (CLGF), I was involved professionally in dealing with fragile or failing states and in supporting the building of inclusive and democratic institutions. I did this following the first-ever democratic multi-party local elections in Tanzania in 1995. My task in Tanzania was to equip hundreds of freshly elected local councillors, who had little experience or idea of their new role and responsibilities, with basic training. I was able to do this through an innovative programme of distance learning. This involved self-teaching manuals, local tutors and radio broadcasts which could reach the vast rural outback of the country.

This activity, for which I negotiated EU funding, was conducted by the Dar es Salaam-based Southern African Extension Unit. The latter was run by a dedicated Tanzanian Director, Elizabeth Ligate, with whom I had previously cooperated in supporting South African and Namibian political exiles. It was satisfying to see the success of this outreach programme, which laid the foundations of local democracy for the first time.

In Sierra Leone, which had then not yet relapsed into its tragic civil war, I worked with the United Nations Development Programme, UNDP, to provide Commonwealth expertise. Our aim was to revisit local legislation on decentralisation of public service and to assist with legislative reforms. Here, as in much of Africa, new local democratic structures had to consider the role of traditional chiefs. These tribal leaders still hold much sway in rural areas and decide issues such as land rights and arbitrate local disputes and deal with minor crimes.

To understand their role better, I commissioned research on traditional leadership in different countries in Africa; this was then shared across the continent in order to promote good practices and then shared across Africa. I found that Botswana a good model. Here chiefs have an official role alongside elected local councils, thereby encouraging cooperation with elected councillors rather than rivalry. They also have formal representation at national level.

Countries like Malawi, where I was much engaged, saw considerable suspicion and conflict between newly elected councillors and traditional leaders as well as with local MPs. MPs in particular saw councillors as interlopers, especially if they represented rival political parties. Such disagreement is also common in Europe and elsewhere and not limited to developing counties. However, in new democracies there is little experience of working together across political parties for the common good. It was this conflict between local councillors and parliamentarians that led Malawi to put its newly established system of local democracy on ice for a whole decade until, with much advocacy work, I helped to have it re-established.

Addressing the needs of fragile states and building inclusive institutions is a long-term project.

21.

Post-apartheid Transition

I WAS TO WITNESS HISTORY IN THE MAKING WITH THE DEMISE of apartheid. This transition to democracy gathered much momentum in the early 1990s.

The collapse of communism had eased US and Western fears about Marxist insurgency in southern Africa. This had had its origins in the support the Liberation Movements had received from Moscow and was due to the strong political position of the South African Communist party within the ANC. In consequence there was a gradual winding-down of the vicious civil wars that had raged in Angola and Mozambique since their independence from Portugal in the 1970s.

Both Mozambique and Angola have been victims of the power play of the Cold War. Both were destabilised greatly by the apartheid regime in neighbouring South Africa. Their respective civil wars were fuelled by foreign attempts to topple their then Moscow-friendly governments by arming and supporting the rebel opposition forces fighting in the bush – UNITA in Angola and RENAMO in Mozambique. The end of the Cold War reduced the extent of direct external interference, but the damage had been done. I recall only too vividly the decrepit and scarred buildings I saw in Maputo and Luanda in the early 1990s, the poverty and deprivation and the destroyed infrastructure, much dating back to the departure of the Portuguese.

It was with great pleasure that on my subsequent visits to Luanda and Maputo I witnessed economic progress and improvements in city architecture and services. Poverty and associated problems such as urban blight and public corruption remain, however, in both cities. But on a lighter note, I must recommend the wonderful and tasty king prawns served in the many small Maputo seafront restaurants. These are easily the biggest I have ever consumed, being each the size of a small lobster.

Angola has never been a member of the Commonwealth. Following the ceasefire between the communist-backed MPLA and the western-supported UNITA in the Angolan civil war in 1991, I took part in the only official Commonwealth mission to go to Luanda. This was designed to see if a Commonwealth programme could be instigated there, like the one I had helped to implement for Mozambique under the Special Commonwealth Fund for Mozambique after 1988.

Unfortunately, the resumption of hostilities soon after my visit prevented this happening. Angola, unlike Mozambique, did not become a Commonwealth member. I am however proud that, as Secretary-General of CLGF, I got Angola to join the CLGF as an associated member and it took an active part in our work. I also developed a friendship with the minister for decentralisation, Bornito d'Souza, a charming man, who later hosted an important CLGF regional event in Luanda and subsequently became Angola's Vice President.

It is my belief that two factors brought about the subsequent collapse of apartheid once the global threat of Soviet communism had vanished. One was the increased liberation struggle by the ANC, PAC and above all by the internal United Democratic Front, UDF and the Congress of South African Trade Unions, COSATU. The other was external pressure applied through economic sanctions by Western governments, edged on by the UN and the Commonwealth, which generated international business concern about the security of their investments in South Africa.

After Nelson Mandela's transfer to the mainland from his harsh and windswept Robben Island prison off the coast of Cape Town, which I had occasion to visit some years later and is now a museum, negotiations took place with Pretoria regime. A breakthrough in early 1990 led to the un-banning of the African National Congress and other banned parties. Then on 11 February 1990, Nelson Mandela himself was released from prison.

I remember watching with great excitement the live TV transmission of Mandela's release from prison in my London home. Here he gave his first speech as a free man, broadcast across the world. He was flanked by my old comrade-in-arms, Cyril Ramaphosa, who now as ANC Secretary-General was to take on the mantle of the main ANC negotiator. The end of apartheid suddenly seemed in sight, although it was to take another four years for it to be realised.

In response to this dramatic development, I saw an opportunity to re-focus our Commonwealth *Victims of apartheid programme,* building on the support I had already been able to secure for the 'agents of political change', the Black trade unions. I penned an internal Secretariat memo on 28 February 1990 where I argued for "an Enhanced Commonwealth Programme for South Africans", the aim of which "would be to provide a collective response to the needs for technical, training and other forms of assistance which South African victims of apartheid will require both in the period leading up to liberation and following the establishment of a democratic South Africa which has returned to Commonwealth membership".

The 1987 CHOGM had set up the Commonwealth Committee of Foreign Ministers on Southern Africa. This aimed to coordinate sanctions; support the Liberation Movements by reaching into South Africa through our training programmes and to promote political dialogue in line with the concept originally proposed by the EPG and CTUC in 1985. This Committee received regular reports on our work and in turn reported to the CHOGM in 1989 and 1991.

In a 1990 confidential report, the Committee noted that whereas the majority of supported trainees were exiles, "the main exception is trade union training, which has involved trainees from inside South Africa". It now recommended that with the prospect of a post-apartheid South Africa, "training could take place both outside and inside South Africa" in the case of major agents of change such as trade unions. Hitherto, such support had been restricted to the exiled ANC and PAC, with no training supported inside South Africa. I was pleased that I was in a position to drive forward these strategic policy reforms in line with what COSATU and the UDF had been advocating. This new policy would soon open up the door for me to travel to South Africa again in support of my old comrades.

Meanwhile, Namibia, or South West Africa, as it was known, was moving toward freedom.

The country is marked by the vast and barren Kalahari Desert. It had originally been a German colony until 1918. During this period the German administration had exercised a genocidal policy of great cruelty against the native population. Namibia then came under South African administration after 1918 as a virtual colony, and after 1948 suffered the same racist apartheid policies imposed by Pretoria within South Africa. It does however retain a German legacy on account of the exceptionally good 'Windhoek lager' and a few Munich-style beer gardens in the capital city Windhoek which I have had occasion to enjoy.

I had worked closely with its Liberation Movement, SWAPO, both its exiled and internal branches in our Commonwealth programme for the victims of apartheid. I had also met with its trade union and political leaders to ensure they received support. My reward was a personal invitation to the Independence celebrations held in Windhoek in 1990. This was an exciting and joyous event. A highlight was the presence of Nelson Mandela, just released from prison, who received huge cheers, standing alongside a beaming Sam Nujoma, Namibia's first democratic President.

At the time there were insufficient hotel beds for all the overseas guests in Windhoek, but this mattered little, and we were well looked after in private accommodation. Prior to the celebrations I met the CTUC Chairperson, Canadian Shirley Carr, also a guest at the celebrations. Together we toured some of deprived and poverty-stricken townships on the outskirts of Windhoek. These showed that here, as in South Africa, the grim legacy of apartheid would take time to overcome.

Chief Emeka Anyaoku, the recently elected Commonwealth Secretary-General, was also in Windhoek. Emeka had spent much of his career as an official at the Commonwealth Secretariat, having started, like me, as Assistant Director. His only interlude was a brief spell as Nigeria's foreign minister which was cruelly curtailed by a military coup. Happily, his old job in London had remained open and he was able to return and resume his career there. The Chief, as he became affectionately known, played a key role on the South African issue. He was also supportive of my work at the Secretariat in this important area. During his tenure in office Chief Anyaoku oversaw a growth in the Commonwealth's mandate in support of democratic transition and good governance, including, with much courage, in respect of his own country, Nigeria.

I had already known Emeka in my CTUC days when he was campaigning to succeed Sonny Ramphal as Secretary-General. I may have been able to give him modest assistance when he dined at my London house together with my friend the late Joseph Rwegasira, then foreign minister of Tanzania, and secured East African backing for his candidature. During my time at the Secretariat, I developed high respect for the diplomatic skills and dedication of the Chief who I came to regard as a friend as well as boss.

Following Namibian independence, attention switched to the political transition in South Africa. This focused on supporting negotiations between Nelson Mandela and President F.W. de Klerk aimed at achieving democratic election based on the principle of 'one man (and woman), one vote'.

The next four years, until 1994, would see many ups and downs in South Africa. Internal conflict erupted with resistance by die-hard white Afrikaners. There were also violent clashes provoked by the Inkatha Movement of Zulu Chief Buthelezi. Buthelezi was backed by Pretoria together with some Western Governments like the UK as a less radical option to Mandela. These disturbances left at least 7,000 dead and the situation threatened to spiral out of control and derail progress towards democratic elections scheduled for 1994. I had a close shave when I ended up in the middle of a violent confrontation between ANC and Inkatha supporters in the heart of Pretoria. This was turning nasty, and I hurriedly sought refuge in a nearby doorway to avoid the angry masses and a rapidly advancing Casspir armoured military vehicle.

By 1993, internal political negotiations under the specially established South African Transitional Executive Council were making real progress. April 1994 had been set for the first-ever 'one person, one vote' democratic elections; most external sanctions had been lifted. This was to be underlined when Nelson Mandela and F.W. de Klerk jointly received the Nobel Peace Prize in recognition of their efforts for a peaceful transition.

It soon became apparent that the legacy of apartheid, especially the economic and social deprivation foisted on the Black majority for over forty years, would take long to overcome. I was to become closely involved in work to identify the formidable problems which would face a Black majority government and in designing ways of overcoming these. Key to this work was the establishment of a Commonwealth Expert Group on human resource development for post-apartheid South Africa, which compiled its report *'Beyond Apartheid: Human Resources in a New South Africa'* during 1990-91. The idea of the group had been endorsed at a meeting of the Commonwealth Committee of Foreign Ministers on Southern Africa in Abuja in May 1990, in response to our suggestions for an enhanced Commonwealth programme to support the transition to post-apartheid.

On the proposal of the Canadian government, my good friend John Harker, now heading up a Canadian NGO training Black South African leaders, was made chair of the Group. My boss, Mohan Kaul, was its secretary but I, with my wide range of personal South African contacts was responsible for the actual work, including commissioning research and undertaking initial drafts of the Group's report. As a result, I undertook frequent missions to South Africa in the early 1990s to consult a wide range of parties and organisations, including my old trade union comrades in COSATU.

The Expert Group included eminent individuals such as the British writer Anthony Sampson who I had first met as a student in London. It also contained two prominent South Africans, Papie Moloto from the ANC and Professor Francis Wilson from Cape Town University. Our work involved researching vital areas such as education policy, where we worked especially closely with the late Professor Harold Wolpe. I was in Harold's Cape Town home to share the huge excitement and jubilant celebrations when the results of the April 1994 elections came through. This showed a decisive ANC victory under Nelson Mandela and the dawn of the new post-apartheid era.

The Group had got underway quickly in 1990 and was able to present an interim report to the Commonwealth Committee of Foreign Ministers on Southern Africa in February 1991 where I attended and took minutes. This meeting also reviewed the recent moves in South Africa to dismantle apartheid, but took the firm view that sanctions need to be maintained while the process was underway. The Committee noted, "there was an urgent need to take action now if there was to be a smooth transition to the promised non-racial democracy."

In its subsequent report to the 1991 Harare CHOGM, the Committee agreed that the goals of human resource development should contribute to:

"The process of political change;
The education and training of members of the deprived majority to equip them to occupy positions which will be crucial to creating a new democratic, political, economic and social order.
The immediate advancement and transformation of education and training institutions and organisations committed the building of a non-racial post-apartheid South Africa was also required.
It was accordingly decided that this would entail an enhanced Commonwealth programme of education and training in the following strategic areas:
Public administration both at central and local levels
Non-government and community organisations
Trade unions
Key professionals in public and private sector, such as engineers, information technologists, managers, etc.
Staff development and teacher training in the area of education".

The Group's report was to provide ground-breaking material on the large number of Black South Africans which needed to be recruited into central and local government. It highlighted the scale of the problem which would face Mandela and proposed that 600 of the top 6,000 positions in South African government departments be filled by members of the deprived majority as soon as possible. This was a matter about which the Pretoria regime under de Klerk was highly sensitive. Prior to his taking office, it forced Mandela to make significant concessions, ensuring that many of the senior white, mainly Afrikaner, positions in the civil service were held onto for a transitional period. However, these concessions helped to smooth the way forward for a peaceful transition to Black majority rule.

We saw our report being of practical use, a hands-on, not an abstract academic document. We therefore geared it towards implementation measures to be supported by the international donor community. This led me to what was my last major activity as Commonwealth diplomat, the organising of the first international donors' conference in support of the new South Africa, in Cape Town in October 1994.

The initiative had been first proposed in 1991 and was an example of collaboration between the Commonwealth Secretariat and the United Nations and involved my flying to New York and liaising with UN colleagues. The Cape Town conference was convened jointly between the Commonwealth Secretariat and the UN, with support from UNDP, and involved participation of a wide range of donors interested in assisting post-apartheid reconstruction. While the conference did not result in the major new Commonwealth programme we had at one time hoped for, it brought together all the major donors. A key achievement of the conference was to help Mandela's government establish an overall framework, based on our report, for securing significant donor support for the democratic transition.

In preparation for the conference, I consulted closely with the new South African government, especially my friend Jay Naidoo, former COSATU General Secretary, who had been given ministerial responsibility for the National Reconstruction and Development Programme. Another notable South African we engaged with was Professor Makele Ramphele, then Vice Chancellor of the University of Cape Town, who later took on a senior role at the World Bank in Washington. She had earlier been the partner of the freedom fighter Steve Biko, who had died under brutal circumstances in police detention.

As with the Expert Group report, on whose recommendations it was based, the preparation of the 1994 donor's conference involved frequent visits to South Africa in 1993-94. I usually stayed at the plush Carlton Hotel in the heart of Johannesburg and hired a car to drive myself up the motorway to nearby Pretoria for meetings. The Carlton was to shut down later owing to the decline of the city centre as a business venue, and the shift of much commercial life to the outlying suburb of Sandton. Happily, 'Jo'burg' city centre has since undergone a revival under successive ANC mayors, which I encountered in my subsequent local government work.

My frequent shuttling back and forth to South Africa during this period made up for the time when, prior to 1990, I had as Secretariat official, been prohibited from travelling to the country. On one occasion this had involved turning down a personal invitation from Jay Naidoo, then still COSATU Secretary-General, to attend his wedding. It meant that I was now able to take up another personal invitation to what must have been one of the great political events of the 20th century, the Inauguration of Nelson Mandela as President of the Republic of South Africa at the Union Buildings in Pretoria in April 1994, following his successful election victory.

The Inauguration was an occasion when I truly saw history being made. I was fortunate to be seated in the VIP section, just one seat from President Nyerere of Tanzania. Everywhere you looked you saw prominent world leaders.

The Inauguration and Nelson Mandela's swearing in as President took place under clear blue African skies. It was a wonderful event to have witnessed. I was able to meet many old comrades-in-arms including former Australian Prime Minister Bob Hawke, British Labour Leader Neil Kinnock and anti-apartheid activist Archbishop Trevor Huddleston. My one real regret is that I never got a personal photograph with Nelson Mandela. But I am proud of the memory of having encountered the most iconic and inspiring political leader of my lifetime, including on subsequent visits to South Africa.

Fidel Castro, a long-standing supporter of the Liberation struggle, got the loudest cheer from the crowd when he gave his familiar clenched fist salute. I briefly met Castro a few years later arriving in Kingston, Jamaica and being rushed to an open-air rally which he was addressing. Giving one of his shorter speeches – under two hours – he recalled the fight against apartheid and the Cuban-led advance into Angola, driving the South African military machine back to its own borders. He dramatically disclosed that Soviet intelligence, which he amusingly referred to as his 'then friends in Moscow' had warned him that Pretoria was threatening to deploy atomic weapons against the advancing troops. A spine-chilling revelation, which I have never heard reported elsewhere, but it was later revealed that Pretoria had destroyed its secret nuclear capacity prior to Mandela taking over in 1994.

I was privileged to have attended one of the great political events of the twentieth century.

22.

Fair and Free Elections

A CORE COMPONENT OF THE POST-COMMUNIST ERA WAS holding fair and free elections. This emerged as a key theme of the Commonwealth's work in the 1990s.

I was uneasy about the brazen free market philosophy which underlay public sector reform initiatives in the 1990s, but I had no such qualms about the new emphasis on democracy, human rights and fair and free elections.

The 1991 *Commonwealth Harare Declaration*, later added to by the 1995 *Millbrook Programme of Action,* set out basic principles concerning respect for democracy, human rights and the rule of law and other key aspects of a free society by Member States. It was to ensure the transition of the Commonwealth from an organisation in 1990 containing nine One-party or military regimes to a situation in 1999 where almost all of its then 54 members could claim to be democracies. In truth, there were still very dubious cases like Eswatini (Swaziland) and especially Brunei which I am not sure has ever met the Commonwealth's core principles, given it has no form of democracy whatsoever and subscribes to *sharia* law. I have visited both countries and was to some extent successful in supporting local democracy in Eswatini, but I frankly wonder how they can justify being a member of the Commonwealth.

To help bring about democratic transition, the Commonwealth was to develop a highly pro-active policy of support for the democratic process, masterminded by Secretary-General Anyaoku. This involved providing political as well as technical support to countries undergoing democratic transition from One-party or military rule, the monitoring and supervising of democratic elections and, on a modest scale, providing capacity-building support for the new democratic structures and in support of good governance.

This policy meant cajoling military regimes back to democracy, backed, if necessary, by sanctions and suspension from Commonwealth membership, as in the case of Nigeria and also Fiji and Pakistan. The Commonwealth Ministerial Action Group (CMAG), composed of foreign ministers, established after 1995, proved an important instrument to co-ordinate activities in this regard. It was a body to which I subsequently submitted a number of representations about violations of democratic rights.

The Commonwealth, with a direct means to supervise and, if necessary, sanction its members, was thus ahead of other international institutions like the UN. However, ultimately the deployment of CMAG and the Secretary-General's so-called 'Good Offices' mediation were dependent on the necessary political will by member states. It also required direct intervention by a forceful Secretary-General – someone who famously was more a 'General' than a 'Secretary'.

As a Secretary-General myself, I have personally always tried to be more of a 'General' directing and initiating policy. This is something which British and Canadian members, used to a technocratic, non-political, chief executive, who runs organisations under the direction of a political leadership, were often uncomfortable with. In contrast, most other countries understood the wider political leadership role of an international Secretary-General and lent their support to me. Although I did not request it, I often received formal ministerial-level status on visits abroad, with the provision of official cars with drivers on call and protocol and security officers assigned to me, as well as airport VIP reception, making travel a lot easier.

In the 1990s, the Commonwealth undertook around thirty election monitoring missions which were at the cutting edge of the democratic process. During this period, I was to take part in four Commonwealth election monitoring groups: Ghana (1992), Pakistan (1993), Nigeria (1998) and then Pakistan again (2000). This work involved checking if the pre-conditions of fair and free elections, such as freedom of the media and unrestricted campaigning by all political parties were present, that technical preparations for polling and an accurate voters' register were in place, and that the actual election processes, not least the counting of votes, was transparent.

A monitoring team has to make hard choices as to whether the overall process has been fair and free – not only the actual election, but all the procedures leading up to it. In doing this, observers are aware that they cannot do more than monitor a microcosm of the entire process, especially in larger countries. They can however draw on a wide range of local opinions and sources, as well as the findings of other monitoring groups, including domestic observers.

In 1992, our Ghana observer mission oversaw the transition of Flight-Lieutenant Jerry Rawlings' military regime to one with a democratic mandate. As with many other elections of this nature, nothing is perfect and afterwards the opposition parties cried foul and criticised the Commonwealth – and other observers – for judging the election process to have been essentially correct.

I can give a personal anecdote of how things can get exaggerated in the heat of an election campaign. On my pre-election day rounds in eastern Ghana, I was confronted by angry members of the opposition, who demanded that I witness a clear case of attempted electoral fraud. They pointed me to a single domicile which had almost 100 voters on the electoral register. Yet when we inspected the house in question, it turned out to be hostel with well over 100 residents. The opposition had not done its homework and had jumped to undue conclusions.

A footnote to the election in Ghana is that it coincided with the 1992 Presidential election in the USA. This saw the return of the Democrats to the White House for the first time in twelve years with the victory of Bill Clinton. I was informed about this by excited members of the American monitoring team from the Carter Center, set up by Jimmy Carter, the loser to Ronald Reagan in 1980, now a highly respected global statesman.

Pakistan in 1993 proved a difficult election to monitor. The country was returning from military rule and Benazir Bhutto was successfully running for election. Elections here were prone, as always, to outburst of violence. Apparently several hundred killings during a campaign was normal.

Pakistan is a 'dry' country where alcohol is banned. I realised I was in an unusual place when on arrival my police bodyguard offered to sell me illegal Indian whiskey. When I declined, I was shocked to be asked if I would prefer heroin instead. Apparently, illicit Indian whiskey is 'imported' across the desert by camel at night. The story goes that once in a while the Pakistan police try to intercept smugglers, just to prove a point. At this stage, the smugglers, seeing the police Land Rover on the horizon in the moonlight, force a bottle of the vile stuff down the poor camel's gullet. Thereupon, the unfortunate animal takes off at such a speed that no four-wheel drive can keep up with it. Having once tasted this dreadful brew, I can well believe it.

At the election I was posted in the most difficult part of the country, Hyderabad in Sindh, which had been the scene of an insurgency by the MQM separatist movement. My companion was an trade union friend, now a parliamentarian from Barbados, Bobby Morris. Although good buddies, we declined our host's strange suggestion of sharing a bed at the government guest house where we were to be put up, opting instead for two single rooms – and beds.

I soon learnt of the complexities of Pakistan politics when we met a local candidate from Mrs Bhutto's PPP party, which is a member of the Socialist International. Young and Harvard-educated, he was keen to impress us with his progressive politics. However, it turned out he was also the local landowner. His enlightened image was spoiled when, on leaving his campaign headquarters, to his great embarrassment two of the domestic servants prostrated themselves in front of him in a gesture of submission to their feudal master.

A serious incident occurred a few days before the election. Without warning, the local commissioner of police flung thirty political activists, who had been involved in nothing more than normal political canvassing, into preventive detention. When we met him, a military man with a nasty scar across his face, of the type one imagined would be good at pulling out prisoners' fingernails, his excuse was that they were all 'troublemakers'. Despite our vigorous protests, he refused to release them until after the election. I suppose the only good thing was that he was not biased – those detained were all drawn from different political parties.

My memories of Pakistan in 1993 include causing havoc in a local restaurant when our police bodyguards, Bren guns at the ready, insisted on sitting at the next table to us. I also had to endure seemingly endless amounts of sugary soft drinks and sickly-sweet cakes, offered whenever we called on one of the many political parties. To refuse would have been very impolite and undiplomatic. Perhaps I had, after all, become more of a diplomat after five years accreditation to the Court of St James.

Election day was tense, long and hot, with temperatures soaring up in the high 30s centigrade. There were a few local political killings, but happily we were not in the middle of them and overall the election passed reasonably peacefully.

Before leaving Pakistan, we committed the ultimate diplomatic sin. Our prominent blue Commonwealth flag was fixed onto a short pole on the front of our official car. When we were driving, it fluttered along nicely, but being much too long, dragged on the ground whenever we slowed down. This did not matter until we passed through the Karachi fish market. The resulting fishy smell on the flag was just too much even when we wrapped it up in plastic to take it back to London. I only hope it got a good dry-cleaning on returning home.

Being an election observer in a complex environment like Pakistan brings home the fragility of the democratic process.

23.

Party Political Lotteries

SINCE MY FIRST INTRODUCTION TO POLITICS, I HAD THOUGHT about entering Parliament as a British Labour MP. I now sought to realise my goal.

I, however, never viewed Parliament as the sole way to exercise political power. I certainly did not seek status or look for a slippery slope of career advancement, resulting in ministerial office for its own sake. I do confess to having been attracted by the historical glamour of the House of Commons, but all my early political and trade union experiences made me see the parliamentary work as being complimentary to democratic extra-parliamentary action. To my mind Labour MPs had to work in close collaboration with unions, NGOs and interest key groups such as environmental and human rights organisations, as well as with their local governments, all part of the rich heritage of our democratic governance.

I regard a parliamentarian who is cut off from civil society and the local community with suspicion and I have nothing but contempt for those who use their elected position for commercial or personal profit. I think it a scandal that some MPs can earn fortunes from outside consultancies, directorships or media appearances when they are already getting a decent salary from the taxpayer. This greedy practice should be curtailed in its entirety as it is both unethical and unjustifiable.

Looking back, my time living abroad in Brussels and my subsequent frequent professional absences overseas prevented me from pursuing a classic political career path. This would have involved first becoming a local councillor to make your name in your local CLP – the Constituency Labour Party, and then winning your spurs fighting an un-winnable Tory seat at a General Election. Only then would you normally be selected by your party to fight a winnable seat. But you cannot attend your local ward or council meetings when you are organising training courses in Tanzania or Papua New Guinea, thousands of miles away.

I had also not counted on two decades of Conservative Party ascendancy from 1979 to 1997. In 1987, Labour lost the General Election in the UK for the third successive occasion since 1979. My earlier dream of entering British parliamentary politics seemed dim and impractical, given that the number of winnable Labour seats had been significantly reduced, although Labour's 1987 election result was better than the disastrous showing under Michael Foot in 1983.

Even in those dark days I did not lose faith in the Labour Party and was never tempted to join former political associates and friends in the new Social Democrats. The latter failed to achieve a political breakthrough and merged with the Liberal Party to form the Liberal Democrat Party. During this time, I continued to engage with the Labour Party on global issues and helped to shape its policy on international development by advising on a number of policy papers.

I was attracted by the determined leadership of Welshman Neil Kinnock, who had, despite losing in 1987, fought a good election campaign and was revitalising and modernising the Labour Party. I also much admired the commitment of his wife, Glenys, and in 1987 was to become the founding Treasurer of a radical campaigning charity, One World Action, set up under her leadership. In this connection I got to know Glenys and Neil Kinnock and visited their home in Ealing on several occasions. In 1988, I contributed to a publication *Voices for One World* alongside other prominent authors such as Gro Brundtland and Michael Manley; the proceeds of the book went to support solidarity to Labour Movement initiatives in developing countries.

I was prompted to be more pro-active in my search of parliamentary selection by initial disappointment of working at the Commonwealth Secretariat after 1988. This was before I was given key responsibilities to deal with South Africa and Namibia after 1990. I found a politically like-minded colleague in a fellow Secretariat employee, Val Shawcross, an intelligent and committed Labour Party activist working in the Gender Division.

Val had previously pioneered the establishment of All-Women shortlists at the Labour Party and was to leave the Secretariat earlier than me and, successfully contesting local elections, became a highly able local councillor. Rising to Leader of the London Borough of Croydon, she was subsequently elected member of the Greater London Assembly and ended up as London's Deputy Mayor in charge of London Transport, a very senior portfolio; she is someone I have much admiration for, both on account of her professional dedication and her clear-headed politics.

One of my memories relates to the day of Margaret Thatcher's resignation, when I was parking my car on The Mall and saw the Prime Minister's car speeding to Buckingham Palace to see the Queen. This was truly a cause for us having a celebratory drink together. Val and I became very close friends, encouraging and supporting each other's attempts at political advancement. Over the years we attended many Labour Party events and participated together in overseas workshops and visits, including to India, where Val was advising on training women councillors, and to the USA where we attended the Democratic Party Convention in Chicago.

My most serious attempt at a parliamentary selection took place in the north Wales seat of Delyn, near Deeside, in 1989-90. The seat, which had been a Tory marginal, went Labour in the 1992 General Election, and remained so until 2019. The real battle pre-1992 was over the Constituency Labour Party (CLP) nomination to be the Labour candidate, not so much the actual election which was something of a forgone conclusion. I was to come within an inch of winning the Labour nomination.

At the time I was on the prestigious TGWU Parliamentary Panel, and I had been tipped off about Delyn by George Wright, TGWU Welsh Secretary. This was to result in the absurd rumour, put around by my opponents, that George, as my namesake, but no relation, was an uncle and he was 'looking after the family'. I however managed to secure solid support from most of the Deeside unions, using all my old trade union links to the hilt. This proved invaluable as at that time unions still held around 40 per cent of votes of the electoral college set up to nominate Labour candidates. In the process I made clear my determination to work with the local unions as MP and looked to them to provide me with future organisational support and setting up a full-time constituency office.

I spent many weekends commuting from London to Delyn, living on fish and chips takeaways, and got to know key local party activists, to say nothing of the railway timetables. I secured active support from several, including the amiable local chairman, a retired printer with a heart of gold, Penmaen Griffiths. Such support on the ground is essential and a key to any success: no candidate wins on good looks or intelligence alone.

I took a risk with party rules, as most successful would-be candidates do, by getting myself in the local media attacking the sitting Tory MP. On one occasion Adele came along and managed to win the local dog show so we ensured that this success, and of course my political interest, was duly headlined in the local paper. Such media exposure is obviously invaluable to make yourself known and demonstrate your potential ability as MP.

In the end, the field of candidates was a tough one and was eventually reduced to six, and all of them, apart from myself, subsequently became MPs. Never being much of a great public speaker at the time – I have improved a lot since – I had limited impact at local ward meetings. I therefore only managed to secure one ward nomination, Flint. However even that was ruled ineligible on a technicality engineered by my opponents and meant that I only had trade union nominations.

When it came to the final selection vote, it was a close call. Despite all the manoeuvring by my rivals I nearly made it. I only lost by one single vote. In the final ballot round the votes of the candidate I beat into third place, London Left-winger John McDonnell, who later became shadow chancellor under Jeremy Corbyn, went to the local man, David Hanson. The latter had the advantage of having already stood as Labour candidate in 1987; he went on to win at the 1992 election. My narrow failure to be selected for Delyn was a great disappointment.

After such a close run, I was perhaps too confident at finding a safe seat to fight. These were running out fast with an election approaching. I rejected an offer to stand in nearby Colwyn Bay, a more marginal seat which went Labour in the 1997 landslide. All that remained was a last-minute opportunity to put my name forward in Wallasey, another marginal seat on Merseyside. This was not far from Delyn, which I hoped would bring me local contacts. The sitting MP was none other than Tory Overseas Development Administration (ODA, now DFID) the amiable Minister Lynda Chalker (now Lady Chalker). I naively thought that local activists might be impressed by my international credentials and nominate me to stand against her, but I was very wrong.

Wallasey was a complex exercise as the candidate previously selected by the local party had been deemed a Left-wing extremist and ruled ineligible to stand, much to the disgust of local activists. Instead, the Labour Party National Executive Committee, NEC, imposed a specially vetted panel of candidate, including me, for selection by the local party members. At the NEC interview we were all asked to confirm that we 'had no skeletons in our cupboard'. Happily, I was able to oblige.

As TGWU parliamentary panel member, I counted – as in Delyn – on TGWU and local union votes for support. I had reckoned without the machinations of the Merseyside hard Left. While the local TGWU branch was obliged to back me, they did so by sending out the union recommendation in my favour by second class mail – making sure it dropped in members' letter boxes only after the vote. As a result, and because, unlike the winning candidate and eventual 1992 election winner, Angela Eagle, I had no local backers, my vote was derisory. In retrospect Wallasey, unlike Delyn, would have been a political bed of nails and would have required much sweat and tears in sorting out the Trotskyite activists.

The wrath I incurred from the hard Left on account of Wallasey made itself felt later when the TGWU failed to renew my membership of their parliamentary panel. By that time, however, unions had lost much of their formal influence on the parliamentary nomination process. Nonetheless they still retained much indirect clout in nominating and supporting candidates and no longer being on the union's panel was a personal blow.

At times my political activities had their farcical side. I recall once arriving by train in Brighton for an important trade union dinner. As I descended on the station platform, I heard a nasty tear where the back of my trousers had suddenly split. I was obviously having too many good business lunches. What to do? There was no time to return to London to change and local shops had already closed so no replacement was possible. I decided to go to the poshest hotel in town, the Metropole, and ask if they could help me out 'as a frequent guest', omitting to say I had only stayed there once or twice. Within minutes my split trousers were repaired, all 'on the house', and I was able to proceed to my dinner.

In the period leading up to the 1992 election, I put considerable efforts into helping the election of my local candidate, the Oscar-winning actress Glenda Jackson, in Hampstead and Highgate, a seat that went Labour for the first time since 1970. I was then the Vice Chair of the Constituency Labour Party (CLP), and was able to co-ordinate fundraising. This helped to pay for an employed party worker and I also got my union, the TGWU, to provide a party office; neither had existed previously and proved vital for our campaign. Adele also organised a fundraising event for Glenda with some of the kids from her dance school.

I was to spend a bit of time with Glenda on the campaign trail and was witness to her chain-smoking habit. It was said that in the age of New Labour, she was one of the few MPs who still smoked untipped Woodbine cigarettes and drank Guinness beer. Once elected, although in many ways a conscientious constituency MP, she did not do much to engage or socialise with party activists who had worked hard to get her elected. I do not even recall her buying us a drink to say thanks after her election. Not a good practice for a local MP.

Although successful in Hampstead, Labour lost the 1992 election which was hugely disappointing, given we had earlier seemed on course for victory. Neil Kinnock resigned as Leader and was replaced by John Smith. I occasionally reflect that if I had stood and been elected in 1992 at the age of 42, this would have been an ideal time to have entered Parliament and make a mark before the eventual Labour victory under Tony Blair in 1997.

My old Welsh schoolfriend Gary Smith had a similar experience in running for the Labour nomination in his native Pembrokeshire. Here, like me in Delyn, missed narrowly in a seat which also went Labour in 1992. One of his key selling points was his experience of the oil industry, which had a significant presence in the local Milford Haven refinery. However, I learnt that some of his electioneering methods were quite unconventional. He also publicly criticised Neil Kinnock's leadership which could hardly have endeared him to the party establishment and local members.

Having missed out on Westminster, my eye turned to the forthcoming European Elections due in 1994. With my strong Labour credentials and European and international experience, this seemed in some ways more suited than Westminster. I therefore felt confident of success in getting a Labour nomination and becoming a Member of the European Parliament (MEP) and pursuing a political career in the EU, returning to some of my old haunts of the 1970s. I however underestimated what little emphasis party activists place on international experience – your knowledge of local, often quite parochial, issues is what matters.

My first attempt at a nomination was in the East Midlands, as I had a contact in the local Euro-CLP through my former CTUC colleague Dave Clement. Like all Euro-seats, this covered a large area with some ten different CLPs, stretching all the way from Stafford to Leicester. I had however left matters a little late, and despite some early successes and was unable to secure the necessary CLP nomination to go into the final ballot.

Another opportunity soon arose in my home base. Here the sitting Labour MEP, Stan Newens, was regarded as inefficient and out-of-touch, as well as being too much of the Old Left. I therefore put my hat in the ring, being careful this time to assemble a strong team of local supporters in my own CLP. I received overwhelming support in Hampstead and Highgate, although when it came to the vote on the CLP nomination, there was tactical voting to block me in favour of a dynamic young newcomer, Oona King, who was to go on to become MP in Tower Hamlets in 1997. This almost denied me my nomination, but I prevailed in the end. Another unsuccessful aspirant at the time was Jan Royall, who had worked with Neil Kinnock and was later to get a peerage and become Labour Leader of the House of Lords.

While having strong support locally, it was much more difficult to get effective support in the other eight CLPs that made up the London Central Euro CLP, ranging all the way from Islington in the east to Hammersmith in the west.

At one stage Newens looked very shaky when he lost five of the nine CLP nominations. All these were however split between me and three further candidates, including the gay actor, Michael Cashman, from the BBC TV soap *East Enders*. Michael only secured his nomination onto the final ballot at the last minute. I had already been negotiating with his campaign manager, Stephen Twigg, later to become the unexpected victor over Tory hate-figure Michael Portillo in 1997, to attract his supporters. In the event we and the other two candidates split the votes, allowing the incumbent Stan Newens to win the nomination and serve a final term as MEP. This was another big disappointment.

Paradoxically, I had received an unsolicited approach from the East Kent Euro-CLP while I was running for London Central. I felt it unethical to go for two seats at the same time and a Labour victory in East Kent seemed highly improbable. Yet the seat was won by Labour in 1994 and on reflection it would, given my personal connections and country home in the area, have been a great seat to have held.

After the European Elections, the selections for the next General Election in 1997 were looming. In mid-1994, I had just started my new job setting up the Commonwealth Local Government Forum and this was preoccupying me, involving much overseas travel. After some hesitation, I decided to have a go at being nominated in Gravesend, Kent, a marginal Tory seat which was won by Labour in 1997. I was able to attract some local support and set about building this up. In the middle of this process, the NEC decided in their wisdom that Gravesend was to be designated as a women-only seat and short of having a sex change, my strategy collapsed.

Following a High Court challenge, ironically on grounds of discrimination, Gravesend was again opened up to selection by both sexes and I sought to re-establish contact. But I had lost a lot of momentum in the process. I was dismayed and a little hurt that I failed to get the necessary ward nomination to get onto the final ballot. The absurdity of the nomination process came home to me when, flying back from warm tropical Bombay to freezing sleet in Kent, I missed the nomination by a single vote at a ward meeting attended by a paltry twelve members.

I was pleased when Tony Blair moved to modernise the antiquated nomination process and reduce the scope for manipulation by small cliques of party activists. I remain a little upset by my experience in Gravesend, which I recall when I pass it by car on the way to my home in Kent, as it appeared to put the seal on my long-held ambition of parliamentary selection. I did subsequently achieve a place on the party's approved panel of parliamentary candidates and put out some half-hearted feelers in some other instances, including Canterbury, which finally went Labour in 2017. But by then I had decided to concentrate on the international work I loved, to focus on what I was good at and where I was having an impact.

Parliamentary selection is a lottery, and success requires quite a few rolls of the dice.

24.

The 1990s Remembered

THE 1990s WERE KICK-STARTED WITH THE GLOBAL COLLAPSE of communism, which hardly anyone had anticipated. This geopolitical step change had ramifications throughout the world, including in Southern Africa, where the apartheid regime was forced to relinquish power.

The end of the Cold War affected countries within the Commonwealth and beyond, which now gravitated towards establishing new democratic and inclusive government, with a blossoming of the rule of law, free media and civil society, resulting in the growth of liberal democracies around the world. Whereas previously the ideological competition between East and West had frozen out possibilities for change, the flood gates of democratic reform burst open. My professional work in the Commonwealth changed to supporting democratic transitions globally, especially in fragile states, where I helped to build new inclusive public sector institutions, notably at local government level. Examples included Malawi, Sierra Leone and Tanzania, as well as in South Africa post-1994. My activities also involved monitoring fair and free elections at national and local government level and saw me acting on Commonwealth Election Observer teams in Ghana, Pakistan and Nigeria, often under difficult and dangerous circumstances.

As always, my activities were a mix of supporting grass roots activism and engaging in high level diplomacy. It was exciting to have been at the cutting edge of so many historic developments and transitions. In South Africa our past emphasis on supporting the Liberation Movements and Black trade unions in their freedom struggle switched to building the post-apartheid transition. The landmark Commonwealth report on human resource development for post-apartheid and organisation of the 1994 Commonwealth Secretariat/UN donors' conference in Cape Town, which I was intimately involved with, consolidated this process.

My work involved many visits to South Africa and strengthening further my already close links with the leaders of political change inside the country. Having attended the Namibia Independence celebrations in Windhoek in 1990, it was a delight to be invited to witness Nelson Mandela being sworn in as President in Pretoria in 1994. The Inauguration provided a fitting conclusion to my period as Commonwealth diplomat and my long-standing anti-apartheid work over several decades, and I left the formal employment of the Secretariat shortly afterwards. As a reference I cannot do better than the letter I received some years later from the wonderful and charismatic late Archbishop Desmond Tutu. In it he praised my engagement in the anti-apartheid struggle and concluded most generously that, "Mr Wright is highly competent and skilled in diplomacy and navigating the sometimes turbulent waters of international affairs."

During my seven years on Her Majesty's Diplomatic List, 1988-1994, I had remained a grass roots activist at heart, even as I polished off a few rough edges. I was truly an unlikely diplomat. My role at the Commonwealth Secretariat did sharpen my management skills, my ability to deal with significant funding allocations and gave me an insiders' view of the workings of the intergovernmental Commonwealth structures which was to be of much benefit in my future tasks. I also got invaluable experience serving on Commonwealth election observer teams, especially in difficult political environments like Pakistan.

In 1990, I came very close to realising my youthful ambition of becoming a Labour parliamentarian. Here the real contest was over the party nomination as candidate, as the subsequent election itself would have been assured. It was not to be. Securing parliamentary nomination, whether at Westminster or Strasbourg, requires much determination and local engagement. Many successful MPs have ten or more nomination battles before they succeed. The main barrier to my success was my constant international travel, which prevented me from getting well known in a particular area and building up the local support necessary for selection.

By the mid-1990s I was heading towards the age of fifty. The prospect of being backbench MP, or a junior minister should Labour get into power, was increasingly less attractive. The high-level work I was doing internationally provided me with professional and personal satisfaction. It was where my talents and my passion lay. I doubt that as a Westminster MP or Brussels MEP, I would have had such job satisfaction or such a worthwhile career, interacting as I did in my Commonwealth work with so many interesting personalities, including numerous Prime Ministers and Presidents. I certainly would not have enjoyed the immense public pressure, ruthless media exposure and often vindictive and personalised nature of party politics.

The 1990s were a decade marked by rapid technological change, requiring me to acquire new skills. This was driven by the IT revolution, the onset of widespread access to the internet, personal PCs and use of mobile communications – emails – which by the middle of the decade started to make it into my office.

These new technologies had been rare at the beginning of the decade, but by the year 2000 they were everywhere. Bulky PCs and cumbersome cell phones got ever-smaller, ever-more powerful and even more mobile. Skype calls suddenly allowed real time video conferencing. Television sets shed their voluminous frames to become flat-screen and smart with a vast choice of many new channels, even if most offered low quality programmes not worth viewing. Compact discs took over from cassettes, with the Sony portable Discman becoming a bestseller. Video games and games consoles made their appearance although I must admit I have never been tempted by computer games and prefer to get stuck in a good old-fashioned book or a political journal like the *New Statesman* and the *New European*.

The internet was soon to provide a wonderful means of accessing a limitless source of information and data; it was also to lay the foundations for the medium of social media, such as Facebook, Instagram and Twitter, which took off in the early 2000s but took a while for me to master fully.

Not only technology but also global and geopolitical changes were accelerating – history clearly did not end with the collapse of communism.

PART IV

LOCAL GOVERNMENT CAMPAIGNS
(towards 2000 and beyond)

Promoting People Empowerment

"All politics is local"

THOMAS P. 'TIP' O'NEILL,
SPEAKER OF THE US HOUSE OF REPRESENTATIVES

With the approach of the new Millennium, I set up the Commonwealth Local Government Forum, campaigning for people empowerment, local democracy and good governance. During this time, I met many grass roots activists, politicians and officials.

25

Challenge for the New Millennium

ON LEAVING MY ROLE AS COMMONWEALTH DIPLOMAT, I FACED a new challenge: establishing a new Commonwealth body. This was the Commonwealth Local Government Forum (CLGF).

The history of the CLGF goes back to 1994 and the final days of my work at the Commonwealth Secretariat. Its formal establishment in 1995 would involve my continuing with global action but with a local dimension – thinking globally but acting locally, to adopt the slogan of the environmental movement. Prime focus was building democratic local government and this task took up all my time and energies until my formal retirement as CLGF Secretary-General in 2016.

I had previously developed contacts with the overseas arm of UK local government, the Local Government International Bureau (LGIB) working with its Director Paul Bongers and his amiable deputy, the late Vernon Smith. This had involved supporting its activities, notably an African workshop on local government, held in Zimbabwe in late 1992. The workshop had indicated an interest in establishing a Commonwealth local government network or forum with a small office in London to undertake lobbying and operational activities overseas. This initiative was not unlike the Commonwealth Trade Union Council, CTUC, which I had set up in 1980.

There is a tradition of local government working internationally, spearheaded by great urban centres like London or New York. World cities increasingly operated on the global marketplace, competing for jobs, commerce, investments and tourism, in some cases independent of the nation state. These cities often maintained close links with each other and there had been a proliferation of city-to-city 'twinning' in Western Europe after 1945 to foster friendship between former wartime enemies, such as France and Germany, as well the UK.

After the fall of the Berlin Wall in 1989, city twinning began to extend to Eastern Europe. There were also the beginnings of twinning with cities in the developing world, through what has become known as 'decentralised cooperation', although this was then still at an early stage. Originally seen as ways of cultivating youth and civic exchanges, such twinning is sometimes criticised in the media as overseas 'junkets' for mayors and councillors. Such criticism ignores the positive links being forged between peoples, resulting in genuine human friendships. It also fails to recognise the real benefits for trade, investment and tourism for both partners, engaging local businesses.

I decided to meet the challenge of setting up the new local government organisation as its Director and later Secretary-General and was given a six-month secondment in 1994 from the Commonwealth Secretariat to do this.

As with the CTUC, I started in a tiny office with a single staff member, Dzifa Tay, from Ghana, who was always very diligent and supportive. We were based at the headquarters of the UK Association of Metropolitan Authorities (later to merge into the Local Government Association) in Great Smith Street, Westminster, alongside the LGIB, not far from Parliament. The CLGF was launched in style in the elegant Blenheim saloon at Commonwealth headquarters, Marlborough House, in the presence of the Commonwealth Secretary-General and Commonwealth High Commissioners in late 1994.

An important distinction of the new organisation was that it was quasi-governmental, not non-governmental like the CTUC or other Commonwealth bodies, given it represented a local sphere of elected government. However, it was also not a formal intergovernmental organisation, or IGO, set up by legal treaty, like the Commonwealth Secretariat. This mixed status had many advantages. While having direct access to government and many of its resources, we managed to avoid the more rigid bureaucracy typical of many IGOs and could take action quickly and without undue red tape.

Our core members were individual cities, local authorities and country-wide local government associations, represented by mayors and senior elected councillors. Unlike other international local government organisations, however, we also had national ministries of local government as full members, represented in most cases by senior ministers of cabinet rank. This served to enhance our profile and political clout and helped us with much of our in-country work and advocacy in the Commonwealth. There were also associate members such as universities, professional associations and public sector unions connected with local government such as UNISON from the UK, represented by a former trade union friend, Keith Sonnet.

By 1997, Tony Blair had just assumed office and Board members now included the responsible UK Secretary of State for local government, Hilary Armstrong, an old Labour Party acquaintance with a strong commitment to overseas development. Another key ministerial supporter was Kwamena Ahwoi, the then Ghana minister of local government, who had undertaken major decentralisation reforms and became a powerful advocate of our work. Kwamena liked to tell the story of how, by decentralising local decisions to local government, he had rid himself of endless queues of community leaders and chiefs outside his office seeking favours. This allowed him to get on with the strategic national issues more suited to central government and avoid local micro-management: a powerful argument for decentralisation and community empowerment for the mutual benefit of central and local government.

We later went a step further and recruited prominent heads of government as our honorary patrons which gave us considerable political influence within the Commonwealth. These included Prime Minister Helen Clark of New Zealand; Prime Minister Portia Simpson-Miller of Jamaica; Prime Minister Kamla Persad-Bissessar of Trinidad and Tobago; Prime Minister Enele Sopoaga of Tuvalu; President Yoweri Museveni of Uganda; and President John Dramani Mahama of Ghana. I was able to keep in touch with our patrons and meet them regularly and developed good links with them. The only problem was that the patronage was linked to the office held, so we had an awkward situation when, as happened twice in Jamaica, our very supportive patron, Prime Minister Simpson-Miller, was in and out of office after losing and then winning an election again.

I met with many Commonwealth leaders over the years. One of the first back in 1994 was Jerry Rawlings of Ghana, a highly focused politician. Rawlings had originally taken power in a military coup in 1979 and again in 1981, before being elected as President in democratic elections in 1992, which I had witnessed as a member of the Commonwealth election observer team. I was subsequently to engage with numerous other leaders from all parts of the Commonwealth.

Some of our local government members, like the Canadians and their francophone international affairs director Jacques Jobin, were initially suspicious of giving a voice to central government ministers, but they began to see the advantage, even the necessity, of working in partnership with central government. Indeed, for some mayors, CLGF meetings provided them with a wonderful opportunity to interact informally with their own ministers and officials and reach domestic deals.

At the same time, we ensured that the chair of the organisation was always held by a senior mayor and during my time this included two chairpersons from Uganda (Christopher Iga and John Otekat), two from South Africa (Collin Matjila and Nomaindia Mfeketo), two from the Caribbean (Bobby Montague from Jamaica and Zenaida Moya from Belize), two from New Zealand (Basil Morrison and Lawrence Yule) and one each from the UK (Len Duvall) and Botswana (Mpho Moruakgomo). Such regional rotation is essential in any international organisation.

I always had a close and cordial relationship with Board members and Patrons and sought to involve them in our work as much as possible. Quite a few like Helen Clark, Basil Morrison and Adolf Mwesige from Uganda visited my home in Kent and we became good personal friends. My Treasurers were, for practical reasons, senior UK local government officials and included Jeremy Smith, Mike Ashley and Simon Baker; all were diligent in their support, helping to ensure our finances were sustainable, and Mike in particular became a close friend.

My good links with Chief Anyaoku, the Commonwealth Secretary-General and Mohan Kaul at the Commonwealth Secretariat, would prove to be of advantage to the new organisation. They provided me with significant resources initially to undertake workshops, symposia and research in different parts of the Commonwealth. The first important CLGF event was held in Accra, bringing together local governments from across Africa. This was followed by a Caribbean event in Port of Spain in Trinidad. Both took place in 1994, while the CLGF was still operating on an interim basis prior to its formal establishment in 1995. This put us on the map and helped to recruit members.

I soon discovered that running a not-for-profit, voluntary organisation was tougher in the 1990s than in the heady days of the 1980s when I ran the CTUC, and that attracting funds was considerably more difficult.

I managed to secure initial funding from the LGIB and the Federation of Canadian Municipalities. At the time a friendly Tory MP, Jim Lester, had steered a private members bill through the House of Commons under which local authorities were legally permitted to engage in international work. With his help we secured funding from Lady Chalker's Overseas Development Administration, ODA (later the Department for International Development, DFID). I was also able to obtain grant funding from the Carnegie Foundation after meeting them in New York. Following consultations in Brussels I further negotiated significant EU funding, which over the years became ever-more important and eventually exceeded what CLGF was receiving from DFID.

As our funds grew, I was able to recruit more staff. Among the early employees recruited were Lucy Slack, a young, enthusiastic UK national, full of ideas, who later became my deputy, and Sam Teyki-Berto, a Ghanaian who became an able and diligent Finance Director and who never failed to ensure that the finances were in order.

I employed several PAs, including Lorna Nicholas (from India), Bernie Dare (from Singapore) and Claudia Bultman (from Sierra Leone), who were all highly reliable and loyal. Other staff included Gareth Wall, who in addition to research, liaised with academic Board members such as Dr Phil Amis from the University of Birmingham's esteemed international development department. More recent recruits included Chaminda Kevitiyagala (from Sri Lanka), as finance officer and Shraddha Kaul (from India) who made a major contribution to our communications and conference work.

We sought to attract academic expertise on local government, not only from the UK but other Commonwealth universities such as KwaZulu-Natal, the University of the Pacific and the University of the West Indies. These included such outstanding academic experts like Professor P S Reddy from South Africa and Dr Bishnu Ragoonath from Trinidad. I was further able to draw on competent local government practitioners from across the Commonwealth such as Terry Parker from Australia who worked for me in a range of different countries.

A key strategy, similar to what I had done at the CTUC, was to set up small regional offices. These were staffed by locally recruited personnel to oversee our work in different parts of the Commonwealth. This had the advantage of decentralising our work, encouraging local ownership of our programmes and having a presence on the ground. It was also a way of attracting local donor support for our work and meant that the organisation and its staff was truly Commonwealth in nature, unlike many other UK-based Commonwealth bodies.

As most of these offices only had a small number of staff, coordination and supervision was a challenge. I therefore ensured that where possible our offices were located with our member organisations in the countries concerned, who also provided oversight as well as practical facilities. Over the years, this led to us having regional offices in Ghana (Accra), South Africa (Pretoria), India (Mumbai), Fiji (Suva) and Trinidad and Tobago (Port of Spain); we further had country programme offices, for example in Colombo, Sri Lanka and Harare, Zimbabwe.

I was fortunate in the staff I recruited. They included Nyasha Simbanegavi (from Zimbabwe) in Pretoria, Karibaiti Taoaba (from Kiribati) in Suva, Anuya Kuwar (from India), in Mumbai and Sandra Singh (from Trinidad) in Port of Spain, all highly capable and professional women appointed on merit. CLGF was therefore a trailblazer for women's empowerment across the world which was underlined further when Lucy Slack became its Secretary-General in 2021.

By the year 2000, the CLGF network had 160 fee-paying members in 49 of the 54 Commonwealth countries. Only a few counties, like Barbados, Brunei or Singapore which had no formal local government structures, were not represented in our membership, although we tried to involve them in CLGF meetings where possible.

By then our members were either umbrella national associations of local government, bringing together the individual councils in their country, or the respective national ministries of local government or urban and rural development. I was also successfully secured membership by key Commonwealth cities like Delhi, Durban, Kingston (Jamaica), London, Melbourne and Windhoek. However, given that in most countries we already had the national local government association as members, which comprised their cities, recruiting individual cities as separate members proved difficult. One exception was the UK, where we did secure a large number of individual city and local council as members including big cities like Birmingham, Cardiff, Glasgow, Leeds, Manchester and county councils like Kent.

To facilitate more city engagement, I later established a *Commonwealth Inclusive Cities Network*; this was relaunched as the *Commonwealth Sustainable Cities Network* at a meeting in Singapore in 2015. The network provided a vehicle for engaging city members, in the light of rapid urbanisation and growing international interest on cities as engines of economic growth.

This new global focus on cities was reflected by the adoption in 2015 of the UN's Sustainable Development Goal SDG 11 to make cities and human settlements inclusive, safe, resilient and sustainable, and UN

Habitat's New Urban Agenda in 2016, both initiatives I was involved with. I also brought CLGF into membership of the Cities Alliance, a global network to develop practical responses to what the writer Richard Florida has termed the 'new urban crisis'.

I further instigated a category of observer membership to cover non-independent territories and countries which were not members of the Commonwealth, but wished to work closely with us, especially at the regional level. These observers benefitted from and participated in all of our activities but did not have statutory voting rights; they included countries like Gibraltar, the Cook Islands and Angola.

With the approach of the new Millennium, CLGF was, after five years, well on the way to establishing itself. On New Year's Eve 1999, together with Adele and some friends, we headed down to central London to see in the new Millennium, alongside hundreds of thousands of revellers. Here we watched a spectacular Millennium firework display lighting up the banks of the River Thames. One of my abiding memories of the night is traipsing over the river's bridges after midnight trying to avoid countless broken and discarded champagne bottles. It was an exciting moment.

Some years later my CLGF office was on the top floor of an old building in Northumberland Avenue, just off Trafalgar Square, overlooking the Embankment and the river. It was right opposite the London Eye – the 'Millennium Wheel' – from which ever-more amazing firework displays were launched each New Year's Eve.

Having a small balcony, this was the ideal spot to have a private New Year's Eve party and watch the clock ticking down to midnight, something I made use of on several fun-filled occasions. After 9/11 security around the Embankment was tightened up. To get to my office on New Year's Eve, I had to convince the police that I was actually living in Northumberland Avenue, which, given the amount of time I spent there, rarely leaving work before 7 or 8pm, was almost true.

My Westminster office was certainly in a super location and within a short walk from Whitehall ministries, Parliament and our UK member, the Local Government Association. It was much better than the previous offices I had had at the Association of London Government in Southwark. Here I had been stuck a poky and claustrophobic little windowless room, costing an arm and a leg in rent. This is why I moved CLGF to superior but cheaper commercial premises in Northumberland Avenue.

Of course, being in an old London building has its drawbacks. On one occasion we had an infestation of rodents. I was having a meeting with my Chairperson, the youthful Mayor Zenaida Moya from Belize, when a mouse streaked across my office. Zenaida gave a little gasp and I tried to reassure her that nothing had happened. However, dealing with rodents was the least of my worries.

With the turn of the Millennium many new challenges and opportunities still lay ahead.

26

Networks and Partnerships

AS A COMMONWEALTH ORGANISATION, OUR PRIME FOCUS was networking with Commonwealth governments and the Commonwealth Secretariat. However, we soon looked at other partnerships, especially with the UN and the EU.

I had been able to achieve formal political endorsement for CLGF's establishment by the 1995 Commonwealth Heads of Government Meeting (CHOGM) in Auckland. I had flown there to meet with and lobby the hosting New Zealand Prime Minister, Jim Bolger. Many years previously, I had met Jim when he was minister of labour in the government of Robert Muldoon and my past contact was helpful. On that occasion, having just arrived from a gruelling 36-hour flight from the UK with my luggage lost, I had to see him in grubby clothes and an old pair of jeans – not that he had minded. Happily, I was better attired this time around.

The 1995 CHOGM proved a key stepping-stone and provided important political recognition for our new organisation within the Commonwealth. I was able to secure formal acknowledgement for our work in the official Auckland communique as well as official accreditation. This was followed up at subsequent CHOGMs: Edinburgh 1997; Durban, 1999; Coolum, 2002; Abuja, 2003; Valletta, 2005; Kampala, 2007; Port of Spain, 2009; Perth, 2011; Colombo, 2013; and Valletta, 2015. I attended all of these apart from Coolum. Adding the CHOGMs I participated in when I was CTUC Director, I have been to thirteen in total since 1981, plus some regional CHOGMs, perhaps not quite an all-time record, but quite a good score.

Of course, all this required much advance advocacy and lobbying of the Commonwealth Secretariat and individual Government officials and ministers: ultimately it was essential to have at least one or two governments, prompted by our respective Board members, to speak up on our behalf at the relevant CHOGM drafting sessions. These included presentations at the pre-CHOGM preparatory meetings of senior officials of the Committee of the Whole, with the wonderful acronym COW. A good deal of my time was always spent on this advocacy and it bore good fruit and helped significantly to raise our profile.

I made a point of keeping up close links and regular meetings with the Commonwealth Secretaries-General and involved them in key CLGF conferences and events. After the departure of Chief Anayoku, I had good relations with both Don McKinnon from New Zealand and Kamalesh Sharma from India; the arrival of Baroness Scotland coincided with my retirement in 2016.

I further made it my task to develop close relations with senior Secretariat staff, like Mmasekgoa Masire-Mwamba from Botswana, Steve Cutts from the UK and Nabeel Goheer from Pakistan, all highly able and committed officials. We worked especially closely with the Political Affairs Division and cooperated together to promote local democracy, for example in the Maldives, Pakistan, Sri Lanka, Malawi and Nigeria. I was fortunate in being able to deal with a series of open-minded and supportive Directors such as Australian Matthew Neuhaus and Indian Amitav Banerji, who became good friends.

Despite our generally cordial relations, it was sometimes a battle to convince the Secretariat, ever jealous of its own perceived exclusive intergovernmental status, that CLGF was not an NGO or a professional association but had governmental status. Here, I had the advantage of having previously worked in the Secretariat and knew exactly which buttons to press.

After much lobbying, a breakthrough came in 2002 following the Coolum CHOGM. It was agreed that CLGF – and a small number of other Commonwealth quasi-governmental organisations would receive enhanced accreditation status at future CHOGMs separate from NGOs. We were subsequently given the designation of Associated Organisation or AO. By 2011, I had taken on the task of convening and chairing regular meetings of AOs to ensure that we coordinated our positions, for example to agree to joint submissions to CHOGM.

Our new status meant that we were given official Delegation status, allowing us access to the actual CHOGM venue inside the main security exclusion zone alongside national delegations. We were also able to sit in on the foreign ministers meeting at CHOGM as an observer, and later had dedicated exchanges with them. This was a big improvement on the previous situation when we had been relegated to the outside along with NGOs and the media.

There remained petty restrictions such as not being provided with official documentation; in addition, the actual meetings of the Heads – the Executive Sessions – understandably remained private. Nonetheless, our new status meant having direct access to the national CHOGM delegations which was vital for advocacy work, aimed at securing political endorsement of our work in successive official CHOGM communiques. It also provided an opportunity of having bilateral meetings with national delegations.

What was lacking for quite a while was better institutional division of labour and on-the-ground coordination with the Secretariat, especially its governance division – ironically my old department. In the early 2000s the latter initiated its own local government activities, appointing a full-time local government adviser and duplicating our work. This caused confusion among our members, as well as representing a poor use of resources, given that CLGF had the relevant expertise in the area.

We did finally manage a better collaboration largely thanks to the positive attitude of the Secretariat's local government adviser, Dr Munawwar Alam, who saw the importance of CLGF and his boss Max Everest-Philips, a former DFID official. However, unlike previously, Secretariat funds were normally not provided directly to CLGF.

In this issue we were not alone – other AOs like the Commonwealth Parliamentary Association, CPA and the Commonwealth Association of Public Administration and Management, CAPAM, had similar problems. In the case of CAPAM this even involved the Secretariat taking over responsibility for meetings of public service ministers which probably contributed to the CAPAM's eventual demise.

The temptation for the Secretariat to lump the AOs together with the CSOs and professional associations was always present. I constantly had to guard against this, especially when the Secretariat appointed a very junior official to 'liaise' with all Commonwealth bodies. While this may have been helpful to the smaller Commonwealth CSOs, it was hardly the kind of person who I or my Board members, comprising senior mayors and ministers of cabinet rank, would wish to go through in our dealings with the Secretariat. I therefore continued to ensure direct access to the Secretary-General and senior staff.

It took a number of further CHOGMs decisions, which I lobbied for, to effect change in our work with the Secretariat. The 2011 Eminent

Persons' Group, which had reviewed the Secretariat's work, called for better collaboration between the work of the Secretariat and other Commonwealth organisations. This was endorsed by CHOGM and led to the Secretariat discontinuing its local government work in recognition that this was the responsibility of CLGF.

On occasions we partnered or collaborated with specific Commonwealth bodies such as the Commonwealth Foundation, CPA, CAPAM, Commonwealth Telecommunications Organisation (CTO) as well as the Commonwealth Business Council (CBC; later the Commonwealth Enterprise and Investment Council), the Commonwealth Association of Planners (CAP), the Commonwealth Human Rights Initiative, the Commonwealth Human Ecology Council (CHEC), the Royal Commonwealth Society (RCS) and the Commonwealth Round Table.

Apart from the Secretariat, CLGF partnered with a range of Commonwealth national development agencies These included the development agencies of the UK (DFID), Canada (CIDA, later DFAIT), Australia (AusAid, later DFAT) and New Zealand (New Zealand Aid, later MFAT). At various stages I was able to cooperate and negotiate funding for our work from all of these. DFID was the most generous, providing around £1 million in grant funding to us annually, subject to strict programme evaluations which we generally passed with flying colours.

In addition, I had to cultivate leading London-based High Commissioners and their staff. This was not an easy task given the numbers involved and the constant change in personnel. Happily being invited to Secretariat and High Commission receptions provided an opportunity of doing some serious networking – while avoiding drinking too many cocktails.

Occasionally some funny things happened. I recall a CLGF reception in London being addressed by the Commonwealth Deputy Secretary-General. Unfortunately, the speech he was reading from came into proximity with a lit candle on the table next to him. Suddenly the bottom of his papers started emitting ominous dark smoke, yet unaware of this, he ploughed on with his address. It needed a glass of wine held by one of the adjacent High Commissioners to quickly douse the incipient flames. This incident caused great merriment among the London diplomatic corps.

Throughout this time, I continued close policy engagement with the EU, especially the European Commission and DEVCO – its Directorate-

General for Development which had a small department dedicated to working with local authorities and NGOs. This bore fruit in diverse places like Africa, the Caribbean and the Pacific (ACP) where the EU has a long-term partnership under the EU-ACP Cotonou Agreement, 2000-2020. Here I linked up with Jean Bossuyt of the influential European Centre for Development Policy and Management (ECDPM) and Jean-Pierre Mbassi of the Africa section of United Cities and Local Government, UCLG, to ensure that when the Cotonou Agreement was reviewed in 2005, local government was formally included as 'state actor' under article 4 and eligible for funding.

I discovered that central governments in ACP countries are generally opposed to having their local governments access overseas donor funds directly, especially if the latter are controlled by an opposing political party. They were more relaxed about seeing these funds channelled through a Commonwealth organisation like CLGF, especially given that their government was already a member of CLGF through the local government ministry, and providing they were fully consulted. This gave us some leverage, also with the EU.

Accessing EU support is linked to much advocacy and lobbying with frequent visits to Brussels. Ultimately it is about being able to influence EU policy and being accepted as a partner, not just about receiving money. I recall in the lead-up to our 2015 EU partnership agreement working hard to secure high level political endorsement of a ground-breaking EU Communication on Empowering Local Authorities, agreed in 2013. This involved my flying to Dublin to meet the Irish minister of development policy who was at that time chairing the EU Council on Development and getting his support. I was also able to get the Commission to attend the 2013 CLGF Conference in Kampala and use the occasion to officially announce the new EU Communication.

It was a similar story with the United Nations Development Programme, UNDP, where I was able to cultivate our partnership. This was made easier when Helen Clark, the former New Zealand Prime Minister who had hosted us in Auckland in 2007, took over the top post of UNDP Administrator in New York. My advocacy and Helen's support resulted in signing a formal MOU of cooperation between CLGF and UNDP which bore fruit especially in our work in Africa. While UNDP funds rarely went through us directly, we were able to partner in some highly strategic joint activities and contribute to important UNDP policy initiatives.

Helen, as our CLGF Patron, made a point of attending all our CLGF conferences between 2011 and 2017 and we became good friends. She and her husband Peter stayed with us at our home in Mill House in Kent in 2017 and I arranged for her to be the keynote speaker at the annual UN Peace Service held at Canterbury's historic cathedral that year which she enjoyed. Sadly, she was unsuccessful in her bid to become UN Secretary-General, where I am sure she would have made a first-rate leader of the organisation. Helen continues to play a prominent international role in many capacities, and I hold her razor sharp intellect and political know-how, which I have witnessed on numerous occasions, in the highest respect.

Other UN agencies which CLGF partnered with were the UN Department of Economic and Social Affairs, UN-Habitat and the UN Capital Development Fund, UNCDF. UN Habitat has a sizeable staff, devoted to dealing with issues relating to urban development including housing; it is located in beautiful green gardens on the outskirts of Nairobi in one of the nicest working environments I have seen.

For a while CLGF working in partnership with other Commonwealth organisations under the umbrella of *Comhabitat,* set up to engage with UN Habitat and link with Commonwealth ministers meeting in Nairobi. I attended a number of the big UN Habitat conferences in places like Istanbul, Vancouver and Naples, but found that these were frankly too massive to allow effective interactions, bringing together as they did thousands of participants, many from the non-governmental sector rather than local government.

In our work I ensured we partnered with like-minded local government bodies, notably the International Union of Local Authorities (IULA), headquartered in The Hague, and some of its individual members such as the Dutch local government association. The Dutch had a strong international department headed by the experienced Peter Knap with whom I later jointly visited the Philippines. In fact, we took advantage of the global IULA Congress being held in The Hague in 1995 to convene our first CLGF General Meeting of members there, and for a while continued to hold such meetings on its fringes as many of our own members were in attendance. I guess the quaint guild houses and waterways of this old Dutch city provided an odd venue for the founding event of a new Commonwealth body.

Relations with IULA, which was strongly Anglophone in membership, were close, but later IULA merged with the separate mainly francophone

United Cities to form UCLG – United Cities and Local Governments and relocated to Barcelona. UCLG was headed initially by a French Secretary-General, Elizabeth Gateau; its important African section was also headed by the francophone Jean-Pierre Elong Mbassi. Problems were especially acute in Africa, where there was continuing tension among its anglophone (mostly Commonwealth) and francophone UCLG members. Here CLGF was often perceived as a rival, including in securing external partner funding. As a result, owing to the new UCLG wanting to assert itself globally, relations got less cordial.

After a while and with more cooperative UCLG staff, these difficulties subsided. I was able to ensure that CLGF and UCLG cooperated for our common aims, whether at political level at the UN, through a Global Task Force, or in seeking funding from bodies like the EU. This involved visits to Barcelona and attending key UCLG meetings, working with senior UCLG staff like the highly competent Emilia Saiz, who is now UCLG Secretary-General. I also good links with Frederic Vallier, Secretary-General of the Council of European Municipalities and Regions, which under his leadership played an important role within the EU. I further attended various regional events like Africities, held in a range of different African locations like Johannesburg and Dakar.

Cooperation between Commonwealth and like-minded global organisations is not only sensible and avoids unnecessary duplication and harmful rivalry, it ensures more impact in political advocacy, whether with the UN, the EU or other intergovernmental bodies. It further opens the door for jointly attracting vital external funding, as donors do not like being faced with competing rival organisations.

I was always on the lookout for new partners. I was hopeful of forging closer links with local government in the Irish Republic, which had been a Commonwealth member until 1949, albeit when it was still the British Commonwealth. Many in the country had not caught up that the 'British' Commonwealth no longer existed, and I had to dispel this misconception on my visits to Dublin – and indeed sometimes at events in the UK.

An opportunity occurred in 2014 when I managed to get the Lord Mayor of Dublin to host a CLGF event. I can genuinely claim that this was the first Commonwealth meeting which has ever taken place in the Irish Republic. It was held in the prestigious venue of Dublin's Mansion House, site of the first Irish Dail (Parliament) in the 1920s, a highly symbolic place for Irish nationalists.

The Dublin event was a meeting of CLGF European members and brought together our members from the UK, including the devolved Governments of Scotland and Wales, and from Cyprus, Malta and Gibraltar. Significantly, there were representatives from Northern Ireland, the (then) Sinn Fein Mayor of Belfast and a senior Ulster Unionist local government leader. Apart from the Lord Mayor of Dublin, we also had top representatives of political parties from the Irish Republic, not least the *Tanaiste*, the Irish Deputy Prime Minister, who addressed us.

The meeting was a resounding success and contributed towards the later establishment of a Dublin branch of the Royal Commonwealth Society, which I attended, travelling to Dublin with the RCS President, Lord Howell, for its launch. These initiatives need follow-up, ideally resulting in a return of the Irish Republic to the Commonwealth, with which it has so much potential political alignment.

Many of these meetings had their moments. At the 1999 CHOGM in Durban, South Africa. I wanted to present a retirement gift to outgoing Commonwealth Secretary-General Chief Anyaoku to thank him for all his support. This gift turned out to be a limited-edition sketch of *Madiba* – Nelson Mandela – by a famous South African artist, acquired locally and which for some unknown reason was set in a large picture frame.

I and my then CLGF chairperson, UK councillor Len Duvall, were carrying this rather big object up the driveway to the Hilton Hotel, where the Chief and many VIPs were staying. On approaching the Hilton, we were stopped by a stern Black policewoman, who demanded to view what we were carrying. On seeing it was a sketch of *Madiba*, she spontaneously snatched the portrait from us and in sheer delight kissed it on the lips. Truly a symbol of the deep affection in which Nelson Mandela was – and still is – held by his people.

I discovered networking and partnerships are as vital at international level as elsewhere.

27

Advocacy for Local Democracy

TO MY DELIGHT, MY WORK IN SUPPORT OF LOCAL DEMOCRACY brought me back into contact with grass roots politics. It provided a powerful vehicle to promote the kind of people empowerment I have always believed in.

Local democracy had, by the year 2000, taken on real significance throughout the world. Following the conclusion of the Cold War and the move away from centralised government command economies, public sector reform programmes had been initiated in many countries. Governments increasingly decentralised services and functions from central administrations and ministries to local government where there was a closer link to the people. Similarly, the transition of highly centralised One-party structures to multi-party democracy frequently entailed a rediscovery of democracy at local level and the holding of democratic local elections for the first time, especially in Africa. However, I found that the process of establishing local democracy on the ground was a lengthy one.

I was always clear that the drive to reduce poverty and to ensure basic services to the community cannot be undertaken only by the private sector or by civil society organisations; a minimum of governmental infrastructure, funding and direction is essential. Arguably the most effective system for this is democratic local government, led by elected grass roots politicians in touch with and responsible to their local communities. This in turn requires local transparency and accountability and the enforcement of high standards of ethics among mayors and local elected representatives, as well as among paid council officials. Such standards are not guaranteed and need to be worked at and encouraged.

I believe that effective local democracy and decentralised, inclusive, institutions with efficient delivery of basic services to the community are vital for achieving successful developmental strategies; they form the building blocks of true participatory democracy. In consequence, one of my early achievements was to get the Commonwealth Secretariat to publish a pamphlet setting out the importance of local democracy. The ongoing struggle to achieve local democracy and the persistence of fragile and failing states, of economic, and of political and religious fundamentalism, demonstrates yet again that history is far from over and can never really end.

A significant part of my political advocacy for local democracy and local campaigning entailed election observation. This involved taking part in or contributing to Commonwealth election observer teams across the world. However, election observation is really a quite small part of the day-to-day work to support democracy. I was also involved many other international political initiatives. Here the unique membership structure of CLGF, embracing both local and central government, proved to be of much advantage. Not only did it give us entry points where NGOs might have been shut out, but on quite a number of occasions I was able to deploy senior Board members, both mayors and ministers, to apply peer pressure on their counterparts in the countries we were concerned about.

The other comparative advantage enjoyed by CLGF is being part of the Commonwealth network and having close working links with the Commonwealth Secretariat. For example, at one meeting of foreign ministers under the Commonwealth Ministerial Action Group, CMAG, CLGF submitted a report on local government developments in Fiji, Pakistan, the Solomon Islands and Zimbabwe, highlighting areas of concern. We were then able to follow-up various practical actions to address our concerns in collaboration with the Secretariat.

In 2005, I drafted and oversaw approval of the Commonwealth *Aberdeen Principles on Good Practice for Local Democracy and Good Governance* which has become a landmark policy document. These cover constitutional and legal recognition of local government, the ability to elect local representatives, accountable, transparent and inclusive government and much more. The *Principles* provide a key political reference point in those instances where governments, having previously endorsed them, deviated from them, for example by not holding the regular democratic local election stipulated.

Following adoption by our conference and members in Aberdeen in the presence of the inspirational Archbishop Desmond Tutu, we got the *Principles* formally endorsed by Heads of Government at the 2005 CHOGM. This gave them a high-level political status; I was also able to have them incorporated into the *Commonwealth Charter* some years later. As a result, many of our members implemented the *Principles* in practical policy measures and in some cases, through national legislation in their respective countries. I was later able to work with the Commonwealth Secretariat in undertaking reviews on how the *Principles* were being implemented on the ground in countries such as Pakistan, Rwanda and Uganda.

An example of advocacy on local democracy involved South Africa. Following the democratic elections of 1994 much needed to be done to consolidate local government and ensure it was operating on a fully non-racial basis. During this time, I travelled to the country many times and attended the founding congress of the South African Local Government Association, SALGA, which was addressed by Nelson Mandela. I also organised for Commonwealth experts to visit and advise, and was able to assist the process of having local government entrenched in the new South Africa constitution, something we also encouraged in other countries. This was to lead to the ground-breaking innovation of having local government defined as 'sphere' of government, not just a 'level', thereby implying equal recognition of its role alongside central and provincial spheres of government. Having such formal constitutional recognition made it difficult for central governments to ignore or dissolve local government.

We were also much engaged with Malawi. Here local elections had been suspended in contravention of the *Aberdeen Principles*. I engaged in a variety of non-antagonistic ways, organising visits for Malawi MPs to neighbouring countries like Uganda and Zambia to have them look at working systems of local democracy, sending consultants to the country to advise on local government issues and funding the Malawi local government association. With support from the Scottish Government, I also provided external technical expertise to improve local government services through city twinning with UK counterparts and by organising policy events inside the country.

I repeatedly met senior Malawi ministers, including at CHOGMs, to try and persuade them to re-instigate local democracy in the country. It was only with much Commonwealth Secretariat engagement and marshalling peer pressure from neighbouring countries like Zambia, that we were finally able to get the Malawi government to restore elected local government through democratic local elections. This was an important advocacy success for CLGF.

Establishing democratic local government in The Maldives was another political advocacy I undertook in support of the *Aberdeen Principles*. These beautiful islands, mostly tiny atolls, are just above sea level and stretch over a thousand miles along the deep blue Indian Ocean. It makes absolute sense for a local community in one of the islands to provide local services to its population or to take basic decisions, like building a new fishing jetty, without having to refer this for approval to the capital Malé, hundreds of miles away. Hence the case for having decentralised and democratically empowered local government even in a small island state like The Maldives.

The country had suffered from lack of democracy and authoritarian rule for many years. At our 2007 Auckland conference, a progressively minded minister, Mohamed Deen, attended and asked me to help set up a system of democratic local government. Following a number of visits and working with the local UNDP office, I was able successfully to do this, cumulating in democratic local elections being held, monitored and endorsed by a joint CLGF/Commonwealth Secretariat election observer team led by our Chairperson Zenaida Moya.

One of my fond memories of The Maldives was being invited for a very special dinner by a later minister of local government. I assumed this would be at a local restaurant. However, on meeting up at the minister's office in Male we walked a few metres to the nearby seafront and boarded his personal yacht. We were then whisked to a tiny tropical island not far away. This seemed quite deserted apart from a formal table laid out with a sumptuous dinner on the beautiful sandy beach where we had moored. Quite an exclusive occasion.

Around this time democratic national elections also took place in The Maldives. This resulted in the coming to power of dynamic young President Mohamed Nasheed, who had been imprisoned under the previous regime and had been an Amnesty Prisoner of Conscience. One of the key issues Nasheed championed was action on climate change, given that pretty well all of his country would disappear under the waves if there was even minimal global warming. One of his great stunts, loved by the international media, was to hold a meeting of his cabinet underwater to draw attention to the issue of climate change. When I met him in his office in Malé, I asked how they had been able to communicate with each other underwater. With a smile he replied, "Ah, Mr Wright, we all learnt sign language."

President Naheed impressed me at a Commonwealth meeting when he was asked by the press if supporting development was more important than supporting democracy. This is a highly topical issue within the Commonwealth where the developed countries like the UK have sought to focus on the latter, including human and LGBT rights, while developing countries have expressed their preference for the former. He provided the perfect answer, saying that one was dependent on the other, giving his own example of having been a political prisoner and only being able to pursue his developmental goals such as climate action on his release once democracy had prevailed. In other words, democracy and development are totally interdependent. Unfortunately, I am not sure if all Commonwealth countries have really understood this.

Disappointingly, the democratic tenure of Nasheed did not last long. He was brutally ousted from office in what was to all intents a *coup d'etat* and marched from his office at gunpoint. He was then denied regaining a democratic mandate in highly dubious elections which were basically re-run until his political opponents got their hands onto power. Once in charge, the new regime proceeded to harass and arrest political opponents including Nasheed who was only freed after much international pressure and allowed to go abroad in exile. The same tactics were deployed against local government leaders aligned to Nasheed's party, including the Mayor of Malé. Even the local government minister, who had been a member of the CLGF Board, fell foul of the regime and was imprisoned.

These developments led me to adopt a dual strategy: staying in close contact with local government colleagues in Malé and providing as much support to them as feasible, including by sponsoring them to attend relevant CLGF events; and urging the Secretariat and Commonwealth Governments to pressurise the regime to relent its persecution of opponents.

On a number of occasions, Commonwealth and the UN sought to apply pressure and offered to mediate. They were to my mind not forceful enough. India, which as the adjoining regional power, could have easily intervened, was concerned about driving its strategically located neighbour into the arms of China, its geopolitical rival. There was also the danger of strengthening local Islamic fundamentalism. This led to the temporary departure of the Maldives from the Commonwealth, but it was readmitted again after the previous regime was voted out of office in democratic elections.

The situation in Zimbabwe which has now been out of the Commonwealth since in 2003, nearly twenty years, remains more complex. Despite this, I ensured that CLGF engaged in support of local democracy in the country throughout this time, which kept the flame of democracy alive, although it often flicked weakly. The events in 2018, when the Mugabe government was ousted, have opened the door back to democracy but there have also been backward steps since. The resumption of Commonwealth membership by Zimbabwe will require a clear indication that human rights and democratic norms are again in place.

As with Zimbabwe, I felt that CLGF should reach out to countries currently not Commonwealth members, but which might want to join. I undertook what I felt were ground-breaking missions to South Sudan in 2011 and Myanmar in 2012, designed to initiate support for local democracy and inclusive governance in those countries and encourage their interaction with CLGF and the Commonwealth.

When I visited Juba, the capital, South Sudan had just got its independence and had not yet disintegrated into internal strife. It had expressed an interest in Commonwealth membership and during the 2011 CHOGM in Perth I had been instrumental in helping to draft a sentence to this effect for inclusion in the official CHOGM statement. Juba and the country were desperately poor, with only one good, tarred road in the capital. It struck me that what was needed was a system of decentralised local governance, charged to provide effective local services. I was able to secure some small EU resources for an initial programme and benefitted from generous expert support from neighbouring Uganda, but the work was cut short by the erupting internal conflict in the country.

As often, the visit had some lighter moments. In the departure lounge of Juba airport, itself a glorified aircraft hangar, I discovered I needed to go back to the check-in desk to get a departure stamp in my passport prior to boarding. Returning via a non-existing security control, I found there was nobody present at the check-in desk. However, I soon realised I could simply stamp the passport myself, using the materials left conveniently on the desk, as other would-be passengers were doing.

Myanmar – or Burma – had been a British colony. Unlike her neighbours, it had never joined the Commonwealth and had languished under military rule for many years. My fact-finding mission to its capital Yangon was in anticipation of forthcoming democratic elections and to explore what support could be given to establish democratic local government structures. I had previously met with representatives of Aung San Suu Kyi's National League for Democracy, NLD, in London and had arranged for them to be sponsored to participate in a recent CLGF Asian event in Sri Lanka. This gave me political credibility.

I now saw a chance of getting the country to learn from Commonwealth democratic practices and was hoping to bring expertise from India as well as South Africa, drawing on the latter's experience of achieving democratic transition in 1994-95. Travelling to Yangon with its gleaming golden domed pagodas and orange robed Buddhist monks, I met with NLD and other key political representatives, as well as the UK Embassy and UNDP. I got endorsement for my ideas at my subsequent 2012 Board Meeting in Belize – including from the senior Indian minister attending – and I subsequently arranged for CLGF staff members to visit the country to try to develop a programme; I also later briefly met Aung San Suu Kyi herself in London.

Regretfully, my initiative was stifled by lack of funds and donors already having developed their own programmes. It was also a shame that the Commonwealth as a whole did not show more interest. I sometimes wonder if there had been real progress in setting up democratic local structures whether the persecution of the Rohingya Muslims in Rakhine State would have been as acute. However, I am probably underestimating the extent to which the military still pulled the strings, even after Aung San Suu Kyi became Prime Minister. The latest brutal military takeover and imprisonment of Aung San Suu Kyi shows just how fragile the embryonic structures had been and calls for determined concerted international action to help restore democracy.

I was to initiate collaboration with the Commonwealth Secretariat in a number of important political ventures to promote local democracy. These included the monitoring of local elections in Nigeria in 1999 and in Pakistan in 2000/2001, both of which I participated in.

Nigeria undertook a complex election process for its transition to democracy, starting with local government elections in December 1998, followed by State and Federal elections in 1999. I and several local government colleagues including the Mayor of Cape Town and Sandra Pepera from the Commonwealth Secretariat – whose daughters attended Adele's dance school – were part of our Commonwealth monitoring team for the local elections. After a few days in the opulent surroundings of the Lagos Sheraton, we soon came down to earth in a run-down hotel in downtown Ibadan, in a politically volatile area.

The local elections were remarkably well organised and overall passed off fairly peacefully. What was less peaceful was not so much political violence, as ongoing mob violence. During three days in Ibadan, I witnessed several attempted mob lynchings. On one occasion, we were just a few metres away from an angry crowd. They were about to beat a young man, probably a petty criminal who had been caught, to death. Luckily for him, our female police escort intervened and dispersed the crowd with a bullwhip she carried. Our presence saved the young man's life.

As we sped on the motorway, I was stunned to see drivers using the four-lane expressway like two parallel roads with oncoming traffic on both sides instead of sticking to one side or the other. Even more shocking was the sight of corpses lying next to crashed motor cars. Our driver cheerfully remarked that he had seen them there a few days earlier.

Nigeria has an endemic problem with violence and can at times be a little chaotic, although it is not the only place in the world in this respect. On my frequent visits to the country, mostly to the capital Abuja, I was lucky to be met off the plane by a government official. I was then escorted to the VIP lounge and had all entry formalities and transport to my hotel taken care of; the same happened on my departure.

Occasionally things would go wrong. I remember being in a posh government car speeding to the city from the airport when the vehicle broke down. My accompanying officials, to their great embarrassment, had to flag down a decrepit old taxi and transfer me and my luggage into this.

Another time, I was in a smart government Mercedes in the centre of Abuja around noon when we got stuck in traffic. Suddenly, my car door was flung open – it was not locked – and an AK-47 rifle was pointed a few inches from my stomach. A Nigerian soldier demanded a bribe to allow us to proceed. This is when things really got dangerous. My accompanying government minder was outraged. He started shouting at the guy whose fingers looked twitchy on his gun. I was all set to give the soldier whatever dollars he wanted, rather than die a hero, but fortunately he backed away.

There was a further occasion during the 2003 CHOGM in Abuja, when I and my Chairperson Len Duvall were accommodated in a shambolic hotel which had just re-opened after renovation. The renovation was very much ongoing. On our first night, the room was only equipped with a bed and basic furnishings, the second day other artefacts arrived, and the third day we got a fridge. The last day, just as we were leaving, a TV arrived, but there was no discount at the checkout.

Nigeria also has problems around corruption, often at the highest levels of government, although it is again not unique in this. A troublesome incident happened after another visit to Abuja. I had met the federal minister to ensure that membership fees owing to us by his government would be transferred on my return to London. Back in my office I received a fax on official letterhead apparently from the Nigerian Auditor-General wanting to pay the money onto our account. I was suspicious as he was asking for full bank account details, which had already been provided. When I got my PA to check the matter, it turned out it was indeed a scam, clearly involving someone privy to my private conversation with the minister and wanting to access our account to siphon off funds.

Yet it is worth emphasising that Nigeria also has a highly vibrant, cultured and politically diverse society with a vigorous media, academia and civil society, including wonderful writers and artists and journalists. Its size, diverse ethnic and religious groups and large population make it difficult to govern. As always, colonial legacies and current commercial structures – many having their origin in the UK – hold much responsibility for many of the problems faced by the country since independence. Nowhere is this more the case than with the country's great oil wealth which foreign companies have exploited, encouraging bribery and corrupt practices in the process.

My other election observation experience around this time, together with another Secretariat colleague, Chris Child, was in Pakistan. The election was held on New Years' Eve 2000 which involved travelling immediately after Christmas, and as so often curtailing my holidays, something Adele was not pleased about.

The security situation had become a lot worse in the country since my last election observation there in the early 1990s, so this time a full-time bodyguard was assigned to me. He was armed and accompanied me everywhere, even sitting outside my posh Islamabad hotel bedroom door all night.

This resulted in a funny incident when I wanted to leave the hotel and cross the street to a shop selling leather goods, which I had previously visited. My bodyguard insisted that I wait. Suddenly a whole contingent of heavily armed Pakistani soldiers arrived with AK-47s at the ready. They then escorted me across the road to the shop. To my embarrassment, the poor shopkeeper was so intimidated that I did not have to haggle over price but got a really good deal straight away.

Election day in Pakistan was spent far away from the capital in Punjab, near the town of Multan – the furthest place Alexander the Great managed to reach in his excursion into Asia in 325 BC. All day we experienced strong winds and driving rain. This produced thick mud everywhere, at times threatening to get our vehicle stuck on the road. It was a miserable occasion.

Trudging around as many polling stations as we could manage, we checked correct ballot procedures, met with returning officers and party-political representatives and watched if the public was able to vote fairly and freely. As always, we were under strict instructions to only observe and merely note any incidents – of which there were none – but not to intervene ourselves. We then went to a local polling station in the middle of nowhere to await the announcement of the results at one of the polls and make sure all was done correctly. This took us late into the night.

Arriving exhausted back at our hotel at the stroke of midnight, I had hoped to see in the New Year of 2001 with a beer. However, despite staying at a Holiday Inn, no alcohol was on offer, even to foreigners, and the best we could do was Coca-Cola. The only excitement happened at 3am when the fire bell suddenly sounded, and we were dramatically evacuated from our rooms – it was a false alarm. This was certainly seeing in the New Year with a difference. On our return journey to the capital, Islamabad, we had a bonus stop to see fascinating ancient ruins of Bronze Age Indus Valley peoples. These dated back to around 3,000 BC – long before Alexander the Great – and were a stark reminder that Europe is not the only cradle of global civilisation.

Pakistan was to be a key focus of our ongoing work to build local democracy and had many ups and downs, with democratic local government being dissolved and then finally, in part thanks to the CLGF's advocacy, being fully restored. During this time, we organised a series of events in the country, drawing on experts from Canada, South Africa and elsewhere and marshalling support to the umbrella Punjab local councils association.

Building local democracy is hard work and is no short-term project.

28.

Knowledge-sharing and Good Practices

AN IMPORTANT PART OF THE CLGF'S MANDATE IS TO SHARE knowledge and transfer local government good practices. This requires practical exchanges of policies.

I have always resisted the idea that developing countries should be instructed by developed countries like the UK, Australia or Canada. In fact, most learning should be among developing countries themselves, as they have more in common with each other. I feel that highly top-down British system of local government, with excessive financial and other powers controlled by Whitehall, is not at all a model to be emulated elsewhere. On most occasions I therefore deployed experts from other developing countries – Ghanaians advising Sierra Leone, Trinidadians advising Belize, South Africans advising Pakistan and so forth.

Developed countries can also learn from developing countries. The South African Local Government Association, led for many years by its savvy chief executive Xolie George, has much to teach others. In the late 1990s I organised for UK local government minister Hilary Armstrong to visit South Africa. As a result, she picked up interesting South African practices, which I understood subsequently found their way into British local government legislation. Here was an example how Commonwealth interaction can have beneficial and result in practical policy reforms.

This has not changed. At the CLGF Board meeting in Kigali in 2018, our British colleagues were astounded by the many progressive social measures in place in Rwanda. These were ahead of what they had at home in the UK, for example banning all plastic shopping bags and organising car-free Sundays. Clearly, Africa and other parts of the developing world can teach the older developed Commonwealth countries a thing or two.

As a key strategic aim, I sought to encourage the Commonwealth-wide adoption of inclusive public sector policies. These should promote local democracy and seek genuine decentralisation in line with the

Aberdeen Principles. Such policies had to include fiscal decentralisation, as having powers without resources cannot achieve much. I promoted this not in an academic way, but through addressing topical issues and policies and then having our members, both local governments and ministries, adopt them at home through their own practices or legislation.

I was able to achieve this by bringing together thousands of key stakeholders and policy makers, mayors, ministers and senior officials at high-level events. This initially involved a number of regional symposia for senior policymakers between 1995-2000 in a wide range of locations including Harare, Islamabad and Port Moresby. In addition, we held specialised regional workshops on subjects like the role of traditional leaders in Botswana, local government training policy in Kenya, and local government in small states in Malta.

We also organised regional events in Africa, the Caribbean and Asia-Pacific on enhancing the status of women in local government – not only electing more women councillors but supporting them once elected and encouraging women to take office, such as becoming mayors. Later examples of more specialised CLGF events included local democracy and good governance, in Suva, 2004; better local services in Kuala Lumpur, 2005; innovations in municipal infrastructure, Vancouver in 2008; and access to development funding, Johannesburg, also 2008.

We held at least one Board meeting in a different venue each year, hosted by local members. This soon became a mini conference with fifty or more high-level participants across the world at venues as far apart as Belize City, Kingston, Vancouver, Abuja, New Delhi and, of course, London. One of my less fortunate early choices was Nassau in The Bahamas during the hurricane season. This was marked by a palm tree crashing across the hotel's swimming pool, much to the dismay of our Board members who had not envisaged their exotic Caribbean trip being quite like that.

Another bizarre story happened at a Board meeting in Delhi. At the end of our meeting our Indian hosts had taken Board members on a trip to see the Taj Mahal. Unfortunately, on the bus coming back our South African female Board member was bitten by a rat which was running loose. On return to the hotel, I quickly called for a doctor to give her a tetanus shot. Waiting for medical attention the first knock on the door was from a tailor wanting to deliver a ready-made suit. Eventually the doctor arrived but threatened to go into a long discussion about whether the bite was from a rural or an urban rat. I just told him to get on with it.

In fact, this was not so serious as a later Board meeting, also in Delhi, where virtually the entire Board apart from myself went down with a serious case of food poisoning – the so-called 'Delhi belly'. Clearly CLGF meetings had their dangers.

Once every two years I organised our statutory General Meeting of members during our main CLGF conferences; these approved our reports, accounts and elected the new Board. Initially, Board places were relatively uncontested but as the organisation developed and grew in stature, the competition for places grew. One occasion I had to stop two senior African ministers coming to physical blows arguing over who should sit on the Board. The issue was only resolved by getting the ministers to consult their respective capitals overnight and bartering a compromise between them the next day.

Our Board members were high-level politicians who proved to be invaluable supporters for our young organisation. A good deal of my time was spent staying in close touch with them and briefing and consulting them on important developments. The Board meetings were always carefully prepared with detailed policy papers for members to consider. Occasionally we had a controversial Board member. Minister Dhanraj Singh from Trinidad was known as 'The Sheriff'. In 1998, he had his firearm taken by the police and was subsequently arrested for the alleged murder of a local government chairman. As a result, we agreed a code of conduct for all our Board members to which they had to subscribe.

Our initial meetings had 'piggy-backed' onto other international events, like the congresses of IULA. However, we soon felt the need to organise our own stand-alone Commonwealth Local Government conferences. These rapidly grew in size and importance and soon we were attracting 500-600 top government policy makers. Typically, these included dozens of city mayors and up to twenty or thirty national ministers. Quite soon, CLGF conferences had established themselves as a prime international event for local government globally and attracted stakeholders such as development partners from the UN, DFID and EU, the private sector and academics interested in local government studies. Our conferences were relatively unique as most other global events tended to be either intergovernmental or, alternatively, local government, in nature, whereas CLGF, drawing on its mixed membership, managed to combine both.

The first of these new-style CLGF conferences took place in 2000 in London, co-hosted by the recently elected Mayor of London, Ken

Livingstone, and the Government of Tony Blair. The latter had just created the new office of directly elected mayor for London, alongside an elected London Assembly. While our conference was a success, it took place at a strange moment in time when there was a temporary oil and energy supply crisis in the UK. This interrupted travel and at one stage it looked like we might not be able to get our delegates to move around London, but we succeeded including to enjoy a splendid dinner at the Mansion House in the City.

There was a little local difficulty in that Mayor Livingstone had been elected as an independent candidate, in opposition to the ruling Labour Party. This put him in conflict with the Labour Government's Deputy Prime Minister, John Prescott, who was addressing the conference.

John Prescott was known as 'Two Jags John' on account of his love for Jaguar cars, whereas Livingstone in contrast made a point of travelling on public transport. On this occasion roles were reversed. Prescott was taking public transport owing to the oil supply crisis, while the mayor had an official car, which had just whisked him in from London City Airport. A funny scene ensued on the steps of the conference hall in Canary Wharf on their departure. Livingstone offered to give Prescott a lift back to Parliament in his car, but 'Two Jags John' determinedly refused the offer, stating firmly that he was taking the Underground. The story caused quite some amusement in political circles.

My next big event was timed to precede the CHOGM planned for 2001 in Brisbane. All arrangements had been made and air tickets issued to delegates. I had, however, not anticipated the 9/11 terrorist attack. This happened just before our conference and threw all plans into confusion and the CHOGM itself was delayed until 2002.

Postponing our own Brisbane event would have incurred major financial losses and presented organisational difficulties; luckily most delegates had already made their travel plans. I vividly remember being in Australia in the week before the conference and spending most of the three-hour car journey between Canberra and Sydney on my mobile phone to all corners of the globe, urging delegates to attend. Although my phone bill was high, I was successful in getting a 90 per cent turnout at a time when fears of further airborne terrorist attacks was preventing much business travel.

Thereafter, I oversaw successful conferences in Tshwane/Pretoria (2003); Aberdeen (2005); Auckland (2007); Freeport (2009); Cardiff (2011); Kamala (2013) and Gaborone (2015). The 2015 conference had originally been confirmed for New Delhi but had to be abandoned owing to the 2015 Indian election. Happily, I got Botswana to step in at short notice and they facilitated an excellent event.

In selecting venues, we encouraged our members to formally bid to host us and generally received good bids which allowed us to pick the best offer. Each bid involved political considerations about how the event could benefit the local governments hosting us. We also tried to encourage events in different regions of the world. Finances of course also played a key role and we ensured that hosting governments underwrote the conferences, as well as attracting private sector sponsors.

Our conferences attracted heads of government and big names like Archbishop Desmond Tutu in 2005. Tutu was a truly wonderful man who had the amazing humility to write to me after the event thanking me for inviting him. In fact, we were the ones honoured by his presence. Other keynote speakers included Professor Jeffrey Sachs in 1997, and successive Commonwealth Secretaries-General, including Don McKinnon, Kamalesh Sharma and Patricia Scotland, and Helen Clark, as well as other leading UN and EU officials. In 2015, I was also able to arrange for a special video message from HRH the Prince of Wales with whom I had met in advance.

Each conference had a particular political or economic theme relating to local government. For example, our 2005 conference, which adopted the *Aberdeen Principles*, focused on promotion of local democracy and good governance. In 2011, we looked at local economic development strategies, approving the *Cardiff Consensus for Local Economic Development*. Given the ongoing UN negotiations on what became the SDGs, our 2013 and 2015 conferences placed major emphasis on the local government role in sustainable development.

My own role as conference secretary was incredibly tough, overseeing logistics and finances, but above all the VIP protocol and negotiation of sometimes controversial conference statements. If that was not enough, I had to fit in many bilateral meetings with ministers, mayors and development partners present and ensure that the accompanying CLGF Board and the statutory meetings of members went smoothly, not least the often quite hotly contested board elections. There was certainly little time for socialising apart from the formal dinners and receptions; and the events left me pretty exhausted. Luckily, I had hard-working staff to support me who I often had to chase out of our office at 10pm in the days preceding our events, and who worked into the early hours during the conference. Of course, it also helped that I had prior experience in how such events need to run from my work at the UN and elsewhere, and what mistakes to avoid.

Our conferences proved valuable and focused, with intensive policy exchanges among senior local government practitioners from central and local government and other stakeholders. But I was mindful that they should have concrete outcomes. In the first instance these outcomes were the final conference policy statements adopted. These had added weight in that in addition to local government leaders, they had been agreed by ministers and central government officials attending. This meant that there was an obligation on both mayors and ministers to seek to implement the policies agreed on their return home, which we sought to both encourage and monitor.

The official opening by the country's President or Prime Minister, with whom I and my senior Board members would meet privately, and the presence of the Commonwealth Secretary-General gave further weight to our deliberations. On several occasions I was moreover able to invite the incoming the host of the next CHOGM like the Presidents of Uganda and Sri Lanka and the Prime Minister of Malta. This all facilitated our strategy of getting the statements formally endorsed by the subsequent CHOGM, which gave them yet more political clout. This in turn would set the scene for deploying the statements in our ongoing advocacy work for promotion of local democracy and other strategic aims. It was also then reflected in our practical capacity-building programmes once I was able to raise the necessary funds.

Apart from the main conference, we incorporated a policy exchange specifically for our associate academic and professional CLGF members, usually hosted by the local university. These would allow consideration of more in-depth policy and peer reviewed papers, usually related to the overall CLGF conference theme. This discussion provided a valuable forum for our associate members. It successfully bridged the gap between academics and local government practitioners. It often led to greater domestic deployment of local academic expertise, as when Birmingham or Durban City Councils engaged their local universities to undertake studies or evaluations.

The conferences had their lighter moments too. In Tshwane, I recall that there were not many takers for local specialities offered one lunchtime – deep-fried chicken claws and what looked like slimy boiled slugs. In Aberdeen, my PA received a call from London from the fifty-strong

Nigerian delegation which had just arrived at Heathrow, enquiring which London underground line they should take to Aberdeen. At the same event we had to urgently purchase shoes for our South Pacific delegates in place of their open sandals when the Scottish snow set in.

In Auckland, I had organised a private consultation with our keynote speaker, President Museveni of Uganda and incoming CHOGM Chair. I had carefully prepared the agenda. I got more and more anxious when nearly our entire meeting with the President, who was a cattle farmer, developed into a discussion with our New Zealand colleague Basil Morrison, also a farmer, about the merits of different breeds of cattle. Time was ticking away. Happily, the President was so delighted with the subject matter of cows that at the end he readily agreed all the various proposals I had put to him.

Some years later in Kampala we had an Army tank stationed outside the conference entrance which I felt was a bit excessive security. Here it was the turn of President Museveni to open our conference. This he duly did but only after some considerable delay in arriving. Unfortunately, the local band assigned to play at the opening had a limited repertoire. We must have heard each musical number played half a dozen times until the President arrived. Gaborone went very smoothly apart from an outdoor evening reception at what was the height of the Botswana winter. Temperatures were near freezing with Helen Clark, Adele and quite a few of my staff almost catching pneumonia.

Apart from these high-level conferences and the numerous CLGF regional and national events, often linked to particular local government programmes being undertaken, we sought to disseminate information and data on good local government practices. This went to our members on a regular basis through an active communications policy. The information was to prove invaluable for many members, who used it to shape their own local government practices and legislation, in areas like municipal finances.

My professional activities and our knowledge-sharing work were made easier by the IT revolution and the vastly improved nature of international communications. Back in the 1980s, I had relied on old fashioned typewriters and a personal secretary would type letters, then post them physically by airmail. International phone calls had to go through central telephone exchanges with the operator taking for ever to connect us and were prohibitively expensive. The bills were especially costly if you called from your hotel as this involved a massive service surcharge. As a result, international communications were extremely slow and sporadic before the onset of direct dialling and the internet.

A breakthrough happened with the introduction of fax machines in the 1980s. Initially these were prized possessions. I remember working at the Commonwealth Secretariat with 400 staff sharing just one single fax machine. The procedure was for your personal Secretary to type the letter, which would be put in an out-tray on your desk. It would then be collected twice a day by an office messenger whose sole job was to physically take the letters to the main building to be faxed out. They might then come back two days later with a little note attached. This often said it had not been possible to get them out – a far cry from the instant SMS or email responses demanded by today's high-speed world.

By the 1990s and 2000s, we had the internet and our own website, instant email communications, as well as mobile phones. There is now the ability to Skype, to Zoom or deploy WhatsApp free of charge. Social media, especially Twitter, plays a growing role and after some initial struggle, I became proficient in these essential modern skills, helped by my communications staff, especially Shraddha Kaul. There, however, remained logistical problems when seeking to organise a Skype call with Board members across many time zones. It was difficult to find a common time for colleagues as far apart as New Zealand and Canada to speak together. The furthest away, usually our New Zealand friends, usually drew the short straw, having to take the call at 5am local time.

One of our successes was the online *Commonwealth Journal of Local Government* which has exceeded 100,000 downloads. However, despite the growing use of e-communications, members valued receiving our policy papers and research reports as hard copies. This was the case with our authoritative *Commonwealth Local Government Handbook* which I had initiated in 2002 with a launch by the Commonwealth Secretary-General, and which the research staff regularly updated. Although available on our website, it was published in book form every two years and provided concise country profiles of the local government systems of all fifty plus Commonwealth countries. Being quite a substantial publication and rather bulky, I was pleased to have been able to have negotiated a good deal with our publishers, UK Publications, whereby they met the entire publishing and distribution costs through commercial advertising in the handbook.

Without global knowledge-sharing, we would be re-inventing the wheel and fail to learn from others' successes and mistakes.

29.

Building Local Capacity

AT THE HEART OF OUR WORK WAS PROMOTION OF GOOD local governance. That meant ensuring efficient local services for the 2.2 billion people living in the 54 countries of the Commonwealth.

Much of the CLGF's practical work revolved around support to local governments in Africa, the Caribbean and the Asia-Pacific through programmes of institutional development and capacity-building. These programmes often entailed building-up expertise in national local government associations and to help them secure their own funding from the EU and other development partners – on the time-honoured principle of 'helping a man to fish'. We also sought to encourage international peer learning and to undertake regional and global exchanges of good practices. It was my job to identify and oversee the initiation and implementation of such programmes in consultation with our members and to find the resources to fund them. This was not an easy task.

Our work could have its dark side. I was sitting in my hotel room in Durban early evening on 20 September 2008, looking out at the calm blue waters of the Indian Ocean beyond the golden beaches of the city, when suddenly my phone rang. The message I received from London was dramatic and harrowing: there had been a massive suicide terrorist attack at the Islamabad Marriott Hotel with dozens of fatalities reported.

For a minute or two my mind numbed with horror. I had just sent my good friend and colleague Mike Ashley to Pakistan to do work for me in the country. I knew he had booked in at the Marriott. Was he at the hotel when the attack had taken place, was he injured or even worse and how could I find out?

What made my blood freeze was the recollection that only a week previously, Mike and his wife Pauline had been to my London house for dinner. Pauline had expressed concern about the security situation. I had assured her that the hotel where I always stayed and where Mike would be put up, the Islamabad Marriott, was very safe. Mike then flew off to Pakistan while I departed for South Africa. With the horrible news I had received, I now felt a terrible burden of responsibility.

I sprang into action and called UK Foreign Office and my staff in London. I finally managed to reach personal contacts in Islamabad by phone. There was total confusion. It seemed there was not a trace of Mike. I now had the difficult task of contacting Pauline who was clearly beside herself with worry. Meanwhile, I discovered that an al-Qaeda truck laden with explosives had crashed through the security barriers and had detonated. Over fifty people had died and nearly 300 were badly injured; most of these were innocent Pakistani families having an evening meal together, including women and children. Things were looking grim.

About an hour later – it seemed like an eternity – I got through to Islamabad again by phone.

To my immense relief I got the news that Mike was safe and sound, although greatly numbed and shaken up. Luckily, he had been at the back of the hotel when the explosion went off. Although not harmed himself, he had seen the devastation, the flying glass and the bloodied bodies. I then went into overdrive to get him back home to London as soon as possible. British Airways had, not very helpfully, cancelled their flights to Pakistan, but my wonderful personal assistant, Lorna Nicholas, managed to find an alternative routing to get him back home. It was a truly harrowing experience.

Not so many months later I had an invitation to go to Pakistan for a key political event.

My wife, Adele, was against my going and I was not exactly enthused after what had happened to Mike. After some hesitation and negotiation with my government hosts it was agreed I would proceed. I would be accommodated for the two days of my stay in the official government 'Green Zone' for diplomats. This was supposed to be ultra-secure.

With trepidation, I proceeded with my visit to Islamabad. At the conclusion of my first day, I was glad to be escorted to the secure surroundings of a large Government apartment inside the Green Zone. I found its entrances guarded by fierce-looking soldiers sat behind ample sandbags for protection, with machine guns poised at the ready. I seemed to be well protected from any terrorist incident.

I soon went to sleep after a long overnight flight from London and a busy day of meetings. When I woke up the next morning, I felt disorientated. In fact, I seemed to have a bad hangover. Yet, Pakistan is not a place you drink alcohol, at least not on an official visit. I became conscious of an acute smell coming from the kitchen; there was a gas leak. I got outside quickly, anxious to breathe clean air. I then realised that I could so easily have asphyxiated in my sleep. But it would have been the gas, not the terrorists, who would have got me. Not as awful as what had happened at the Marriott, but fatal nonetheless.

In the late 1990s, I initiated our *Commonwealth Local Government Good Practice Scheme.* The Scheme supported local government exchanges based on technical partnerships around a particular project activity, normally a council service such as improvement of financial management, waste management, urban safety or promotion of local economic activity. It therefore represented a development of the more informal and less focused town twinning activities of earlier years and marked joint partnership working, not just a loose exchange visit.

The Scheme was coordinated very effectively by my deputy, Lucy Slack, with support from other project staff, including those overseas. I delegated much of the work of drawing up detailed proposals and then implementing the programmes to her, although I kept an oversight of the content and helped with troubleshooting. It also usually fell to me to ensure the necessary final advocacy to secure our major long-term funds, which on occasions required personal approach to DFID ministers like Hilary Benn and using my old EU contacts in Brussels.

In the early years of the Scheme, many UK councils teamed up with counterparts in Africa, Asia and the Caribbean and a parallel scheme was set up between Australian and Papua New Guinea local government, supported by the Australian Government. As the Scheme progressed, the exchanges included 'South-South' and 'South-North-South' interactions between councils in developing and developed countries, as well as exchanges between national associations of local government on broader policy issues.

Examples of the Scheme projects included Orange (Australia) collaborating with Mount Hagen (Papua New Guinea) in drawing up a city plan; Birmingham (UK) linking with Vadodara (India) on municipal waste; Tower Hamlets (UK) cooperating with Sylhet (Bangladesh) on economic development; Torfaen (Wales) partnering with Oostenburg (South Africa) on tackling social exclusion; the Ghana LGA working with its Uganda counterpart on improving organisational capacity; and the Association of London Government assisting the Caribbean Association of Local Government Authorities to develop publicity and membership strategies. All of these had practical aims and sought tangible outcomes.

The Scheme had its amusing moments. On one occasion a group of UK councillors from Warwickshire were on their way to visit their counterparts in Bo Municipality, Sierra Leone. They had just arrived in the country and were making the sea crossing from the airport to the capital Freetown on an ex-British hovercraft now in service there. To their distress, the ageing craft suddenly deflated in mid-flight and sprung a leak. Luckily, a local fisherman spotted them and was able to tow them towards the shore. It did, however, require them to all jump into the water when they got close to dry land. I guess it could have all ended in a less funny way. The only alternative transport from the airport was a decrepit old ferry boat, which took forever, or ex Soviet army helicopters. I only took the latter once, learning that they had a nasty habit of crashing.

By 2000, some sixty Commonwealth partners were linked under the Scheme, which had been formally endorsed by Heads of Government in 1997 and 1999. At its conclusion in 2010, over 1,000 local government practitioners had been directly involved in Scheme projects and many more indirectly. It proved to be a highly successful model of decentralised cooperation between local councils or city administrations.

The UK Government, through DFID, provided a multi-million pound support for the Scheme for the best part of ten years and its strict end-of-project external evaluations always showed up the cost-effectiveness and developmental relevance of the programme. These found that the Scheme resulted in local government contributing £4 in staff time and support for every £1 made available by DFID. This meant the £1 million initially provided by DFID generated another £4 million or £5 million in total. The external DFID evaluations accordingly demonstrated the value and cost-effectiveness of our work and were in contrast to some of the critical evaluations DFID had done of the Commonwealth Secretariat's activities.

The Scheme had an important impact, raising awareness of development issues in the participating communities. I was able to obtain additional EU funds to allow us to develop special educational materials for use locally and in UK schools. Although the Scheme was local government focused, it often encouraged parallel partnerships with NGOs, schools, church groups and business, looking for investment and export opportunities. It therefore had a broad developmental education impact and made good business sense.

By its nature decentralised cooperation has the limitation of being highly localised. It is therefore restricted in its wider geographical and developmental impact in the countries concerned. In addition, in the light of the growing government austerity programmes, especially in the UK after the crash of 2008, local governments in developed countries found it increasingly difficult to release staff for overseas partnership work, even if, as was the case under the Good Practice Scheme, air fares and local costs and sometimes salaries were covered. Brexit may accentuate this trend in the UK unless it is consciously counteracted, for example by renewed city-to-city exchanges in collaboration with EU and other partner cities as is happening between Leeds, a long-standing CLGF member, and my old home city of Dortmund in Germany.

After 2010, we decided to adopt a more broad-based capacity building approach, limited to a small number of countries only, based on specific defined areas of activity such as the promotion of local economic development. Outcomes of individual projects would also be shared and disseminated nationally by the responsible local government associations and ministries which were CLGF members. This has had a bigger impact than individual development cooperation or partnership projects at council level only and was preferred by DFID and most development partners which find supporting lots of small-scale projects too cumbersome.

The Scheme-type mechanism of deploying local government expertise and peer-to-peer learning is still at the heart of this new approach, for which I and Lucy secured further DFID funds. However, it depends less on formal city-to-city or council-to-council partnerships, but a more ad hoc deployment of local government expertise according to the requirements of the programme involved.

Capacity-building work at country and regional level included a bilateral Malawi/UK partnership (1996-2000); a Caribbean training programme (1998-2000); establishing a Southern African regional local government information centre (1999-2003); local governance and democracy training for South Asia (mid 2000s); and a Pacific regional programme (2000-2016). We also partnered in other initiatives including under the African, Caribbean and Pacific Local Government Platform (ACPLGP, 2000-2014), involving a range of activities in all the different regions.

The CLGF helped to establish and fund the EU ARIAL programme in partnership with Dutch local government, designed to strengthen national local government association. It facilitated, with the help of Jamaican Prime Minister Portia Simpson-Miller, a Caribbean programme to promote economic development undertaken by our member, the Federation of Canadian Municipalities, which was launched at our Board in Belize. The CLGF further helped implement an extensive programme in Eastern and Southern Africa involving high-level regional events in Windhoek and elsewhere, supported by UNDP and the UN Capital Development Fund, UNCDF, to promote decentralisation and local governance.

With help from India, I was able to attract funding from the UN Democracy Fund to review the implementation of local democracy and good governance based on the *Aberdeen Principles* in South Asia. This involved a number of capacity-building events, working closely with national training institutes and included the production of a trainers' manual. Here India had a quite advanced system of local government and expertise through organisations like the All-India Institute of Local Self Government, but in many of it states it was still weak and often controlled by central or State government. A notable exception was Kerala which had a good decentralised system. Bangladesh, which I visited on several occasions, also faced many challenges, in part related to its divisive political structures; and while Malaysia had local government, there were no democratic elections , with mayors being appointed from above by State Governors.

Many of our capacity-building programmes were specifically targeted at strengthening the umbrella national associations of local government, given that these brought together most, if not all, local governments in a particular country and were CLGF members. We also placed a high emphasis on the training of newly elected councillors, given that there is a high turnover of councillors after each local election and many of these need basic induction training.

All these programmes made significant contributions to strengthen local government, although a few, like the ACPLGP, encountered political and staffing problems and did not prove sustainable. They required much travel by myself, Lucy and other staff to initiate and oversee the work, although our structure of regional offices allowed local implementation.

On reflection, I wonder how in all those years and many hundreds of flights, I hardly ever missed a connection. There was one occasion when I was refused check-in on a flight from Johannesburg to Luanda when South African Airways rejected point blank to accept a letter of entry, signed by the hosting Angolan minister that I had been given in lieu of the required visa. I thought the matter would be resolved when the South African minister, who I knew well, and was travelling to the same event, appeared at the airport and offered to vouch for me, but to no avail.

I had to wait 24 hours in South Africa to get a visa. I arrived in Luanda the next morning for my conference speech, then left again for London that evening. The hosting Angolan minister had dispatched a police motorcycle escort to get me through the heavy traffic from the airport quickly. This they did at terrifying speed, stopping all the traffic along the way. At one instance, a car did not get out of the way in time. To my dismay, my police escort, looking sinister in his dark glasses and black leather jackboots, got off his motorbike and kicked the 'offending' vehicle, leaving a big dent. I suppose I can be glad that he did not shoot the poor driver.

Apart from the above programmes, I was able to initiate and implement important country activities in Zimbabwe and Sri Lanka, both of which had a significant political dimension.

The Zimbabwe programme started in 2004, at the time when Robert Mugabe, stung by criticisms about election fraud and his human rights record, quit the Commonwealth. It was therefore touch and go if the programme would continue. We could however demonstrate that our work would enhance local democracy in the country and in fact much of local government in the main urban centres including Harare was run by the opposition MDC party.

The MDC was headed by Morgan Tsvangirai, who I had first known when he was heading the Zimbabwe trade unions. Our programme was to be cross-party and support also local governments in the rural areas, controlled by Mugabe's ZANU-PF party, as well as MDC-run urban councils. After high-level consultations, it was agreed to proceed, facilitated by the active involvement of Southern African partners, as well as UN Habitat. We could therefore not be accused by Mugabe of being a tool of the UK Government. On its conclusion in 2008 the programme, funded by the EU, received a highly successful external evaluation, conducted by the ECDPM.

When, in 2009, Tsvangirai and the MDC took part in a Government of National Unity to address the economic meltdown Zimbabwe was facing, there were high hopes. It looked as if the country was getting back on its feet and returning to real democracy and possibly re-joining the Commonwealth.

In London, I helped to set up and then chair a Commonwealth Organisations' Committee on Zimbabwe. This Committee sought to marshal Commonwealth support for our counterpart organisations in the country and fund scholarships for Zimbabweans. We also held a seminar in Johannesburg attended by senior Zimbabwe politicians. While the Zimbabwe economy did improve somewhat, the political situation did not, and our broader Commonwealth engagement petered out.

I had an opportunity to visit Harare around this time. I recall all too well the misery and rampant inflation; I have a hundred trillion Zimbabwe Dollar note ($100 000 000 000 000) to remind me. I am thus able to tell my friends I am now not just a millionaire or billionaire, but a trillionaire, although the hundred trillion dollars were worth less than a US dollar.

In the meantime, I continued to engage with Zimbabwean local government, as well as the dubious local government minister Ignatius Chombo, one of Mugabe's hardliners. Chombo took a dislike to me. On one occasion he had me evicted from a southern African meeting in Luanda which CLGF had sponsored. I shed no tears when political change came in 2017 and he was arrested for corruption, with vast amounts of cash and other valuables apparently found at his home.

I was pleased that shortly before I left CLGF in 2016, I was able to start another local government programme in Zimbabwe. This involved establishing a Harare office with three staff and which has continued to provide an important link between the Commonwealth and Zimbabwe, ready for the time when the country will again be a member. The office gave important logistical support to the Commonwealth election observer team at the 2018 Zimbabwe elections which contained two CLGF Board members.

The Commonwealth Committee was recently revived with the help of my Commonwealth colleague Mark Robinson who is now its chair in anticipation of possible re-admission of Zimbabwe to Commonwealth membership, although the road back is proving very difficult. My last personal recollection of Robert Mugabe was when I was at the Mozambique 40th Anniversary celebrations in Maputo in 2015. There I unexpectedly found myself standing next to Mugabe. Needless to say, I quickly moved to avoid being seen in the same photograph. Like many leaders, and not only in Africa, he should have departed gracefully from office much earlier.

Sri Lanka presented more political challenges. For much of the past decades the country had undergone a bloody civil war between the majority Singhalese, who are Buddhist, and the minority Tamils in the Northern Province around Jaffna, who are Hindu, and were seeking independence. Civil wars are always ugly affairs and this one was no different. The Sri Lanka Government and its Army has been accused of serious human rights violations and massacres, notably at the end of the war when it finally managed to subdue the Tamil insurgents on the battlefield. The Tamil Tiger fighters had blood on their hands too – it is often forgotten that they and their women indiscriminately pioneered the suicide vest in civilian areas long before Islamist extremists ever did.

As with Zimbabwe, there was a question if it was wise to have a Commonwealth programme on the ground in the prevailing circumstances. However, I saw an opportunity in 2012/13 when the war had just concluded. My aim was to help bring past combatants together at the community and local government level, in the same way as had happened in Northern Ireland and other former conflict zones.

As it happened, our main local government member in the country was the national federation which embraced both Singhalese and Tamil mayors, including from Jaffna and was headed by the experienced Hemanthi Goonasekera. To ensure that our planned programme was inclusive, I took the initiative to fly to Jaffna and meet the Tamil mayors concerned. The trip was not without risk, as the city had only just been 'liberated' and there was much destruction. In particular, there were potential deadly hazards such as unexploded roadside mines which were just being cleared up as I drove past.

My visit to Jaffna proved ground-breaking, and we were able to start a national programme as planned. I hope it has genuinely helped to build bridges among the two communities at a grass roots level. What was problematic was that the programme was launched around the same time as a CHOGM was being held in Colombo in 2013. This resulted in the Commonwealth being heavily criticised by human rights groups for holding the Summit, given that the Sri Lanka Government was being accused of war crimes at the UN.

I was subjected to the most difficult interview of my career on Sri Lanka television. Defending and explaining our engagement in Sri Lanka made the BBC's *HARDtalk* seem like a soft touch. I was, however, encouraged that the TV presenter was so forthright and was able to voice his criticism of the Sri Lanka Government without apparent restriction.

I feel that ultimately, whatever the crimes on both sides, the people of Sri Lanka benefitted greatly from the peace. Not so long before I had recalled seeing the beachfront outside my Colombo hotel shut off with barbed wire and patrolled by machine gun-wielding soldiers on the lookout for would-be terrorists. It was a pleasure now to witness instead families picnicking and having fun at the seaside.

Sadly, the Islamic terrorist attacks of 2019 have set the country and its economy back and forced CLGF to cancel the conference it had planned there. I felt desperately sorry for the people of Sri Lanka and those, like my good friend Ali Moulana, CLGF Board member, whose constituency was targeted by the terrorists. One positive piece of news after the election of 2019 was that an old associate and thoughtful politician, Dinesh Gunawardena, returned as senior government minister. I can only hope that this beautiful country and its wonderful people will soon recover from their ongoing traumas, although political warning signs are flashing yet again.

Travelling and working in many parts of the world is no easy task.

30

The 2000s Evaluated

THE CLGF'S MANDATE IS PROMOTING DEMOCRATIC LOCAL government, sharing good practice and strengthening capacity. I believe we fulfilled this mandate during my tenure.

As far as possible I sought to link the different elements of our mandate in line with the strategic aims of our three-yearly business plan. A local democracy advocacy campaign would be re-enforced by sharing good practice policies and by subsequent capacity-building programmes. In the case of capacity-building, it was our aim to avoid one-off activities and implement more substantial multi-annual programmes, preferably on a regional basis through our local CLGF offices. There were also more generic and cross-cutting activities, such as our efforts to ensure the localisation of the UN's Sustainable Development Goals and address climate change and to reach Zero Carbon.

It was important that as many as possible of our members in the 54 Commonwealth countries, big and small, developed and above all developing, benefitted from the diverse range of our programmes, so that they saw value in our organisation. At the same time our limited resources meant that we had to prioritise certain activities and countries, especially those places requiring help to set up their local democracies and decentralised governance systems.

I was further aware that the majority of Commonwealth countries, especially in the Caribbean and the Pacific, but also in Africa and Asia, were small vulnerable states, which were often neglected by big donor organisations and deserved particular support. I therefore made it a point of speaking on their behalf at EU and other meetings and seeking resources to undertake capacity-building and other work for them. I also ensured that they had representation on relevant EU and ACP bodies.

Unexpected events such as sudden political upheavals – as occurred in The Maldives – which impacted on our local government members would require us to rapidly adjust our plans. Nor could we be immune from wider global events, whether terrorist attacks or major health problems like Ebola or, more recently, Covid-19. Much of our work was dependent on securing donor agency support and sudden changes in policy, as happened in the case of New Zealand and our Pacific programme in 2015, could be highly detrimental. International work is therefore generally more vulnerable than work at local or national level, although it does also have a potential advantage in being able to draw on resources from different countries and agencies. However it is not feasible to simply replace one donor by another overnight.

By the early 2000s, the CLGF was well grounded and was receiving regular membership fees from its Commonwealth members, including from the smallest countries such as Dominica, Kiribati and the Seychelles, based on a sliding scale of contributions according to population size and gross domestic product. The fees, even for larger countries like the UK, were relatively low and did not fully cover our core staff and administration costs. This meant I had to secure additional external income from government grants, conference fees, private sector partnerships and other sources, even book sales. In this we were operating very much as a small not-for-profit business.

Government grants were normally earmarked for specific activities so raising money for salaries and administration overheads was never easy. I was pleased that over the years we always managed to balance our books and build up a reasonable level of financial reserves, ensuring financial sustainability even during tough times. Certainly, at no time did the organisation go into debt.

Inevitably, the UK through DFID remained our main source of funds for most of the time. I was also able to attract support from the development agencies of Australia, Canada and above all New Zealand, as well as from UNDP and other international organisations. I did sound out some other agencies, where I took part in a number of events held by DELOG, bringing together various development partners, chaired by the German development ministry, but was less successful; however, attendance at these events in Bonn and Berlin raised CLGF's profile.

Given my past links with the EU, where I had secured funds for my trade union work at CTUC in the 1980s, I paid special attention to deploying my contacts at the European Commission in Brussels to attract funding. This required frequent trips to Brussels, which provided an opportunity to meet up with old friends, although the city holds many bitter-sweet personal memories for me.

Usually, we had to compete for funds with others in a bidding process or tender which stretched our capacity to deal with the extensive paperwork and red tape involved. Fortunately, staff like Lucy Slack excelled at putting together good funding bids. Annoyingly, really big tenders for local government work issued by donors like the EU or DFID are frequently won by large commercial consultancy firms. The latter have a lot of resources to write up tender bids but little expertise of how to implement local government work – not a sensible way of spending public aid money in my view.

On one occasion – our early Zimbabwe programme – I got the European Commission to accept that CLGF had a 'monopoly' and was therefore eligible for direct funding. Later, in 2015, along with other international local government organisations, we were able to negotiate a six-year 'framework partnership agreement' with the Commission. This allocated EU funds directly to us in recognition of our 'monopoly' and local government status, avoiding the bidding process. We are some way off before our local government members in individual countries or regions of the world can secure donor funds directly. This remains work in progress and CLGF has an important role to help its members in this task.

It has been said that the Commonwealth has a lot in 'common' but lacks 'wealth'. There is indeed much to link its members, especially legal and cultural, but most are poor developing countries with few resources. While this is true, one of its great strengths is that the Commonwealth is not only an intergovernmental network, but has a wide range of quasi-governmental, professional and civil society networks covering just about any conceivable subject and area of activity. CLGF is just one of these. This broad global network provides a source of know-how and expertise from across the world, especially from the developing counties which make up the great majority of Commonwealth members, including its thirty plus members from small and vulnerable states whose needs are often neglected.

When CLGF celebrated its 20th birthday in 2015, it had achieved formal status within the Commonwealth and was regarded as an important global organisation for local government. It had delegation status at high-level CHOGMs and had the opportunity of inputting to the work of important Commonwealth ministerial events such as CMAG, Finance

Ministers, Education Ministers and Ministerial Meetings on Small States. Subsequent to this, I and my colleagues would confer with Secretariat staff about appropriate follow-up actions. Examples of the close cooperation with the Secretariat were our observer missions to local government elections in Nigeria, Pakistan and The Maldives, funded by the Secretariat and having local government representatives on other missions. This marked a new departure from what had hitherto been exclusive Commonwealth focus on national elections.

In my role as CLGF Secretary-General, heading a significant Commonwealth organisation, I gained the status and confidence to liaise directly at the senior-most political levels in the Commonwealth. This led to individual meetings with Commonwealth leaders, many of which were sympathetic to local democracy and public sector decentralisation and the work of CLGF.

Yet all this was done with minimal staff and few resources; outside colleagues were always amazed at how few resources CLGF had – by 2016 our full-time staff complement was only some 25, of which half were based in London. Much of our success was due to the active support of our Board members and the dedication and long and late hours put in voluntarily by our staff, including those based overseas. In this I cannot commend our staff too much. I hope too that I was able to provide the necessary leadership for my team while maintaining a relaxed management style, although sometimes I perhaps pushed them too hard.

Building up the new CLGF organisation took up all my energies in the 2000s. It meant I ceased my pursuit of parliamentary selection and direct involvement and later my membership of the British Labour Party. Such party involvement was also not appropriate given the non-party nature of my professional work. At the same time, I still benefitted from my close personal associations with senior ministers of the Blair and Brown Governments after 1997, such as Hilary Armstrong, Nick Raynsford, Hilary Benn and George (now Lord) Foulkes.

Indeed, it was during this time that I first passed through the hallowed portals of 10 Downing Street for a reception hosted by Prime Minister Blair and for meetings with Number 10 policy advisers. Although it looks small from the outside, Number 10 encompasses the surrounding buildings and is surprisingly large inside, including the Cabinet Room and its substantial reception rooms. It is a bit like the Tardis time machine in the BBC *Dr Who* science fiction TV series which I first watched as a young lad-tiny from the outside but huge inside.

My work in local government involved strategic thinking and making sure that all our members felt engaged. It accordingly entailed extensive advocacy and travel to maintain close links with our far-flung membership across the world. Apart from holding our own events, including our increasingly high-level biennial conferences, it involved attending conferences of key members, especially, but not only, in countries like Australia, Canada, India, New Zealand, South Africa and the UK. This meant absurd schedules with time and travel cost dictating that I try and take in as many countries as feasible on one overseas mission – a bit like a country a day. As most travel was by economy class, this was gruelling.

I was frequently amused by friends who would ask me if I had a wonderful time on my overseas travels to what they saw as exotic holiday locations. My choices for travel were limited as so many Commonwealth countries, especially in the Caribbean, are also tourist centres. I reminded my friends that my schedule involved departing at weekends and flying long distance overnight, going to a hotel for a short rest, and then non-stop, early morning-to-late-night meetings and social events with just a few hours for sleep. I would then fly onto the next destination, again with no pause. Here there would be the same hectic schedule. While travelling I would need to keep in constant touch with my London office and keep up with current events, responding to endless emails, often late into the night.

By way of example, I have probably visited Australia forty times professionally, usually only for no more than two or three days, and mainly to Canberra or Sydney. I have never yet made it to either the Great Barrier Reef or Ayers Rock (Uluru). Tourists sitting by the hotel pool in their Bermuda shorts and bikinis must have thought I looked odd, dashing around in a formal suit, shirt and tie and clutching my briefcase, papers and laptop under my arm.

My overseas visits presented an opportunity to address and to meet CLGF members and senior Council leaderships, local government ministers and officials and, on occasions, with their Prime Ministers and Presidents. Such international travel and events are essential if intimate and confidential talks are to be held. Without it, bodies like CLGF could not function effectively. Telecommunications and video conferences can play a role in minimising unnecessary travel and provide ongoing exchanges as Covid restrictions on travel demonstrated. But Zoom cannot replace the vital person-to-person contacts and small talk, often resulting in specific joint projects and securing funding applications. Such direct interactions also lead to long-standing personal friendships, cemented over late-night drinks.

Our reputation soon extended beyond the Commonwealth and meant I also had an opportunity to represent local government interests at the UN, the EU and other global bodies, in collaboration with partners like UCLG. This resulted in my being asked to chair key international conferences and to address important gatherings of stakeholders. All this demonstrates the complex interplay and cooperation between non-governmental/professional organisations, quasi-governmental bodies like CLGF and intergovernmental structures at international level. This is a nexus of activities which generally little-known but is ever-increasing in importance internationally in every conceivable area of specialisation.

I could have easily spent my whole time travelling and living with a suitcase but made a rule only to go to events where I had a clear role, such as being a keynote speaker or securing new funds. Otherwise, I sent a CLGF staff member, preferably from our nearest regional office or simply gave our apologies. I had to remember that many of my staff already had busy travelling schedules to initiate and oversee our various programmes around the world. I further tried to avoid large global mega-events where it was difficult to meet colleagues or achieve much. To have done otherwise would have meant neglecting office management and jeopardising my home life more than my frequent absences abroad already did.

Travelling around the world in often difficult and uncomfortable circumstances was far from glamorous or jet-setting. It was sometimes downright dangerous too. According to official statistics road accidents account for among the largest number of deaths in developing countries, way ahead of killers such as malaria or HIV-AIDS. India is top of the list for fatalities and a staggering 181,000 were killed on the roads in one year alone (2019). I accordingly have never felt comfortable on long road journeys in countries known for their high accident rates. I tried to avoid travelling on roads by night when the worst accidents occur and when huge lorries can come hurtling towards you without lights. I have been in a few nasty situations, but luckily never anything too serious, although being in a minibus with failing brakes on a steep hillside outside Port Moresby in Papua New Guinea and rolling backwards towards a precipice – before the driver recovered control – was not too pleasant.

One occasion I was proceeding by road from Nairobi in Kenya to meet with the East African Community in Arusha, Tanzania. The road was not too bad apart from where it hit the dusty 'Wild West-lookalike' border town, with the local Masai going around in their traditional dress carrying spears. We were wildly ambitious in thinking we could do the return journey to Nairobi the same day. On our way back we hit the frontier just as dusk was approaching. It would be at least three hours travel in the dark before we could have made Nairobi. Our driver advised we should stay overnight rather than proceed. I assumed that was because of the dangers of night-time traffic, but he enlightened me by informing me that it was because of 'bandits'. Apparently, they would put nails across the road, ambush you and take your car and belongings and then leave you to the mercy of the lions. This was not an attractive prospect and we decided to stay the night. This entailed accommodation in a tiny roadside hostel, totally blacked-out as it lacked electricity and our spartan beds covered by mosquito nets. But at least we were safe from bandits and lions.

Local taxis have their problems too. I remember taking one from my hotel in Delhi around midnight to go to the airport. On departing the driver proceeded without any headlights on and kept crashing his gears, announcing that he was a trainee driver. In Lilongwe our taxi's back doors did not open from the inside and it had different, ill-fitting tyres on all four wheels. In Rabat it was more a case of avoiding being charged the triple rate. There were many similar instances.

Not that flying on certain airlines is much better. I had to do this during my visits to Nigeria in the knowledge that the British Embassy had banned all staff from taking local airlines because of their frequent crashes. I once had a particularly close shave in Dar es Salaam when, just before take-off, all the power in our plane gave out. Happily, the plane was still on the runway. I have been on dodgy old propeller planes in places like Fiji where amusingly the passengers as well as the luggage are weighed before departure, which could be embarrassing to some.

Against these incidents, there are excellent airlines in developing countries which I have flown without any worry, such as Ethiopian Airlines and RwandAir, to say nothing of the superb Middle East airlines like Emirates and Qatar Airways. However, wherever possible, I stuck to British Airways, in part because it provided the fastest direct air connection from London.

Yet one of my worst experiences was a landing at Heathrow airport, probably still the world's busiest air hub. As we were about to land with the plane's wheels down, our pilot pulled back up steeply at the very last minute. When we recovered from the shock, he calmly announced that he had to perform this sudden manoeuvre to avoid a plane in front of us on the runway.

By 2010, I had been heading CLGF for fifteen years. It was also the year of my 60th birthday which I celebrated in true Commonwealth style at the Royal Overseas League Club with vibrant African drummers from Ghana and gentle Pacific Island dancers from Kiribati welcoming our guests. The Commonwealth Secretariat was represented by Mmasekgoa Masire-Mwamba, its Deputy Secretary-General, and it was great to have friends and family members present including from overseas.

We received and read out congratulatory greetings from across the world. These included a message from former Secretary-General Sir Shridath 'Sonny' Ramphal who most kindly noted that, "You gave invaluable service to ... numerous Commonwealth and United Nations committees and expert groups, as well as on election observer teams" and "You have been a true Commonwealth exemplar."

A wonderful endorsement by the most distinguished Secretary-General to have served the Commonwealth.

PART V

NEW REALITIES
(to the present time)

Unravelling of the Post-1945 Consensus

"Silence in the face of evil is itself evil".
DIETRICH BONHOEFFER, MURDERED BY THE NAZIS 1945

9/11 changed politics as did the global economic crash, leading to political populism, Brexit and Trump; then Covid-19 hit the world. But there were positive trends towards sustainable development and addressing the climate emergency.

31

9/11, 7/7 and Violent Extremism

BLOODY CONFLICTS CONTINUED UNABATED INTO THE 21ST century – in Afghanistan, the Congo, Chad, Colombia, Iraq, Kosovo, Libya, Palestine, Sierra Leone, Sudan, Syria, Sri Lanka, Yemen, Ukraine – the list goes on. What was new was the intensity of violent extremism and the spread of terrorist attacks perpetrated by al-Qaeda and ISIS in Western and other cities.

The new realities marking the turn of the century were underlined in 2001 by the 9/11 terrorist attack on the World Trade Center in New York and the Pentagon in Washington. This was a geopolitical game-changer. It was a demonstration of how non-State actors were challenging the post-1945 consensus, based on the international rule of law and multilateralism and ordered relations between nation states.

I was in Brussels on 11 September 2001, having meetings at the European Commission. I first knew something big was up when the EU official we were meeting rushed off to phone his daughter in New York. We soon heard the dramatic news from the US and the rest of that day Brussels was turbulent and confusing.

I had flown to Brussels; I now take the much more pleasant and environmentally friendly Eurostar train, but in 2001, flying was still an option. On 9/11, I faced the worrying prospect of taking to the skies to return to London right in the aftermath of the attacks. The evening taxi journey to Brussels' Zaventem airport was adventurous and lengthy. The motorway, which passed NATO headquarters, had been closed by the armed forces in case of attack. There were inevitable delays at the airport, but we did eventually take off. This was amidst all sorts of rumours of new airborne attacks. I must admit I did not feel very secure in the air that fateful day. I was relieved when we touched down safely on solid ground at Heathrow.

I had previously visited the Twin Towers, having ascended the observation level with its splendid views across Manhattan. Since the terrorist attacks, I have been back to New York many times. The 9/11 memorial site *'Reflecting Absence'* at Ground Zero where 2,983 people perished is harrowing and thought-provoking with a strange sense of peacefulness.

I can well understand how the 9/11 attack affected the psyche of the USA; at the time the whole world was in solidarity with its people. It is a tragedy that this support was dissipated by the indiscriminate 'War on Terror' and endless entanglement in Afghanistan with trillions of dollars of military expenditure. As the events of 2021 in Kabul showed, not much was finally accomplished.

The subsequent attack on Iraq, aimed at regime change led by George W Bush, in violation of the UN, and foolishly supported by Tony Blair, was a huge blunder. Its aftermath led to the unnecessary loss of so many civilian lives and countless refugees and opened the door to ISIS and other extremists. The forced rendition of terrorist suspects, their torture by water-boarding and worse, and their illegal incarceration without trial in Guantánamo Bay undermined the Rule of Law and soiled the reputation of Washington and her allies.

In some instances, external military intervention is necessary to protect human lives. In 2000, I supported the Blair Government sending troops to Sierra Leone to back up the UN mission there and promote peace; this subsequently allowed me to resume CLGF support for the country. Intervention should be strictly in line with the UN doctrine of Responsibility to Protect (R2P), agreed in 2005, which authorises humanitarian intervention by the international community when there is a real risk of mass killings or genocide; unfortunately, this came too late for Bosnia and Rwanda. If politicians or indeed foreign soldiers, including British or US, have individually committed war crimes, for example in Northern Ireland, the full force of the law, including through the International Criminal Court, established 2002, has to be applied – there must be no double standards. This, too, applies to Russia today.

The Commonwealth addressed issues of terrorism, extremism, conflict and violence in a landmark 2007 report on *'Civil Paths to Peace'* chaired by Professor Amartya Sen. This argued that cultivating respect and understanding is important in itself and in reducing violence and terrorism. It looked at methods of counteracting disaffection and violence and highlighted the importance of diversity, which it felt was fundamental to the values of the Commonwealth. Our own CLGF work in implementing the 2005 *Aberdeen Principles*, with their focus on promoting local democracy and good governance were designed to encourage political consensus and democratic paths to peace.

A direct consequence of Western unilateral intervention in the Middle East post 9/11 was Islamic radicalisation, an increased number of terror incidents and the rise of ISIS. One of the most brutal attacks was the train bombing in Madrid in 2004 which left 193 innocent people dead. Further attacks were to follow in London, Paris, Brussels, Berlin and other European cities. It was to lead to reprisal terrorism by far-Right extremists as was seen in a growing number of highly violent incidents in diverse countries like New Zealand, Norway and the USA.

Many more terrorist killings take place in the Middle East and in developing countries than in the West, with Afghanistan, Iraq and Syria top of the list. I remember too, the callous attacks in Mumbai in 2008 which took 175 innocent lives. This caused me to seek urgent contact with my Mumbai-based CLGF colleague, Anuya Kuwar, who I was relieved to discover was safe. Nairobi, too, where I had many friends, suffered badly from terrorism. Pakistan has been yet another major target. It is ordinary people, including women and children, who are most likely to be victims of violent extremism and our thoughts should be with them.

Nigeria has the bloody Boko Haram insurgency which started in the Muslim north of the country and has spread to neighbouring countries. It is notorious for its abduction and abuse of innocent schoolgirls and has claimed many lives through brutal terrorist acts. In the capital, Abuja it has bombed the UN offices which I had previously visited. It was not long after such an attack in 2014 that we had scheduled a meeting of my CLGF Board in Abuja. Several Board members got cold feet on account of the security situation, and I was asked to reconsider holding the Board meeting elsewhere. I, however, felt that this would be giving in to terrorism and letting down our Nigerian members who were keen to host us.

At any rate Nigeria was not the only country facing terrorist threats and I decided to proceed with the Board meeting. As expected, we received good treatment from our hosts who greatly appreciated my decision, and we were accompanied by armed soldiers whenever we left our hotel. In fact, on quite a few visits to Commonwealth countries in past years I have been given personal armed security alongside an official driver and car. The latter is always invaluable, but the former – the bodyguard – is often more a matter of protocol.

Our 2014 CLGF Board meeting adopted the *Abuja Declaration on Local Democracy and Development in the Commonwealth.* Recalling the 2005 *Aberdeen Principles*, the Declaration pledged full solidarity with the people and Government of Nigeria and other countries which have had to confront terrorism and associated itself unequivocally with the call to 'bring back our girls' – who had been kidnapped by terrorists. It pointed out that no amount of misguided ideology can undermine fundamental human rights, including the universal and equal right to education for girls and boys.

Terrorism takes place mainly in big urban centres as we have seen in Mumbai, Nairobi, Paris and many other places. Mayors and local government leaders have a key role to work with the national government and the emergency services to prepare their cities for terrorist incidents. During the 7/7 attacks in London, a well-prepared emergency plan by the London Mayor immediately sprang into action which, if it had not existed, would have resulted in many more casualties. Our *Abuja Declaration* accordingly committed the CLGF to assist its members in sharing the expertise of local government and linking with federal and state governments in dealing with civic and emergencies responses in national conflict resolution and peace-building efforts.

On a lighter note, visiting Nigeria in 2012 allowed me to compliment my collection of African bronze figures, which I have collected over the years and take pride of place at home. On this occasion I acquired a beautiful, almost life-size bronze leopard with a strikingly protruding tail. As a VIP guest of the government, I did not have to go through the regular airport security check and took my acquisition under my arm as hand luggage directly onto the plane. I caused great alarm to the BA staff when I put it in the overhead locker as they felt that my leopard's protruding metal tail could seriously injure other passengers if it fell out. I did, however, get my prized acquisition back safely and it now adorns my Kent house along with many other beautiful artefacts from Commonwealth countries around the world.

The role of local government in conflict resolution, promotion of democracy, good governance and the rule of law has increasingly been recognised. This also applies to the wider responsibility of local government to fulfil human rights, especially, where it has powers for local policing and security. This issue was set out in some detail in a report submitted to the UN Human Rights Council in 2015.

While preparing for violent terrorism is vital, it is better to try to prevent it in the first place.

This is done by actively promoting community cohesion, in cooperation with local religious and civil society groups and strengthening the resilience of institutions of local democracy in line with the CLGF *Aberdeen Principles*. Mayors and civic leaders have a great responsibility and need to promote social integration and inter-communal understanding in their cities, especially among alienated youth and marginalised groups. Having lots of CCTV and an armed police response is no answer on its own. Local leaders must take all action to counter any sign of religious or racial intolerance or xenophobia, such as that directed against refugees, minority groups and migrants, and to promote an inclusive society.

Ideally, I would have like to have secured more resources to strengthen CLGF work to allow our local government members to exchange good practices in this sensitive area. In 2016, I had suggested that Commonwealth Secretary-General Patricia Scotland should help take this forward, but this did not happen. Of course, funding from Commonwealth governments was always highly limited and often, as in the case of Zimbabwe, I was more successful in securing EU funds.

Some of our earlier work had addressed related issues of community security and policing, for example under our *Good Practice Scheme* we had funded an exchange in this area between Leeds in the UK and Durban in South Africa. Back in 2009, I had had correspondence with British Foreign Secretary David Miliband in seeking more funds for our work in support of local democracy, notably in Pakistan and Zimbabwe. I had got to know David a bit and regretted that he narrowly missed the Labour leadership after 2010 as he would have made a good Prime Minister.

I seem to have a knack of avoiding terrorist attacks by a hair's breadth. Back in the mid-1970s, I narrowly missed being a victim of the IRA's Chelsea Barracks bombing in London, one of the first big IRA attacks on the capital that decade. I had just driven in from Brussels and parked my car nearby and was about to enter Tite Street in Chelsea, where my in-laws lived. Then without warning a loud bomb went off. This blast was so powerful it shattered all the windows in the flat of my in-laws but luckily, I had not yet turned the corner into the street. If I had walked a bit faster at the time, I would not be here today.

Once the street had been cordoned off, I remember talking to an MI5 undercover agent – he was dressed in jeans and an old leather jacket and spoke in a thick Irish accent. On another occasion I was in London's West End with Adele and her parents near Oxford Street at Christmas time when we were hurried on by the police to evacuate because of an IRA bomb scare.

I was in London on the day of the July 7th Islamist terrorist attack in 2005. Here, again, I narrowly missed being a victim. On the morning of that fateful day, I was travelling to work on the busy Underground. As our train approached Bond Street station, a major network interchange, it ground to a halt. A loud announcement instructed all commuters to evacuate the station immediately. Fortunately, the evacuation was calm and without panic.

As I emerged at street level on Oxford Street in the bright morning light there was total confusion. It seemed the entire Underground system had been closed. But no-one knew what was going on. Not finding a taxi, I jumped on a bus. A few minutes later I heard police and ambulance sirens. I was only a few streets away from Tavistock Square, where a suicide bomber had just blown himself up on a London bus killing many others. It was the fourth suicide bombing that took place that day, in a coordinated attack on London's transport system that resulted in the deaths of 52 UK residents.

I still shudder to think how close I was to all this terrible carnage. At this stage Adele managed to call me on my cell phone. I then learnt to my dismay what was actually going on, and she was much relieved to learn I was safe, at least at that moment.

I proceeded to my office near London Bridge, at the Association of London Government (ALG) building. Being a government institution, we were deemed a potential target and were instructed to stay indoors all day. It later fell to me to get on the phone to alert the ALG Chief Executive, Martin Pilgrim, who was away at an event outside London. He was a member of COBRA, the Government's emergency task force, and needed to be briefed about the developing crisis in the capital.

That evening, much of the London Underground network was still closed, so I took a long walk to the nearest over-ground train station to get home. The next morning my fellow commuters were quiet and reflective, but it was good to see Londoners refusing to be intimidated by terrorism.

More recently, in 2016, I was at the exact location of the dreadful Brussels metro terrorist attack only one week after this occurred. Later that same year Adele and I were on the precise spot of the Berlin Christmas market just one week before the terrorist attacks, also taking many lives.

It is worth remembering that violent crime kills many more than terrorism or armed conflict. According to the UN, in 2017 crime killed

464,000 people, armed conflicts 89,000 and terrorism 19,000. Nor should it be forgotten how many millions die globally of preventable diseases, in childbirth or famines; as well as in natural disasters, of which the 230,000 death toll from the 2004 tsunami is a grim reminder.

I am fortunate that, in my extensive travels around the world, I have never been seriously attacked, and I always tried to be careful wherever I went. It is, therefore, ironic that the only place I was assaulted was right outside my very own front door in the prosperous London district of West Hampstead. This happened on a dark winter evening in February when, walking back from the local Kilburn Underground station after work, I realised I was being followed by two hooded youths. I felt uneasy.

Before I knew it, they jumped on me outside my house and flashed a knife, instructing me to be quiet and hand over my belongings. Foolishly, I shouted out loud and pushed past them to get away. I only got as far as the bushes of our neighbour Kaye's front garden just across the road. My assailants then caught up and upended me, so I landed roughly on the ground. By great fortune, Kaye happened to be at her front door and, noticing my predicament, shouted at my assailants. This startled them and they ran off, snatching my briefcase which contained just office papers.

I was not hurt, only shaken. Kaye gave me a cup of tea to allow me to calm down while we phoned the police. There was an amusing ending to the drama. The police arrived at my house quite quickly, but they were in plain clothes: jeans and black leather jackets. Adele, who had not heard about the incident, refused to open the door to them. On reflection, it is odd that of all places in the world I would get assailed in what was a normally safe and pleasant part of London.

I have been lucky to escape death many times and perhaps I have a guardian angel watching over me.

32

Economic Crash, Austerity and the New Populists

ANOTHER DEFINING MOMENT WAS THE GLOBAL ECONOMIC crash of 2008. The resulting Government-induced austerity gave rise to widespread social discontent and led to the poisonous political populism exemplified by Brexit and Trump.

Despite the warning of the earlier dot-com economic crash in 2000, by 2008 the USA, UK and other Western countries had become too lax in their regulations of the banking and financial sectors. The ensuing global crash was a consequence of the excessive market liberalisation started by Thatcher and Reagan under the so-called Washington Consensus which was not sufficiently reversed by Clinton, Blair and other centrist political leaders.

Ironically, the main perpetrators of the crisis, the bankers and City whizz kids, were bailed out by the public purse as they were deemed too big to fail. It was the ordinary people that suffered and, in my case, my projected pension income took a big hit. Scandalously, those responsible continued to pay themselves oversized bonuses regardless of their awful performance. Very few if any countries followed Iceland which had the guts to put those responsible on trial for the misery they had caused, and to impose fines or imprisonment. If more had done this, the public might not have become so disillusioned with the political system and its elites.

It was a close-run thing in 2009-10 whether the crash would develop into a major worldwide depression as happened in the 1930s. This was only prevented by newly elected US President Barack Obama and British Prime Minister Gordon Brown coordinating international efforts to apply almost forgotten Keynesian economic remedies with massive quantitative easing of the money supply. Economic disaster was prevented, but at considerable cost.

After 2008, many countries would feel the bitter consequences of government austerity programmes, increased unemployment, and often massive cutbacks in essential public services. These included the health and social services sectors, many of which are administered and delivered directly by local government. Economic growth in Western countries was stalled for much of the next decade and there were inevitable social consequences, hitting the poorest hardest. Within the Eurozone there was an acute crisis, severely affecting several countries, notably Greece.

Globalisation had brought benefits through trade liberalisation, reduced costs of imports and a glut of cheaply priced consumer goods from emerging economies like China. It had however impacted on many traditional industrial areas such as the US 'rust-belt', the north of England and south Wales, decimating production and creating unemployment. This led to a feeling of being 'left behind' in those areas and growing political alienation.

Insofar as there was alternative employment, this often entailed low-wage, insecure, non-union jobs, marked by zero-hour contracts providing little or no benefits. As a result, an underclass of workers and their families had been created, especially in the UK and the USA. These did not benefit from globalisation but saw it as a threat to their living standards and way of life. Foreign immigration, whether from Mexico or Eastern Europe, created further tension by being perceived as undercutting wages and putting pressure on public services.

In the UK, I witnessed how the new Conservative-led coalition government in 2010 under David Cameron and his Chancellor George Osborne imposed severe austerity in public finances. UK local government was directly affected as the Westminster government, having overall control of local finances, simply offloaded public sector cuts onto local councils.

A 2015 report by the UK's Joseph Rowntree Foundation showed that between 2010/11 and 2015/16 local authorities in England overall lost 27 per cent of their spending power in real terms, resulting in cuts of up to 14 per cent in social care spending. In consequence, many big UK cities faced 30-40 per cent budget cuts in the ensuing years. This had huge impact on vital local services, not least those supporting the young, elderly and socially disadvantaged, which has not yet been repaired. There was also severe under-funding of the British National Health Service which had consequences for the UK's ability to cope with the 2020 Covid-19 pandemic – the third big global shock post-2000, after 9/11 and 2008.

The impact of 2008 was to affect the last years of my professional work, making international work and access to government resources yet more difficult than previously. I had, for the first time, to put our London staff, as well as myself, on a four-day week with reduced pay for several months while awaiting new funds. I was unwilling to erode the financial sustainability of my organisation by exhausting our small reserves or incurring undue debt. Happily, it was not too long until I was able to successfully secure longer-term funds for our work and we were able to return to normal working and regular pay.

It proved increasingly much more difficult to get my UK members, even the Local Government Association, to devote resources or time to international work, given the savage budget cuts they were battling with domestically. The LGA disbanded its International Bureau and many councils that had previously allocated resources to activities such as town twinning or Agenda 21 promotion, now cut them. Soon the only justifiable international activities were those that brought in resources, such as having staff based in Brussels to secure EU grants. As a result, quite a few UK councils dropped out of CLGF membership which had a knock-on effect on our finances.

I realised that it was necessary to re-orientate CLGF programmes to have a greater focus on the economy – local economic development. This was an area of interest to DFID and other donors and provided practical benefit to our members at a time of economic downturn. Underlying this concept was that mayors and local leaders could play a key role in boosting local development by proactively encouraging investment by business or promoting their city or region for as a tourist, conference or shopping centre. Of course, this was easier in countries where, as in South Africa, local government had significant powers to act autonomously, having integrated local development plans and the ability to offer businesses incentives, to cut red tape or to set up tourist infrastructure.

Local government partnerships with the private sector, notably in the delivery of services was not a new concept. It had been the main focus of our 2003 CLGF conference in Tshwane, South Africa which had produced a strategy on 'local government service partnerships', a terminology we preferred to the more common 'private-public partnerships'. It had also been the subject of more detailed strategic deliberation, such as our 2005 Asia-Pacific Symposium in Kuala Lumpur.

In consequence our 2011 Conference adopted the *'Cardiff Consensus for Local Economic Development'*, highlighting the importance of having a clear national framework for local economic development, creating the necessary enabling environment through legislation, and having local strategies for promotion of such development, together with appropriate partnerships with the private sector and other partners. Our ongoing knowledge-sharing and capacity-building programmes henceforth had an important local economic development component and by the end of the decade CLGF had become a lead organisation in this area.

The economic crash and subsequent austerity cuts produced an inevitable political backlash. It was not the left of centre parties who benefitted. Many of them, like the New Labour Party of Tony Blair and Gordon Brown, were seen as complicit in the old discredited financial system and the bankers and were dumped from office. Instead, there was an upsurge of new, far-Right and neo-fascist political parties with populist leaders promising to sweep away the old system and provide a better tomorrow. Access to social media allowed wide public audiences to be reached, which had previously been denied to them, permitting them to spread their poisonous fake news.

The ugliest aspect of the new populists was their xenophobia, intolerance of minorities, immigrants and foreigners; demonising 'the other'. There was a focus on crude nationalist solutions like 'Make America Great Again' or 'Global Britain'. Much of this entailed an underlying distain of international cooperation, through the UN, the EU and opposition to overseas development assistance. This was often accompanied by the demand to obey 'the will of the people', with uncomfortable echoes of 1930s fascist ideology.

Populist governments in Hungary and Poland passed anti-democratic legislation eroding traditional legal and social rights and even progressive countries like Denmark, Sweden and the Netherlands were not immune from this harmful political virus. Nor was populism verging on authoritarianism and fascism confined to Europe.

I saw this worrying trend at first hand in many of the countries I visited at this time like Brazil, India, Philippines and Turkey. The changes in India under Prime Minister Modi, with brazen attacks tolerated against the indigenous Muslim population, has been particularly worrying, given the country's hitherto proud democratic record; it was also accompanied with a loss of interest in Commonwealth cooperation, illustrated by failure to honour India's earlier commitment to host our own CLGF conference in 2015.

It is not surprising that the most dramatic political impact was in the two Anglo-Saxon countries, the UK and the USA, which had led the world in deregulation and had been the key champions of neo-liberal economics. For a while, President Obama was a beacon of light as first Black US President and seemed to stem the populist tide. But he was succeeded by the ultra-Right Presidency of Donald Trump in 2016. Only in 2020/21 was there a significant change with the election of Joe Biden as US President. However, the toxic political legacy of Trump remains strong in the USA as shown by the assault on Congress in early 2021. In addition, as the Black Lives Matter movement has highlighted, an underlying strand of institutional racism persists in the country.

I started off these recollections recalling my early time in Brussels in 1973 as one of the first Brits working in Europe. It seems history has come full circle. Since 2016, I have been deeply concerned about the political direction of the UK dating from the irresponsible decision of Prime Minister David Cameron to hold a referendum on British membership of the EU. In the run-up to the referendum, I warned about the negative impact of Brexit not only on the UK, but on especially our Commonwealth partners. I had also spoken out against giving a public platform to UKIP, for example at a meeting of the Commonwealth Round Table. Doing so was, I felt, a form of appeasement to demagogic far-Right forces which would undermine the consensual nature of British politics. In this I was proved correct.

The 2016 EU referendum campaign was ugly and dominated by Nigel Farage of UKIP, and Tory politicians Boris Johnson and Michael Gove hyping up prejudices against immigrants and telling lies about how much money would go to the British National Health Service if the country left the EU. They also said that they did not care about 'expert' opinion on the economic consequences of Brexit. There were moreover dark rumours of Russian interference in support of Brexit using social media. The campaign ended tragically with the murder of a young Labour Member of Parliament, Jo Cox, by an extreme Right-wing fanatic. Yet the populist UK newspapers could not bring themselves to call this act for what it was: namely, a cold-blooded political assassination.

On the 'Remain' side, the campaign was too negative with hardly a mention of the positive aspects of EU membership; how it provided opportunities for our young people; how it was a force for peace; and how it boosted British business. Instead, the focus was on an unattractive series of scare stories about the economic dangers of leaving. There was a lack of effective engagement for the Remain campaign by Labour

Leader Jeremy Corbyn, which failed to counter ill-informed pro-Brexit views of voters especially in the north of England and Wales.

I remember with a shudder staying up the night of the referendum results. In the early morning hours, I heard the awful news that there had been a tiny 52 per cent majority vote in favour of leaving the EU. Such a fundamental decision surely should have warranted a two-thirds requirement for approval.

The first message I received came from my old friend Basil Morrison in New Zealand who asked if we had gone totally mad. I was to hear the same refrain from numerous other Commonwealth friends and contacts, often at the highest level of politics. So much for the idea that Brexit would be welcomed by Commonwealth countries – the reality was quite the opposite. Most, especially smaller Commonwealth countries like those in the Caribbean, were also deeply concerned to lose the UK voice speaking on their behalf in Brussels. Few saw value in new bilateral trade deals with the UK, with echoes of what was sarcastically deemed 'Empire Mark 2'.

After the referendum the new British Prime Minister, Theresa May, pandered to the extreme Brexiteers of the far-Right Conservative European Research Group by going for a 'hard' Brexit rather than a 'soft' Brexit, with no close association with the EU, no membership of its Customs Union, the Single Market or freedom of movement of workers. She was then shackled to the Northern Irish Democratic Unionist Party (DUP) after her failed attempt to win a majority at the 2017 General Election. Only when her Brexit deal had been defeated three times in the House of Commons by historically large margins, did she attempt to find a compromise deal with support across Parliament. This was too late as the extreme Brexiteers had smelt blood.

Following May's resignation in mid-2019, Boris Johnson, the former Mayor of London, who I had met in that capacity, took over as Prime Minister and achieved a big parliamentary majority in the election of December 2019. The Johnson Government, composed of dogmatic Brexiteers, opted for an even more uncompromising 'hard Brexit' with only minimal trade links with the EU.

The new bureaucratic obstacles to trade with the EU, made the EU-UK deal the only such international deal which actually made trade and business more, not less, difficult. Johnson's populist Government represented a swing to the hard and xenophobic Right of politics, and Brexit came fully into force in 2021, after a transitional period in 2020.

To the dismay of genuine 'One Nation' Tories who were side-lined, Johnson's Tory Party has morphed into the English National Party with Union Jack flags in prominent display behind every ministerial media appearance.

I encountered the new xenophobia when I witnessed how Polish and other EU citizens were pilloried in the way Black citizens had been in the past; and how new waves of anti-Semitism and Islamophobia were unleashed. I saw political debate become debased and prejudiced, and disdainful of knowledgeable experts; how populist newspapers attacked High Court judges, parliamentarians, and those whose legitimate decisions they disliked; and how the Johnson Government sought to shut down Parliament illegally and ignore obligations under its own EU treaties. Even the BBC has lost much of its objectivity in my view, being obsessed with political 'balance' in its coverage and dumbing-down much of its reporting.

Thirty years after the Berlin Wall came down, we are building new walls.

33

A Little Local Difficulty

BY 2009/10, THE CLGF HAD EXISTED FOR FIFTEEN YEARS AND had established itself as a significant Commonwealth organisation. However, in 2009, I faced an unexpected personal challenge which nearly ended my career.

The CLGF is a non-party political with representatives of many different parties and ideologies from across the Commonwealth democratic spectrum – although happily never from the extreme Left or Right. Although I had my own strong political views and long-standing links with the British Labour movement, I did not, and could not, let this interfere with my role as CLGF Secretary-General. By the late 2000s my party-political ambitions were long behind me, and I no longer held an active Labour Party position.

UK local government is highly party political and in 2007, when the Labour Government was still in power nationally, control of the leadership of my main UK member, the Local Government Association, LGA, switched to the Conservatives, which had gained a control over a majority of local councils. The genial Labour LGA representative on my Board, Cllr Ken Bodfish from Brighton, was replaced by the new LGA Leader, Lord Hanningfield, the Tory leader of Essex and a member of the House of Lords. Hanningfield attended our CLGF Board meetings in Delhi and Kampala and I felt I had a reasonable rapport with him.

It was unfortunate that in the immediate aftermath of the 2008 economic crash our 2009 CLGF biennial conference was scheduled for Freeport in The Bahamas. While The Bahamas had been chosen through competitive bids and Freeport, as the name suggests, is a port, not a tourist venue, for many 'The Bahamas' immediately conjures up an exotic holiday location. It was no surprise that unlike on previous occasions no British minister dared to attend our event at a time of national economic crisis.

The conference did not start well when the local police found Nigerian delegates with counterfeit US dollars. This hit the local media but did not have anything to do with CLGF and soon blew over. I was more dumbfounded when my CLGF Chairperson, Basil Morrison of New Zealand and his predecessor, Bobby Montague of Jamaica, came to me to tell me that Hanningfield was conspiring to have me sacked, and that he was going to propose this at the forthcoming Board meeting in Freeport.

The reasons were never clear – the organisation was doing well, and I had not committed any grave management mistakes. Insofar as there was any motivation, it seems Hanningfield had discovered my earlier Labour Party and trade union background. He had, however, appeared to overlook the fact that I was a Commonwealth, not British, official, and not beholden to him or the UK Government.

Hanningfield may have felt I was 'too big for my boots' and had taken objection to my having shown an interest in a future House of Lords appointment. Back in 1997, just before the election of Tony Blair, Lord Stanley Clinton-Davis, a respected former Labour minister and EU Commissioner had, out of the blue, suggested including my name in a list of possible Labour peers. This had been submitted to the new Prime Minister for consideration, but I had heard no more. Now ten years later, I felt it time to revive the issue. I however made a point of applying under the new transparent system of non-party political appointments to the UK's second chamber. This was supposed to be based on merit and not on party-political affiliation as a party nominee.

Prior to 2008, the then UK Board member of CLGF, British local government minister Nick Raynsford, had sounded me out if I wanted a 'gong' or national honour. Senior UK local government leaders and officials receive such honours as a matter of course. I made it clear to the minister that this was not something I was much interested in. I felt that the UK honours system is not fit for purpose, with top honours mostly going to political or civil service timeservers regardless of merit. Worse still, honours are given to political cronies or to rich donors who give funds to party coffers. My friend, Gary Smith, recalls how a senior New Labour figure had offered him a peerage if he was to donate a large sum of money to the Party. He rightly refused.

I, however, did express to Nick Raynsford my interest in the House of Lords. I did not see being a member of the House of Lords as an 'honour', but rather a practical opportunity for active political engagement and advocacy on behalf of the Commonwealth and international work once I had retired from the CLGF. I have never had the slightest interest in absurd feudal titles like 'Lord' or the fancy privileges. Many of my contemporaries, like Dianne Hayter and Dick Newby, were now in the House of Lords, as were former trade union colleagues like David Lea, so I did not regard this as such a special deal. Many members of the House of Lords do serious and valuable parliamentary work and I felt that while it existed, it should be made use of, but also felt it needed to be replaced by a democratically-elected second chamber.

In applying for consideration to the Lords as a non-party political appointment, I took into account my CLGF role. I first consulted both Basil Morrison and Bobby Montague and was actively encouraged by them to proceed. I then acquired a lengthy list of high-level personal endorsements from within and outside of the UK, including other CLGF Board members and political associates. These included formal letters of recommendation from Prime Minister Helen Clark of New Zealand and President Museveni of Uganda addressed to Gordon Brown, now the Prime Minister. Inexplicably these letters from senior heads of Government were – to my knowledge – never acknowledged, odd diplomatic protocol to say the least.

After a lengthy wait, and a short time prior to the Freeport conference, I received a letter informing me I had not been selected for a Lords appointment. No reason was given, but I strongly suspect a political hand in this, not least because the appointments panel included a senior Tory 'grandee'.

Thanks to Hanningfield, I spent stressful days in Freeport when I had to run a major conference. But I need not have worried. In his address to the conference, Prime Minister Bruce Golding of Jamaica paid me a warm public tribute, saying: "I would also like to commend Carl Wright in recognition of his tremendous zeal, commitment and passion with which he has infused the practice of local government and I would like to commend him for the work he continues to do". All my non-UK Board members, especially Basil and Bobby, rallied behind me. At the end of the conference, my Board met and passed a resounding vote of confidence in me with twenty votes in favour and only one abstention: Hanningfield. He then departed early to the UK, muttering how he would stop our British DFID funding of CLGF.

Hanningfield would, however, again become a focus of attention. A wide-ranging parliamentary expenses scandal had blown up in the UK media. This exposed British MPs and peers who were abusing their parliamentary expenses by making false claims for the daily allowance for staying overnight in London when attending Parliament. Those accused included Hanningfield who, it was claimed, had pocketed the not insubstantial allowance when not actually attending the House of Lords.

It was with supreme irony that I was interviewed on the matter by Scotland Yard who requested me give a witness statement and provide the minutes of our Board meetings in Delhi and Kampala. How could I refuse such a reasonable request by police investigators?

The minutes proved his Lordship had attended these meetings abroad and was not eligible to claim his London allowance at this time.

The matter came to court and Hanningfield was convicted and sentenced to nine months in prison. After his release, Hanningfield hit the papers again when he was photographed 'clocking in' to the House of Lords to collect his attendance allowance and then immediately leaving.

Questions were asked as to whether peers should be allowed to continue in their role after having served a prison sentence. It is no wonder the British public has lost faith in many politicians and is wary of the political system.

To reassure external partners, including funders like DFID, our Board with my active encouragement decided that CLGF should be subject to a full strategic external review of its work and objectives. This review would reflect on my performance and stewardship as Secretary-General. It was at any rate due as the organisation had been in existence for over ten years and would benefit from such an assessment. The review was undertaken by a distinguished academic from India, Dinesh Metha and the Vice-Chancellor of Birmingham University, Michael Clarke. It involved a thorough consultation with members, funders and other stakeholders.

The exercise took the best part of a year and produced useful governance and other reforms which we adopted. It strongly commended the organisation and myself for doing an able job with minimal resources in line with what was desired by our members. I therefore got a full clean bill of health. The review was followed by a detailed Business Plan for 2011-2014 which set out clear and transparent aims and outcomes for our core strategic objectives. Not long afterwards this positive endorsement was further underlined by an external DFID review of our work strongly endorsing our work and by allocation of new DFID funding for three years.

In 2013, I was moreover to receive a wonderful recognition of my life's work when I was given the distinction of an honorary doctorate in public administration from the University of KwaZulu-Natal in Durban. This was in recognition not only of my current work on local government, but also of my commitment to human rights including the anti-apartheid cause over many years. The graduation ceremony at the University was attended by good friends and colleagues like Rev Mpho Moruakgomo, the CLGF Chairperson who had flown down from Botswana, and looked splendid with his large Christian cross on his chest, Professor PS Reddy from the University and Mike Sutcliffe who had been chief executive of the city.

In my acceptance speech, I reminded the young South African graduates about the successful fight against apartheid, something which was already history for many for them. Yet it was the reason why so Black students were now present and had been able to study and graduate. I also touched on contemporary local government and wider global issues and expressed the hope that young people would be committed to internationalism. My *honoris causa* was the one honour I was truly proud to accept, very different from the often-superficial awards under the British honours system. It was, as one of my British Board members aptly put it, 'a gong really worth having'.

While the CLGF strategic review strengthened my hand, damage had been done. I was informed by political friends that a prominent Labour MP with a marginal seat had been encouraged to take over my job once I was removed, although she denied this when I confronted her. In addition, ministers had been briefed negatively about me by a senior civil servant in the local government ministry who I had previously fallen out with. As a result, the UK ministry ceased its formal engagement with CLGF, although once I was fully vindicated, the UK Government, now under Prime Minister Cameron, resumed its CLGF membership through DFID.

Despite being fully exonerated and getting the unanimous confidence of my Board, the matter left a bad taste. My feelings were hurt because I felt I had not had the support of Labour ministers who I had previously engaged with and had an idea that some of my own senior work colleagues had known of the plot to remove me, ready to stab me in the back.

In the flow of the wider global events post-2008 this episode was not more than a little local difficulty, a political ripple soon resolved. But it was symptomatic of a deeper malaise in political structures in relation to democratic accountability, patronage and propriety in the use of public funds. It reminded me of the battles Sonny Ramphal had previously had with the British Government, which often forgets that it is only one of 54 equal Commonwealth member states.

A few years later, shortly before retirement, I again put my name forward for the non-party Lords appointment. This was on the active encouragement of Lord Howell, himself a senior Conservative grandee and long-standing champion of the Commonwealth, who acted as personal referee. Again, nothing materialised.

It seems the non-party system of appointment on merit is restricted to a derisory two or three appointments a year and is swamped by continued appointment of large numbers of purely political appointees by the Prime Minister and Opposition leader of the day. In fact, if anyone deserves an honour for selfless dedication and working with generations of young people for little personal reward, it is my wife, Adele. Yet when grateful parents and friends put her name forward for consideration for a UK honour on her retirement, the establishment was not interested.

Politics can be a dirty game.

34.

Millennium Development Goals to Sustainable Development Goals

DESPITE THE GLOBAL SHOCKS OF 9/11 AND THE 2008 ECONOMIC crash, there were countervailing forces seeking to strengthen multilateralism and give new momentum to tackle such vital global issues as climate change, sustainable development and rapid urbanisation. These were all areas I was intimately involved with.

In 2000, the UN had adopted the Millennium Development Goals (MDGs), eight international development goals with specific targets to be achieved by 2015. They dealt with eradicating extreme poverty and hunger, universal primary education, gender equality, child mortality, maternal health, combating HIV/AIDS and other diseases, environmental sustainability and a global partnership for development. The MDGs were ambitious goals and while some countries did achieve the targets set, many did not. Some specific global targets, for example reducing numbers of slum dwellers, were realised, but this reduction was overtaken by increases in the total number of slum dwellers during the period – a case of one step forward and two steps back.

Nonetheless, the MDGs provided a global developmental framework for the UN, international developmental agencies and aid charities. They did not however challenge the fundamentals of the global neo-liberal economic system and addressed only the results, not the causes, of the problems they reflected. Despite these limitations, I quickly realised the importance of the MDGs for local government. In developing countries local government was responsible for the delivery of many MDG targets, for example on housing, primary education and primary health care and disease eradication.

By the mid-2000s, I had been able to hold several activities highlighting local government approaches to implementing the MDGs. In 2005, I had arranged for evidence to the *Commission for Africa*, set up by Tony Blair, which was formally acknowledged by the Prime

Minister. Then in 2006 I organised a CLGF symposium in Kampala which adopted the *Kampala Agenda for African Local Government.*

A key element of our strategy was what we called 'localising the MDGs' by local government through planning and service delivery. This was a terminology originating from meetings of UN Habitat's earlier Urban Development Programme which I had participated in. At this time we had considerable interaction with UN Habitat through ComHabitat, designed to address urban development and engage with Commonwealth ministers on housing and urban development.

In 2007, MDG implementation featured prominently in the discussions at our 2007 CLGF Auckland Conference. Here leading MDG advocate, the economist Jeffrey Sachs, who I had invited as keynote speaker, made a strong public case for local government involvement stating: "the role of local government in the Millennium Development Goals is paramount ... and the empowerment of local government to get this job done is absolutely at the core of the Millennium Development Goals". This was the message contained in *'The Auckland Accord: Delivering Development through Local Leadership'* adopted by the conference and subsequently submitted to and endorsed by Commonwealth Heads of Government in Kampala in 2007.

In 2010, I participated in the UN's review of the MDG implementation at the *Global Forum on Local Development,* also in Kampala. The Forum noted the threat posed to MDG implementation by the 2008 economic crisis and explicitly recognised "the potential comparative advantages of local governments in delivering basic social services such as health, education, water and sanitation, promoting local economic development, responding to climate change and managing natural resources, ensuring gender equality, and contributing to state-building in post-crisis situations, and the direct and strong impact that local governments action in these areas could have on the achievement of the MDGs."

The 2010 Forum called on all partners to pursue what it termed *'Local development through Local Government (LDLG) approach'*, sometimes called the 'territorial approach to local development' by the EU, OECD and others. This provided a powerful endorsement of what CLGF had argued for in 2007 and subsequently, notably in the CLGF 2009 *Freeport Declaration on Improving Local Government; The Commonwealth Vision,* agreed at our 2009 conference in The Bahamas.

From 2012 onwards, serious thought was given by the UN and the international community as to what should follow the MDGs on their expiry in 2015. Developmental thinking had moved on since 2000 and the neo-liberal system had undergone a major shock with the crash of 2008. Economists like Thomas Piketty were documenting the extent to which income and wealth inequalities had spiralled under neo-liberalism. This opened the door to more interventionist economic strategies to tackle global development. There was also mounting worry about environmental and climate challenges, for example at the 2009 CHOGM in Trinidad, which I attended, and which preceded the UN Climate Summit in Copenhagen.

Growing global concern about sustainability was to lead to the concept of the Sustainable Development Goals (SDGs), building on the MDGs and the, by then, well-established concept of environmental sustainability, but taking it much further. The SDGs are to be implemented between 2015 and 2030 and were approved after several years of in-depth negotiations by the UN General Assembly in 2015 under the *2030 Agenda for Sustainable Development*.

Following much discussion, initially resisted by developed countries, the goals were expanded to a total of seventeen to cover the various concerns of all countries, including our Commonwealth small island states, not least on climate change (SDG 13) and sustainable use of the oceans (SDG 14). Significantly, the Agenda contained politically controversial goals on tackling corruption (in SDG 16) and on reducing income inequalities within and among countries (in SDG 10) – directly echoing the demands made back in the 1970s for a *New International Economic Order*. I was also pleased that there was further reference to ILO standards in the goal relating to economic growth and employment (SDG 8).

A key difference to the MDGs is that the new SDGs apply to all countries, developed as well as developing, in other words, the UK as much as Uganda, New Zealand as much as Nigeria. Their scope is therefore truly global, making the point that development is interdependent and cannot be seen in isolation.

The 17 SDGs, which have specific 169 targets for 2030 and many accompanying indicators of performance, are:

• SDG 1 No poverty
• SDG 2 Zero Hunger
• SDG 3 Good health and well-being
• SDG 4 Quality education
• SDG 5 Gender equality

- SDG 6 Clean water and sanitation
- SDG 7 Affordable and clean energy
- SDG 8 Decent work and economic growth
- SDG 9 Industry, innovation and infrastructure
- SDG 10 Reduced inequalities
- SDG 11 Sustainable cities and communities
- SDG 12 Responsible consumption and production
- SDG 13 Climate action
- SDG 14 Life below water
- SDG 15 Life on land
- SDG 16 Peace, justice and strong institutions
- SDG 17 Partnerships for the goals

One SDG I was especially involved in getting agreed was SDG 11 – Make cities and human settlements inclusive, safe, resilient and sustainable, to give it its full title. This has ten targets covering such issues as affordable housing, safe transport systems, integrated planning, safeguarding cultural and natural heritage, air quality, climate change and disaster risk reduction. SDG 11 clearly spoke to the local government work I was engaged with, and its adoption was a recognition of the importance of cities and local governments in SDG implementation.

As important as getting SDG 11 agreed was securing an understanding that all 17 SDGs, to be successful, required a bottom-up implementation at local community and especially local government level. They should not be imposed top-down by national governments or the UN but grounded in local realities. A study by the Technische Hochschule (technical university) of Berlin, later confirmed by the OECD, found that 66 per cent of all the 169 SDG targets require local application to be successful. As with the MDGs, this concept became to be known as 'localising the SDGs' and I and my local government partners found ready allies for this approach among civil society, academia and key UN agencies such as UNDP and UN Habitat as well as the EU.

In this global advocacy, I collaborated closely with United Cities and Local Governments and other partners in the *Global Taskforce of Local and Regional Governments* of which I was a founding member. The Task Force was set up in 2012 and held its first substantive meeting in Istanbul; many of the subsequent meetings were held in New York to provide opportunities to lobby key governments involved in the UN negotiations on the SDGs.

This necessitated frequent flights across the Atlantic between 2012-2015. During these visits I met with senior Commonwealth UN Ambassadors from countries like Botswana, Jamaica, Samoa and Uganda and secured their support, assisted by the able help of my Board members from those countries who I brought along to New York. I further benefitted from the excellent facilities of the Commonwealth Small States office, located close to the UN, and on several times sat in the official Commonwealth UN observer seat during the SDG negotiations.

The Commonwealth Secretariat had hosted an early meeting on what was to become the SDGs at Marlborough House in London. Yet a common complaint I encountered from the Commonwealth UN Ambassadors in New York was that the Secretariat was absent from the ongoing SDG negotiations and was not providing the expected technical advice. Indeed, apart from one short high-level event held by the Secretariat, it seems my organisation, CLGF, was the only Commonwealth body active during the actual negotiations, which I felt was a shame.

Apart from interactions at UN meetings, I sought to ensure that our own CLGF activities were geared to engage our members and partners on the SDG issue. Both our 2013 Kampala and 2015 Gaborone conferences had a major focus on the SDGs and were attended by Commonwealth Heads of Government from Uganda, Botswana, Rwanda, Sri Lanka and Malta, as well as leading UN figures like Helen Clark from UNDP.

In 2013, we adopted the *Kampala Declaration on Development Local Government,* together with a statement on Local Government's role in the post-2015 development agenda. These made the case for putting local government at the heart of development and the 2030 Agenda.

These ideas were elaborated in *The Gaborone Declaration – Local Government Vision 2030*, agreed by our conference shortly before the final adoption of the SDGs by the UN in 2015, setting out in detail our strategies for implementing the 2030 Agenda and localising the SDGs. The Statement called for clear acknowledgement and definition in respect of:

- "The key role local government has to play in setting, implementing and monitoring SDGs. The necessary enabling legal and policy framework needs to be in place.
- Strong intergovernmental relations between local, central, state/provincial government (horizontal and vertical) and

clarity of roles and functions, including with key sectoral ministries such as water, education and health, are essential to successful localisation of the SDGs."

Local government associations which are key CLGF members have a vital role to play in providing a voice for local government in these intergovernmental relations, as well as encouraging crucial capacity building activities of good practice sharing and training. This role should be supported and strengthened to support localisation of the SDGs.

As part of my SDG advocacy work, I took part in many international policy events. These included participating on a high-level UN panel alongside Heads of Government in New York and moderating a conference session on SDGs with UN Secretary-General Ban Ki-moon in Turin. At the latter event, I amused the Secretary-General by trying, not very successfully, to quote a proverb in his native language, Korean.

Helen Clark's UNDP had become an early champion for supporting local government engagement in SDG implementation and I liaised closely with her and her staff. Helen saw the value of local government and, as CLGF Patron, was an avid supporter of our work. Prior to the adoption of the *2030 Agenda* in 2015, UNDP undertook a series of country studies on how future SDGs could be localised, and I was asked to co-chair a key international consultation dealing with this issue, also held in Turin.

I co-chaired another important dialogue on institutional capacity-building for SDGs in Chisinau, Moldova, co-organised by UNDP, ILO and the German BMZ development ministry. At the time, Moldova was marked by the sad aftermath of communism with a bleak legacy of drab residential tower blocs, pot-holed streets and a general sense of decline. However, the local Moldovan wine, which has a history dating back to 3000 BC, was excellent.

The outcome, the 2015 *Chisinau Outcome Statement on Strengthening Capacities and Building Institutions for the Effective Implementation of the Post-2015 Development Agenda*, was broad-ranging but I was able to ensure a paragraph highlighting the need for empowering local government and their associations through capacity building. I also achieved the inclusion of the linkage of "localisation of resources alongside localising the SDGs", a concept I had coined earlier and which emphasises that local government needs resources to achieve its aims, not only 'unfunded mandates'. As such I was able to reflect our Global Taskforce's policy on SDG implementation.

Then there was the *Addis Ababa Conference on Financing for Development* held mid-2015 in Ethiopia which was an integral part of the 'means of implementation' of the SDGs and where I was accredited as a member of the official Commonwealth team. This was the first time CLGF had been formally part of a Secretariat team at a key intergovernmental event, a further example of our close interaction. At Addis we were able to get adoption of a substantive section on sub-national and local government financing into the final communique (under paragraph 34), a resounding advocacy success.

It was interesting to note how much Addis had improved since I had visited the city quite a few years previously, and I was also impressed by the gleaming new African Union headquarters where we had meetings with AU officials. Following my attendance in Addis I had to fly straight onto a series of meetings in Australia and the Pacific, on a very hectic and gruelling itinerary.

This time saw extensive collaboration with UN Habitat, headed by amiable former Barcelona Mayor Joan Clos. At the same time as the UN negotiations on the SDGs I and my Taskforce colleagues were involved in preparations for the 2016 UN *Habitat III Conference* in Quito, which was to adopt the *New Urban Agenda*, a substantive and detailed action plan, which complemented SDG 11.

These UN policy events allowed me to help ensure that the local government interests on the SDGs were heard loud and clear at the most senior level. Likewise, I participated in important EU meetings in Brussels on the SDG negotiations; the partnership I negotiated with the European Commission for 2014-20 contained financial support to allow us to pilot SDG localisation in Commonwealth countries in Africa and the Caribbean. I later also got involved in OECD policy work in Paris in relation to localisation of SDGs.

In late 2015, I took part in the ground-breaking *Paris Climate Summit* which set global targets for the deduction of carbon emissions. Climate issues including the vital need for adaptation and mitigation had been addressed in previous CLGF policy statements like our *Statement on Natural Disasters and Climate Change,* adopted by the CLGF Board in Vancouver in 2008, but was now taking top priority in local government work, leading many councils to declare their own 'climate emergencies' with specific targets for reducing local carbon emissions. The Paris Summit was held just after the Commonwealth Summit in Malta. Here Commonwealth Governments had agreed on a common position on climate change which, at our urging, included reference to local government, and this provided a springboard for a similar endorsement in Paris.

In Paris there was an accompanying high level local government meeting to input into the main event and ensure due reference to the local government role in tackling climate change. Among those addressing the mayors was Al Gore, former US Vice President and now leading advocate on climate action. During his session, the female journalist moderating suddenly collapsed unexpectedly into his arms. Apparently, this was not because of his male charms, but because of the excessive heat in the room. Happily, she soon recovered.

While in Paris, I and other colleagues joined the Mayor of Paris, Anne Hidalgo, in paying homage to the many innocent young fatalities of the appalling Paris terrorist attack which had just taken place. This involved a sombre occasion where I, alongside others, deposited a flower in memory of the victims at the Place de la République, another reminder of the new brutal realities of the 21st century.

The mounting worldwide concern over our Climate Emergency, demonstrated that any global warming above 1.5 C would be catastrophic. Not only for our Commonwealth small island states, but globally. The jury is out if Governments – and indeed individuals – will take the necessary carbon-reducing actions to reach zero carbon, and if an active adaption policy will be agreed to ensure that the change to clean energy is made.

As Greta Thunberg has highlighted, time is short if climate disaster is to be averted.

35

Final Acts and New Roles

IN 2016, I REACHED THE AGE OF 66. ALTHOUGH FIT AND STILL top of my game, I felt it was time to let new blood take over at CLGF and take on a different role.

One of my final acts before formal retirement was to negotiate new offices for CLGF at the Commonwealth Secretariat headquarters in Pall Mall, called Commonwealth House, and ironically the very same building where I had spent six years as Assistant Director. Apart from sharing common services, it was my hope that this location would further enhance the status of CLGF and lead to yet stronger inter-meshing and cooperation with the Secretariat and other partner bodies.

Our new office was alongside the Commonwealth Games Federation and the Royal Commonwealth Society in what was deemed the 'Commonwealth Hub' and was launched in grand style by no less a person than HM Queen Elizabeth II, Head of the Commonwealth, at a splendid event at Marlborough House where I briefed Her Majesty on our work. I felt I had left CLGF in 2016 with a sound and secure base for its future activities.

My official retirement party took place in July 2016 in the regal splendour of the Blenheim Saloon of Marlborough House. This was a venue I had been on innumerable past occasions and where CLGF itself had been launched back in late 1994. I was privileged to have the attendance of HRH the Prince of Wales, Prince Charles, the new Commonwealth Secretary-General, Patricia Scotland and my CLGF Chairperson, Rev Mpho Moruakgomo. All said nice things about me and my work, and I was proud when Prince Charles publicly praised my record of service and the work I had done for the people of the Commonwealth. I was also gratified at the warm messages I received from friends and colleagues from around the world.

My Board members, staff and various High Commissioners and dignitaries were present at my retirement party, together of course with

Adele, family members, including my German godson Johannes, his mother Heide, and Gary Smith and other close friends. My family and friends, not least my nephew Robert and his wife Rosie, were excited when I presented them to the Prince of Wales, the next King of England. I was impressed by the time and care Prince Charles took in talking to them, it being my task to escort him around and do the introductions.

As farewell, I was given two superb gifts from Botswana by my Chairperson and by the Botswana minister which they had transported all the way from Gaborone to London. These were large framed wall hangings which contained Botswana handicrafts, including an ostrich egg, and which now adorn the walls of my home in Kent, alongside many other Commonwealth mementos. It was a wonderful occasion which was rounded off by an intimate private dinner with family and friends.

I was pleased that my political or local government engagement did not stop with my full-time retirement from CLGF in 2016, although this has nearly all been *pro bono*. When I first had announced my intention to retire, quite a few of my Board members urged me to stay on and were worried about my succession. It was therefore agreed that I should help with appointing my successor and to continue to guide the organisation strategically as ex-officio Board member with the title of Secretary-General Emeritus. However, I was clear that this must not involve interfering with the role of my successor or getting engaged in operational activity unless requested.

The new CLGF Secretary-General turned out to be Dr Greg Munro, a South African, who impressed our appointment committee. While our choice was made on merit, I was happy that we chose a non-British Secretary-General, to emphasise the Commonwealth nature of our organisation. I was further pleased we chose a South African, given my own long association with the country.

Brexit has cast a dark shadow over CLGF and its ability to attract resources. By 2016, we had forged a strong partnership with the EU and were receiving more funds from them than from DFID and other Commonwealth governments combined. Over the past years I have met with Greg Munro and Lucy Slack and discussed issues where I hope I was able to provide useful strategic advice. In particular, I have advised CLGF that we must make it clear to the EU that CLGF is a Commonwealth, not British organisation, with remaining EU Commonwealth members in Cyprus and Malta, as well as in many of the

EU's ACP partner states and therefore deserves continued EU support. I was pleased to see that CLGF has now established an office in Malta to maintain an EU presence and EU support has continued. Partnership with the EU is too important to be destroyed by British Brexit policies.

I was disappointed that Greg Munro left CLGF in 2021, just at a time the organisation was experiencing significant difficulties on account of Covid and around funding problems. I was however encouraged to see the organisation being put into the capable hands of Lucy Slack as the new Secretary-General, given her long-standing experience and commitment to CLGF and look forward to giving her appropriate support.

It looks like my engagement with CLGF and local government is set to continue.

36.

Post-2000 Appraisal

TWENTY YEARS HAVE ELAPSED SINCE THE TURN OF THE NEW Millennium in 2000. A lot has happened.

Interacting with senior Presidents, Prime Ministers, the UN and Commonwealth Secretaries-General, European Commissioners and heads of other important intergovernmental organisations, as well as HM the Queen and HRH Prince Charles had become almost routine. Of course, I never took this for granted. I also valued my close engagement with elected mayors, local community activists and grass roots civil society campaigners at least as much. This allowed me to keep my feet firmly on the ground while mixing with esteemed company.

I need to acknowledge the generous organisational and political support I received from so many of my Board members, mayors, ministers and others like our academic associate members such as Professor P.S. Reddy from South Africa. I am especially appreciative of the close operational and indeed friendship I developed with some of my Chairs and Vice Chairs like Basil Morrison and Lawrence Yule of New Zealand, Bobby Montague of Jamaica, Adolf Mwesige of Uganda, Len Duvall from the UK and Philip McPhee of The Bahamas. But there were many others too, like Kwamena Ahwoi from Ghana and the quixotic Peter Woods from Australia, going right back to the establishment of the CLGF in 1995. Without their active engagement, CLGF would not have made the remarkable progress it did.

At the same time, I never forgot that ever since I started my career as a youthful activist in 1972, my aim in life has been to effect radical change and to run local campaigns. It was not to rub shoulders with the rich and powerful, still less with royalty. It was not to receive Government honours. As I have got older, I may well have mellowed and matured as far as my interactions with those of different views and dispositions were concerned. However, my core political beliefs centred on democratic socialism, combatting social inequalities and internationalism, including trade unionism, have remained firm and have not been compromised. I feel in that I kept true to the promise to keep the faith which I made to Jack Jones and my Labour Movement friends back in 1988.

I had founded and with the help of Lucy Slack and my dedicated staff built-up the CLGF as a significant international body over a period of more than twenty years with an annual budget of £4-5 million and overseas programme offices around the world: Accra, Pretoria, Harare, Columbo, Mumbai, Islamabad, Suva and Port of Spain. I was also able to achieve a unique organisational structure – not IGO yet with much of the clout – but not bureaucracy – of an IGO.

Apart from the Associated Organisation status we had at CHOGM and Commonwealth Ministerial meetings, we had established partnerships with important development partners like DFID and the EU and with private sector companies like Microsoft. In addition, we had strong links with key IGOs like UNDP and UN Habitat and worked closely alongside like-minded local government organisations like UCLG and CEMR/PLATFORMA.

Attending our biennial conferences, I realised the importance which top policy makers from all over the world, including local government leaders and senior ministers attach to these high-level CLGF events, and their policy recommendations which have been regularly endorsed by Commonwealth Heads of Government. Of course, the reason I was able to gather such senior policy makers and global leaders was due to the prestige of CLGF, backed up by the active engagement of our high-level Patrons and Board members as well as of our hard-working staff. Nonetheless, I take quiet satisfaction having started the institution from scratch in 1994 and I recall that colleagues jokingly referred to CLGF as 'Carl's Local Government Forum'.

To undertake our work, we required government funding as apart from some occasional programme finances, we did not receive funds through the Commonwealth Secretariat. Back in 2005, Prime Minister Tony Blair had highlighted the support the UK was giving for our, "work on local elections, elections monitoring and building the capacity of local councils" and had acknowledged "the value of your work to poor people". In 2011, Prime Minister David Cameron had said, "Local democracy, as promoted by the Commonwealth Local Government Forum, is a key component of the core Commonwealth values" and "we look forward to strengthening the UK partnership with the Commonwealth Local

Government Forum". We had received the similar endorsement from many other Commonwealth Leaders.

Gareth Aicken, a former Secretariat colleague, then employed by DFID, had been seconded to us in 2007 to help develop our strategic partnership with DFID and I regularly had close interaction with senior DFID and other Whitehall officials. In fact, for a while I was able to instigate joint meetings with DFID, the Foreign Office and the local government department to discuss CLGF's work and agree joint positions regarding CHOGM.

I was able to secure regular annual DFID grant support for our programmes averaging around £1-2 million annually, under successive Labour and then Conservative governments, and this was very welcome. But I was not able to achieve the kind of serious levels of funding from the UK or other Commonwealth Governments which I felt our work merited. I was particularly disappointed with Canada, which had funded the establishment of CLGF but then failed to give us support, yet quite happily gave regular grants to our francophone equivalent, the AIMF, in Paris. No doubt this was to appease local Quebec politicians. Australian and New Zealand support for our work was also somewhat erratic and I felt other large countries like India and South Africa could have done more.

Certainly, CLGF did significantly better in securing official funding, also from the EU and the UN, than most Commonwealth organisations. I, however, found it dishonest when donors told me that many millions of their public aid funds were devoted to local government capacity-building. In fact, these resources were more often than not pumped through large private consultancy firms charging huge fees, companies with little or no local government know-how, to the exclusion of ourselves and our members in the countries concerned. Yet CLGF working with its members in-country could have provided expertise and project management at a fraction of that cost to the public purse.

Globally, the MDGs of 2000 marked a cautious move away from neo-liberalism and the Washington Consensus. The 2015 SDGs were more of a bold break with the past and heralded a new-found faith in international engagement on core developmental issues, including addressing income inequalities. I was reminded of the deliberations back in the 1970s on the *New International Economic Order* and pleased to see this more interventionist approach re-enforced by a series accompanying global initiatives, most notably at the 2016 Paris and 2021 Glasgow Climate Summits.

Looking back, my past engagement first with the MDGs and then, more substantially, with the SDGs and other global events, such as the Paris Climate Conference, represented the pinnacle of my international career and professional work. I take much pride in what I was able to achieve in those years. I am especially happy that I was in a small way, together with other partners, able to contribute to the adoption of the SDGs and their subsequent implementation by local government.

After 2015, all UN member states are expected to incorporate the SDGs and their targets into their respective national planning and related instruments. They are further to report back to the UN regularly on their implementation through what are called voluntary national reviews. In addition, many cities are now submitting their own voluntary local reviews on SDG implementation. Well over 100 countries have presented national reports to the UN, the UK being one of the last to do so in 2019. However, it is by no means certain how many of the 169 SDG targets can be reached by the designated date of 2030 and the situation has been made worse by Covid-19 bursting onto the global stage and diverting resources.

Although the UK through DFID was a leading advocate of the application of the SDGs overseas, domestic implementation of SDGs has been poor. In 2016, I was asked to give evidence to the House of Commons Environmental sub-committee on how the SDGs were being implemented in the UK, and the committee went on to criticise how little had been done. A subsequent study by UK Stakeholders for Sustainable Development Network showed only 24 per cent of 143 relevant SDG targets being met with 57 per cent being adequately met and 15 per cent not all. In part this is because of the highly over-centralised governance structures in the UK, with most powers vested in Whitehall, unlike the situation in many other countries. Much can clearly be done locally to ensure sustainable development. In other words, to implement the SDGs from the bottom up, not top down, in line with the 2015 Chisinau recommendations.

Of course, effective decentralisation and local community empowerment is not the answer to everything. In the UK and elsewhere, economists and political scientists are now calling for more radical solutions to address social inequalities and decisively break with discredited neo-liberal policies, for example by provision of a universal basic income and moving to a four-day working week. However, the community and local government level is not a bad place to start.

The last years have seen the Commonwealth Secretariat under Secretary-General Baroness Patricia Scotland, a former minister under the Blair Labour government, face many difficulties. A particularly inflammatory political issue blew up just before the 2018 London Commonwealth Heads of Government Meeting, which damaged Commonwealth relations. This was the callous deportation of Caribbean citizens who had lived in the UK virtually all their lives since childhood, but never acquired formal British citizenship. Hardly a good advertisement for Britain taking over the chair of the Commonwealth that year.

UK Government decisions to pull out of the EU, downgrade the role of DFID and abandon the 0.7 per cent ODA target is also hurting the Commonwealth and poorer countries. I can only hope that the UK will keep its commitment to support the Commonwealth, including through bodies like CLGF and reverse its bilateral aid cuts to member countries, especially to the many vulnerable small states of the Caribbean and Pacific. To do otherwise would underline further how much the concept of 'Global Britain' is just a farce.

Patricia Scotland has also faced much direct criticism since taking office. She got off to a bad start at an inauguration party at Marlborough House at which I attended in 2016. The event was graced by Cherie Blair and other New Labour luminaries – something used against Scotland by Right-wing newspapers like the *Daily Mail*. There have since been repeated serious media questions over her appointments of consultants, dismissal of staff and spending on the Secretary-General's official residence, about leaked audit reports and formal employment tribunal judgements. These were issues that caused much concern to friends of the Commonwealth which found their expression in the articles of the Commonwealth Round Table and elsewhere.

More seriously the UK, Australia and New Zealand have followed Canada by slashing their funds to the Commonwealth Secretariat, creating an unprecedented financial crisis and reduction in staff numbers, claiming the organisation was badly run. I was particularly disappointed in 2019 when Commonwealth House and the Hub, so grandly launched by HM The Queen in only 2016, could no longer be sustained financially by the Secretariat. I am also sure this must have upset the Palace. In consequence, the CLGF and other Commonwealth partners had to find new offices.

While some funding has been restored, many Governments seem to have lost interest in the Secretariat and as a result, the Commonwealth is now a shadow of its former self. In the absence of a new vision and leadership, I genuinely fear for its future of the wonderful organisation to which I have devoted forty years of my life.

By 2020-21, the Covid-19 pandemic dominated everything with millions of deaths around the world, damaging economic shutdowns and huge potential social and political consequences with the poorest social groups most hit. There has been a failure to ensure the necessary international support for vaccine roll-out and at the time of writing only some 5 per cent of Africa has been vaccinated, leaving most of the continent's populations hugely exposed to the virus.

There had been ominous warnings in past years which had not been heeded. These included the 2002-03 Severe Active Respiratory Syndrome (SARS) and bird flu after 2009. I recall attending a WHO event in Washington back in 2010 where we looked at urban health inequities and how local government can play a role in combatting the spread of disease and epidemics. Unfortunately, inadequate resources have been put at the disposal of local government, which are at the frontline in the fight to tackle pandemics.

Ultimately, there will be a political reckoning for those governments which failed to take decisive action on Covid-19 or took the wrong steps, resulting in tens of thousands unnecessary deaths. Much is likely to depend on global economic recovery. If this is inadequate, the lessons of the 1930s, which saw the rise of extremist regimes are grim. Already political populists everywhere are poised to undermine liberal democracy and destroy what remains of international cooperation.

At the same time, Covid-19 has exposed the vital need for social solidarity, and for universal approaches to healthcare and social services. It has highlighted how essential workers like cleaners, shop attendants and bus drivers are more valuable than billionaires or hedge-fund managers. It has demonstrated that it is only the State and the public sector that can provide the necessary level of mobilisation to avert social breakdown. It has shown that viruses do not discriminate between poor and rich – although the latter may be able to isolate themselves a bit more in the short-term. This might just lead to a return to more social democratic and interventionist politics, pledged to address economic and social inequalities, as happened in the aftermath of the Second World War before the onset of neo-liberalism. Clearly government interventions and remedial actions are vital, a reliance on market mechanisms is not enough.

In 2022, the global community faces serious new geopolitical and security challenges on account of Russian aggression in the Ukraine.

The situation in China and the Far East also remains tense. Everywhere the post-1945 world order based on the Rule of Law and multilateral institutions appears under siege. The very foundation of global cooperation, which I had spent my entire life supporting, is under threat.

Today, the case for international cooperation to promote peace, democracy and the Rule of Law is greater than ever.

PART VI

ECHOES AND IMAGES
(Old Memories and New Plans)

"After climbing a great hill, one finds there are many more to climb"

NELSON MANDELA, PRESIDENT OF SOUTH AFRICA

My life was shaped by my childhood and younger years, especially as a teenager in the 1960s. Nor is it possible to separate work from home life, as the two interact, for example when Adele and I attended official functions.

37

Royal Encounters

PEOPLE AROUND THE WORLD THINK IT AMAZING TO MEET with HM the Queen, HRH Prince Charles and senior members of the British Royal Family. I did this many times.

As Queen Elizabeth II is the Head of the Commonwealth, encountering her and her family members was not unusual during my Commonwealth career, and I must have met with her on over a dozen occasions. Our encounters were mostly at official receptions, often Commonwealth events held at Marlborough House or at Buckingham Palace, and by their nature involving small talk. There was one occasion in 2016, when she launched the Commonwealth Hub, which I had helped to set up, when I had an opportunity of a longer chat with her. During this conversation, as always, her vivid interest in diverse Commonwealth organisations was evident.

The Queen has played an important role within the Commonwealth and opens the biennial CHOGM meetings, where she makes a formal address and engages with the leaders. Her commitment to the Commonwealth is apparent and she did not shy away from confronting Prime Minister Margaret Thatcher over issues like apartheid South Africa or the US invasion of Grenada. I recall attending the Royal Banquet at the 2009 CHOGM – having hurriedly had to secure a black-tie outfit for the occasion in downtown Port of Spain. The Queen had only arrived in Trinidad that morning and had already done official engagements. Yet she was full of energy, even to the extent that some tired elderly heads of government were looking to see when they could finally leave the banquet, it being strict protocol not to depart before Her Majesty.

All the times I have met the Queen she has been elegant, dignified and attentive and she is someone I have much respect for. Adele and I were privileged for many years to be seated alongside Her Majesty and the Royal Family in the central quire of Westminster Abbey during the multi-faith Commonwealth Day Service each March. This is a wonderful annual occasion when the Commonwealth is celebrated by all the main religious faiths, with much accompanying music, singing and cultural displays. It included Caribbean steel bands, Indian classical dancers and contemporary musicians and artists. The service starts with a Commonwealth Day Message given by HM the Queen, followed by an address by a well-known personality, such as the young Pakistani Nobel Laureate Malala Yousafzai in 2014. The British Prime Minister, Leader of the Opposition and all 53 Commonwealth High Commissioners are normally in attendance as well as many excited young schoolchildren from across the UK.

Prince Charles is also someone I have much regard for. I have had a number of personal encounters with him when we have talked in-depth about his concerns on the environment and urban planning, issues he cares passionately about. I found him serious-minded and paying attention to detail. I was very honoured in 2016 at my official retirement reception at Marlborough House London, when he was the main guest and made highly complementary remarks about me and the work I had done for the Commonwealth. He is now taking on major Commonwealth duties from his mother, especially where it will involve overseas travel. I hope he will give the Commonwealth the shot in the arm which it needs.

Other members of the Royal Family I have had detailed conversations with are the late Prince Philip and Princess Anne. As is well known, Prince Philip always liked to crack a joke, often not in the most politically correct manner, and he certainly enjoyed a bit of banter. Adele, too, has had amusing exchanges with him. Princess Anne, in contrast, has a serious nature and takes her duties, especially as Chancellor of London University, most conscientiously. I did see the late Princess Diana on a number of occasions as well.

I am less impressed with Prince Andrew, the Duke of York, who has always seemed more interested in commercial matters and whose unsavoury personal entanglements have recently been exposed in the media. This was underlined when The Queen stripped him of much of his royal and other duties in 2022. I once encountered Prince Edward, the Earl of Wessex, at a Commonwealth reception but failed to recognise him. I then committed the ultimate faux pas of asking him what he did for a living. I cannot recall being given a clear answer – it was probably not a question he was used to being posed to him. I was fortunate not to be blacklisted from Commonwealth receptions or locked up in the Tower of London for my insolence.

A strange interaction with the Royals occurred some years ago. Adele was asked out of the blue to put on a ballet show with her best pupils at a private birthday party of Princess Beatrice, the daughter of Prince Andrew and Sarah Ferguson. This took place at their home near Ascot and all the kids were excited to take part, with Adele remarking how casual and relaxed the royal couple had been. Yet within just a few days after this happy family event, all hell was to break loose. This was when 'Fergie' was photographed in a highly compromising position with her American adviser, who Adele had seen at the birthday party.

The royal scandal was splashed all over the popular media. Somehow the press found out Adele had been at the royal household just a few days previously and started hounding her for comment and gossip. This she resolutely refused to give. It got so bad, that we decided to hide away at our country cottage in Kent until the media frenzy had blown over. I guess the fees for newspaper interviews might have paid off our mortgage, but it would not have been the right thing to do.

I respect British institutions and The Queen's role in the Commonwealth, but I have never been an avid royalist; if anything, I was a republican in my younger days. I have now come to appreciate the role and value of a constitutional monarchy as practiced by the House of Windsor and have seen the dedication and hard work of HM The Queen, Princess Anne and of Prince Charles, including the wonderful work being done by the Prince's charitable foundations. I am impressed by the modern approach of the younger Royals like Princes William and Harry. At the time I was encouraged by Harry's marriage to Meghan Markle, and her progressive and feminist ideas, which I felt could have been a real asset to the Royal Family. Sadly, the unfair abuse she was subjected to by the British media led her and Harry to opt out of their royal duties and live aboard.

Where I part company is with the wider group of royalty beyond the immediate core royal family. I do not think that they should receive State income or have special privileges. There should also be an examination of whether the vast amount of feudal property and possessions held by the Royal Family should be acquired and owned by the State. Here, the model of the Scandinavian and Dutch Royal Families with their modest lifestyle seems more appropriate.

As I have already recounted, I feel that the current British royal honours system is a farce. It has been misused by successive Governments to reward their own political class, financial donors and other cronies. I would not go as far as the late John Lennon who turned his 'gong' – it was an MBE, Member of the British Empire – into his doorbell. But the current system should be scrapped and replaced by something more transparent and modern. Any new awards should have less pompous and have modern titles perhaps with the word 'Excellence' replacing 'Empire'.

It has been a long time since the 'British Empire' was dissolved.

38.

Shaping My Life

AS A YOUNG BOY I WAS ONLY VAGUELY AWARE OF GLOBAL geopolitical changes. Growing up in different countries, however, exposed me to diverse cultures from an early age.

My birthplace was the then West German industrial city of Dortmund, just five years after the end of the Second World War in 1950. Following the Nazi dictatorship of 1933-45 and the extensive destruction during the Second World War, US troops of the 95th Infantry Division fought their way through bombed ruins to occupy the city in April 1945.

Dortmund was then assigned to the British zone of occupation until the establishment of the Federal Republic of (West) Germany in 1949, the year I was conceived. The British Army of the Rhine (BAOR) were however to remain another forty or so years, initially as occupiers, then as close allies under the NATO umbrella until the end of the Cold War. It is to its presence in Dortmund and Germany that I owe my move and subsequent upbringing, education and professional life in Britain.

My childhood and young years up to 1973 were divided between living in Germany, England and Wales. Growing up in countries with different, although common European, historical and political perspectives had its intellectual and cultural benefits. I became bilingual in English and German, although sadly I never learnt Welsh as my family lived in an Anglicised part of Wales, South Pembrokeshire.

These diverse cultural identities deepened my understanding of history and encouraged me to have an internationalist and European outlook on life and become a Global Citizen. This found its reflection in my later professional career and personal relationships. It gave me a sense of ease when encountering other nationalities and cultures and allowed me to forge close friendships across the world. It included long-standing attachments with many non-European colleagues in Africa, the Caribbean, Asia-Pacific and elsewhere, without preconceptions or, I hope, prejudices.

As a young child, I grew up playing in the post-war rubble from the aftermath of the war. I heard horror stories of the wartime bombings and destruction and how my German family had huddled in our basement to escape death while bombs were falling all around them, while neighbouring houses were set alight. Even today, ugly remnants of that period remain and only a few years ago a 4,000-pound bomb was defused, requiring a temporary evacuation of 20,000 inhabitants – as still happens in London and many towns in Europe. I heard less of what terrible devastation and plight Germany had inflicted on the rest of Europe during the war, especially the horrors perpetuated following its invasion of the Soviet Union in 1941, or about the atrocities of the Holocaust.

This was a time of shortages and austerity. It is ironic that West Germany, as the defeated country, was able to dispense with post-war rationing of food as early as January 1950, a month before my birth. In contrast, Britain, the victor, had to endure rationing until July 1954, a whole year after the coronation of Queen Elizabeth II in 1953.

By the time I first entered primary school in 1956 at the age of six, things were really beginning to look up. Economic recovery was well underway and unemployment levels were coming down. As elsewhere in war-devastated Europe, building reconstruction was booming. Dortmund regretfully lacked resources to reconstruct old historical medieval buildings in their attractive original style. Much of the city became blighted by bland and sometimes Brutalist 1950s architecture, although a softer design has taken over in later years.

If I have one abiding early childhood memory it is that everything appeared in shades of black and white. Dortmund, in the heart of Germany's industrial Ruhr, was a city of heavy industry – iron, steel, engineering, coal mining, as well as beer brewing. It had ugly bombed-out dwellings and eerie, shadowy ruins. They were devoid of colour, the air was filled with obnoxious fumes from innumerable coal fires and steam railway engines, the skies were dark from thick pollution emitted by factory chimneys, and buildings were blackened by soot and smoke. Nor was it in any way unique. I recall seeing London's Whitehall, long before it was cleaned up, and thinking it could more aptly have been called 'Blackhall'.

Contemporary media lacked colour. Photographs were black and white, as were the movies you watched at the cinema. That exciting innovation, television, presented the same monochrome world. Even automobiles were mostly black in coating and people, especially elderly men at work and sad, widowed women, wore black clothes and shunned bright colours – or so it seemed.

My first eight years until 1958 were spent in my grandparents' house in downtown Dortmund. My mother, Ilsemarie, had been divorced when I was only three, so I grew up in a one-parent family. I was never hungry, even if meat was often only served on weekends. I still recall the sickly smell as my elderly great-grandmother, who lived with us, singed the feathers off a freshly slaughtered chicken in the kitchen ready for our Sunday treat.

Weekdays involved hearty soups and potato-based dishes; we also enjoyed such delicacies as dark rye bread with butter and sugar on top, rather than jam. Despite these dietary restrictions, there was flour available to make sumptuous and delicious home-made cakes and biscuits. This was an austere, but basically healthy diet with plenty of vegetables and there was never any takeaways or fast food. As I had to walk on foot literally everywhere, with little sitting down watching TV, still less in front of non-existing computers, I was never overweight, let alone obese.

Our spacious turn of the nineteenth century terraced family house had three substantial stories. It also had a frighteningly dark cellar leading to a tiny back yard and small garden with a big horse chestnut tree at its end. The cellar housed an old-fashioned, blazing coal-fired boiler which supplied the ancient but effective central heating system. I recall big dirty lorries, laden with coal, tipping their heavy produce down a long chute which connected the outside of the house directly to the boiler room. I also recollect my dear grandmother in her dressing gown and slippers going into the cellar at the depth of a cold winter's night to shovel coal into the roaring boiler, so as to keep the flames going and the house warm. Certainly, I never grew up wanting in the comforts of heat or hot water to wash or bathe with.

I was surprised that when I moved to England, central heating was often still an exception rather than the rule and seen as a luxury item. The Army quarters which we inhabited for the ten years between 1958-1968 were frugal and had no central heating. Likewise, my later wife Adele's parents never had central heating in their substantial, but often cold, West Hampstead home until the day they died at the turn of the century. Nor did we shower, given we had no shower cubicles in any of my childhood homes. Instead, you would lie and soak for ages in a big bathtub in hot soapy water. This is unlike today where my house in Kent now has a spacious walk-in shower but no bath.

My mother's German family was professional middle-class and my grandfather, Dr Werner Franck, was a respected dental surgeon, always called 'Herr Doktor'. After the war they were not particularly wealthy. Following a serious road accident, when my grandfather was disabled and no longer able to work, my grandmother went back to her old pre-war job of teaching. She also rented out rooms to make ends meet, while my mother did simple secretarial work. While money was short, it was a comfortable time with a wide circle of uncles, aunts and family friends.

I had a loving grandmother, Ilse Franck, who greatly spoiled me all my life and was very much a second mother to me, given the absence of a father after my mother's early divorce. This was also because her only son and my mother's sole sibling, Werner, had been conscripted into the German Reichswehr at the very end of the war, aged a tender seventeen, and tragically was killed in action in April 1945 just a few short weeks before the German surrender in May. I was, therefore, a second son to her. Likewise, her own mother, Marie, my great-grandmother, who was to reach the age of 94, was a loving influence, stimulating my imagination with exciting stories of adventures in her early youth many years ago.

In 1958, we moved to England when my mother married my stepfather Donald Wright, a lowly private in the British Army from a working-class family in east London. He was in the Royal Electrical and Mechanical Engineers and would progress to the rank of Staff Sergeant; being of no mean intelligence he later successfully took a bachelor's and master's degree at the Open University.

My new life in England involved living in spartan, Army married quarters near Reading, and we had very little money, only supplemented by occasional support from my grandmother. At times this involved my mother doing menial work as she did at Huntley and Palmers biscuit factory, which had the advantage of her bringing home broken biscuits, which could not be packaged, for our tea. I also recall our icy cold rooms at our Army quarters in Wales. In winter, the only source of heat was in our living room through a single small paraffin stove, emitting unpleasant and smelly fumes which left an ugly black mark on the ceiling. It was so damp that the salt and sugar in our kitchen bowls often solidified.

My parents never owned or drove a motor car. Many of the things we now take for granted – refrigerators, washing machines and dishwashers, telephone and television – came into our household only much later. Household machines were expensive in the 1950s and 1960s. I remember that our first black and white TV in the early 1960s was rented, not bought, a common practice in the days when ownership of a TV cost a small fortune.

Indeed, in those days it was normal to lug washing to the local launderette. Here you would wait until a washing machine was free, insert coins to pay for the wash, and read a magazine while it took place. You then hauled the clean washing back home. I also well recall squeezing into a red telephone box located at the end of our street together with my mother to place an overseas call to my grandparents each Christmas, often with snow outside. There would be a pile of shillings, which had been saved up, to pay for a short three-minute call.

In 1968, when I was just finishing grammar school, Donald left the Army to work in electronics in the private sector. Thanks to help from my grandmother my parents were then able to buy a small modern terraced house in Bracknell New Town in Berkshire. Frau Franck, as she was known, also left Germany to live in a little house of her own near my parents. Only then did their living standards improve.

Regretfully, I never got on with my stepfather, and having merely vague recollections of my real father, who had never even lived much with my mother, lacked a father-figure throughout my life. Donald was a recluse, and we had virtually no contact with his own family, from which he was estranged, having left home at a very young age to join the Army. This was a different and tougher life from what I had enjoyed in my younger years in Germany. However, my dear mother was always loving and devoted to me until her very untimely and painful death from throat cancer at the age of 67. As it happened, she died the same weekend in 1997 as Princess Diana had her fatal car crash.

As a child I grew up at the height of the Cold War and frequent East-West tensions. I sensed the deep anxiety and fears of grown-ups around me whenever major international crises occurred when armed forces were suddenly put on alert and when acute nuclear conflict threatened. The absurdity, but also the dire danger, of the nuclear weapons age was aptly portrayed in Stanley Kubrick's brilliant anti-war satire *Dr Strangelove or: How I Learned To Stop Worrying And Love The Bomb*, released in 1964 and starring Peter Sellers. It is a movie still all too relevant today given the new Cold War tensions with Russia.

This constant sense of global tension was not something I can easily forget. It was especially acute during the 1962 Cuba Missile crisis, when we were living on a British Army base in Manorbier, Pembrokeshire in west Wales. The base had been set up back in 1937, originally as an

RAF station and School of Artillery, linked to a top secret installation at nearby Lydstep for radar-controlled anti-aircraft guns, then a new technology.

Being on Britain's remote Atlantic coast, Manorbier Army base contained state-of-the-art early warning radar systems to detect incoming Soviet missiles. It also housed Thunderbird surface-to-air missiles. Much of this was hidden deep inside the rugged cliffs of nearby Skrinkle Bay, where I would go swimming, together with other NATO military hardware. As a result, we would have been a prime target in any nuclear attack.

Happily, sanity prevailed. A compromise was found between Washington and Moscow over Cuba, which resulted in a cooling of tension. It involved removal of nuclear missiles, and installation of a 'hot line' between the two capitals. It was quite a few decades before the ever-ominous threat of atomic obliteration truly eased. In 1983, Armageddon was again narrowly avoided when the Soviet Union nearly launched nuclear missiles, having mistaken a NATO military exercise, Able Archer, as preparations for a first strike against them.

This constant Cold War worry provided a daunting background to a young teenager growing up in the 1960s. My part-German background, with its acute awareness of the monstrosity of the Nazi past, also evoked deep feelings of guilt about the war and the Holocaust. It led me to hold anti-war sentiments and an intense dislike of all things military. This was perhaps not the best attitude for the stepson of a member of the British Armed Forces. In truth, despite his Army uniform, Donald was more of an electronics technician than an arms-carrying soldier and to be fair he did not really try to change my views.

For much of my childhood right up to my early teens, family entertainment was based on reading books and listening to the radio, given we did not have TV until 1962. The radio – or wireless – had only a few limited BBC stations and included programmes such as *Two-Way Family Favourites*, a music request show which linked up service families in the UK with those stationed in Germany and elsewhere. There were also comedy shows like *The Navy Lark* and *Hancock's Half Hour*. *The Archers* radio soap actually started in 1950 and is still going strong today after more than seventy years.

By the late 1950s, cultural life and culinary tastes began to change. I recall my first-ever visit to the only Chinese restaurant in Reading in 1959. 'Exotic' foreign food was still a rarity, and it was a while before

Indian cuisine became popular; and there were few takeaways other than from traditional fish and chip shops. The only other type of 'fast food' was the rather flaccid Wimpey burger, taken with mugs of weak instant Nescafé, coming as it did many years before the age of McDonald's and Starbucks.

In the late 1950s, a weekly cultural highlight was a visit to the local cinema for Saturday morning pictures (movies). This was designed for younger kids and featured action films starring such notables as Robin Hood, the Lone Ranger, Superman and Batman. It was an event I eagerly looked forward to each week. Although I was only nine or ten years old, it was normal for me and other children to hop on a bus and or walk everywhere on our own, without being chaperoned by our parents. It was a more innocent and safer age.

My family was secular and not churchgoing, and Sundays were boring. When it rained, there was little else to do apart from listen to the radio, read books or play with my toy soldiers or my electric train set. We had no car, buses were on restricted services and all shops were shut, excluding any chance of going out for retail therapy. Not having a family car meant that we took few trips away from our immediate surroundings with only rare excursions into the countryside. I never even experienced the seaside until our move to coastal west Wales in 1962 when I was twelve years old.

My frugal upbringing influenced my later support for the underdog and instilled a desire to get on, academically and professionally. This was perhaps re-enforced by being an only child. I attended numerous schools between 1956 and 1968. These included a miserable stint at an austere Army Boarding School during a brief return posting by Donald to Germany in 1961. The school aped the public-school system, discouraging parental visits, and had a harsh physical education regime and corporal punishment for minor misdeeds. I was useless at practical subjects, and I recall a woodwork teacher at a later school who would bash my head against a wall if I got something wrong: not quite in line with today's progressive teaching methods.

I remember when I first moved from Germany to England near Reading in 1958, I was mocked at school for having a German accent and for 'having lost the war'. Although only just about conversant in English since 1958, I still scraped through the Eleven-plus selective exam a couple of years later. I then proceeded to one of the UK's first fully comprehensive and mixed sex establishments, Greenhill School in Tenby, Pembrokeshire in 1962.

My school results improved each year, and I got the school's top GCE O-level results in 1966. That same year my family moved near Wokingham in Berkshire where I went to the all-boys Forest Grammar school. Ironically, I was now teased about my recently acquired Welsh – not German – accent and my O-level results were looked down upon as 'being only from Wales'. I thus made sure I got the school's best A-level results in 1968 to prove a point.

These experiences served to re-enforce my sense of straddling different cultures and I never really fitted into any typical English – or indeed German – stereotype. This probably made me averse to identifying with any tight-knit social or national group. If anything, my personal and cultural associations are closest to Wales. It was here where I spent happy formative teens, playing rugby and dating my first girlfriend, Susan Griffiths. Here I felt accepted and respected as an individual on my merits and not judged by class, nationality, or accent.

The mid-1960s was the time Wales dominated the rugby world. There were superstars like Barry John, J.P.R. Williams and Gareth Edwards and Cardiff Arms Park – the Millennium Stadium had not been built – rarely saw happier times with the scarlet jerseys of Wales regularly crossing the try line to score for their country. I have avidly supported Wales ever since.

I soon got into the game, starting as a forward in the scrum front row and progressing to second row and finally wing forward or flanker. To my own surprise, I ended up in the school 1st XV at the young age of 16, apparently quite an achievement. Here I played alongside an older schoolmate, Jim Shanklin who was soon to be capped for Wales and then become the captain of the renowned London Welsh rugby team when this was the top rugby club in England. As a rugby forward, I guess I was pretty tough, once returning from a match with a blood-soaked jersey, much to the dismay of my mother. But I was lucky never to have suffered serious injuries or breakages while playing.

It was in Tenby at school where I met Garfield – later Gary – Smith. We spent time early on travelling overseas together and having much fun. Our friendship was consolidated by my inviting Gary to come to my old family home in Dortmund in 1966, his very first overseas trip. This was an enjoyable visit, crowned by an exciting live Rolling Stones rock concert in Dortmund's big Westphalia Hall, just when the famous group had hit the big time.

Gary later went on to work in the Oil Trade and lived for some years in the Arab world and we differ in our political opinions and social attitudes. We married at around the same time and were the best men at each other's wedding. His wife Andrea became a close and dear friend, and their children, Martin and Megan, are godchildren to me and Adele; both have both now progressed to successful careers and have their own children.

I was a teenager in the 'Swinging Sixties', a decade when things changed much for the better. This applied to the vast majority of the population, not only the young, at least in Britain, the US and in Western countries. A foremost cultural influence on me, and so many millions of others, was The Beatles rock group – and not just their wonderful music, which I adore, but also their hairstyles, fashions and views which I avidly followed and adopted.

Soon I had every 'Fab Four' record, bought in the case of 'singles' vinyl records for the princely sum of six shillings and eight pence. This I purchased at the one and only record shop in Tenby from my scanty pocket money. To buy the long-playing LPs or albums, I had to save up the larger amount of one pound, twelve shillings and three pence, but a shorter EP – extended play – with four songs-only cost eleven shillings and eight pence. I bought as many Beatle souvenirs and nick-knacks as I could afford and was a fully paid-up member of the official Beatles Fan Club.

Even to this day I have a fascinating collection of innumerable newspaper clips and photos of the Fab Four from the years 1964-65 when I was fourteen, assembled in several bulky scrap books. They are probably worth a small amount at any Beatles memorabilia auction.

The Beatles were the spearhead of a wide range of new musical talents, starting with fellow rock groups of the 'Merseyside sound' and soon blossoming into other rock stars like the Rolling Stones, The Who, Pink Floyd and many more. The group themselves were influenced by artists such as Bob Dylan, whose early music I much enjoyed. The exciting Tamla-Motown 'Black' music of the 1960s also impacted greatly on their work.

It was the time when to my delight pop and rock music finally got an outlet on the radio and TV. Pop had originally been confined to a few sparse weekend slots on BBC radio, but this monopoly was broken by Radio Luxembourg. Its non-stop pop music could be best received at night, this being the time before digital radio or even FM. I often listened at night under the bedsheets to my little battery-run transistor radio when my parents had ordered me to go to sleep – which could be as early as 9 pm. Then, starting in 1964, it was the turn of the so-called pirate radio stations like Radio Caroline, broadcasting illegally from old Second World War Sea Forts in the Thames Estuary, just outside UK territorial waters – and not far from my later Kent home.

The new youth-centred culture helped to breakdown rigid class and social barriers of the past. It was facilitated by ordinary, especially working-class, people benefitting from economic prosperity and their growing wage packets. The 1960s saw a wide range of progressive social reforms which included the decriminalisation of homosexuality, introduction of the contraceptive pill which led to greater sexual freedom, the emergence of women's rights, labour and employment reforms and student's participation in governance at universities.

The voting age, too, was brought down from 21 to 18 and I voted in my first General Election in 1970 when I was twenty. Ever since then I have chosen progressive Left/centre parties, whether Labour, Liberal Democrat or Green Party, depending on who was best placed tactically to win in whatever constituency I happened to be registered to vote.

A striking feature of the 1960s was the relaxation of the previous strict censorship laws in the arts and literature. This was signified by the decision to allow the publication of D H Lawrence's *Lady Chatterley's Lover*, copies of which soon circulated among my teenage school friends. We were less interested in its obvious literary merit, but rather its description of explicit sex acts. This was a time when such material was still illicit and difficult to acquire, quite unlike today's prevalence of easily accessible online pornography.

The late 1960s saw widespread challenges to established authority by student, youth and feminist movements, which came to a head in 1967-68. Within this heady mix was a growing and vociferous global opposition to the Vietnam War while in the US, policies of racial segregation were finally being challenged and dismantled in the deep South and across the country.

It was the time when the New Left, represented by writers like Herbert Marcuse and revolutionaries like Malcom X, who distained old style Marxism as much as Social Democracy, was in the ascendancy. One of the leading lights of the student and youth movement at the time was the Marxist Tariq Ali, and his recollections, *Street Fighting Years*, provide a vivid insight into both the exuberance and ideological debates of the 1960s.

The year 1968 was the peak of the student and youth movement of the 1960s. The *soixante-huitards* (sixty-eighters) had a big impact everywhere and in France almost brought down the government of General de Gaulle. This was the very year I started my BSc Undergraduate studies in Geography at University College London (UCL), which is part of the University of London.

UCL is the oldest English university college in England after Oxford and Cambridge and was set up as a radical alternative to the established universities. It was the first university to proudly open its doors to non-conformists, Jews and free-thinkers and took in women students from an early stage. This was a legacy of eighteenth-century philosopher, Jeremy Bentham, famous for his philosophy of utilitarianism – achieving 'the greatest happiness for the greatest number'. It is consistently rated among the top academic institutions of the world, alongside Oxbridge, Harvard and Yale and its academics and scientists recently played a prominent role in the fight against Covid-19.

One of the more unusual and little-known sights of London is the mummified body of Jeremy Bentham. This sits on a chair in a wooden-doored and glass-fronted 'telephone kiosk' in the main hall of UCL looking like the 'Tardis' time machine from the BBC TV series, *Dr Who*. Like some other great men, Bentham seems to have gone a little funny in the head at an old age. Before he died, he left precise instructions for his mummification, stipulating precisely the white trousers and red coat he wished to have his preserved remains dressed in. This was in order to ensure that 'his physical presence was there to inspire future generations'.

Today, the only artificial bodily part of Mr Bentham is a Madame Tussauds-like wax head – the actual skull sits in a wooden box nearby. It used to be tradition for students from UCL's rival Kings College London, to steal the skull. In what must surely rate as one of the more unusual university rituals, the body of the great man is brought forth once a year before the assembled UCL Vice Chancellor, academic staff and student body. He is then indeed present physically to 'inspire' the current generation and its thoughts and deeds.

In my Geography undergraduate studies, I focused on regional and urban economic planning, complemented by applied economics. This involved writing mini-dissertations, one of which was on the regional economic impact of Birmingham airport. My studies entailed a fair bit of research and reading of numerable books and articles, mostly the University of London's library in Senate House. The year 1968 was long before the onset of the internet, and I spent many laborious hours in the library. My work on city planning also led me to cast a critical eye on the urban environment of our family home in Bracknell, one of the London New Towns, set up after 1945 to accommodate overspill population from London.

As part of my Geography studies, I had to undertake field work. Among the more interesting trips I did was to visit Landkreis (county council) Unna in Germany. Unna is large semi-rural council east of Dortmund on the eastern periphery of the Ruhr conurbation. The Chief Executive Officer of the council, Dr Lothar Voit, was a close friend of my grandmother's brother, great uncle Willy Ackermann. Dr Voit took a liking to me and offered me a summer job working in his council's planning office.

I proceeded to make good use of this opportunity to research the district's recreational policy, the provision for parks, sports facilities and the like, and setting out fairly innovative criteria for future development in a report. Dr Voit was sufficiently impressed by my work, which I had written in German, that he had it published as an official council document. In retrospect, it was a foretaste of my much later local government work.

In London, I lived in a male student hall of residence in Camden between 1996-71 which became mixed male/female in my third year there. This was quite a revolutionary step at a time when the sexes were often still segregated. One of our self-indulgent decisions as a collective student body was to vote to have a new colour TV installed in the hall. Colour TV had only recently started in the UK and we loved seeing our favourite cult comedy shows like *Monty Python's Flying Circus* in all its glorious technicolour each week.

The 1960s were a time when drugs became freely available. These were mainly soft drugs like marijuana – 'pot' – not harder drugs like LSD or cocaine. UCL was no exception and there were many occasions when the sweet smell of pot pervaded my hall of residence. Unlike later US President Bill Clinton, I neither smoked nor inhaled. This was not on account of any puritanical streak or lack of opportunity; I always hated losing control and have only been drunk on very few occasions. Having grown up in tiny Army quarters, filled by my parent's tobacco fumes, I had also developed an early aversion to smoking, and have never smoked a cigarette in my life. I am sure if I had instead been offered nicely baked 'pot cake' I might well have taken it – and swallowed.

A funny incident occurred at the official opening of UCL hall of residence. This was done by the University's Patron, HRH the late Queen Elizabeth, the Queen Mother, accompanied by the Vice Chancellor and various assorted dignitaries. As witnessed by Alan Scheifla, a school friend from Tenby, HRH was being shown student rooms when she was intrigued by loud music from one of the rooms – where the students were smoking pot. Luckily, they were not too stoned to put their joints away before the royal party descended on them, but the room was blanketed in the sweet smell of marijuana. While the Vice Chancellor and his entourage must have been in something of a panic, HRH's knowing comment was along the lines of, "What a nice room, but wouldn't it be a good idea to get some fresh air in here?"

It was during my time at UCL when I found, belatedly, my first serious girlfriend. She was a young Danish au pair, Annelie. I had met her on a night-time venture to one of London's many trendy discos, the Scotch Club of St James. At that time such discos were not over-expensive to visit. Its Wikipedia entry describes it as a "historically significant meeting place for London's rock elite in the 1960s", but I was certainly no member of the rock elite.

On graduation at UCL in 1971 and in tune with the prevailing spirit of student rebellion, I did not bother to attend the graduation ceremony for my Bachelor of Science BSc (Hon); I received a 2.1 grading, apparently being a highly borderline First. In retrospect not going for graduation was unfair on my proud mother. I then had to decide what to do with my life and how to earn a living.

I was able to postpone the day of reckoning by choosing to continue my academic studies. This time I selected a subject involving politics and economics, deciding to do a Master of Arts (MA) in Contemporary European Studies at Reading University, having by now become hooked on the issue of 'Europe'. I preferred the one-year MA to a longer two- to three-year MPhil or PhD doctorate course at Sussex University, which was also on offer. Here I might have run across a young Thabo Mbeki, future President of South Africa.

At Reading I wrote two mini dissertations. One was on the political position of the British Labour Party and the EEC, something I had by now gained personal insights into and I recall discussing this with my tutor, Avi Shlaim. The other was on the consequences of European economic and monetary union on regional policy, where I co-authored an in-depth research paper with another tutor, Geoffrey Denton. The latter paper made a strong argument that with a European Monetary Union peripheral regions and Eurozone countries would suffer economically on account of investment being drawn to central areas such as Germany.

I further served as research assistant to renowned academic historian Professor Hugh Thomas, compiling what was frankly an academic pro-EEC propaganda book, *Europe the Radical Challenge*. He gave a most generous attribution in the acknowledgments saying: "…this book owes a great deal to my research assistant … many of the good ideas are his … he guided me brilliantly over some tricky ground". Having just missed out on a First at UCL, I was proud that on attaining my MA in 1972, I scored the top academic result of our year.

I soon realised that there was much more to a university or higher education than just formal study but an opportunity to shape your personal and intellectual horizons. Higher education should never be a job-production factory. I am grateful for having had the opportunity to have an academic education at a highly formative time of my life, benefitting from a generous state grant and absence of any tuition fees, unlike those burdening today's students in England.

Increasingly, I began to understand the political and economic forces which lay at the heart of our society, about which I had previously not thought deeply. This experience shaped my consciousness and contributed to my becoming politically engaged and a grass roots activist. My university years 1968-72, influenced my future outlooks, especially my subsequent dedication to progressive Left-leaning politics. I became what is now sneered at as a 'metropolitan liberal elite'. Yet frankly this strikes me in line with mainstream European and global Enlightenment values and vastly preferable to being an 'illiberal populist xenophobe'.

Looking back, my early life and student experiences marked the beginnings of becoming a Global Citizen.

39.

Greek Colonels and other Foreign Adventures

MY FIRST REAL TASTE OF FOREIGN TRAVEL WAS IN THE EARLY 1970s when I nearly ended up in a fascist jail. It seemed I liked youthful activism from a young age.

My first visits to West European countries was as a student in the late 1960s to the three centres of European institutions: Brussels, Luxembourg and the birthplace of my grandmother, Strasbourg. Most of these trips involved attending student conferences. I recall in particular my fascination with the unique Gallic atmosphere of Paris on my first stay in France; eating sweet-smelling warm croissants and delicious freshly baked baguettes accompanied by steaming-hot *café au lait*.

There was much of Europe I had not seen. On completing my MA in 1972, I decided on a whistle-stop tour of central and southern Europe by train, together with my friend Gary Smith. Our European tour in 1972 was a formative experience and embraced Switzerland, Austria, Hungary, the then Yugoslavia and Bulgaria, something like a country a day. Our 'Grand Tour' ended in Athens, Greece. I subsequently flew to Izmir in Turkey for a few more days to visit the ancient site of the fabled city of Troy. I then went by overland bus to Istanbul, my first encounter with the exotic East and its colourful bazaars, aromatic spice markets and golden-domed mosques.

At the time Greece was, like Spain and Portugal, under totalitarian military rule. The brutal Greek colonels had viciously repressed political opposition in the birthplace of democracy. It was not a logical choice of holiday venue for a progressive student activist and should have been out of bounds. I, however, had a serious mission to accomplish in Athens which could have resulted in imprisonment.

One of my other tutors at Reading University, George Yannopoulos, was tied up with the exiled political resistance. Learning I was going to visit the Balkans on holiday, he urged me to go to Athens to pass a confidential letter to the student opposition in Athens; this was after all long before emails or the internet. I realised that this was a risky exercise which could have landed me in deep trouble if I had got caught.

Having agreed, I arranged to include Greece on our tour of Europe. When Gary and I arrived in Athens there was much cloak and dagger activity. After making contact with local student activists, I had to go through various intermediaries. They vetted me closely before I was deemed safe enough to see their leader. When we eventually did meet, it was in circumstances not dissimilar to a thriller set. It was at night-time, and we were sitting in an inconspicuous unlit car, parked on a dark hillside overlooking the beautiful panorama of Athens and its magnificent Acropolis. It was an appropriate place to meet and hand over my clandestine letter.

Gary and I managed to do some sightseeing in Athens, but frankly I was looking forward to leaving, having accomplished my undercover task. I was therefore glad when we reached the airport. Imagine my alarm when having just gone through passport control, the sinister looking emigration official with dark glasses insisted on calling me back. For a moment I feared the worst. Happily, it was only to stamp my passport, so I was able to depart and avoid rotting in a fascist jail.

I was to have ongoing correspondence with the Greek students after my return to England and helped to draw attention to their struggle. Two years later in 1974, student activists in Athens successfully confronted the colonels and led the restoration of democracy. It turned out that the student leaders I had met played a central role. I was now living in Brussels and joined my European colleagues to celebrate the collapse of the hated dictatorship. There was further jubilation at the demise of the fascist regimes in Portugal and Spain in 1975. These were heady days and we cheered loudly the establishment of new democratic governments after years of repression.

My delight about the new democracies in Europe was tempered by the news of Pinochet's bloody regime seizing power in Santiago in 1973 and the killing of the democratically elected President Salvador Allende. There had clearly been CIA involvement. The news from Chile got progressively worse with political executions and torture. Before long we were trying as best we could to give support and solidarity to an ever-growing flow of political exiles from Chile. Many of these found refuge in London and I was to become good friends with a number of them and I am reminded of their fate today when I see the desperate plight of refugees today, whether from Africa, Hong Kong or the Ukraine.

The instability in Athens had had repercussions on Cyprus where Turkish troops invaded and occupied the north of the country. As a result, the island has been tragically carved up between a Turkish north and Greek south as I witnessed on a number of later visits. It is something about which I remain deeply concerned, especially when I correspond with my good friend Lazaros Savvides, a former mayor and senior government official from Cyprus.

Eastern Europe, in the meantime, remained under the thumb of Moscow. Elsewhere, especially in Africa and Latin America, brutal one-party tyrannies prevailed, backed respectively by the superpowers that were the USA and USSR in the name of Cold War expediency.

The 1970s saw terror-related political agitation in Europe. At the heart was the Palestinian-Israeli conflict, leading to hostage taking and the callous killings of Israeli athletes at the 1972 Munich Olympics. Far-Left groups like the West German Baader-Meinhof cell undertook a prolonged series of bombings, political assassinations and kidnappings, directed at what they perceived was a fascist state having ex-Nazis in positions of public prominence.

When the leaders of the Baader-Meinhof cell where caught and imprisoned, this led to further hostage takings and plane hijackings, as in Entebbe in Uganda. I remember still seeing the shot-up hijackers' plane at the side of the Entebbe runway when I landed there some years on. Terrorism was met with resolute counter measures under German Chancellor Helmut Schmidt. The ultimate failure of terrorist actions led to the suicide of Baader, Meinhof and other cell members in a futile attempt to achieve political martyrdom.

While I can comprehend the political motivation of the Far Left, I condemn terrorism in the strongest terms. This sort of action can never be justified in European democracies any more than far-Right terrorism. I have always stayed clear of extremist politics, as a student and later. Only where there is no alternative to democratic reform, as was the case in apartheid South Africa or brutal Latin American dictatorships, would I condone revolutionary or violent measures. But such action must be aimed at the repressive regime and its armed forces and not harm innocent civilians. For the same reason, I could never accept the violence of the IRA and its bombings of civilians, which I encountered myself, although I have sympathy for the historical desire for Irish unity.

I became a committed socialist, but a democratic socialist, respecting parliamentary sovereignty and Rule of Law.

40

Facing Superpower Rivalries

NOT LONG AFTER MY INITIAL EUROPEAN TRAVELS I WOULD venture further afield. This was to take me to the USA and USSR and introduce me to the two rival superpowers and their dark arts.

I had early encounters of East-West confrontation when I had visited my grandmother's other brother, German great-uncle Curt Ackermann in West Berlin as a child. This was to leave a lasting impression on me. In 1961, the East German Government with Soviet backing closed all border crossings between East and West Germany and built the notorious Berlin Wall, with its barbed wire and death strip – its so-called 'anti-fascist bulwark'. The Wall was fortified with floodlights, guard dogs, trip-wire machine guns and patrolling soldiers with orders to shoot on sight. It had been constructed to stop the flood of East Germans emigrating to the West, which was having a catastrophic impact on the East German economy.

The cruel division of the city separated families and loved ones. Over the nearly thirty years of its existence the Wall saw many attempts at escape to the West, resulting in 171 deaths and numerous imprisonments. Remarkably around 5,000 East Germans did manage to flee successfully from East Germany during this time, often in adventurous circumstances. On several trips to Berlin, I was a witness to the Wall's inhuman nature, running like a bloody gash across the heart of the city. I did on one occasion cross the Wall which was possible if you were a Westerner going East, but not if you were an Easterner wanting to go West.

The Cold War tensions I had experienced as a boy in the 1950s and 1960s remained in the 1970s. However, the decade saw a thawing of the hitherto icy relations between East and West because of Willy Brandt's *Ostpolitik*. By the mid-1970s I was actively engaged at global level, and I was soon comfortable finding my way around the labyrinth-like UN conference centres of Geneva and New York where the two superpowers confronted each other through diplomacy. I also travelled to other exotic and not-so-exotic overseas venues.

I rapidly became an expert on last-minute airport check-ins and how to try and get the most comfortable economy seat – if there is such a thing – on long overnight transcontinental flights. Unlike today, air travel was less stressful. Prior to 9/11, check-in and airport security were minimal, and airlines had not yet learned how to pack-out every seat. There was a good chance of finding room next to you and even stretching out over three seats. This was also the time of the so-called 'mile high club' of intimate encounters in the skies, although I never quite managed that kind of thing.

In the summer of 1971, I travelled for the first time across the Big Pond to the USA – something I was to do regularly in future, on occasions four or five times a year. The country was under the controversial rule of President Richard Nixon, with its bloody embroilment in Vietnam; just a few years later in 1974 the Watergate scandal was to force Nixon's resignation from the Presidency in disgrace. However, the new US engagement with communist China guided by Henry Kissinger helped defuse global tensions.

My first impressions of New York were just how big everything was: the skyscrapers, the freeways and the automobiles and, of course, the Big Mac hamburgers and sumptuous ice cream sundaes. I was enthralled by 'The Big Apple' eagerly exploring the many sights, pounding the pavements and criss-crossing Manhattan. It was a city I was to visit dozens of times, mainly on UN business. It is a place I never failed to enjoy, with its vibrant, multi-ethnic and cosmopolitan population. I can safely say that after London, it is my favourite global city, followed by Paris and Berlin.

My American visit involved a student summer job in Atlantic City, New Jersey, for a full two months. This was quite a difference from my previous holiday jobs hiring out deckchairs on Tenby beach, doing the Christmas postal rounds in Bracknell or being bored out of my mind in an office physically sticking national insurance stamps into certificates all day long.

I had a distant family contact in Atlantic City who helped me get a position as a general dogsbody in a small seaside motel just off the city's famous seafront boardwalk.

Even at that time, before casinos came in a big way, Atlantic City had its fair share of the Mafia. On one occasion I was woken up in the middle of the night by loud gunshots. Another time a sinister-looking guy walked into the motel reception and demanded to see the manager. When the manager appeared, they sneaked off to the back of the office where I saw a big bundle of dollars being handed over from the safe, no doubt protection money.

My memories of New Jersey were of long and hot summer days, and a sweltering heat I had never experienced in Europe; of beautiful sandy beaches; and of failed romances with pretty American girls. I was still quite shy in those days. I also struggled with American English. On one occasion I nearly got beaten up by a guest's angry husband. His wife had asked me to give her a wake-up call in the next morning, and I duly asked at what time I could 'knock her up'. This was an innocent phrase in UK English, but with quite a different meaning in American English.

I made an American friend, Scott Berkey, who later became an airline steward and whose air miles put mine in the shade. He graced my 1975 wedding, a posh event with morning suits, standing out in the most loud, bright orange checked jacket imaginable.

Atlantic City was followed by a hectic solo tour right across the States by overland Greyhound bus. My travels must have set new endurance records. In only three weeks, I visited stately Washington DC; Birmingham, Alabama and the deep South; New Orleans with its jazz haunts; San Antonio, Texas and the famous Alamo; and the Grand Canyon in Arizona with its breathtaking beauty. I then crossed the Rio Grande to Chihuahua to get a flavour of Mexico. I went on to bustling Los Angeles in California, staying with another distant family friend, a retired movie cameraman, in the heart of Hollywood, seeing Disneyland and Sunset Boulevard.

My last stop on the west coast was colourful San Francisco. In 1971, the city was at the tail-end of flower power. I was put up by an ageing hippy who took me to an impromptu 'happening' in a fringe theatre with performers dancing naked on stage, fuelled by pot. California was followed by a rapid return via the Mid-West, with fleeting stops in Chicago and Detroit. I often slept in cheap motels or travelled overnight by bus to save money. I became an expert on Greyhound timetables and the location of downtown bus depots. Finally, I got the flight back home from New York to the familiar territory of Old Europe, having savoured my first exposure to the New World.

Just a few years on, I was to take an almost similar routing across the USA. This was however courtesy of the US State Department and the generosity of the American taxpayer. It took place under its 'Young Leaders Programme', a US Cold War initiative to influence promising young foreign leaders, most likely vetted by the CIA. I had just taken on quite a key position at the International Confederation of Free Trade Unions, so perhaps this had elicited some interest at CIA Headquarters in Langley. I however took the visit more seriously than most and undertook an intense programme of meetings across the country, which I was free to choose myself, with initial briefings and meetings in DC at the Brookins Institute and the US Labor and State Departments.

Apart from discussions in Washington, I had exchanges with US union officials engaged in industrial struggles, such as garment workers in New York City, textile unions in South Carolina, farmworkers in California and autoworkers in Chicago. Now I travelled in luxury by air and was put up in good hotels with all expenses paid. I can however vouch for the fact that you see more of the real America on Greyhound buses, and by staying in run-down motels.

My early venture to the USA must have given me a taste for the exotic and the wider world. In the summer of 1973, my friend Gary and I decided to travel East, not West, embarking on a tour of the Soviet Union. Our itinerary embraced the austere capital Moscow, graceful Leningrad, Kyiv in the Ukraine and then flying thousands of miles east to exotic Tashkent and Samarkand in the heart of Soviet central Asia.

In retrospect, the Soviet trip was a little odd. It was supposed to be a standard *Intourist* private package holiday and was fully paid for ourselves. I should have been wise to the fact that normal package tour tourists are not met by luxury limousines at each airport, booked into top hotels and provided with personal guides to show them around. One of our guides was a young Russian girl who spoke good English, but whose otherwise pleasant appearance was marred by an entire set of gold front teeth. This made me think that I was in a James Bond movie.

Originally our *Intourist* trip had been fully booked, but miraculously two places materialised. This was after I had spoken to a contact at the Soviet Embassy in London given to me by Gwyn Morgan, with whom I was working in Brussels. The diplomat was Victor Kubekin, political attaché and a popular figure at Labour Party Conferences. Years later he was – surprise, surprise – revealed to have been a senior Colonel and alleged KGB operative at the Embassy. Maybe the fact that I had just started quite an important position at the European Commission had been of interest to the KGB.

Our Soviet visit turned out to be much fun. On arrival in Moscow, we were put up at the grand Metropol Hotel just off Red Square. Here each floor was overseen by a large austere Russian lady who kept a close watch on all who came and went. At the time we did not really focus much on politics or ideology. I did however notice that our breakfasts were rationed to a single cup of coffee. Consumer goods in the shops also appeared scarce. One evening in the hotel restaurant we were invited by a drunken Russian to join in the vodkas at a wedding party and render a 'British folksong'. Well lubricated by vodka, we chose that well-known Welsh ditty, 'Lloyd George knew my father, my father knew Lloyd George'. Our Russian hosts got the tune and the song reverberated across Red Square into the night.

In Leningrad, now again St Petersburg, we saw rich European heritage, lovely waterways, fabulous museums and beautiful Tsarist palaces. I admit that I fell in love, at least for one night, with an attractive young Russian lady I had met at the hotel disco and one thing led to another. I did keep up brief correspondence on returning home and when I last heard from her she was working at the Soviet Embassy in Kampala. Perhaps she had not been such an innocent liaison after all. I was just a red-blooded young bachelor in those days, without a care in the world, so there could be no consequences and I never heard any more of the matter. Of course, I was never under any illusions about the dirty tricks of the KGB and the repressive state mechanisms which underpinned most of the Communist world. But in our youthful naiveté, we noticed little of this at the time.

The ensuing flight to Kyiv was eventful, with stormy turbulence rocking the plane back and forth in a frightful manner. Matters were not helped by the overhead lockers being overloaded. I seem to recall that these held live chickens clucking excitedly in their cages. In those days internal Aeroflot flights in the USSR had a dodgy reputation for safety. In retrospect I shudder at what we had let ourselves in for. Happily, we made it down safely. Kyiv and its architecture reminded me of central European cities and underscored the common culture and heritage we share with Russia and the Ukraine. Situated on the mighty Volga river, the capital of the Ukraine had impressive war memorials commemorating the success of the Red Army in World War II. It is so sad to see it facing destruction and destitution some fifty years later in 2022.

Next, we set off on the long flight across the Ural Mountains on to far-away Central Asia to rediscover the ancient Silk Road on the tracks of Marco Polo. In Tashkent we found a local disco with Western-style music and danced with American girls also touring the Soviet Union. Samarkand, with its strong Islamic traditions and beautiful, blue-domed mosques and exotic Eastern bazaars, was the highlight of our tour. Walking around the hot, dusty unpaved side streets with their shabby houses, we saw just how different the local culture was from what we were used to. We witnessed much poverty, although not as acute as what I was to encounter on my subsequent trips around South Asia.

I sometimes wonder whether MI6 or the CIA got wise about me and my Soviet adventure. Quite likely notes were added to the political blacklist they probably already had compiled on me when I was a Lefty student at university, or so I like to think. This idea is not so ridiculous as it might sound as this is what happened to many student activists. MI6, as revealed by ex-operatives such as Peter Wright in his book *Spy Catcher*, was paranoid about the student Left. It engaged in illicit surveillance of such notable 'Leftists' as Jack Straw and Peter Mandelson, both to become pillars of the political establishment in Tony Blair's Labour Government.

The CIA may have got more concerned about me when, by chance, I met one of their most damaging renegade operatives, Philip Agee, at a Left-wing political conference in Brussels in the mid-1970s. Apart from facilitating the overthrow of President Salvador Allende in Chile, the CIA was, according to Agee, up to much mischief in Latin America and elsewhere.

Years later when I was Director of the Commonwealth TUC, I had the distinction of being visited in my London office by a CIA 'spook'. This happened just after I had phoned to check on my trade union members in Grenada, following Ronald Reagan's 1983 invasion of the small Commonwealth Caribbean island. My organisation had publicly denounced the US invasion of Grenada, but this was hardly a radical position. Indeed, the same sentiment was shared by much of the Commonwealth, including its Head, HM Queen Elizabeth, who had angrily summoned Prime Minister Thatcher from a Cabinet meeting in Downing Street to Buckingham Palace to demand to know in no uncertain terms what was happening. Likewise, when I met Prime Minister Indira Gandhi not long afterwards in New Delhi, she expressed to me her strong disquiet about the unilateral US military action.

My creepy Embassy visitor proceeded to justify the US invasion. Showing me a photocopy of internal minutes of the ruling New Jewel

Movement of Maurice Bishop, he in all seriousness pointed to what he termed 'Marxist terminology'. After listening to this nonsense for a while, I dispatched the hapless operative with the thought that perhaps the US constitution should not be judged by Richard Nixon's Watergate tapes and all its depleted expletives. He was not much amused by the comparison.

During the years of East-West conflict both US and Soviet Embassies in London sought to excel themselves at hosting lavish receptions to which I was invited. I tried to be even-handed in my acceptances and it was a shame that at the end of the Cold War these lively events largely ceased. My subsequent invites, as Commonwealth diplomat, to the annual Queen's Garden Party at Buckingham Palace, were very distinguished. But they did not really match up to the lavish superpower hospitality celebrating the 4th of July Independence Day and the October Revolution. Certainly, the whiskey bourbons and the icy vodkas served were more fun than drinking cups of English tea on the Palace lawns.

As a child of the Cold War, I gained early experience of superpower rivalries.

41.

Private Interludes and In-between Pastimes

MY FRANTIC PROFESSIONAL LIFE INVOLVED DEPARTING FOR overseas missions at weekends with long overnight flights to Africa, Asia, the Americas or further afield. As a result, my personal life often felt like short private interludes and mere in-between pastimes.

When I was back to my office in London from overseas, I would be travelling across the UK to meet people and attend conferences. Once I took responsibility for local government after 1995 this involved the annual conferences of the Local Government Association of England and Wales (LGA) the Convention of Scottish Local Authorities and the Society of Local Authority Chief Executives. I still attended the annual Labour Party Conference, where now I was classified as a distinguished 'overseas' diplomatic guest rather than party member, but slowly my attendance petered out.

Inevitably, these many absences from home took a toll on my family and social life. Luckily, my wife Adele was very engaged with her highly successful dance school. She would spend much of the time when I was away with her mum, Bobby, who lived next door. In fact, we eventually got around to putting a gate between our back gardens, so these were interconnected. Bobby was an elegant and astute elderly lady, who, after her husband Max, a master builder, had died, went on to live to ninety in robust health; this was no doubt facilitated by the support she received from Adele. Bobby represented the artistic side of Adele's family; she had been a dancer back in the 1920s and was good in writing sweet little poems and stories; a skill which Adele has inherited.

Adele's younger brother, John, followed his father into the building trade and lived not far outside London in Surrey with his first wife Catherine and two sons, Robert and Edward. John was to go through a divorce and married a Danish woman, Mette, and went on to have two children, Thomas and Mathilda. John now has a unique business of engraving bricks for charities. His older son Robert proceeded on to an extraordinarily successful career, setting up a specialist furniture and woodwork business. He married his wife Rosie, and has three lovely children of his own, Isabel, William and Reuben. He is astute and hard-working and is our favourite nephew.

In 1979, my stepfather Donald had got a job in aerospace in Munich and he, my mother and grandmother moved from England to the Bavarian village of Neufahrn where my beloved grandmother Ilse Franck was to die in 1983. I had regular visits to Germany to see them, often linked to excursions to the beautiful Bavarian Alpine mountains and lakes.

In 1990, they returned to the UK and went to live in Whitstable, Kent. Here, Donald now ran a small high street newspaper shop with, to my dismay, crammed and uncomfortable above-shop accommodation. I still cannot understand why after a good career in electronics he chose this path. Sadly, my mother, who frankly should have retired by now, did much of the unsocial hours involved, often at considerable physical effort, but she never once complained. It also meant Adele and I did not see her as much as I had hoped, and her excessive workload may have contributed to her early death.

The year 1997 was a bad one. Adele's sister, Yvonne, a lovely jolly lady and a talented Royal Academy-trained painter, died in March of bowel cancer at a much-too premature age of sixty. Then, in August, my dear mother Ilsemarie passed away from throat cancer aged just 67, after unsuccessful hospital treatment and a short stay in a hospice in Canterbury. Both Adele and I were deeply upset at our family losses. All this stress placed serious strain on our marriage, not helped by my being immersed in politics and spending time away from home.

I last saw my mother at the archaic Kent and Canterbury hospital on a hot day in late August 1997. I was appalled at how the National Health Service had deteriorated and become run-down after eighteen years of Tory Government; Tony Blair's government, which was to plough much money into the NHS, having only assumed power that year. She was in a large public ward with truly third-world conditions, overcrowded and with over-stretched nurses. There was no air conditioning or even fans despite the intense summer heat, with poor Ilsemarie herself resorting to putting wet towels on herself to keep cool.

A day later, my mother died suddenly during the night in circumstances never quite explained. I suspected something had not been quite right, as she had certainly not been on her deathbed. I would have liked an autopsy, but my stepfather did not want to go through this. Donald died only a few years later, a lonely man, spending much of his time in pubs, again only in his late sixties. Adele and I had tried to engage with him after my mother's death, but these encounters were tense and unproductive, so we became detached from each other.

Ilsemarie's death led me to reconnect with our German family in Dortmund: Peter Ackermann, the sole son of my grandmother's brother, Willy, and his two children, Dieter and Heide and their spouses Christa and Markus. It was nice to see that they made up for our lack of family offspring when they had, respectively, four and three children. Two, Cleo and Johannes, became my godchildren. Thereafter I kept up regular contact, especially with Peter and also Heide, who is a lovely person of whom I am very fond. It was nice to have my relatives from my home town attend my 60th birthday celebration in 2010 and my retirement party in 2016. Prior to Covid, I visited the city of my birth once a year, often around Christmas time to see the traditional Yuletide markets with the alluring smells of mulled wine and roasted almonds.

I also re-established warm contacts with my father's family in Berlin, my dear aunt Rosemarie Winckler (née Wilms) and her husband Bert who is now 92, with Rosemarie just a few years younger. I had sought to contact my birth father, Rosemarie's brother, Karl Helmut Wilms, with whom I had had no links since I had been a young child in Germany, only to find that he had died a few years earlier. Looking back, it was ironic that I had been a naughty page boy at Rosemarie and Bert's wedding in Detmold, Westphalia in 1955 at the age of five, but that had been my last contact with them.

Since meeting them in 2009 in Berlin and their attendance at my 60th birthday in London, I developed a close and warm relationship with Rosemarie and Bert, their two sons, my cousins, Eckhart and Gerald, and the latter's sons, Julius and Leon, with frequent visits to Berlin, a vibrant and exciting city. Regretfully, I never met my other aunts like the late Anno Wilms, who was an accomplished professional photographer in Berlin. I did however attend a retrospective of her work some years later. Rosemarie, became a real surrogate mother to me and has been very kind; despite her advanced age she sends me regular WhatsApp messages accompanied by topical videos and photos.

Bert Winckler, although too young himself to serve in the German Army, had suffered greatly because of the war. One of his older brothers had been killed in action and the other had died of typhoid in captivity.

Most dramatically, when the Red Army entered Berlin in May 1945 and reached his family home, they discovered that his father, now elderly, had been a German officer. Without any trial, his father was taken into the street and shot dead in the presence of his traumatised son.

This wartime suffering, which was widespread in Germany, does not diminish or excuse the horrors which the German Army and the Nazi regime had inflicted on innocent civilians, and above all the Jewish population, throughout Europe, especially in Poland and Russia. Despite having been schooled and raised for much of my life in Britain, where I studied, worked and married, I have always felt a deep personal shame and abhorrence about the atrocities committed by Germany in the Second World War and the Holocaust in particular. Once I moved to Britain, I sought to play down my early German upbringing and later shortened my surname to Wright.

This inherent guilt about the War has troubled me throughout my life, especially when I have been with Jewish friends and colleagues. It is not something I can forget or come to terms with, even though I value and enjoy much of Germany's rich culture and traditions. This is why I abhor any form of anti-Semitism or racial prejudice, especially where it is directed at refugees or immigrants.

After 1991, summer weekends and mid-year holidays were spent at our lovely little country cottage in Hoath, East Kent. We were often joined by Gary and his wife Andrea and their children. Adele's mum Bobby would, on occasions, visit, together with her little barky Yorkshire terrier and her adopted tortoise, Horace, nearly 100 years old, who we were to inherit. Once returning, late at night to London by car, loaded with our two dogs, my mother-in-law, her dog and tortoise, we broke down on the motorway. Informing the AA breakdown service that we had an elderly lady, three dogs and a tortoise in the car caused great amusement. It meant that the AA arrived remarkably quickly to fix us up.

During the 1990s, Adele and I became regular visitors each winter to the pretty little Austrian Alpine village of Maria Alm, an hour's drive south of Salzburg. I had learnt to ski in the area in the late 1970s at a relatively late age. Through Adele's London friends, Vicky and Jeff Alexander and their talented daughter Sara, who is an actor and writer, we became good friends with Anna and Peter Hattinger, who owned a grand family chalet in the village, where they rented out luxurious *en suite* rooms during the winter season. Anna was a Czech émigré who had left her country after the Soviet invasion of 1968, and Peter was Austrian.

Our early trips to Austria involved much snow and sub-arctic temperatures, but in recent years, global warming meant good conditions for skiing were not guaranteed. By 2015, we had visited so many times that the local mayor presented us with a 25-anniversary year medal, some flowers and a jolly feathered Austrian hat to acknowledge our loyal patronage. We had great fun in Austria and I was pleased to return there for my first post-Covid overseas trip in 2022.

A highlight was New Year's Eve, with vibrant fireworks and seeing the traditional *Pechtentanz*. Performed on a remote mountain top, the 'dance' sees local villagers don foreboding traditional costumes and beautifully carved wooden masks. Posing as demons and witches holding leather whips and broomsticks, they seek to drive away the bad spirits of the old year. In the process they whip curious tourists and onlookers, spooking them badly.

On occasions, things would get boisterous. I recall making a fool of myself when I partook in a local tradition of rolling naked in the cold snow after a hot sauna. I promptly found my back seized up, preventing further skiing that holiday. In truth, we enjoy the cosy ambiance, hearty food and local folk traditions, the après-ski – as much as the skiing. Adele herself never really got into the sport. Once I had accomplished the big downhill ski runs, I found the quiet solitude of cross-country skiing more attractive. Even in 2020, at the age of seventy, I enjoyed 25-kilometre cross-country hikes, skiing on high mountain runs, often climbing up to 1000 metres. Admittedly I usually had a few 'pit stops' at local inns for liquid replenishment.

Before the Covid lockdowns of 2020-21, we took much advantage of London, engaging in the capital's fabulous cultural pastimes, the West End theatre, ballet at Sadlers' Wells, classical concerts at the South Bank, Barbican Centre and Albert Hall, and visits to the British Museum and art galleries. A particular favourite is the amazing Tate Modern, housed in a massive old turbine hall on the south bank of the Thames. At one stage, I managed to see Wagner's entire Ring cycle at the Royal Opera House, Covent Garden, a sublime musical experience. Adele is less keen on such musical endurance tests, but did join me for rather different, but equally enjoyable, live concerts by my old pop idol, Paul McCartney several times, including an open-air performance in Hyde Park where we rocked on the lawns to vibrant Beatles songs. It is good to have variety in your life and London as the most wonderful city in the world offers these in plenty.

Occasionally, I get a ticket to see Wales play rugby and go for a few pints of ale at the London Welsh rugby club, near Twickenham, where I am a member. Previously these social occasions were limited by my inability to plan and book ahead of time as I was likely to be getting on a plane to the other end of the world. However, I was often near a TV set for a live rugby transmission and exchanging views by text about ongoing score-lines with my good friend Basil Morrison in New Zealand who was watching from the other end of the world. Once Basil and I attended the players' private post-match reception in Cardiff following an All Blacks-Wales encounter. It was amusing to see the muscular rugby players with their battle scars, including black eyes and bruises, all dressed up in smart suits and ties.

Over the years Adele and I have been fortunate to visit many countries and have friends in all corners of the globe from The Bahamas to New Zealand. In 1997, a global local government event was held on the beautiful Indian Ocean state of Mauritius, which despite its small size, has a thriving multi-party system of local government. A member of the Commonwealth as well as of the Francophonie, Mauritius is bi-lingual in English and French and has inherited fine French cuisine. It is blessed with attractive sandy beaches and a lovely climate. Adele's older sister, Yvonne, had recently died. I accordingly arranged for Adele to join me in Mauritius for a bit of a break and we stayed at a beautiful seaside resort, La Pirogue.

While I was at my meetings, Adele befriended a scraggy little stray dog on the beach. She soon bonded with us and would follow us around and we called her 'Mini Minor'. We decided to take Mini to a local vet for anti-flea treatment but were horrified to be told strays should be 'fed to the crocodiles'. Adele left for home before me, and it was heartbreaking to see Mini run and run after our departing taxi until she collapsed exhausted on the roadside. Sure enough, on my return, she was loyally waiting for me in front of my beachside hotel room. As a result, I took the decision to take Mini back with me to London.

This was no easy task as she had to get UK Ministry of Agriculture clearance and on arrival, she was forced to spend a miserable six months in quarantine; unnecessary as Mauritius is rabies free. Back she did come, flying on British Airways at some considerable expense, to say nothing of the subsequent quarantine fees. Once in England, Mini put on weight and the quality of her fur improved. However, we were in for a shock. One rescued dog turned into five when she unexpectedly bore four puppies. At this stage I thought I may have to re-mortgage our house to pay for all the new kennel fees. Absurdly, the puppies, having been born in the UK, were released from quarantine after only a few weeks while poor little Mini had to stay on without her pups.

This touching story hit the UK media with special features in the Sunday papers and Breakfast TV came to our garden to film the playful puppies. Soon we were deluged with requests to take in the sweet little dogs and were sent donations from across the country, which we forwarded to the Mauritius dog charity MSPCA to help other strays. All the puppies found a home and we were delighted when Mini finally came out of quarantine. She was to spend many happy years with us, far away from her hungry existence on a beach in Mauritius.

Although we had many opportunities to travel together with my work, Adele was normally busy running her dance school in London and could only leave during school holiday time. She was also frankly not too keen to sit around alone at a hotel swimming pool waiting for me, all day, to come back from meetings late at night. It was moreover expensive to have her accompany me around the world as I never earned a large salary and we always paid for ourselves. What we did do was to arrange for her to join me at the tail end of one of my overseas visits, maybe once a year, and we would then spend quality time together.

Most of our vacations have involved a fair bit of sightseeing as we do not like just sitting on a beach. Sometimes we were truly foolish. On one occasion we got out of our car in the middle of the Kenyan bush to take photos, despite lions being present in the area. Another time a massive python-like snake wriggled closely past us while we were sunbathing on the beach at Lombok. Looking for big hippos on foot in the bush by Lake Malawi was not too bright either. I furthermore think Adele was not too amused when she discovered, on our first trip to Sri Lanka, that we were in an active war zone, or when we landed in Georgetown, Guyana, during a spate of kidnapping of foreigners.

Adele and I attended many official functions together, both in London and abroad. On one notable occasion we were being entertained by the Deputy Prime Minister of Singapore at a splendid banquet in our honour. We were sitting on either side of the deputy PM, who wore an immaculate white suit. Adele was struggling desperately with her chop sticks and launched a slippery piece of fish into the air which on its descent just missed the deputy PM's unblemished white suit. Highly embarrassed and red-faced, Adele asked to be excused to the ladies. She returned to find that the entire room had 'downed tools' and had stopped eating until her return, which embarrassed her even more. Although she loves Chinese food, she has avoided chop sticks ever since.

Another time we were invited to the grand wedding in New Delhi of the daughter of a good friend, Mani Shankar Aiyar, then holding the high office of Federal Minister of Rural Development of India. Indian society weddings are amazing affairs at the best of times, usually lasting many days and involving lavish expense. Being the wedding of the daughter of such a senior minister held in the heart of Delhi meant literally thousands of guests. There was wonderful food as well as endless supplies of alcoholic drinks. So far, so good, except I chose to wear a smart white suit for the occasion. This proved a dreadful faux pas, because in India you wear white at funerals, not weddings. Unfortunately, I learnt this only afterwards.

Following this minor debacle, that nevertheless amused my Indian friends, we had a nice holiday in the beautiful southern state of Kerala. This is the part of India has the largest proportion of Christians with many big Catholic churches, strangely interspersed by buildings and signs bearing the communist hammer and sickle reflecting the State's strong Marxist political tradition. It reminded me of 1950s Italy portrayed in the amusing *Don Camillo* TV sitcoms I used to watch in my youth, featuring a Catholic priest and a Communist mayor.

Neither Adele nor I are religious, but we appreciate and respect local cultural beliefs and customs. For us, Christmas especially is a time for both reflection and for celebration among family and friends, regardless if you happen to believe in a particular God or not. We also enjoy the many traditions of Christmas such as decorating a real fir tree and the family Christmas lunch.

Kerala was one of the few times we have been away from the UK over Christmas. On Christmas Eve, we attended a Midnight Mass in the local Indian church, arriving in a somewhat precarious tok-tok taxi, which is basically a motorbike with two seats attached. The service was very different from what we were used to in the UK. Men and women sat separately on the floor, although we were supplied with chairs. Exotic Indian music rather than hymns accompanied the Mass. There were flashing lights inside the church, but these unfortunately suffered from a sudden power cut halfway through the service when we were plunged into deep darkness. It was quite an occasion.

In 2012, we acquired a beautiful country residence, Mill House, set in its own grounds on the edge of our small local East Kent village and surrounded by many trees. It is not far from culturally rich university and cathedral city Canterbury and the pleasant seaside resort of Herne Bay on the North Sea coast, with fashionable Whitstable nearby. As the name suggests, Mill House, built over 200 years ago, was the site of an old windmill which collapsed 100 years ago, and of which I still have old photographs; charmingly the ancient millstones from the former mill are incorporated into the pathway in front of the house.

Apart from a sizeable garden of two acres, including a tropical garden boasting banana trees, all planted by Adele, and which is her pride and joy, we were fortunate to inherit a large outdoor swimming pool. Given the English climate our pool is now suitably covered and heated geothermally and has a saltwater pump, dispensing with the need for chlorine. We thus have the great luxury of year-round swimming. By 2016, my hectic travel schedule was beginning to slow. In retirement we have a pleasant and privileged lifestyle which I could not have imagined at the time of my frugal and modest youth.

What satisfies me is that our personal achievements and any material comforts gained have been has been attained purely through our own efforts and hard work, not privilege.

42

A Luta Continua

FAST-FORWARD TO 2022. I DO NOT SEE RETIREMENT FROM full-time work stopping further political engagement and grass roots activism. Indeed, quite the opposite when faced with challenges like Brexit and Climate Change.

In 2016, the Rt Hon Helen Clark, former New Zealand Prime Minister and UNDP Administrator, was kind enough to write: "Carl has much still to offer in public service to the United Kingdom, and indeed to the international community."

I have also had a range of additional personal testimonials from leaders from across the world. These included HE President Yoweri Museveni of Uganda, who wrote: "I would like to commend Mr Wright who played an important role in the Commonwealth and Africa, in particular in advancing the cause of local democracy (and) good governance."

On my retirement in 2016, I was approached to see if I wanted to take on the role of Director-General of the Royal Overseas League Club in St James's, Piccadilly, but I did not want to take on another full-time position. I recall with a wry smile how in my youth I had been disdainful of Pall Mall Clubs; but they do offer a pleasant and intimate alternative as business venues to expensive West End restaurants and are now much more inclusive than they were in the 1970s, when many still banned women.

As CLGF Secretary-General Emeritus and with my continued CLGF Board membership I have maintained my CLGF and local government links. Shortly after retiring I participated in an event organised by the South African Local Government Association, SALGA, in Johannesburg. This held many fond memories for me, not least recalling the excitement when Nelson Mandela had officiated over the founding congress of SALGA. I was also delighted by a warm public tribute paid to me at the opening ceremony by my old comrade Cyril Ramaphosa, the Vice President of South Africa, shortly to assume the high office of President.

Not long afterwards I participated in the congress of our partner organisation, United Cities and Local Governments, UCLG, in Bogota. It took place at an interesting time when Colombia had recently undergone a peace process to end years of domestic conflict with the FARC guerrillas which had cost many lives. It was pleasing to hear President Juan Manuel Santos, who opened the congress, describe the progress achieved.

In Bogota, former mayor of Johannesburg, Parks Tau, was competing for the presidency of UCLG against a rival mayor from Kazan in Russia backed by the Putin Government. I had been asked by the Russians to invite the Kazan mayor to our CLGF Board meeting in London earlier that year, given that it was being attended by Parks Tau, but I reminded them that as Russia was not a Commonwealth member, this was inappropriate.

I was drafted into the Tau election campaign team at the Congress and bore witness to dirty tricks by the opposition. This included the distribution of a fake UCLG election pamphlet comparing the two candidates, falsely giving the impression that Tau had no qualification for the position. More seriously, there were allegations of brown envelopes with large amounts of cash being passed to delegates in get them to vote for the Russian, to say nothing of a rumour claiming that the services of local prostitutes had been offered to wavering delegates. This was perhaps a flavour of the kind of unsavoury things the Putin government condoned.

When it came to the actual vote, Tau, to my delight, won decisively. This was despite awful chairing by the UCLG President, the Mayor of Istanbul, allowing a chaotic voting procedure which almost stopped the voting, which may well have been his intention. Clearly, Bogota was a lesson of how democracy should not be run – but at least the good guy won.

A year later in 2017, I attended the CLGF biennial Conference in Malta together with Adele and then I participated in a Board meeting in Rwanda in 2018 and other events such as our CLGF European members' meeting in Belfast before Covid called a halt to these. I also travelled with CLGF Secretary-General Greg Munro to Malaysia at the invitation of the Minister of Local Government and CLGF Board member to address a major local government event. Malaysia is the only large Commonwealth country which does not have elected local government and although the minister was sympathetic to see local democracy elections, to date this has not happened.

Since stepping down as full-time CLGF Secretary-General in 2016 I have continued to collaborate with UCLG, now headed by the very capable Emilia Saiz, in undertaking a number of studies for them and by attending some of their meetings. This has included being asked to co-author the influential UCLG GOLD V report chapter on SDG implementation in Europe, reviewing local government trends and SDG implementation across the continent.

I have further maintained my long-standing links with the EU and Brussels. In 2017, I undertook a consultancy for PLATFORMA, which groups together European and global local government bodies engaged in development work, including CLGF. This involved a review on how local and regional government had benefitted from the 2000-2020 Cotonou Agreement between the EU and 79 African, Caribbean and Pacific (ACP) partner countries and to make recommendations on future engagement post-2020.

In doing this study together with a colleague in Africa, I conferred with senior EU officials and local and central governments as well as EU delegations in a wide range of ACP countries. Other assignments on EU issues and dealing with SDG implementation were to follow. This work sometimes involved conducting Skype interviews with local government colleagues across the world including Latvia, the Philippines and Turkey.

This work has kept me in touch with current policy thinking and with overseas colleagues and has augmented my meagre pension a little, having not qualified for a generous UK end-of-salary civil servant pension. It involved meetings in Barcelona, Paris and repeated trips to Brussels where I also meet with EU officials. My activities involved close collaboration with my old friend Jean Bossuyt at ECDPM, and I have been made a *pro bono* adviser to the Centre which continues to do much important work with the EU. I have also had engagement with the OECD in Paris and its growing work on local government.

I serve on a number of Commonwealth bodies in an advisory or trustee capacity. These include the Commonwealth Parliamentary Association, now headed by my old political friend and former Labour minister, the very capable Stephen Twigg and the Commonwealth Round Table, in which I have had a number of articles published. I have, however, been disappointed by the failure of the Commonwealth Secretariat to make use of my experience, instead of deploying consultants with often little real Commonwealth know-how.

I am also a trustee of the Ramphal Institute, a Commonwealth think-tank, headed for many years by the late Patsy Robertson, a vibrant Jamaican who became a true Commonwealth icon. I have furthermore been active on the campaigns board of Amnesty International in its fight for human rights, an organisation I hold in the highest respect. I maintain academic links by being a Senior Research Fellow at the Institute of Commonwealth Studies of the University of London and a Visiting Practitioner to the University of Kent and have been chairing the MBA advisory board of the Kent Business School.

I have twice been elected as trustee of the UN Association of the UK, UNA-UK, helping the organisation regain financial stability and reform its membership structure. It meant meeting with local UNA branches and attending the annual commemoration service and wreath-laying at London's Cenotaph for UN Peacekeepers, a moving event which salutes UN 'blue berets' who died in the line of duty.

In 2018, I visited Belfast and Armagh for UNA events, the latter being close to the North-South border and had been so-called 'bandit country' during the Troubles. It seemed a bad omen that on the eve of Brexit in 2019, terrorist bombs started going off again and that a local journalist was murdered in Derry by an IRA offshoot.

I am ashamed of British history in Ireland. I well recall the 'Troubles' of the past decades and feel strongly that everything should be done to preserve and consolidate the fragile 1998 Good Friday Peace Agreements. It is sad to see the fear generated by Brexit and a possible return to a 'hard' border between the north and south of the island of Ireland, which belongs together. Perhaps 100 years after the division of Ireland, one of the consequences of the need to maintain borderless links between North and South will be to encourage national unity alongside Commonwealth – and EU – membership.

Brexit has dominated much of my thinking over the past years since the 2016 referendum. I regard the UK's departure from the EU as contrary to all my deeply held beliefs about internationalism and global citizenship. I was appalled that, in 2019, Prime Minister Boris Johnson sought to prorogue Parliament to quash parliamentary debate and joined public demonstrations in central London against this outrageously undemocratic action. Happily, this unconstitutional measure by Johnson was ruled illegal by the British Supreme Court but it did much damage to Britain's international reputation, a standing further undermined by Johnson attempting to go back on his own EU treaty agreements in 2020-21.

Having in my early twenties marched on the streets of London in support of our joining Europe, I could never have imagined that nearly fifty years later I would be doing the same in my late sixties in the cause of our staying in Europe.

Together with Adele we joined 700,000 others on the streets of London in 2018 to protest against the absurdity of Brexit and to demand a new Peoples' Vote. Many of anti-Brexit signs were home-made and bore witness to the British sense of humour: 'Don't Brexit – Fix It', 'Grannies for Europe', 'Europe is rather good' and 'March to end (Prime Minister) May'. Adele and I especially liked the earthy 'Bollocks to Brexit'. By March 2019, and again in October 2019, our number had swelled to over one million, the largest post-war demonstrations held on the streets of the UK. In addition, over six million signed an online petition to revoke Brexit, but this meant little to the hard Brexiteers of the Tory Party and UKIP living in their fantasy land of 'Global Britain' and 'taking back control'.

Although seen as a 'Brexit Election', the outcome in 2019, like the 2016 referendum itself, was more a reflection of the acute dissatisfaction of the declining left-behind regions of the UK and intense dislike of Labour's Leader Jeremy Corbyn. Yet these are the very regions, including impoverished north Kent, which had benefitted from EU funds. It is they which will be most seriously hit by disinvestment and unemployment if the UK fails to maintain close economic and trading links with the EU. There was at least a little good news with the re-election of Canterbury's pro-European MP, Rosie Duffield, who had at the previous election in 2017 become the first non-Tory MP in the city since 1803 and with whom I have met on a number of occasions.

I hope that despite the dogmatic Brexiteer views in the Johnson Government, economic sanity will ultimately prevail. At minimum this requires a closer EU-UK partnership, a 'Soft Brexit' with EU Customs Union and Single Market membership and return to freedom of movement. This is vital to ensure EU access for business and the dominant UK financial and services sector.

I hold much hope in our young generation who overwhelmingly voted to reject Brexit; who have a more internationalist outlook than their parents and grandparents; and who are taking to the streets throughout the world to warn about the impending global disaster of climate change. I am certain Brexit itself will be reversed in the not-too-distant future and am confident that our youth will spearhead the 'Rejoiner' movement.

In the meanwhile, I am using my local government expertise to champion British mayors and local communities taking the initiative in revitalising people-to-people links, building on long standing town twinning contacts with European cities and setting up new European Local Partnerships. Holding a German as a well as a British passport, I remain an EU citizen, something denied to my fellow British compatriots. I am heartened by the distain which so many people I know share about the narrow nationalism which the UK has descended into and their determination to maintain our European, Commonwealth and internationalist links.

I am now much involved in issues around global sustainability and climate change.

Since 2018, I have helped guide the new *Canterbury SDG Forum.* This involved my presenting a public petition to Canterbury City Council asking the council to engage with us on SDG implementation in the district and working with Rosie Duffield MP. I have also engaged with our other local MP, Conservative Sir Roger Gale, whose One Nation Tory views and generally progressive stands on issues like immigration I much respect.

In 2019, I helped draft a leaflet on sustainable development and the SDGs for candidates at the local elections which called on the City Council to commit to the SDGs, incorporate them in their local plan and appoint a councillor as SDG champion. My work has entailed visits to meet with Kent County Council at their offices in Maidstone and bringing over local government experts from Belgium to share experiences. In addition, Adele has got involved locally and is Vice Chair of the parish council in our local village.

In October 2019, I was honoured to be keynote speaker at the annual UN Peace Service held in the venerable and ancient Canterbury Cathedral. The theme for this prestigious event was *Climate Emergency, Zero Carbon and Global Peace.* I delivered my address from no less a place than the high pulpit from which the Archbishop of Canterbury presents his sermons. Pointing to the dangers of climate change and how it affected everyone, both locally and globally, I also felt obliged to point out that Brexit would undermine international efforts at coordinated climate action. I was pleased that my message was well received by the packed-out congregation.

I am now chair of the *Canterbury Climate Action Partnership (CCAP),* established in 2019 as a not-for-profit Community Interest Company to address the growing global climate crisis. This work is taking up increasing amounts of my time, but I have been much assisted by our dedicated secretary John Yard and other volunteers like our Vice Chair William Rowlandson and fundraiser Yvonne Freeman. Our multi-stakeholder partnership comprises local government, civil society, the churches, our universities, business and youth and student representatives. It has given me much satisfaction to help bring this important forum together and it has hit the ground running. Climate change is about the survival of our planet, and nothing can be more important.

Most recently, in 2021, we held a wide-ranging *Canterbury Climate Action Week* to inform and engage the public, immediately prior to the COP26 Global Climate Summit in Glasgow. This was followed by my leading a delegation to Glasgow, where I was able to attain official UNFCCC accreditation for CCAP, my first real outing since the start of Coronavirus in 2020. Our delegation in Glasgow included our lead councillor on climate change, Dan Watkins and the capable Lisa Carlson, who heads up the Business Improvement District, and two civil society representatives, Yvonne Freeman and Freddie McCormack, thereby ensuring a truly multi-stakeholder representation.

Our attendance alongside 20,000 delegates from around the world was marked our strict Covid testing but proved a very worthwhile experience with much useful interaction and sharing of experience on climate change. COP26 also highlighted the key role which local governments in particular, as well as business, plays in championing the race to Zero Carbon, with the presence of senior mayors like Saddiq Khan of London and important corporate leaders. This was something I have written about in a special issue of the Round Table on COP26. Our priority in 2022 is to launch our new *Canterbury Climate Action Awards* scheme.

The issue of climate change is rightly dominating public discussion, highlighted by the *Extinction Rebellion* movement and the committed engagement of young people. Canterbury City Council has declared a Climate Emergency to address climate change, and I am working with its councillors and officers on its *Climate Action Partnership Board,* tasked to develop a coordinated approach in our district to reach Zero Carbon. I was also able to contribute to the successful 2020-21 campaign to oppose the reopening of East Kent's Manston Airport which would have dire carbon emission consequences. Happily, a Judicial Review has ruled against the airport expansion.

The traumas and lockdowns of the Covid-19 pandemic have brought life to an abrupt standstill in 2020-21 and are only now opening up but with new Covid variants, the situation looks volatile. Adele and I are slowly resuming our normal life post-Covid, spent between Mill House in East Kent, where we have often received family, friends and overseas visitors, and in our townhouse in Golders Green, north-west London, less than thirty minutes by Underground from Whitehall and Westminster. We love cosmopolitan London, with its wealth of diverse cultures and experiences, and its mixing of so many peoples and races. We also enjoy the peace and quiet of the beautiful Kent countryside, close to North Sea beaches – the best of both worlds.

There remains much to do and engage with in coming years. I and Adele and our loveable but slightly scatty English setter Rupert intend to live and enjoy life to the full. I hope to contribute actively to our wider society and engage politically on local, national, European and global issues such as Climate Change. I plan to stay true to the same ideals I have fought for and dreamt of as a grass roots activist and Commonwealth diplomat ever since 1972 and to remain a Global Citizen.

A luta continua – the struggle continues.

EPILOGUE

Imagine

THE SEVENTY YEARS OF MY LIFE SINCE 1950 HAVE BEEN exciting, rich and challenging. I have been lucky to live in a period of peace, prosperity and progress, notwithstanding the conflict, poverty and suffering in many parts of the world. I grew up in modest material comfort with a caring family, benefitted from free education and universal health provision, found rewarding employment and travelled across the globe; I have the fortune to have many friends around the globe.

My career has been one of working with international institutions and colleagues from across the world, of being a Global Citizen. This has, I hope, given me understanding of key global issues and trends and above all of the value – and fragility – of our post-1945 world order. It has also shown me that history continues to evolve, and not always in a positive way.

I have worked as a diplomat in intergovernmental organisations like the UN, EU and the Commonwealth; in hybrid organisations representing elected local government; and as a grass roots activist in the trade union movement. This has instilled in me the strong belief that international cooperation is not – and should not be – confined to purely intergovernmental interactions but is a complex and interacting matrix of many different bodies, such as cities and regions, business, trade unions and civil society.

My fear is that the democratic, economic and social progress of the past decades is being destroyed by political populists and authoritarian regimes in Britain and elsewhere, and by conflict and warfare, most recently through the ruthless Russian invasion of Ukraine which has resulted in a new Cold War between East and West. 9/11 and the 'War on Terror' and the restrictions that resulted on many personal freedoms were dire warnings. So was the impact of the global economic crash of 2008 with its imposition of draconian economic austerity measures. This hit living standards of the poorest while the rich got richer. Now we face the fallout of Covid-19 pandemic which has taken the lives of so many millions around the world.

Unless the vital importance of global cooperation is recognised, we could see the collapse of our post-1945 global structures, the undermining of the EU and the demise of valuable international organisations like the Commonwealth. This will inevitably hit international cooperation activities by non-governmental organisations and their ability to reach out across borders. It will also harm business activity. As a result, the world will be a poorer and more dangerous place.

A core problem is the failure of many politicians and key decision-makers to think globally. My life experiences have taught me that chauvinist attitudes are deeply engrained in official minds, whether they be civil servants, parliamentarians or well-meaning, but often inward-looking, political activists. I encountered these narrow attitudes in my early work in Brussels and throughout my career. Yet when I talk to ordinary people, most are open to engaging with strangers and warm-hearted in their response to global disasters; prone to helping those in need.

Sadly, backward-looking outlooks are prevalent in my own country, Britain. This was demonstrated in ill-informed attitudes to EU membership and brought to a head in the 2016 Brexit referendum. Brexit shows that Britain, having lost its Empire, has still not found a role – although encouragingly most of our young generation rejects outdated historical nostalgia.

Underlying these negative trends has been a failure by political leaders and opinion-formers to inform and educate the public in the realities of the modern world and, in the case of the UK, to explain the political and moral argument for being part of the European Union. The case for Europe was never just about economic interest or the minutiae of custom duties, important though they are. It was essentially about how a medium size country like the UK can join hands with its neighbours to prevent war, and strive for peace and for global advancement.

Chauvinism was also evident in battles I had with government representatives at the UN and the Commonwealth; the latter an organisation which has been greatly undervalued by UK governments of all political shades. It is a body that with all its many professional, academic and other organisations, retains great potential. However, the case for the Commonwealth cannot be based on nostalgia or royal patronage but should reflect the dynamics of a partnership of equal nations.

What lessons do I draw from my life-experience? What remedies are there to our current global malaise? What can I communicate that is of relevance to today's young generation?

All human beings are equal regardless of race, creed or religion

We all have the same emotions, the same desires, and the same problems. I have travelled to over 100 countries and met people from most others. All have more in common than what divides them. The former Governor of Hong Kong, Lord Chris Patten, has argued that there is no such thing as 'Asian values' distinct from 'Western values', there are only 'human values'. I strongly share his view.

The inspiring advocacy work of Amnesty International, and whose boards I have served, reminds us that human rights are applicable to all human beings across the world. The work of such human rights organisations needs to be actively supported and reinforced. The Commonwealth, too, can play a key role here building on the provisions of the Commonwealth Charter. Above all, unlike many other international bodies, it has the ability to suspend those members – like Zimbabwe – which have fallen short of its basic values; it now needs to do this to those member countries which do not adhere to its standards.

To my mind, labour rights of the type I sought to promote for fourteen years as trade union official and at the ILO, are an integral part of human rights. In the age of zero-hour contracts and often restrictive trade union legislation, trade union membership is as important as ever. 'Solidarity' should indeed be 'Forever'. Countries like the UK and the USA accordingly need to restore trade union rights in line with ILO requirements, including at the workplaces of companies like Amazon.

There are, of course, diverse cultural and social traits, and the world would be poorer without them. But I cannot detect any fundamental differences among peoples, races or creeds. I have been privileged to have worked alongside colleagues from many countries from an early age. This has allowed me to form my opinions. I accept that someone who has had little contact with strangers may be subject to preconception or prejudice, but they are the poorer for it.

I respect religious leaders and have met many, including the Pope, the Archbishop of Canterbury, senior Muslim and other faith leaders.

But religion's overall track record is not good, and it is certainly not helped by bigots or fanatics of any faith. What is required is to take the moral compasses of the great global religions and adapt them into our modern social and legal codes. This needs to be done in a way that reflects an open, equal and humane society, devoid of dogma or ritual, deploying the inherent goodness of many genuinely religious people for the common good.

I believe in human progress, not retrogression and I am an optimist by nature. Those on the Right who now sneer about 'woke' culture or denigrate past social advances like those achieved in the 1960s, are reactionaries who belong to a past age. There can be no going back on hard-won women's or LGBT rights, on sexual liberties, on artistic freedom, on citizens' and workers' rights, or on a woman's right to choose.

Equally, excessive culture zealots on the Left, who worry unduly about words and labels or about cultural identity, are narrow-minded and alienate ordinary people. There are more important issues than obsession about gender identity. Political correctness is all well and good but it all too often is an excuse for not taking hard decisions to address underlying inequalities in society. At the same time, our schools, colleges and our educational curricula do need to reflect our modern world and its diversity; they should also not shy away from calling out past crimes such as the slave trade and colonial exploitation in the name of Empire.

Today's younger generation has had the ability to travel internationally, surf the internet and mix and work with young people from across the world in our global cities. Many have forged friendships, loves and affections across race, creed and religion. They are thus in a better position than past generations to refute prejudice and discrimination. In doing so, they will contribute to a better world.

Protecting democratic values is vital

My life experience has convinced me that having democracy and sound, honest government is critical to global wellbeing. Totalitarian, authoritarian or populist models of government are not the answer. Having the right to vote and ensuring good governance, with greater transparency and oversight of political decision-making, is required at every level of government. There must further be strong structures to underpin and scrutinise democracy such as independent courts, a vigorous media and a healthy civil society.

I worry greatly about the rise of political populism, particularly the far-Right and its hate-filled agenda, directed largely at foreigners and immigrants. These are people who are unable to look beyond their immediate neighbourhood, and who revel in past national glories instead of facing up to present global challenges. Together with authoritarian and repressive regimes, like those in China and Russia, the new populists threaten our fundamental liberal democratic values, including the Rule of Law and the free media.

Brexit and Donald Trump are just two manifestations of this ugly trend which is sadly in evidence in all too many countries, not least within many Commonwealth countries. It remains to be seen if the election of progressives like Joe Biden in the US, Olaf Scholz in Germany and Cyril Ramaphosa in South Africa can help protect our democracies and safeguard our core values.

For democracy to function, we must stop abuses in public procurement, favours to political friends, misuse of parliamentary expenses and worse. Redressing the undue influence of big private corporations and billionaires on legislators, their tax evasion and their money laundering, is also essential for a healthy democracy. So too is stopping the manipulation of social media to exert political control and disseminate fake news.

Modern participatory politics requires reforms such as a proportional voting system, a written constitution and an elected second chamber, as well as fairer, state, funding of political parties. Votes should be given to young people from the age of 16, to immigrants and foreign citizens who are full time residents and taxpayers. This is lacking in my own country, the UK.

I do not denigrate elected politicians or public servants, nor am I unduly cynical about Parliament as an institution. I have had my political battles, but there will always be rotten apples – those out only for themselves financially and seeking mere personal self-advancement and status. Most politicians and public servants I have met and worked with hold sincere convictions and strive for the public good. More recently, it has been incredibly heartwarming to see the unselfishness of our essential workers during the Covid-19 crisis, not only our valiant doctors and nurses who have put their lives on the line, but also so many low-paid workers in the public and service sectors who deserve better reward.

It is vital that our young recognise the importance of defending our democracies and rejecting the siren calls of populism, so that history does not repeat the terrible mistakes of the 1930s. This means that they need to turn out to vote, reject fake news, are vigilant and actively engaged in democratic oversight, including by running for political office and taking up public service where possible.

Globalisation is remote to ordinary people and requires more, not less, local decision-making

There is no contradiction here. Despite recent reverses, globalisation is here to stay. Decisions should however be taken at the most appropriate level: whether on climate change, promoting economic and social standards and laws, or the implementation of sustainable development. It is essential that governments ensure decentralisation of public services and empowerment of local communities which I tried to promote with the Commonwealth Local Government Forum. It is vital that they provide the financial powers and resources to facilitate this.

It is encouraging that important international organisations like UNDP, the Commonwealth, the EU and the OECD have highlighted that most, if not all, of the UN's Sustainable Development Goals SDGs require implementation at local level to be effective. In the case of the EU, what is called the principle of subsidiarity – doing best what is best at whatever level of government – is formally enshrined in its Lisbon Treaty.

The SDGs and their targets accordingly need to be fully integrated into both national and local development plans. Primary healthcare, whether in response to a sudden pandemic like Covid-19 or in satisfying more ongoing health needs, is just one example of what is best provided at local community level. Numerous other examples of such 'localist' approaches, many of which I have referred to elsewhere, can be cited. Most national governments now also realise this although they often remain reluctant to relinquish their political powers to local or regional government.

My decades of working with cities and local government have impressed on me the key importance of having a bottom-up approach to development, which engages and empowers people at the grass roots. Democratic, participatory, transparent and accountable local government as set out in the *Commonwealth Aberdeen Principles* provides the foundation for operating a true democracy. 'SDG' should therefore not only stand for Sustainable Development Goals, but also *Start Development at the Ground.*

I fervently hope our young will engage fully in local democratic processes in their cities, towns and villages, and that they stand for election as local councillors and mayors. It is they who need to ensure that globalisation does not leave people behind, but that instead we achieve a fairer and better society through positive change within our communities.

Our international system needs preserving and strengthening

There has been insufficient coordinated international action in response to the Covid pandemic and many countries have reverted to selfish unilateralist approaches. Poorer developing countries have not received the vaccines they desperately need. The pandemic has undoubtedly exposed the fragility of human beings and our dependence on the natural environment.

I hope that the impact of Coronavirus will encourage decisive action to deal with other looming global crises, such as the growing climate emergency and the deep divides between poor and rich countries. Above all that, it will lead to the realisation that we need strong and effective international organisations to tackle global crises and prevent them happening in future. We need to nurture our embryonic structures of global cooperation, whether it is the UN, the Commonwealth or regional structures like the EU. This is a key theme in my recollections of the past fifty years.

International organisations have promoted peace, democracy, advanced prosperity and encouraged economic and social progress ever since 1945. They have provided the framework for Rule of Law, as opposed to the Law of the Jungle, and the means for addressing inter-State conflicts consensually. An example is the World Health Organisation, which is not without fault. Yet its role in giving a response to the Covid-19 pandemic and in facing up to future health threats is surely vital. This global system needs safeguarding.

Of course, reform is always necessary. The outdated composition of the UN Security Council no longer reflects the geopolitical realities of today. It is an example of where changes are required. The 2020 *UN 75 Political Declaration* makes important proposals for change. It is also time a global UN Peoples' Assembly convened to meet alongside the UN General Assembly composed of nations states. At a future stage, this could be elected by universal suffrage in a similar way as the European Parliament is within the EU.

The EU, which I have referred to a lot, requires re-invigoration. Increasingly it is moving towards the kind of Federal Europe for which I marched for as a student. A true European Union must however be built on its many nations, regions and cultures, including countries like Scotland and Wales. It needs to reach out to European countries like Ukraine, Georgia and Moldova. It must not be a centralised monoglot structure controlled from Brussels.

The Commonwealth, with its fifty-plus diverse members, deserves preserving and strengthening, not only by the UK, but by all of its better-endowed members. Its many valuable professional and civil society networks do much to bridge global divides of race, creed and religion. They promote the idea of diversity and stand as a beacon against intolerance. But unless the Commonwealth is endowed with good leadership and proper resources, it will whittle away and die.

In my work I have often encountered a lack of respect for the independence of international civil servants. Many national decision-makers think such international officials are beholden to the beck and call of their respective countries' governments or to those that pay the bills. However, international officials are not mere 'servants', they are guardians of consensus, and their integrity needs to be safeguarded, whether at the level of Secretary-General or of a lowly official. While it would be foolish to ignore the wishes of the minority of larger and more powerful nation states, this cannot be at the expense of the majority of states. At the same time, international officials must, as I have always been, accountable to the relevant multi-national Boards of Directors, representative of all members, big and small.

Young people today are more internationalist than their parents or grandparents. They are more cosmopolitan and open minded. I hope they will recognise that with all its imperfections, the international system established after 1945 – the UN, the EU, the Commonwealth and the many other global and regional institutions – has served us well. I hope they see the need to build on existing international institutions and endow them with greater powers, more resources as well as better democratic structures, and not to undermine or discard them; not to 'throw the baby out with the bath water'.

These are tasks for our young generation: to reinvigorate our world order just as happened after 1945.

We need to address the bigger picture

But what of the long-term changes that happen over decades, over centuries and even longer? The kind of issues which the late Stephen Hawking popularised so effectively in his writings? The things that will determine the future, not just of our young, but the entire of the human race.

Our future will entail many global perils and numerous as yet little anticipated changes. An acute short-term danger for humanity lies in nuclear proliferation and the possibility of atomic warfare, not least with the onset of a new Cold War. There are already many current Great Power flashpoints in Eastern Europe, the Middle East and East Asia. Unless we achieve nuclear arms control, we could self-destruct by nuclear annihilation in a final, Third World War. We must not forget the lessons of 1914 and sleepwalk into a terrible conflict.

Climate change and biodiversity loss are rightly top of the global agenda. This was highlighted at COP26. It is vital that the world achieves zero carbon emissions and adapts to existing change. We are ourselves increasingly experiencing extreme climate events like violent storms, flash floods and abnormal heat and fires. Failure to act now would result in many millions of desperate displaced people from small island states, low-lying countries and places faced with desertification. If not controlled, ecological and weather changes will destroy our planet's wonderful flora and fauna, its rich biodiversity. The very fabric of society would be undermined, and civilisation would collapse, resulting in a new Dark Age. Ultimately, our green and fertile planet could become a barren, lifeless world like our heavenly neighbour, Mars.

Covid-19 has been a grave warning, not least in the speed it has spread across the world, and we cannot exclude future, even more lethal, pandemics. It has shown the health dangers of inter-species virus transmission, especially in situations where animals are cruelly exploited as in the so-called 'wet markets' of Asia. But this is not unique to Asia. We should show due respect to other species, which, as recent research has shown, have elements of intelligence and empathy akin to the human animal. I personally look forward to a time when our meat and major organic foodstuffs are factory-grown, using stem cells and proteins, as is already being done. This would do away with the slaughter of billions of animals, address health concerns and preserve the planetary environment including our fragile oceans where a single plastic bottle takes 450 years to decompose.

Artificial intelligence (AI) and bio-technological advances, too, are ever-accelerating. The deployment of quantum physics in AI will have significant impact on economics and jobs as well as social and political structures. It would entail great danger if deployed for robot warfare. The associated genetic engineering, could even, as the writer Yuval Harari has warned, and is portrayed in the work of the novelist Ian McEwan, result in a new human species, synthetic super humanoids. This is a terrifying thought for the future which recalls the macabre time-travelling visions of H.G. Wells a hundred years ago. We may be nearer to this mind-boggling scenario than we think.

These philosophical and in part futuristic considerations are beyond the scope of my current narrative. As I have grown older and more mature, they have however weighed more heavily on my consciousness. Such long-term reflections put into perspective the pettiness of human political, social and religious squabbles, and of the futility of quarrels among nations. They reinforce yet further the vital need for humanity to cooperate across borders and globally in order to safeguard its long-term future existence.

The young have led in alerting the world to the dangers of climate change. They have taken up many other worthy causes such as nuclear arms control and animal welfare. It is time that their concerns are acted upon and reflected in appropriate government legislation and international regulations. Our youth will need to continue its active engagement in highlighting and overcoming such global challenges, not only for their own sake, but also for the survival of future generations. This, too, will be the task of our young Global Citizens.

Final reflections

The seventy years of my life have seen significant progress in cultural and social matters. I am proud to have been a *soixante-huitards* student, to have experienced the heady excitement of the 1960s, and to have benefitted from the resulting personal and political freedoms. It has been my experience that being an internationalist is deeply rewarding and professionally highly satisfying.

There are numerous lessons set out in this book of what might be termed 'the time Before Coronavirus' – BC.

The young generation of today should learn from the grave errors my generation have made, set out in this recollection of my life. These include the Cold War Arms race, almost resulting in nuclear Armageddon; failure to tackle the abhorrent racialism of apartheid and other human rights abuses; endangering our planet's fragile climate, ecosystem and biodiversity; allowing neo-liberal economics to preside over huge disparities in income and wealth, both within and between countries; and endangering the survival our post-1945 system of international cooperation and the Rule of Law.

Our young must avoid making similar mistakes.

I hope that, looking through these pages, our youth will also come to understand and learn from the idealism, optimism and internationalism which genuinely drove much of my generation. That they will realise that history never ends and that the current xenophobic populist tide can be reversed and defeated. I implore them to fight for political, economic and social justice, to strive for sustainable development and climate justice and to defend personal freedoms and liberties wherever they are under attack.

I am gratified that in 2021 young people across the world took part in *Global Citizen Live* concerts to defend the planet and defeat poverty. I hope that this inspirational initiative, which reflects the core messages contained in these pages, will go from strength to strength. Music resonates globally and has a universal message of love, as it did in the 1960s when The Beatles proclaimed, 'All you need is love'. I look to our young to continue to experience the richness of our diverse cultures and to strive to become Global Citizens themselves.

I conclude with a message of hope with words from John Lennon's iconic song, *Imagine*:

> *Imagine all the people*
> *Living life in peace*
> *You may say I'm a dreamer*
> *But I'm not the only one*
> *I hope someday you will join us*
> *And the world will be as one*

BIBLIOGRAPHY

THE BIBLIOGRAPHY FOR MY BOOK IS NOT A DEFINITIVE OR highly researched set of references, but an idiosyncratic collection of texts relevant to my own recollections and the giving of historical context. They represent a few of the many publications which adore my numerous bookcases at home, much to the despair of my wife, Adele, and are books which I hope are easily accessible for those who want to delve a bit more into the subject matter I have recalled. The various references are accordingly set out for each of the relevant parts of the book.

Insofar as I have provided facts and figures which are not referenced in the text, I can vouch that I have checked these on Wikipedia and other sources out as much as possible. To avoid plagiarism, I admit a debt to a number of chronologies of the twentieth century, which have been helpful in reminding me of specific events and dates. These include:

Gilbert, Martin, *A History of the Twentieth Century, Volume 3, 1952-1999* Harper Collins 1998, 1999
Judd, Tony, *Postwar: A History of Europe Since 1945* Pimlico 2007
Kershaw, Ian, *Roller-Coaster Europe 1950-2017* Allen Lane 2018
Roberts, J M, *Twentieth Century: A History of the World 1901 to the Present* Allen Lane 1999

PART I (CHAPTERS 1-7)

Barnet, Richard J & Mueller, Ronald E, *Global Reach: The Power of the Multinational Corporations* Touchstone 1974
Brandt Commission, *North-South: A Programme for Survival* Pan Books 1980
Brandt, Willy, *Friedenspolitik in Europa* Fischer Verlag 1968
Brandt, Willy, *Writing and Speeches of the Noble Peace Prizewinner* Friedrich-Ebert Stiftung 1971
Carew, Anthony, *Democracy and Government in European Trade Unions* George Allen & Unwin 1976
Commonwealth Secretariat, *Beyond Apartheid: Human Resources in a new South Africa* James Currey 1991

d'Alpuget, Blanche, *Robert J Hawke: A Biography* Penguin Books 1985

Friedrich Ebert Foundation, *Towards One World? International responses to the Brandt report* Temple Smith 1981

Hallstein, Walter, *Europe in the Making* Allen & Unwin 1972

Harris, Geoffrey, *The Dark Side of Europe: The Extreme Right Today* Edinburgh University Press 1990

Hawke, Bob, *The Hawke Memoirs* William Heinemann 1994

Kelly, Paul, *The Hawke Ascendancy* Angus & Robertson 1984

Kitzinger, Uwe, *Diplomacy and Persuasion: How Britain Joined the Common Market* Thames & Hudson 1973

Levinson, Charles, *Capital, Inflation and the Multinationals* Allen & Unwin 1971

Mackenzie, Norman & Jeanne, *The Fabians* Simon & Schuster 1977

Nicholson, Marjorie, *The TUC Overseas: The Roots of Policy* Allen & Unwin 1986

Olle, Werner, *Einfuehrung in die Internationale Gewerkschaftspolitik. Band 1* Verlag Olle & Wolter 1978

Pelling, Henry, *A History of British Trade Unionism* Pelican 1963

Piehl, Ernst, *Multinationale Konzerne und Internationale Gewerkschaftsbewegung* Europaeische Verlagsanstalt 1974

Sampson, Anthony, *The New Europeans* Hodder & Stoughton 1968

Schmidt, Helmut, *Menschen und Maechte* Sielder Verlag 1987

Servan-Schreiber, Jean-Jacques, *The American Challenge* Pelican Books 1969

Sommer, Theo, *Unser Schmidt* Hoffmann & Campe 2010

Spanier, David, *Europe Our Europe: The Inside Story of the Common Market Negotiations* Morrison & Gibb 1972

Spinelli, Altiero, *The European Adventure: Tasks for the Enlarged Community* Charles Knight 1972

Stevens, Philip, *Britain Alone: The Path from Suez to Brexit* Faber & Faber 2021

Taverne, Dick, *The Future of the Left: Lincoln and After* Jonathan Cape 1974

Taylor, Robert, *The TUC: From the General Strike to New Unionism* Palgrave 2000

Tugendhat, Christopher, *The Multinationals* Penguin Books 1971

Wilms-Wright, Carl, *Transnational Corporations: A Strategy for Control* Fabian Society 1977

PART II (CHAPTERS 8-17)

Bourne, Richard (Ed), *Shridath Ramphal: The Commonwealth and the World* Hansib 2008

Bourne, Richard, *Catastrophe: What went wrong with Zimbabwe?* Zedbooks 2011

Commonwealth Heads of Government, Kuala Lumpur Communique, *Statement on Southern Africa,* 1989

Commonwealth Secretariat *'Apartheid Terrorism. The Destabilisation Report'* 1989

Commonwealth Secretariat *'South Africa. The Sanctions Report'* Penguin 1989

Commonwealth Secretariat *'Technological Change. Enhancing the Benefits'* (two volumes) 1985 & *'Jobs for Young People. A Way to a Better Future'* 1987

Gandhi, Indira, *Indira Gandhi on People and Problems* Hodder & Stoughton 1982

Jenkins, Clive, *Clive Jenkins. All Against the Collar, Struggles of a White Collar Union Leader* Methuen 1990

Jones, Jack, *Union Man: The Autobiography of Jack Jones* Collins 1986

Mishra, Pankaj, *From the Ruins of Empire: The Revolt against the West and the Remaking of Asia* Allen Lane 2012

Moraes, Dom, *Mrs Gandhi* Jonathan Cape 1980

Morgan, Kenneth O, *Michael Foot: A Life*. Harper Collins 2007

Ramphal, Shridath, *Glimpses of a Global Life* Hansib 2014

Report of the Independent Commission on Disarmament and Security Issues (Palme Commission) *'Common Security. A Programme for Disarmament'* Pan Books Ltd 1982

Report of the Independent Commission on International Development Issues (Brandt Commission) *'North-South: A Programme for Survival'* Pan Books Ltd 1980

Report of the Socialist International Committee on Economic Policy Manley Commission, *'Global Challenge. From Crisis to Co-operation: Breaking the North-South Stalemate'* Pan Books 1985

Report of the World Commission on Environment and Development (Brundtland Commission) *'Our Common Future'* Oxford University Press 1987

Sanders, Ron (Ed), *Inseparable Humanity: An Anthology of Reflections of Shridath Ramphal* Hansib 1988

Sanghera, Sathnam, *Empireland: How Imperialism has Shaped Modern Britain* Penguin Random House 2021

PART III (CHAPTERS 18-24)

Acemoglu, Daron & Robinson, James A, *Why Nations Fail* Profile Books, 2013

Anyaoku, Emeka, *The Missing Headlines: Selected Speeches* Liverpool University Press 1997

Bhutto, Benazir, *Daughter of the East: An Autobiography* Hamish Hamilton 1988

Clark, Christopher, *The Sleepwalkers: How Europe Went to War in 1914* HarperCollins 2012

Commission on Global Governance *'Our Global Neighbourhood'* Oxford University Press 1995

Commonwealth Committee of Foreign Ministers on Southern Africa. *'Review of Commonwealth Action'* CFSMSA (90) 3; Commonwealth Secretariat April 1990

Commonwealth Heads of Government *'The Okanagan Statement and Programme of Action on Southern Africa'* 1989

Commonwealth Secretariat, *Beyond Apartheid: Human Resources in a New South Africa* James Currey 1991

Fukuyama, Francis, *The End of History and the Last Man* Penguin 1992

Johnson, Phyllis, *Eye of Fire: Emeka Anyaoku* Africa World Press 2000

Kinnock, Glenys, *Voices for One World* Fontana 1988

Mandela, Nelson, *Long Walk to Freedom* Little, Brown & Co 1994

Piketty, Thomas, *Capital in the Twenty-First Century* Belknap Press, Harvard University 2014

Wilson, Francis & Ramphele, Mamphela, *Uprooting Poverty: The South African Challenge* W W Norton & Co 1989

Woods, Donald, *Biko* Vintage Books 1979

PART IV (CHAPTERS 25-30)

Much of the CLGF information bulletins, annual reports, policy statements, conference reports (since 2000) conference reports and other publications including the biennial *Commonwealth Local Government Handbook* (since 2002) and the *Commonwealth Journal of Local Governance* can be downloaded from *www.clgf.org.uk*. By way of example, key CLGF/ related policy statements, research papers and other reports include:

- Venson, Pelonomi (ed) *'Traditional Leadership in Africa: A research report on traditional systems of administration and their role in the promotion of good governance'* CLGF 1997
- *London Statement on Local Government priorities for the New Millennium* CLGF 2000
- *Statement on Local Government Service Partnership* CLGF 2003
- Mkhatshwa, Smangaliso & Otekat, John *'Make it local, make it democratic: The case for local democracy'* Commonwealth Secretariat 2005
- *The Aberdeen Agenda: Commonwealth Principles on Good Practice for Local Democracy and Good Governance* CLGF 2005
- International Academy of Urban Dynamics, All India Institute for Local Self-Government *'Promoting gender equality in local government* (Asia)' CLGF, 2007
- Geddes, Mike & Sullivan, Helen *'Delivering development through local leadership in the Commonwealth'* CLGF 2007
- *The Auckland Accord: Tauritenga o Tamaka. Delivering Development through Local Leadership* CLGF 2007
- Amis, Philip *'Improving Local Government – the Commonwealth Vision'* Background Paper CLGF 2009
- *Freeport Declaration: 'Improving Local Government – the Commonwealth Vision* CLGF 2009
- *'Energising local economies: local economic development around the Commonwealth'* CLGF 2011
- *Cardiff Consensus for Local Economic Development* CLGF 2011
- Slater, R & Yadav, Prabkhar *'Municipal Finance for Inclusive Development'*, CLGF 2011
- Curtis, Donald *'Strategies to promote intergovernmental relations in accordance with the Aberdeen Principles'* CLGF 2012
- *Communication on Empowering Local Authorities in partner countries for enhanced governance and more effective development outcomes* European Commission 2013
- Sansom, G & McKinlay, P *'New Century Local Government Commonwealth Perspectives'* Commonwealth Secretariat 2013
- *Munyonyo statement on local government's role in the post-2015 development agenda,* CLGF 2013
- *'Local Economic Development in Asia Pacific: A Review of Policy and Practice'* CLGF 2014
- *'Local Government and Local Economic Development in Southern Africa'* CLGF 2014

- *'Local government 2030: achieving the vision'* Background Paper CLGF 2015
- *The Gaborone Declaration – Local Government Vision 2030* CLGF 2015
- *Chisinau Outcome Statement on Strengthening Capacities and building effective Institutions for the Implementation of the Post-2015 Development Agenda* The World We Want (United Nations) 2015
- Satterthwaite, David *'Successful, safe and sustainable cities: towards a New Urban Agenda'* CLGF 2016

Commonwealth Good Practice Scheme projects include *'Ekurhuleni enhances local economy through employment'; 'Community development approach to clean water supply in Rajkot'; 'Portmore 2020 – a partnership for strategic planning in Jamaica'; 'Three-way link boosts revenue collection in Wasa Amenfi West'* CLGF 2007

Florida, Richard, *The New Urban Crisis: Gentrification, Housing Bubbles, Growing Inequality, and what we can do about it* Oneworld Publications 2017

Howell, David, *Old Links and New Ties: Power and Persuasion in an Age of Networks* I.B. Taurus & Co 2014

Howell, David, *The Mother of All Networks. Britain and the Commonwealth in the 21st Century* Gilamesh Publishing 2018

Kiyaga-Nsubuga, John & Olum, Yasim, *'Meeting the Challenges of the Aberdeen Agenda – an assessment of local governance and democracy in Uganda'* CLGF 2007

Metha, Dinesh & Pandey, K K, *'Country Papers & Trainers' Manual, Local Democracy and Good Governance Training Programme South Asia'*; CLGF/UNDEF 2007

Sachs, Jeffrey D, *The End of Poverty: Economic Possibilities for our Time* Penguin Books 2005

PART V (CHAPTERS 31-36)

The official account of 9/11 is set out in *'The 9/11 Commission Report' Final Report of the National Commission on Terrorist Attacks Upon the United States'* WW Norton & Company, 2004. A more polemic review of the US Presidency of the time is contained in Singer, Peter *'The President of Good and Evil: The Ethics of George W Bush'* Text Publishing, 2004

Abuja Declaration on Local Democracy and Development in the Commonwealth CLGF June 2014

Bregman, Rutger, *Utopia for Realists and how we can get there* Bloomsbury 2017

Cable, Vince, *The Storm: The World Economic Crisis and what it means* Atlantic Books 2010

Commonwealth Secretariat, *'Better Local Services: Improving local government delivery through innovation and partnerships'* Commonwealth Secretariat/CLGF 2006

Commonwealth Secretariat, *'Civil Paths to Peace. Report of the Commonwealth Commission on Respect and Understanding'* Commonwealth Secretariat, 2007

Commonwealth Secretariat, *'Local Democracy and Good Governance in the Caribbean'* Commonwealth Secretariat/CLGF 2005

Commonwealth Secretariat, *'Local Democracy and Good Governance in the Pacific'* Commonwealth Secretariat/CLGF 2005

Commonwealth Secretariat, *'Local Democracy, Good Governance and Delivering the MDGs in Africa'* Commonwealth Secretariat/CLGF 2007

Conference Report, *Commonwealth Local Government Conference 2007* (pp15-17) CLGF 2007

Grayling, A C, *Liberty in the Age of Terror: A Defence of Civil Liberties and Enlightenment Values* Bloomsbury Publishing 2009

Kampala Call to Action' Global Forum on Local Development UNDP/UNCDF 2010

Kilcullen, David, *Out of the Mountains: The Coming Age of the Urban Guerrilla* C Hurst & Co 2013

Law, Nathan & Fowler, Evan, *Freedom- How we lose it and how we fight back* Penguin 2021

Letter by Prime Minister Blair to CLGF Chairperson John Otekat, 25 July 2005

Mason, Paul, *Clear Bright Future: A Radical defence of the Human Being* Allen Lane 2019

Mazzucato, Marina, *Mission Economy: A Moonshot Guide to Changing Capitalism* Allen Lane 2021

Message by Prime Minister Cameron to Commonwealth Local Government Conference, Cardiff, March 2011

Mount, Ferdinand, *The New Few or a Very British Oligarchy* Simon & Schuster 2012

'Research-based report on the role of local government in the promotion and protection of human rights' UN Human Rights Council Thirtieth Session, July 2015

The background to WHO activity is set out in *'Reducing health inequities through action on the social determinants of health'* Sixty-Second World Health Assembly document WHA62.14, WHO, 2009

'The Cost of the Cuts: The impact on local government and poorer communities' Joseph Rowntree Foundation, 2015

Thunberg, Greta, *No One is too Small to Make a Difference* Allen Lane 2019

UK Stakeholders for Sustainable Development *'Measuring Up: How the UK is Performing on the UN SDGs'* 2018

UN 75th Anniversary 'issue briefs' www.un.org/un75; 2019

United Cities & Local Governments *'Towards the Localization of the SDGs. Local and Regional Government's Report to the 2018 HLPF'* 2028; see also www.localizingtheSDGs

Varoufakis, Yanis, *And the weak suffer what they must? Europe, austerity and the threat to global stability* Penguin Random House 2016

PART VI (CHAPTERS 37-42)

Address made by the author at the *2019 UN Peace Service at Canterbury Cathedral* can be viewed on www.vimeo.com/373748740 (starting minute 29)

Agee, Philip, *Inside the Company CIA Dairy* Stonehill Publishing 1975

Ali, Tariq, *Street Fighting Years: An Autobiography of the Sixties* William Collins Sons & Co 1987

Dimbleby, Jonathan, *The Prince of Wales: A Biography* Little, Brown & Co

Kissinger, Henry, *On China* Allen Lane 2011

Kurlansky, Mark, *1968: The Year that Rocked the World* Vintage 2005

Mayer, Catherine, *Charles: The Heart of a King* W H Allen 2015

Oglesby, Carl (Ed), *The New Left Reader* Grove Press 1969

Pimlot, Ben, *The Queen: A Biography of Elizabeth II* HarperCollins 1996

Thomas, Hugh, *Europe the Radical Challenge* Weidenfeld & Nicolson 1973

United Cities & Local Government *'GOLD V. The Localization of the Global Agendas – how Local Action is Transforming Territories and Communities'*. 2019 (the author was co-author of the chapter on Europe)

Wilms-Wright, Carl, Kreisverwaltung Unna, *'Kreisentwicklungsplan. Untersuchungen zum Freizeitsverhalten'* 1970

Wright, Carl, *Local Government leading climate action*, The Round Table, Routledge October 2021

Wright, Peter, *Spycatcher: The Candid Autobiography of a Senior Intelligence Officer* Stoddard Publishing 1987

EPILOGUE

Appiah, Kwame Anthony, *The Lies that Bind Us: Rethinking Identity* Profile Books 2018

Harari, Yuval, *Homo Deus: A Brief History of Tomorrow* Harvik Secker 2015

Hawking, Stephen, *A Brief History of Time* Bantam Press 1988

Lennon, John, *Imagine* Apple 1971

McEwan, Ian, *Machines Like Us* Jonathan Cape 2019

Patten, Chris, *East and West* Macmillan 1998

Pinker, Steven, *Enlightenment Now: The case for Reason, Science, Humanism and Progress* Penguin Books 2018

Tegmark, Max, *Life 3.0: Being Human in the Age of Artificial Intelligence* Allen Lane 2017

Wells, H G, *The War of the Worlds* 1897

INDEX

2008 Economic Crash, 43, 134, 206, 229, 230, 236, 240, 242-4, 308

7/7, July 7th terrorist attack in London, 222, 225

9/11, September 11 attacks in New York, 174, 197, 221-4, 230, 242, 285, 308

Aberdeen Principles on Good Practice for Local Democracy and Good Governance (CLGF), 185-7, 195, 198, 207, 223, 225, 226, 313

Abuja Declaration on Local Democracy and Development in the Commonwealth (CLGF), 224, 225

Ackermann
- Cleo, goddaughter, 293
- Curt, uncle, 54, 284
- Dieter, cousin, 293
- Peter, cousin, 293
- Willy, uncle, 277

ACP (see African, Caribbean and Pacific states)

ACPLGP (see African, Caribbean and Pacific Local Government Platform)

ACTU (see Australian Council of Trade Unions)

Addis Ababa Conference on Financing for Development, 248

AFL-CIO (see American Federation of Labor-Congress of Industrial Organisations)

African National Congress (ANC), 95-8, 115, 122, 142-4, 146, 147, 149

African Union (AU), 248

African, Caribbean and Pacific Local Government Platform (ACPLGP), 206, 207

African, Caribbean and Pacific states (ACP), 180, 212, 252, 302

Agee, Philip, ex CIA operative, 289

Agenda for Sustainable Development 2030, 19, 244

Agenor, Brussels-based Left-wing journal, 42, 43

Ahwoi, Kwamena, Government minister, Ghana, 170, 253

Aicken, Gareth, Commonwealth & DFID official, 255

Aiyar, Mani Shankar, Government minister, India, 298

Akumu, Denis, General Secretary OATUU, 79

Alam, Dr Munawwar, Commonwealth official, 178

Alexander, Jeff, personal friend, 294

Alexander, Sara, personal friend; actor & author, 294

Alexander, Vicky, personal friend, 294

ALG (see Association of London Government)

Ali, Tariq, activist and writer, 275

ALP (see Australian Labor Party)

American Federation of Labor-Congress of Industrial Organisations (AFL-CIO), 48, 56

Amis, Dr Phil, Director, Institute of Commonwealth Studies, 172

Amnesty International, 303, 310

ANC (see African National Congress)

Andrew, Prince, HRH Duke of York, 263, 264

Angola, 14, 95, 122, 142, 143, 149, 174, 208

Anne, HRH Princess Royal, 263, 264

Anti-fascist, 284

Anti-Semitism; 87, 235, 294

Anyaoku, Chief Emeka, Commonwealth Secretary-General, 75, 88, 96, 112, 114, 145, 151, 171, 183

apartheid, 14, 48, 49, 55, 69, 71, 84, 95-7, 99, 101, 107, 108, 110, 116-8, 120, 122, 142-7, 149, 164, 240, 262, 282, 318
  anti-apartheid, 14, 95, 114, 116, 120, 149, 165, 240
  post-apartheid, 25, 110, 114, 142-9, 164

Armstrong, Hilary, (later Baroness Armstrong) British Government minister, 170, 194, 215

Arndell, Richard, student friend & European Commission official, 25

ASEAN (see Association of Southeast Asian Nations)

Ashley, Mike, LGA official & CLGF treasurer, 171, 202

Association of London Government (ALG), 174, 204, 227

Association of Scientific, Technical & Managerial Staff (ASTMS), 80

ASTMS (see Association of Scientific, Technical & Managerial Staff)

AU (see African Union)

Aung San Suu Kyi, Myanmar leader, 189, 190

Australian Council of Trade Unions (ACTU), 81, 97, 115

Australian Labor Party (ALP), 62, 82

Baader-Meinhof, German terrorist group, 282

Baker, Simon, UK local government official & CLGF treasurer, 171

Ban Ki-moon, UN Secretary-General, 14, 247

Banerji, Amitav, Commonwealth official, 177

Barber, Sir Brendan, TUC General Secretary, 80

Beatles, The, the rock group, 130, 274, 296, 318

Beckett, Margaret, British Government minister, 30

Belize, 104, 120, 171, 175, 190, 194, 195, 207

Benn, Hilary, British Government minister, 204, 215

Benn, Tony, British Government minister, 29, 36, 84

Bentham, Jeremy, eighteenth-century philosopher, 276

Berlin Wall, 49, 114, 127, 169, 235, 284

Beyond Apartheid: Human Resources in a New South Africa, Commonwealth report, 146

Bhutto, Benazir, Prime Minister of Pakistan, 153

Bickerstaffe, Rodney, British trade union leader, 80, 116

Biden, Joe, President, USA, 233, 312

Biermann, Heide, cousin, 251, 293

Biermann, Johannes, godson, 251, 293

Biko, Steve, freedom fighter/anti-apartheid activist, 148

Bishop, Maurice, revolutionary leader, Grenada, 290

Black Lives Matter movement, 233

Blair, Sir Tony, British Prime Minister, 26, 85, 132, 161, 163, 170, 197, 215, 223, 229, 232, 237, 242, 254, 257, 289, 292

Bodfish, Ken, British local government leader, 236

Bolger, Jim, Prime Minister, New Zealand, 176

Bongers, Paul, British local government official, 168

Bossuyt, Jean, official, ECDPM Brussels, 180, 302

Bourne, Richard, Institute of Commonwealth Studies, former Guardian journalist, 123

Brandt Commission on North-South Relations, 60

Brandt Commission Report, 78

Brandt, Willy, Chancellor of the Federal Republic of Germany, 14, 49, 50, 126, 284

Brexit (see EU referendum & Brexit)

Brown, George, British minister, 39

Brown, Gordon, British Prime Minister, 215, 229, 232, 238

Brundtland, Gro, Prime Minister of Norway, 157

Brussels Labour Group, 42

Bultman, Claudia, CLGF official & PA to Carl Wright, 172

Bush, George W, President, USA, 223

Business Improvement District (BID; Canterbury), 306

Buthelezi, Zulu Chief (Mangosuthu), 146

Callaghan, Bill, TUC official, 80

Callaghan, James (Jim), British Prime Minister, 53, 83

Cameron, David, British Prime Minister, 230, 233, 240, 254

Canadian Government, 80, 146

Canadian International Development Agency (CIDA), 179

Canadian Labour Congress (CLC), 60, 73, 80, 98

Canterbury Climate Action Partnership (CCAP), 305, 306

CAP (see Commonwealth Association of Planners)

CAPAM (see Commonwealth Association for Public Administration & Management)

Cardiff Consensus for Local Economic Development (CLGF), 198, 231

Carlson, Lisa, Chief Executive, BID Canterbury, 306

Carlsson, Bernt, UN High Commissioner for Namibia, 75, 114, 115, 123

Carlsson, Ingvar, Swedish Prime Minister, 132

Carr, Shirley, trade union leader, Canada & CTUC Chairperson, 90, 98, 145

Carter, Jimmy, President, USA, 153

Cashman, Michael (later Lord Cashman), actor and MEP, 162

Castro, Fidel, President of Cuba, 14, 149

Ceylon Workers Congress (CWC), 57

Chalker, Lynda (later Baroness Chalker), British Government minister, 99, 159, 172

Channel Tunnel, 20, 132

Charles, HRH Prince of Wales, 13, 88, 89, 92, 198, 250, 251, 253, 262-4

Chaudhury, Mahendra, Fijian union leader and Prime Minister of Fiji, 106, 107

Child, Chris, Commonwealth official, 192

Chiluba, Freddy, trade union leader and President of Zambia, 101

China, 19, 126, 135-7, 188, 230, 259, 285, 312

CHOGM (see also Commonwealth Heads of Government Meeting)

– Abuja 2003, 191
– Auckland, 1995,176
– Brisbane, 2002, 197
– Colombo, 2013, 210
– Coolum, 2002, 177
– Durban, 1999, 183
– Harare 1991, 147
– Kuala Lumpur, 1989, 110
– Lusaka 1979, 92
– Melbourne 1981, 89
– Nassau 1985, 89, 90, 96
– New Delhi 1982/83, 89, 90
– Perth, 2011, 189
– Port of Spain, 2009, 262
– Trinidad, 2009, 244
– Vancouver 1987, 89, 107, 110
Chombo, Ignatius, Government minister, Zimbabwe, 209
CIA (Central Intelligence Agency) (see Secret intelligence services)
CIDA (see Canadian International Development Agency)
Cities Alliance, 174
City twinning, 169, 186
Civil Paths to Peace, Commonwealth report, 223
Clark, Helen, Prime Minister of New Zealand & Administrator, UNDP; CLGF Patron, 14, 17, 170, 171, 180, 198, 200, 238, 246, 247, 300
Clarke, Michael, academic, UK, 239
CLC (see Canadian Labour Congress)
Clement, David, CTUC official, 73, 102, 115, 161
CLGF (see Commonwealth Local Government Forum)
Climate change, 19, 43, 132, 187, 212, 242-5, 248, 249, 300, 304-7, 313, 316, 317
Clinton, Bill, President, USA, 132, 135, 153, 229, 277
Clinton-Davis, Lord Stanley, British Government minister & European Commissioner, 237
Clos, Joan, Mayor of Barcelona & Executive Director, UN Habitat, 248
CMAG (see Commonwealth Ministerial Action Group)
Cold War, 21, 48, 49, 56, 70, 79, 84, 96, 102, 103, 127, 133, 142, 164, 184, 266, 270, 271, 282, 284, 287, 290, 308, 316, 318
Colombia, 138, 222, 301
ComHabitat / *Comhabitat*, 181, 243
Commission on Common Security, 78
Commission on Global Governance, 132
Common Agricultural Policy [of the EU], 33, 43
Commonwealth Association for Public Administration & Management (CAPAM), 178, 179

Commonwealth Association of Planners (CAP), 179
Commonwealth Charter, 186, 310
Commonwealth Day, 263
Commonwealth Expert Group on Jobs for Young People, 91
Commonwealth Expert Group on Technological Change, 91
Commonwealth Harare Declaration, 151
Commonwealth Heads of Government Meeting (CHOGM), 74, 89-92, 96, 107, 110, 115, 119-22, 144, 147, 176-9, 183, 185, 189, 191, 197, 199, 200, 210, 244, 254, 255, 257, 262
Commonwealth Hub, 250, 262
Commonwealth Human Rights Initiative, 123, 179
Commonwealth Inclusive Cities Network, 173
Commonwealth Institute , 88
Commonwealth Journal of Local Government, 201
Commonwealth Local Government Forum (CLGF), 15, 17, 20, 34, 140, 143, 162, 167-9, 171-4, 176-83, 185-90, 193-6, 198-200, 202, 206, 207, 209, 211-17, 219, 223-6, 231, 232, 236-40, 243, 246-9, 250-5, 257, 300-302, 313
Commonwealth Local Government Good Practice Scheme, 204
Commonwealth Local Government Handbook, 201
Commonwealth Ministerial Action Group (CMAG), 152, 185, 214
Commonwealth Parliamentary Association (CPA), 178, 179, 302
Commonwealth Round Table, 179, 233, 257, 302
Commonwealth Secretariat, 14, 67, 73, 81, 88, 91, 103, 108, 109, 111, 114, 116, 120-2, 140, 145, 148, 157, 164, 165, 168, 169, 171, 176, 185-7, 190, 201, 205, 219, 246, 250, 254, 257, 302
Commonwealth Small States Office, New York, 246
Commonwealth Special Fund for Mozambique, 117, 122
Commonwealth Sustainable Cities Network, 173
Commonwealth Trade Union Council (CTUC), 17, 20, 72, 73, 79, 80, 85, 88, 90-3, 96-104, 108, 109, 112, 115, 116, 119-22, 144, 145, 161, 168, 169, 171, 172, 176, 213, 289
Congress of South African Trade Unions (COSATU), 14, 97-9, 104, 115, 116, 120, 143, 144, 147-9
Convention of Scottish Local Authorities, 291

Corbyn, Jeremy, British Labour Party leader, 86, 159, 234, 304
COSATU (see Congress of South African Trade Unions)
Cotonou Convention (ACP-EU), 70, 180, 302
Council of Europe, 64, 135
Covid-19, 17, 19, 213, 216, 221, 230, 252, 256, 258, 276, 293, 295, 301, 306, 307, 309, 312-4, 316
Cox, Bob, European Commission official, 35
Cox, Jo, murdered British Member of Parliament, 233
CPA (see Commonwealth Parliamentary Association)
Crean, Simon, Australia, trade union leader & Leader, ALP, 75, 81, 97
CTUC (see Commonwealth Trade Union Council)
Cuba Missile Crisis 1962, 270
Cutts, Steve, Commonwealth and UN official, 177

d'Souza, Bornito, Vice President of Angola, 143
Dare, Bernie, CLGF official & PA to Carl Wright, 172
Davies, Trevor, British trade union official, 116
Davos Symposium, 32
de Klerk, F.W., President of South Africa, 97, 145, 146, 148
Deen, Mohamed, Minister, the Maldives, 187
Deistler, Christa, ICFTU official, 51
Denham, Pamela, British official, 66
Denton, Geoffrey, academic, University of Reading, 33, 278
Dormer, Terry, Commonwealth official, 110
Dortmund, German city, 206, 266-8, 273, 277, 293
Drain, Geoffrey, British trade union leader, 80
Duffield, Rosie, British Member of Parliament, 304, 305
Dutschke, Rudi, German student leader, 28
Duvall, Len, British local government leader & CLGF Chairperson, 171, 183, 191, 253

Eagle, Angela, British Member of Parliament, 160
Earth Summit, 1992, 132
ECDPM (see European Centre for Development Policy Management)
Edward, Prince, HRH Earl of Wessex, 263
EEC (see European Economic Community)
Election monitoring (Ghana, Nigeria, Pakistan), 152
Elizabeth II, HM the Queen & Head of the Commonwealth, 14, 89, 90, 158, 250, 253, 257, 262-4, 267, 289

Eminent Persons Group (EPG) [Commonwealth], 96, 97, 144
Eminent Persons' initiative on South Africa, 120
End of History (see also Fukuyama, Francis), 20, 125, 126, 129, 132-6, 138
EPG (see Eminent Persons Group [Commonwealth])
ERDF (see European Regional Development Fund)
ETUC (see European Trade Union Council)
EU (EEC) referendum 1975, 67
EU (see European Union)
EU referendum & Brexit 2016, 17, 19, 23, 32, 44, 87, 133, 206, 221, 229, 233, 234, 251, 252, 300, 303-5, 309, 312
European Centre for Development Policy Management (ECDPM), 180, 208, 302
European Commission, 20, 23-5, 31, 32, 34, 35, 43, 47, 48, 58, 63, 67, 84, 179, 213, 214, 222, 248, 287
European Economic Community (EEC), 20, 24, 50
European institutional reforms, 1973, 41, 42, 44
European Monetary Union, 35, 279
European Movement, 24-7, 29, 30, 37, 41, 84
European Parliament, 20, 26-8, 32, 34, 35, 38, 41, 42, 47, 64, 67, 161, 314
European Regional Development Fund (ERDF), 33, 67
European Research Group, 234
European Single Market, 234, 304
European Social Charter, 66
European Trade Union Council (ETUC), 51, 52
European Union (EU), 13, 17, 19, 20, 23, 24, 28, 32, 34, 41, 44, 45, 53, 67-70, 85, 87, 102, 104, 110, 119, 120, 128, 132, 133, 135, 140, 161, 172, 176, 179, 180, 182, 189, 196, 198, 202, 204-6, 208, 212-4, 217, 222, 226, 231-5, 237, 243, 245, 248, 251, 252, 254, 255, 257, 302-5, 308, 309, 313-5
Everest-Philips, Max, Commonwealth official, 178
Extinction Rebellion, 306

Fabian Society, 29, 64, 86
Farage, Nigel, Leader, UKIP, 233
Faulkner, Stephen, CTUC official, 73, 102, 115
FCM (see Federation of Canadian Municipalities)
Federation of Canadian Municipalities (FCM), 171, 207
Federation of Conservative Students, 27
Fiji, 73, 90, 104, 106, 107, 138, 152, 173, 185, 218

FitzGerald, Garret, Taoiseach (Prime Minister) Irish Republic, 27
Flintoff, Ian, European Commission official, 36
Foley, Maurice, European Commission official, 35, 44
Foot, Michael, Labour Party Leader, 84, 157
Foulkes, George (now Lord Foulkes), British Government minister, 215
Fragile States, 22, 138, 139, 141, 164
Franck
– Dr Werner, grandfather, 269
– Ilse, grandmother, 269, 270, 292
Fraser, Malcolm, Prime Minister Australia, 97
Fukuyama, Francis, US academic & writer, 126, 132-6

G-77, 60, 65, 69, 70
Gale, Sir Roger, British Member of Parliament, 305
Gandhi
Indira, Prime Minister of India, 14, 79, 90, 120, 121, 123, 289
Rajiv, Prime Minister of India, 79, 123
Gateau, Elizabeth, Secretary-General UCLG, 182
GCHQ (Government Communications Headquarters), 55
General Election, UK
– 1974 February, 44
– 1979, 86
– 1987, 157
– 1992, 158
– 1997, 162
– 2017, 234
– 2019, 84
George, Xolie, South African local government official, 194
Ghana, 77, 94, 103, 152, 153, 164, 169, 170, 173, 204, 219, 253
GLA (see Greater London Authority [formerly Greater London Council, GLC])
Glasgow Climate Summit 2021, 255, 306
Global Challenge Report, 78
Global Citizen Live concerts, 318
Global Forum on Local Development, 243
Global Taskforce of Local and Regional Governments, 245, 247
Goheer, Nabeel, Commonwealth official, 177
Golding, Bruce, Prime Minister of Jamaica, 238
Good Friday Agreement, 1997, 134, 303
Goonasekera, Hemanthi, local government official, Sri Lanka, 210
Gorbachev, Mikhail, President of the USSR, 126, 127, 129, 130

Gore, Al, Vice President, USA, 249
Gormley, Joe, British trade union leader, 39
Gove, Michael, British Government minister, 233
Grant, John, British Government minister, 102
Greater London Authority (GLA) [formerly Greater London Council (GLC)], 85
Greece, 34, 230, 280, 281
Greece, under the Colonels, 280, 281, 283
Grenada, US invasion of, 79, 262, 289
Grierson, Ronald, European Commission official, 41
Griffiths, Penmaen, British trade union official, 158
Griffiths, Susan, school friend, 273
Group of 77 developing countries at the UN (see G-77)
Gulf War of 1990-91, 134
Gunawardena, Dinesh, Government minister, Sri Lanka, 211

Habitat III & New Urban Agenda, 174, 248
Hanningfield, Lord (Paul White), British local government leader, 236-9
Hanson, David, British Member of Parliament, 159
Hargreaves, Alan, TUC official, 58
Harker, John, CLC official & Chair Commonwealth Expert Group, 73, 80, 146
Hart, Judith, British Government minister, 85, 102
Hattinger, Anna, personal friend, 294
Hattinger, Peter, personal friend, 294
Hawke, Bob, trade union leader & Prime Minister, Australia, 14, 51, 61, 62, 75, 81, 82, 84, 96, 97, 102, 107, 119, 149
Hayter, Dianne (later Baroness Hayter), General Secretary, Fabian Society, 86, 238
Heath, Edward (Ted), British Prime Minister, 24, 29, 30, 41, 42, 46, 60
Hennon (later Harris), Anne, European Parliament official, 34
Holocaust, 139, 267, 271, 294
Hong Kong, 106, 136, 282, 310
Howe, Geoffrey, Sir British Government minister, 84
Howell, Lord (David), British Government minister; President Royal Commonwealth Society, 183, 241
Huddleston, Archbishop Trevor, anti-apartheid activist, 149
Hughes, Nye, European Commission official, 36

ICFTU (see International Confederation of Free Trade Unions)
Iga, Christopher, Uganda local government leader & CLGF Chairperson, 171

IGO (see Intergovernmental Organisation)

ILO (see International Labour Organisation),

ILO Fair Labour Rights, 55, 56, 59

ILO Social Clause, 63

IMF (see International Monetary Fund)

India, 21, 79, 88, 109, 126, 137, 139, 158, 172, 173, 177, 188, 190, 204, 207, 216, 217, 232, 239, 255, 298

Industrial democracy, 48, 52, 56, 64, 70

Inkatha Freedom Party, 146

Institute of Commonwealth Studies, University of London, 123, 303

Intergovernmental Organisation (IGO), 169, 254

International Confederation of Free Trade Unions (ICFTU), 20, 47-53, 56, 58, 60, 61, 63, 65, 68, 72, 79, 95, 98, 116, 121, 287

International Criminal Court, 223

International Labour Organisation (ILO), 47, 55-7, 61-3, 65, 66, 68-70, 72, 91, 95, 98, 122, 126, 244, 247, 310

International Monetary Fund (IMF), 78

International Trade Union Confederation (ITUC; formerly ICFTU), 49, 102, 108, 115

International Union of Local Authorities (IULA), 181, 196

IRA (Irish Republican Army), 14, 134, 226, 227, 282, 303

Ireland, 26, 34, 134, 183, 210, 223, 303

ITUC (see International Trade Union Confederation)

IULA (see International Union of Local Authorities)

IULA Congress, The Hague 1995, 26, 181

Jackson, Glenda, British Member of Parliament, 160

Jenkins, Clive, British trade union leader, 80, 81, 84

Jenkins, Michael, European Commission official, 35, 42

Jenkins, Roy, British Government minister & European Commissioner, 25, 31, 34, 84

Jobin, Jacques, Canadian local government official, 170

John Smith, British Labour Party Leader, 161

Johnson, Arthur, TUC/CTUC official, 102

Johnson, Boris, Mayor of London & British Prime Minister, 36, 84, 233, 234, 303

Johnson, Stanley, European Commission official, 36

Jolly, Sir Richard, UN Assistant Secretary-General, 61

Jones, Jack, British trade union leader, 51, 80-82, 105, 109, 254

Kagame, Paul, President of Rwanda, 139

Kampala Agenda for African Local Government (CLGF), 243

Kaul, Dr Mohan, Commonwealth official, 109, 111, 146, 171

Kaul, Shraddha, CLGF official, 172, 201

Kaunda, Kenneth, President of Zambia, 14, 101, 120, 121

Kelly, Petra, environmental campaigner, 43

Kenya, 52, 93, 195, 217

Kersten, Otto, ICFTU General Secretary, 49, 51

Kevitiyagala, Chaminda, CLGF official, 172

KGB (see Secret intelligence services)

Khan, Saddiq, Mayor of London, 306

Kilroy-Silk, Robert, British Member of Parliament, 38

King, Oona (later Baroness King), British Member of Parliament, 162

Kinnock
  – Glenys (later Baroness Kinnock) MEP, 115, 157
  – Neil, (later Lord Kinnock) British Labour Party Leader, 80, 149, 157, 161, 162

Kiribati, 22, 105, 106, 120, 173, 213, 219

Kitson, Alec, British trade union leader, 58

Knap, Peter, Dutch local government official, 181

Knox, Jim, trade union leader, New Zealand, CTUC Board member, 62

Kok, Wim, trade union leader & Prime Minister, The Netherlands, 14, 50

Kubekin, Victor, diplomat, USSR, 287

Kuwar, Anuya, CLGF official / Asia, 173, 224

Labour Committee for Europe, 29, 38

Labour Party Conference, 29, 38, 50, 84, 291

Labour Party, British, 20, 24, 28, 29, 34-40, 42, 44, 50, 53, 58, 67, 82, 84-7, 108, 112, 123, 127, 156-60, 170, 197, 215, 232, 236, 237, 278, 287, 291

Lancaster, Terry, journalist, The People, 42

Lea, David (now Lord), TUC official, 65, 66, 80, 238

Lee Kuan Yew, Prime Minister of Singapore, 51

Leinen, Jo, German MEP, 26

Lennon, John, musician & Beatle, 123, 265, 318

Lester, Jim, British Member of Parliament, 171

Lewis, Betty, mother of Susan & Labour Party official (37), 36, 53

Lewis, Sue, Labour Party activist, wife of Carl Wright (1975-79), 35-7, 42, 43, 46, 53, 54

LGA (see Local Government Association)

LGIB (see Local Government International Bureau [UK])

Liberal Democrat Party, British, 86, 157, 275
Ligate, Elizabeth, Director South African Extension Unit, Tanzania, 140
Little, Jenny, Labour Party official, 58
Livingstone, Ken, Mayor of London, 85, 197
Local economic development (LED), 198, 206, 231, 232, 243
Local Government Association (LGA), 169, 173, 174, 181, 186, 194, 204, 207, 231, 236, 291, 300
Local Government International Bureau (LGIB) [UK], 168, 169, 171
Lockerbie bombing, Pan Am Flight 103, 79, 114, 123

MacDonald, Donald, President, ICFTU, 51
Macmillan, Harold, British Prime Minister, 21
Mahama, John Dramani, President of Ghana & CLGF Patron, 170
Major, Sir John, British Prime Minister, 112
Malawi, 141, 164, 177, 186, 206, 297
Malaysia, 207, 301
Maldives, The, 177, 187, 188, 212, 215
Malhoutra, Moni, Commonwealth Assistant Secretary-General, 112
Mallard, Wendy, CTUC official, 73, 85
Mandela Inauguration 1994, 14, 149, 165
Mandela, Nelson, President of ANC & South Africa, 14, 95-7, 114, 116, 143, 145-50, 165, 183, 186, 261, 300
Mandelson, Peter (later Lord Mandelson), British Government minister & European Commissioner, 59, 132, 289
Manley, Michael, Prime Minister of Jamaica, 75, 78, 104, 157
Manufacturing, Science & Finance (MSF), 80
Marquand, David, British Member of Parliament, 25
Marshall, Sir Peter, Commonwealth Deputy Secretary-General, 91
Masire-Mwamba, Mmasekgoa, Commonwealth Deputy Secretary-General, 177, 219
Matjila, Colin, South African local government leader & CLGF Chairperson, 171
Mauritius (298), 296, 297
Maxwell-Miles
 – Adele, dance teacher; wife of Carl Wright (since 1981), 19, 74-6, 109, 114, 159, 160, 174, 190, 192, 200, 203, 226-8, 241, 251, 261-4, 268, 274, 291-9, 301, 304, 305, 307, 319
 – 'Bobby', mother of Adele, 291
 – John, brother-in-law, 291
 – Robert, nephew, 291
 – Yvonne, sister-in-law, 292

May, Theresa, British Prime Minister, 13, 87, 234
Mbassi, Jean-Pierre Elong, Secretary-General, UCLG- Africa, 136, 180, 182
Mbeki, Thabo, President of South Africa, 278
McCartney, Sir Paul, musician & Beatle, 130, 295
McDermott, Denis, Canadian trade union leader & CTUC Chairperson, 80, 98
McDonnell, John British Member of Parliament, 159
McGahey, Mick, British trade union leader, 126
McGregor, Joanna, personal friend; concert pianist, 74
McKinnon, Don, Commonwealth Secretary-General, 88, 177, 198
McPhee, Philip, Bahamas local government leader, 253
MDC (see Movement for Democratic Change [Zimbabwe])
MDGs (see Millennium Development Goals)
Meany, George, US trade union leader, 48, 51, 56
Metha, Dinesh, Indian academic, 239
Mfeketo, Nomaindia, South African local government leader & CLGF Chairperson, 171
MI5 (see Secret intelligence services)
Michel, Manfred, European Parliament official, 34
Miliband, David, British minister, 226
Millbrook Programme of Action, 151
Millennium Development Goals (MDGs), 68, 242-5, 255, 256
Modi, Narendra, Prime Minister of India, 232
Moldova, 22, 128, 247, 315
Mole, Stuart, Commonwealth official, 123
Moloto, Papie, ANC official, 147
Monks, John (now Lord Monks) British trade union official, 80
Montague, Robert (Bobby), local government leader & Government minister, Jamaica; CLGF Chairperson, 104, 171, 237, 238, 253
Morgan, Gwyn, European Commission official, 35-7, 39, 42, 45, 46, 287
Morris, Bobby, trade union leader & parliamentarian, Barbados, 154
Morrison, Basil, local government leader, New Zealand & CLGF Chairperson, 171, 200, 234, 237, 238, 253, 296
Moruakgomo, Rev Mpho, local government leader, Botswana & CLGF Chairperson, 171, 240, 250
Moulana, Ali, local government leader & parliamentarian, Sri Lanka, 211
Movement for Democratic Change (MDC) [Zimbabwe], 208

Moya, Zenaida, local government leader, Belize & CLGF Chairperson, 171, 175, 187

Mozambican National Resistance (RENAMO), 117, 142

Mozambique, 14, 95, 110, 117, 122, 142, 143, 209

MPLA (see People's Movement for the Liberation of Angola)

MSF (see Manufacturing, Science & Finance)

Mufamadi, Sydney, trade union leader & Government minister, South Africa, 122

Mugabe, Albert, trade union leader, Zimbabwe, 93

Mugabe, Robert, Prime Minister/President of Zimbabwe, 93, 94, 101, 120, 137, 189, 208, 209

Munro, Dr Greg, CLGF Secretary-General, 251, 252, 301

Murray, Len (later Lord Murray), TUC General Secretary, 51, 58, 65, 80, 98

Museveni, Yoweri, President of Uganda, 139, 170, 200, 238, 300

Mwesige, Adolf, Government minister, Uganda, 171, 253

Myanmar, 189

NACTU (see National Council of Trade Unions [South Africa])

Naidoo, Jay, South African trade union leader & Government minister, 98-100, 122, 148, 149

Nair, Dr Devan, trade union leader & President of Singapore, 51

NALGO (see National & Local Government Officers Association [UK; now merged into UNISON])

Namibia, 14, 75, 95, 96, 114-7, 139, 144, 145, 157, 165

Narayanan, Dr P.P., trade union leader, Malaysia & President ICFTU, 51

Nasheed, Mohamed, President of The Maldives, 187, 188

Nassau Fellowships Scheme, 110

Nassau, 62, 89, 90, 96, 97, 101, 110, 120, 195

National & Local Government Officers Association (NALGO) [UK; now merged into UNISON], 80

National Council of Trade Unions (NACTU) [South Africa], 97

National League for Democracy (NLD) [Myanmar], 189, 190

National Union for the Total Independence of Angola (UNITA), 142, 143

National Union of Miners (NUM), 65, 126

National Union of Public Employees (NUPE) [UK; now merged into UNISON], 80, 116

National Union of Students (NUS), 26

Nauru, 106

Neil, Andrew, British broadcaster, 28

Neo-liberalism (see also Washington Consensus), 72, 86, 113, 119

Neuhaus, Matthew, Commonwealth official, 177

New International Economic Order, 60, 61, 63, 70, 78, 119, 244, 255

New Jewel Movement, Grenada, 289

Newby, Dick (later Lord Newby), Liberal Democrat leader, House of Lords, 86, 238

Newens, Stan, British MEP, 162

Nicholas, Lorna, CLGF official & PA to Carl Wright, 172, 203

Nigeria, 14, 26, 77, 97, 145, 152, 164, 177, 190-2, 215, 218, 224, 225, 244

Nkomo, John, Vice President of Zimbabwe, 94

NLD (see National League for Democracy [Myanmar])

North Atlantic Treaty Organisation (NATO), 135, 222, 266, 271

Nujoma, Sam, President of Namibia, 145

NUPE (see National Union of Public Employees [UK; now merged into UNISON])

Nyerere, Julius, President of Tanzania, 14, 149

Obama, Barack, President, USA, 229, 233

Obasanjo, General (Olusegun), President of Nigeria, 97

OECD (see Organisation for Economic Co-operation & Development)

One World Action, campaigning charity, 115, 157

Organisation for Economic Co-operation & Development (OECD), 65, 243, 245, 248, 302, 313

Organisation of African Trade Union Unity (OATUU), 79

Osborne, George, British Government minister, 230

Oswald, Ron, CTUC official, 102

Otekat, John, local government leader, Uganda; CLGF Chairperson, 171

Our Common Future, Brundtland report, 78

Owen, David, British Government minister, 25, 84

PAC (see Pan Africanist Congress of Azania [South Africa])

Pakistan, 14, 21, 77, 152-5, 164, 165, 177, 185, 186, 190, 192-4, 202, 203, 215, 224, 226

Palme, Olaf, Prime Minister of Sweden, 60, 78, 123

Pan Africanist Congress of Azania (PAC) [South Africa], 96, 97, 143, 144

Papua New Guinea, 21, 46, 77, 156, 204, 217
Paris Climate Conference 2015, 256
Parker, Terry, CLGF official, 172
Patten, Lord Chris, European Commissioner & Governor of Hong Kong, 310
Peel, Jack, British trade union leader & European Commission official, 36
Peltzer, Renate, ICFTU official, 47
People's Movement for the Liberation of Angola (MPLA), 143
Pepera, Sandra, Commonwealth official, 190
Persad-Bissessar, Kamla, Prime Minister of Trinidad and Tobago & CLGF Patron, 170
Persaud, Dr Vishnu 'Bishnu', Commonwealth official, 90, 91, 108
Petersen, Graham, CTUC official, 102
Pettitt, Helga, godmother, 75
Philip, Prince HRH Duke of Edinburgh, 263
Piehl, Dr Ernst, official, German Trade Union Council (DGB), 47
Piketty, Thomas, French economist, 133, 244
Pilgrim, Martin, British local government official, 227
Pindling, Sir Lynden, Prime Minister of The Bahamas, 90
Pitt, Terry, Labour Party official & MEP, 46
PLATFORMA, 254, 302
Pope Paul VI, 15
Prague Spring 1968, 126
Prescott, John, British Government minister, 197
Priestley, Sir Julian, Secretary-General, European Parliament, 28

Quinn, Patrick, TUC official & CTUC Director, 115

Rabuka, Colonel (Sitiveni), Prime Minister of Fiji, 107
Ragoonath, Dr Bishnu, academic, Trinidad, 172
Ramaphosa, Cyril, trade union leader & President of South Africa, 14, 99, 122, 143, 300
Ramphal Institute, 123, 303
Ramphal, Sir Shridath 'Sonny', Commonwealth Secretary-General, 14, 60, 88, 90, 91, 95, 96, 104, 110, 122, 123, 132, 145, 219, 241, 303
Ramphele, Professor Makele, academic, South Africa, 148
Ranche House College, Harare, 93, 116
Rawlings, Flight-Lt Jerry, President of Ghana, 103, 153, 170
Raynsford, Nick, British Government minister, 75, 215, 237
RCS (see Royal Commonwealth Society)
Reagan, Ronald, President, USA, 70, 71, 78, 96, 104, 119, 153, 229, 289

Reddy, Professor P S, academic, South Africa, 172, 240, 253
RENAMO (see Mozambique National Resistance)
Responsibility to Protect (R2P), United Nations, 223
Review of the World Economic Situation, ICFTU, 50
Robertson, Patsy, Commonwealth official, 303
Robinson, Geoffrey, British Member of Parliament, 36
Robinson, Mark, Commonwealth official, 123, 209
Rocard, Michel, Prime Minister of France, 51
Rodgers, Bill, British Member of Parliament, 84
Roper, John, British Member of Parliament, 25
Royal Commonwealth Society (RCS), 123, 179, 183, 250
Royall, Jan (later Baroness Royall), British Government minister, 162
Ruggiero, Renato, European Commission official & Director-General, WTO, 33
Russia, 19, 129, 130, 131, 135, 136, 223, 233, 258, 270, 287, 288, 294, 301, 308, 312
Rwegasira, Joseph, trade union leader and Government minister Tanzania, 75, 97, 145
Ryder, Guy, TUC official & Director-General, ILO, 72

Sachs, Professor Jeffrey, US academic & writer, 198, 243
SACTU (see South African Congress of Trade Unions)
Sahlgren, Klaus, Director, UN Commission on Transnational Corporations, 65
Saiz, Emilia, Secretary-General, UCLG, 182, 302
SALGA (see South African Local Government Association)
Salim, Salim Ahmed, Government Minister, Tanzania & Secretary-General, OAU, 96
Sampson, Anthony, British writer, 25, 147
Santana, Aracelly, UN official, 66, 138
Savvides, Lazaros, local government leader & Government official, Cyprus, 282
Scargill, Arthur, British trade union leader, 65
Scheifla, Alan, school friend, 278
Schmidt, Helmut, Chancellor of the Federal Republic of Germany, 50, 60, 282
Scotland, Patricia, Commonwealth Secretary-General, 88, 198, 226, 250, 257
SDGs (see Sustainable Development Goals)
Secret intelligence services
 – CIA, 48, 70, 126, 281, 287, 289
 – KGB, 127, 287, 288
 – M15, 226

Sen, Professor Amartya, Indian academic & writer, 223

Servan-Schreiber, Jean-Jacques, French writer, 23, 40

Severe Active Respiratory Syndrome (SARS), 258

Sharma, Kamalesh, Commonwealth Secretary-General, 88, 113, 177, 198

Shawcross, Val, Commonwealth official & Deputy Mayor of London, 157

Shearer, Hugh, Prime Minister of Jamaica, 104

Shlaim, Avi, academic, University of Reading, 278

Siame, Alice, trade union official, Zambia, 102

Sierra Leone, 81, 104, 138, 140, 164, 172, 194, 205, 222, 223

Simbanegavi, Nyasha, CLGF official/ Africa, 173

Simpson-Miller, Portia, local government leader & Prime Minister of Jamaica; CLGF Patron, 14, 170, 207

Singapore, 51, 172, 173, 297

Singh, Sandra, CLGF official/ Caribbean, 173, 196

Slack, Lucy, Secretary-General, CLGF, 172, 173, 204, 214, 251, 252, 254

Smith, Andrea, personal friend, 75, 76, 274, 294

Smith, Gary/Garfield, school friend, 75, 76, 81, 118, 161, 237, 251, 273, 274, 280, 281, 287, 294

Smith, Ian, Prime Minister of Rhodesia under UDI, 26, 93

Smith, Jeremy, British local government official & CLGF treasurer, 171

Smith, Martin, godson, 274

Smith, Megan, goddaughter, 274

Smith, Vernon, British local government official, 168

Soames, Sir Christopher, European Commissioner, 35, 44

Social Democratic Party (SDP), UK, 84, 86

Social Democratic Party of Germany (SPD), 42, 49

Socialist Group of the European Parliament, Luxembourg, 38, 47

Sopoaga, Enele, Prime Minister of Tuvalu & CLGF Patron, 170

South African Congress of Trade Unions (SACTU), 115, 116

South African Local Government Association (SALGA), 186, 194, 300

South Sudan, 14, 134, 189

South-West Africa People's Organisation (SWAPO), 96, 115, 122, 145

SPD (see Social Democratic Party of Germany)

Spinelli, Alterio, European Commissioner, 40

Sri Lanka, 14, 52, 53, 57-9, 68, 138, 172, 173, 177, 190, 199, 208-11, 222, 246, 297

Stockholm Conference on the Human Environment, 43

Straw, Jack, British Foreign Secretary, 26, 289

Student politics, engagement in, 19, 26, 29, 47

Students for a United Europe (SUE), 27, 28, 41

SUE (see Students for a United Europe)

Sustainable Development Goals (SDGs) including localisation of SDGs, 68, 198, 212, 242, 244-8, 255, 256, 305, 313

Sutcliffe, Mike, local government official, South Africa, 240

SWAPO (see South-West Africa People's Organisation)

Swinging Sixties, 274

Taiwan, 19, 137

Tambo, Oliver, President of the ANC, 98

Tanzania, 81, 96, 97, 117, 140, 145, 149, 156, 164, 217

Taoaba, Karibaiti, CLGF official/Pacific, 173

Tapiola, Kari, local government and UN official, 65

Tau, Parks, local government leader, South Africa, 301

Taverne, Dick, British Member of Parliament & MEP, 25, 30, 34

Tay, Dzifa, CLGF official, 169

Taylor, Ann, British Government minister, 38

Tebbit, Norman, British Government minister, 83

Teyki-Berto, Sam, CLGF official, 172

TGWU (see Transport & General Workers Union [UK; now UNITE])

Thatcher, Margaret, British Prime Minister, 34, 52, 53, 55, 60, 65, 70, 71, 78, 82-5, 96, 112, 119, 128, 158, 229, 262, 289

The Gaborone Declaration – Local Government Vision 2030 CLGF, 246

Thomas, Professor Hugh (later Lord Thomas), academic, University of Reading, 53, 279

Thomson, Caroline (later Baroness Liddle), BBC executive, 31, 86

Thomson, George, (later Lord Thomson), British Government minister & European Commissioner, 25, 31-5, 38, 40-6

Thondaman, Savumiamoorthy, trade union leader & Government Minister, Sri Lanka, 57

Todd, Ron, British trade union leader, 80

Trade Union Advisory Committee, 65

Trade Union Council (TUC), 38, 47-52, 58, 59, 65, 69, 72, 73, 79-82, 84, 98, 99, 102, 103, 115, 119

Transnational Corporations/Multinational companies, 40, 64, 65, 68, 69 / 40, 44, 48, 50, 60, 63, 67, 70, 122

Transnational Corporations: A Strategy for Control, pamphlet published by the Fabian Society, 64

Transport & General Workers Union (TGWU) [UK; now UNITE], 29, 51, 58, 65, 80, 81, 158, 160

Trotman, LeRoy, trade union leader, Barbados; ICFTU President, 72

Trump, Donald, President, USA, 17, 19, 221, 229, 233, 312

Tsvangirai, Morgan, trade union Leader & Leader, MDC, Zimbabwe, 208

Tudor, Owen, ITUC Deputy General Secretary, 49, 80

Tutu, Desmond, Archbishop & Nobel Laureate, 14, 165, 185, 198

Twigg, Stephen, British Government minister & Secretary-General, CPA, 162, 302

UCLG (United Cities and Local Governments), 180, 182, 217, 245, 254, 301, 302

UCLG World Congress (2016), 301, 302

UDI (see Universal Declaration of Independence [Rhodesia])

Uganda, 103, 107, 120, 139, 170, 171, 186, 189, 199, 200, 204, 238, 244, 246, 253, 282, 300

Ukraine, 19, 128, 129, 131, 135, 137, 222, 258, 282, 287, 288, 308, 315

UN (see United Nations)

UN Environmental Programme (UNEP), 43

UN Habitat, 181, 208, 243, 245, 248, 254

UN Human Rights Council, 225

UNA (see United Nations Association)

UNCDF (see United Nations Capital Development Fund)

UNDP (see United Nations Development Programme)

UNITA (see National Union for the Total Independence of Angola)

United Nations (UN), 13, 19, 28, 43, 47, 55, 56, 60, 64-6, 68-70, 75, 88, 95, 106, 110, 114, 119, 123, 126, 132, 138, 140, 143, 148, 152, 164, 173, 176, 180-2, 188, 196, 198, 199, 207, 208, 210, 212, 217, 219, 223-5, 227, 232, 242-8, 253-6, 284, 285, 303, 305, 308, 309, 313-5

United Nations Association (UNA), 303

United Nations Capital Development Fund (UNCDF), 181, 207

United Nations Commission on Transnational Corporations, 64, 65, 68

United Nations Department for Economic and Social Affairs, 181

United Nations Development Programme (UNDP), 17, 140, 148, 180, 187, 190, 207, 213, 245-7, 254, 300, 313

United Nations Protection Force (UNPROFOR), 138

Universal Declaration of Independence (UDI) [Rhodesia], 92, 93

University College London (UCL); studies in Geography (BSc Hon 1971), 25, 28, 276-9

University of KwaZulu-Natal; awarded Doctorate in Public Administration 2012, 240

University of Reading; studies in Contemporary European Studies (MA 1972), 29, 33

University of the Pacific, 172

University of the West Indies, 172

UNPROFOR (see United Nations Protection Force)

USSR, 23, 127-30, 133, 282, 284, 288

Vallier, Frederic, Secretary-General, UCLG-CEMR, 182

van Miert, Karel, European Commission official & European Commissioner, 44

Vanderveken, Johnny, Deputy General Secretary, ICFTU, 51

Victims of Apartheid programme Commonwealth, 108, 110, 143

Voices for One World, publication, 157

Walcott, Sir Frank, trade union leader Barbados, 104, 109

Walesa, Lech, President of Poland, 127

Wall, Gareth, CLGF official, 172

Walsh, Michael, TUC official, 80, 99

Washington Consensus, 78, 119, 229, 255

Watkins, Dan, British local government leader, 306

Watson, Annie, CTUC official, 73, 115

Werner, Pierre, Prime Minister of Luxembourg, 35

Whitaker, Ben, British Member of Parliament, 39

WHO (see World Health Organisation)

Williams, Marcia (later Lady Falkender), PA to Prime Minister Harold Wilson, 36, 53

Williams, Peter, Commonwealth official, 88

Williams, Rowan, Archbishop of Canterbury, 15

Williams, Shirley, British Government minister, 25, 84

Willis, Norman, TUC General Secretary, 65, 98, 99

Wilms, Karl Helmut, father, 293

Wilson, Harold, British Prime Minister, 24, 25,
     29, 30, 36, 38, 44, 46, 53, 88
Wilson, Professor Francis, academic, South Africa,
     147
Winckler
   – Bert, uncle, 293
   – Eckhart, cousin, 293
   – Gerald, cousin, 293
   – (née Wilms), Rosemarie, aunt, 293
Woke culture, 311
Wolpe, Professor Harold, academic, South Africa,
     147
Woods, Peter, local government leader, Australia,
     253
World Employment Conference (ILO), 61
World Federation of Trade Unions, 48, 79
World Health Organisation (WHO), 258, 314
Wright, Donald, stepfather, 269-72, 292, 293
Wright, George, TGWU Welsh Secretary, 158
Wright, Ilsemarie (nee Franck) mother, 75,
     268-70, 273, 278, 292, 293

Yannopoulos, George, academic, University of
     Reading, 280
Yaounde Convention (ACP-EU), 70
Yeltsin, Boris, Executive President of Russia,
     130
Young European Federalists (YEF), 26
Yousafzai, Malala, Pakistani Nobel Laureate,
     263
Yule, Lawrence, local government leader, New
     Zealand & CLGF Chairperson, 171, 253

ZANU-PF (see Zimbabwe African Union-
     Patriotic Front)
Zimbabwe African Union-Patriotic Front
     (ZANU-PF), 93, 94, 208
Zimbabwe, 14, 92-5, 116, 117, 120, 137, 140,
     168, 173, 185, 188, 189, 208-10, 214,
     226, 310